Workers, Jobs, and Inflation

Workers, Jobs, and Inflation

MARTIN NEIL BAILY, EDITOR

THE BROOKINGS INSTITUTION
Washington, D.C.

Library of Congress Cataloging in Publication data:

Main entry under title:

Workers, jobs, and inflation.

Includes bibliographical references and
index.
  1. Labor supply—Addresses, essays, lectures.
2. Inflation (Finance)—Addresses, essays,
lectures. 3. Unemployment—Addresses, essays,
lectures. 4. Wages—Addresses, essays, lectures. I. Baily, Martin Neil.
HD5707.W66 1982   331.12'0973   82-70891
ISBN 0-8157-0764-9   AACR2
ISBN 0-8157-0763-0 (pbk.)

9 8 7 6 5 4 3 2 1

THE BROOKINGS INSTITUTION is an independent organization devoted to nonpartisan research, education, and publication in economics, government, foreign policy, and the social sciences generally. Its principal purposes are to aid in the development of sound public policies and to promote public understanding of issues of national importance.

The Institution was founded on December 8, 1927, to merge the activities of the Institute for Government Research, founded in 1916, the Institute of Economics, founded in 1922, and the Robert Brookings Graduate School of Economics and Government, founded in 1924.

The Board of Trustees is responsible for the general administration of the Institution, while the immediate direction of the policies, program, and staff is vested in the President, assisted by an advisory committee of the officers and staff. The by-laws of the Institution state: "It is the function of the Trustees to make possible the conduct of scientific research, and publication, under the most favorable conditions, and to safeguard the independence of the research staff in the pursuit of their studies and in the publication of the results of such studies. It is not a part of their function to determine, control, or influence the conduct of particular investigations or the conclusions reached."

The President bears final responsibility for the decision to publish a manuscript as a Brookings book. In reaching his judgment on the competence, accuracy, and objectivity of each study, the President is advised by the director of the appropriate research program and weighs the views of a panel of expert outside readers who report to him in confidence on the quality of the work. Publication of a work signifies that it is deemed a competent treatment worthy of public consideration but does not imply endorsement of conclusions or recommendations.

The Institution maintains its position of neutrality on issues of public policy in order to safeguard the intellectual freedom of the staff. Hence interpretations or conclusions in Brookings publications should be understood to be solely those of the authors and should not be attributed to the Institution, to its trustees, officers, or other staff members, or to the organizations that support its research.

Foreword

In 1979–80 the chief concern of economic policy was the control of inflation. Central to that concern was the behavior of the labor market. Wage increases, for example, slowed during the 1975 recession but accelerated again in subsequent years. Many argued that the labor market had become overly tight during the economic recovery, maintaining that excess demand for labor pulled up the rate of wage increase and contributed substantially to inflation. At the same time, other observers noted that the unemployment rate remained high during the last half of the 1970s and rose even higher in 1980. Unemployment during this period was well above the average for the late 1960s, a period generally conceded to have been one of excess labor demand.

These conflicting signals concerning the labor market led to a conference held at Brookings November 7–8, 1980, financed in part by the U.S. Department of Labor. The conference papers and formal discussions that appear in this volume deal primarily with the measurement of labor market performance, but they range over a number of issues that go to the heart of the policy problems of combining reasonably full employment with price stability. Both theoretical issues and recent economic experience are discussed. The introduction and first chapter provide an overview of the issues raised at the conference.

Since the conference was held, unemployment has increased and the inflation rate has decreased, both substantially. The labor market signals are thus no longer in conflict. However, the lessons of the conference remain relevant for the future as economic recovery begins. When the rate of price inflation fell to about 5 percent in 1976 there was an ill-founded hope that inflation had been cured. Reducing unemployment in the future without reducing underlying wage pressures will once again put a premium on understanding labor market signals.

Martin Neil Baily has been a senior fellow in the Brookings Economic

Studies program since 1979. In previous research he has examined the behavior of wages and employment over the business cycle and developed the theory of implicit wage contracts. Nancy Barrett and Roland Droitsch of the U.S. Department of Labor assisted with the selection of topics and participants for the conference, and Lesley Kalmin and Suzanne Wehrs provided valuable research assistance in preparing the manuscript.

Nancy Davidson edited the manuscript; Penelope Harpold checked its factual content; Diana Regenthal prepared the index.

The views expressed here are those of the authors and discussants, and should not be ascribed to the U.S. Department of Labor, or to the trustees, officers, or other staff members of the Brookings Institution.

BRUCE K. MACLAURY
President

June 1982
Washington, D.C.

Contents

ix

Tables

Figures

MARTIN NEIL BAILY

Introduction

THE EXPERIENCE of high unemployment and high inflation in the 1970s
has prompted an agonized reappraisal of macroeconomic thinking and
policy. The papers in this volume are intended as a contribution to
one part of this reappraisal. In the 1960s it seemed relatively straightforward to evaluate whether there was an excessive overall demand
for labor that could contribute to inflation, or excessive unemployment
that imposed social costs on workers and business. Kennedy's Council
of Economic Advisers targeted a 4 percent unemployment rate as
being achievable by monetary and fiscal policy without causing inflation. And the experience of virtually stable prices from 1959 to 1964,
when unemployment was above 4 percent, and subsequent accelerating
inflation when the rate fell below 4 percent seemed to bear out this
view.

The trade-off approach behind the Kennedy Council's thinking was
challenged in models by Edmund Phelps and Milton Friedman that
postulated a natural rate of unemployment. But the natural-rate view
seemed to make the policymaking process even easier. This view
argued that a unique rate of unemployment exists that is neither too
high nor too low, and if this rate is maintained, wage inflation will not
accelerate. Provided the natural rate of unemployment (sometimes
called the nonaccelerating inflation rate or NAIRU) could be estimated
or found by trial and error, a clear policy target was available.

The experience of the 1970s has buried both the optimism of the
Kennedy Council and the simplicity of the natural-rate hypothesis.
There does not seem to be a stable, unique natural rate of unemployment. Both wage and price inflation seemed to accelerate at times that
were hard to describe as showing excess demand for labor.

Thus began the process of reappraisal described above. The papers
in this volume were selected with the aim of helping policymakers
assess the state of the labor market and of clarifying the shifting

1

linkages between this market and inflation. At the outset there was some hope that it might be possible to break away from the Phillips curve framework that has dominated research in this area for twenty years. (The Phillips curve plots the rate of inflation associated with any given amount of economic slack.) In particular, it was hoped that a measure of labor market performance could be found that was independent of inflation. For example, one could define labor market equilibrium as equality between the number of unemployed and the number of vacancies. However, many of the papers did end up analyzing the determinants of the rate of wage increase and the trade-off between economic slack and inflation. That was probably inevitable, because it is the nature of this trade-off, or indeed the question of whether such a trade-off really exists, that is the fundamental issue for policy.

My own paper is intended to set the stage for the subsequent discussion of issues. I begin by looking at a variety of measures of labor market performance and conclude that the unemployment figures are really the only ones that show chronic slack in the 1970s. Measures of labor turnover and help-wanted advertising suggest that, apart from 1975–76, the 1970s were a period of normal labor demand. There are alternative explanations for this divergence among the labor market signals, but I conclude that the main reason is an increase in structural unemployment. It follows that for purposes of setting macroeconomic policy the conventional unemployment rate can be a misleading guide to the state of the labor market. As a single indicator, the adjusted unemployment rate constructed by George Perry is better, but still not adequate.[1] Information on the amount of unemployment needs to be supplemented by a variety of alternative sources of information, including turnover and help-wanted series that reflect the demand for workers. Were information available on vacancies, this too would be helpful.

The paper continues with a discussion of why structural unemployment may have increased and why labor market slack is a relatively feeble instrument for reducing the rate of wage increase. In both cases, it is argued, these problems are side effects of labor market institutions

1. "Changing Labor Markets and Inflation," *Brookings Papers on Economic Activity,* *3:1970,* pp. 411–41. Perry breaks down the unemployed into their age-sex groupings. He then weights each demographic group by its relative wage to get a measure of market-effective unemployment.

and arrangements that increase the wage and job security of those who are already employed and have seniority. It is not easy to escape the policy dilemmas that this creates. If one could really be confident that a decisive change in policy regime (a strict rule of monetary tightness, for example) would actually result in greater wage responsiveness and an end to inflation without major recession, this would be an attractive option. But the doubts about such an approach are serious. Alternatively, there are incomes policies, but these have not been successful in the past. It may be that a tax-based incomes policy or a system of flexible wage-price controls could be made to work. I suggest combining strict control over aggregate demand with either a flexible incomes policy or measures to make the labor market more responsive to unemployment.

The next two papers take somewhat different approaches to the problem posed by the shifting Phillips curve linking unemployment and inflation. James Medoff and Katharine Abraham argue that the key instability in this relationship is created by the increase in the amount of unemployment associated with a given amount of true labor market slack. They note that the deterioration in the inflation-unemployment combinations experienced in the 1970s is paralleled by a shift in the combinations of unemployment and vacancies that have been observed.

This finding leads them to suggest that there may be a more stable or stronger relationship between the rate of growth of money wages and two measures of unsatisfied labor demand—the quit rate and the help-wanted index—than between wage growth and unemployment. They test this proposition econometrically and find it supported by time-series data from 1956–80. One might have expected that both unemployment—the unutilized supply in the labor market—and vacancies—the unsatisfied demand—would show up as significant determinants of wages. But Medoff and Abraham find that the powerful unsatisfied demand variables seem to make the unemployment rate irrelevant for the inflation outcome. In their view, the unemployment rate can be virtually discarded as a measure of labor market tightness relevant for inflation. Of course unemployment still represents an important measure of the costs of economic slack.

Robert Gordon's paper takes a rather different view of the shifting Phillips curve. He would agree that part of the shift is due to the increase in structural unemployment, so he uses the Perry-adjusted unemployment number rather than the conventional rate as his measure of labor market slack. But the focus of his analysis is on price increases rather than wage increases, and he considers the effect of a variety of shocks to the economy. These include the slowdown in productivity growth, the change in the value of the dollar, the increases in the relative prices of food and energy, the Nixon controls program, and small effects from minimum wage and social security tax rate changes.

In addition, Gordon finds that the rate of inflation is influenced importantly not only by the level of the Perry unemployment rate but also by its change. This means that the rate of inflation declines relatively rapidly during a recession, when the unemployment rate is rising. But once the unemployment rate levels off or starts to decrease again, the deceleration of inflation is reduced and there may even be some reacceleration.

In recent years it has been argued that the nature of the policy regime—the framework in which policy decisions are made—can make a big difference to the effectiveness of a particular policy action. Gordon argues that the change to a flexible exchange rate system in the early 1970s was such a regime change, with implications for inflation control. Flexible rates allow the monetary authority to control the price level more directly than before, through the channel leading from interest rates to exchange rates to prices, instead of waiting for the long drawn-out impact of money on unemployment and then on wages and prices. His paper models the impact of the exchange rate on inflation and hence provides a quantitative assessment of the importance of the policy regime change.

Gordon uses his results to simulate the response of the economy to alternative policy choices. He is also able to determine from his equations which conventional unemployment rate represents labor market equilibrium, that is, what the natural rate is. He finds that in 1972 the conventional unemployment rate would have to have been about 6.1 percent simply to avoid accelerating inflation. This is much higher than the 5.0 percent rate that would have achieved this goal in 1956. By 1978 the natural rate had fallen from its 1972 high, but only by a very small amount—to 5.9 percent. It follows that very high unemployment rates would have been required in the past few years to bring about rates of inflation much below the ones actually experienced. For example, in one simulation Gordon finds that a tight money rule could have reduced the inflation rate by 2.9 percentage points in the fourth quarter of 1980, but at the cost of running an unemployment rate averaging 7.8 percent in 1978–80.

In both the Gordon and the Medoff–Abraham papers, past price increases feed back into current increases in prices or wages. This means that the specifications assume that there is little or no trade-off between inflation and economic slack *in the long run*. The explorations undertaken by the authors are to pin down the shifting short-run trade-off after allowing for the wage-price spiral.

In the fourth paper, John Geweke takes a very different methodological approach to understanding the role of the labor market in the macroeconomy. In the last few years, econometricians such as Christopher Sims and Thomas Sargent have argued that there are major problems in specifying, identifying, and then estimating structural econometric models. As an alternative they have proposed estimation techniques that impose few prior restrictions on the data and include a large number of free parameters. Significance tests then determine whether or not changes or innovations in one variable or a set of variables can predict innovations in another variable. For example, if there is a significant feedback of price inflation into wages, one would expect that price innovations predict wage innovations. Similarly, one can test whether a particular measure of labor market performance— like the quit rate—can actually predict wage movements.

John Geweke has made his own original contributions to this new econometric literature and he applies some of his techniques here. He considers interactions among five variables: the growth rate of the money supply, the wage rate (average hourly earnings in manufacturing), the consumer price index, and two measures of the labor market—the quit rate in manufacturing and the reciprocal of the unemployment rate. Geweke divides his data into two periods, 1955–71 and 1971–78.

Over the period 1955–71 he finds clear evidence that monetary policy does predict future changes in the quit rate and the unemployment rate. Fluctuations in the monetary growth rate over the course of the business cycle lead to cyclical fluctuations in unemployment and the quit rate, but there is no longer-run effect. Over this period, tight money contributed to recession and high unemployment, and loose money to expansion and low unemployment. Geweke also finds important longer-run feedback from the labor market variables to money: it seems that monetary policy did respond to fairly persistent high or low unemployment.

For the same period (1955–71), Geweke then turns to an analysis of the predictors of wage inflation. He finds that a combination of labor market variables plus either the consumer price index or the money supply can predict most of the variance in wages. In a striking conclusion, Geweke finds "no evidence that nominal wages are primarily a monetary phenomenon. In the long run, innovations in the monetary growth rate are estimated to account for about 10 percent of the variation in the wage growth rate, and this estimate is not significantly different from zero." In contrast, the conventional Phillips curve variables do well in explaining nominal wage movements, as noted above.

Unlike Medoff and Abraham, Geweke does not find the quit rate performs better than the unemployment rate as a measure of labor market performance. This is probably because his main results are for the 1955–71 period and because he detrends the data. The unemployment rate is not necessarily showing the correct trend, but it continues to provide an indication of variations in the state of the labor market.

Unfortunately, Geweke's interesting results are not confirmed by the data for the period after 1971. There do not appear to be clear patterns of prediction or causality among these variables in the 1970s. In one sense this is a disappointment and a weakness in the findings. In another sense, perhaps it confirms Gordon's conclusion that exogenous shocks in the 1970s have been pushing the other variables around.

In his discussion of Geweke's results, Robert Hall points to another striking finding. There is apparently no tendency for exogenous movements in wages to cause changes in either the unemployment rate or the quit rate. That fits well, he argues, with recent models of labor market behavior, specifically with efficient-market contract-theory models.

In their paper, Daniel Mitchell and Larry Kimbell seek to understand the importance of wage contracting in determining labor market outcomes, although their view of the role of contracts is not based on the efficient-market literature that Hall described. They first examine labor market institutions, why they occur, and their implications. In all but casual labor markets there are property rights associated with employment. In particular, employers grant certain rights to their employees with respect to both wages and employment security. In some countries most employees are covered by detailed, legally binding, explicit contracts. And of course in the United States, the legal union contract is important. In many cases, however, implicit contracts or understandings govern the employer-employee relation.

Mitchell and Kimbell explore some of the reasons why these arrangements exist. The "threat effect" of unions is very important. Management consultants who counsel firms on how to avoid being unionized usually suggest that they adopt personnel practices like those of unionized firms. A second reason derives from public policy. Employers are required to follow certain practices to avoid discrimination charges, and various programs regulate the work environment.

Mitchell and Kimbell note that current employment practices were not generally followed in the nineteenth century. Current labor force arrangements and institutions are fairly modern. They present a historical review and a survey of the theoretical literature to complete the rationale for the existence of both implicit and explicit wage contracts.

Within macroeconomic models, they see contracts as associated with three characteristics of wage setting: the impact of labor market slack is attenuated, multiyear contracts introduce lags and inertia, and price increases can induce wage increases through explicit or implicit cost-of-living escalation. To demonstrate the impact of these contract effects, the authors use two methods. First they run some simulations using a simple four-equation model with a wage-adjustment equation varied in several ways. They then use the UCLA forecasting econometric model as a basis for similar simulations.

They find that, relative to the base case, reducing the effect of unemployment on wages makes it harder to fight inflation with recession. The same is true if there are more long-term contracts. If there are escalator clauses, however, the fight against inflation is easier, since an initial reduction in inflation quickly feeds back into further reductions in wage increases. This finding about escalators holds out some promise for policy, although of course such escalators make it harder to prevent OPEC-style price shocks from being translated into persistent inflation. In general, escalators make the rate of wage change adjust more quickly up and down.

Within the more elaborate UCLA model, where there are more

equations and generally longer lags, the same basic findings hold, but they come out much less forcefully in the results. This is because the impact of particular parameter changes tends to be absorbed and dampened in a large model.

The paper by Pierre Fortin and Keith Newton examines the importance of unemployment insurance and other institutional factors in influencing labor market behavior. Fortin and Newton examine the Canadian labor market since World War II. They find that, like the United States, Canada has experienced a marked deterioration in economic performance; both unemployment and inflation grew worse in the 1970s. Another common theme is that the demographic composition of the labor force has contributed to a deteriorating unemployment picture. Some Canadian authors have argued that the 1972 amendment of the Unemployment Insurance Act, which sharply increased benefits, raised the unemployment rate by between 1 and 2 percentage points after a lag of a couple of years. From 1975 to 1979 the unemployment rate averaged 7.6 percent, while inflation, measured by the consumer price index, averaged 8.9 percent. After some of the effects of the 1972 amendment were felt, policy backpedaled, reducing the scope of the program. But it remains substantially more generous than the U.S. system.

The authors also argue that upward adjustments in Canada's minimum wage have made structural unemployment worse. The minimum wage rose by over 20 percent in 1974. A high minimum wage plus a generous unemployment insurance program combine to make unstable jobs more attractive and more common.

Because of the demographic and policy changes in the labor market, the authors agree with U.S. observers that the conventional aggregate unemployment rate provides a misleading guide for policy. They look at an adjusted unemployment rate and the vacancy rate. This latter series is available for Canada by linking employment service data for the 1950s, the help-wanted index in the 1960s, and Statistics Canada's Job Vacancy Survey data in the 1970s. The authors also examine other labor market tightness measures, including a measure of labor hoarding and hours worked per employed person.

On the basis of a Canadian wage equation, the authors conclude that an adjusted unemployment rate (either Perry's method or a similar rate developed by Michael Wachter), the adult male unemployment rate, and the vacancy rate all do about equally well in measuring tightness. Other supplementary measures do not seem to add any further useful information. Their results confirm the importance of public policy, with both greater generosity of unemployment insurance and higher wage minima pushing up the natural rate of unemployment. But they find a smaller impact of unemployment insurance than that found in earlier work.

Kim Clark and Lawrence Summers also look at the impact of unemployment insurance, but they take a very different empirical approach in studying its effect on the U.S. economy. They believe it is important to determine how unemployment insurance alters all of the different labor market transitions, that is, movements among the states of employment, unemployment, and nonparticipation.

Unemployment insurance can affect behavior if, for example, it encourages workers to remain unemployed rather than accept new jobs or if it encourages firms to make short-term layoffs every time demand falls. More positively, unemployment insurance can encourage labor force participation by providing more security of income. Clark and Summers also stress that unemployment insurance may simply change the way people report their behavior, rather than actually change their behavior.

In order to estimate the impact of unemployment insurance, Clark and Summers use the March and April 1978 Current Population Surveys. By comparing the two, they can trace the flows of people from one labor market state to another. A detailed computer program developed by the authors estimates the unemployment insurance for any individual in the sample should that person become unemployed. Geographical differences in unemployment insurance benefit levels are considered, as are differences among individuals in marginal tax rates. Tax rates are relevant because benefits were untaxed in 1978 and therefore worth more than the same amount of wage income. Finally, the authors estimate the "transition probabilities" for their model. These measure, for example, how likely it is that someone who is unemployed in the March survey will have a job one month later, given characteristics of the individual, his local labor market, and the level of his unemployment insurance benefit.

The overall results for those who are unemployed do not show that benefits either discourage withdrawal from the labor force or discourage job acceptance. This is counter to the prediction of theory. Clark and Summers speculate that unmeasured individual differences may be causing the problem and they note that for those unemployed workers who are on layoff the expected results hold.

The effect of unemployment insurance on employment decisions appears to be quite strong and in the expected direction. Firms with a variable demand for their product can minimize their labor costs in the short run (that is, for a given wage rate) by varying employment to the full extent implied by the variations in product demand. However, the market encourages firms to take a longer-run view and to provide greater job stability because workers will require compensation in the form of a high wage when their jobs are very insecure. By subsidizing unemployment, the unemployment insurance system reduces the effectiveness of this market mechanism and increases employment instability. Experience-rated taxes are supposed to offset this, but they do not do so very effectively. Clark and Summers do find a substantial effect of unemployment insurance on the probability of job separation, with the greatest effect on layoffs, as one would expect.

Taken together, the two sets of results on transitions from employment and unemployment indicate support for theoretical work that uses implicit-contract and layoff models to study labor force turnover. They do not give the search model of unemployment much support, because the predicted effect of unemployment insurance in extending job search was not found.

To some extent unemployment insurance causes persons who are separated from their jobs to remain unemployed or to report themselves as unemployed, rather than withdrawing from the labor force. Thus, the system should reduce the frequency of transitions from employment to nonparticipation. Clark and Summers do indeed find this result, but the effect seems much larger than is plausible. The implausibly high response is reduced substantially by applying a nonlinear estimation procedure, but still remains higher than one would expect.

The results for transitions into the labor force are also a little surprising. The directions of the effects Clark and Summers find are indeed in accord with one's prior view: unemployment insurance encourages transitions from nonparticipation to unemployment rather than employment. Insurance benefits encourage entrants and reentrants to the labor force to search for jobs rather than accept jobs that are immediately available. What is surprising is that such a job search response shows up for the entrants and reentrants, who are mostly ineligible for benefits.

As their final step, Clark and Summers ask what the overall effect of the system is on unemployment, employment, and labor force participation. They find that the partial effect of the unemployment insurance system has been to raise the unemployment rate by 0.65 percentage point. Primarily because of the strong estimated effect on transitions from employment to nonparticipation, they find that the system has raised the employment-to-population ratio by 0.62 percentage point and the participation rate by 1.11 percentage points. These are partial effects because the role of unemployment insurance as an automatic stabilizer has not been counted, nor has the impact of the taxes used to finance the system.

In 1977 James Tobin and I published a theoretical model of the impact of wage subsidies and public employment on the natural rate of unemployment.[2] A feature of this model was that there were different equilibrium or natural unemployment rates for different classes of workers. It was argued that a wage subsidy would increase the demand for hard-to-employ workers and also lower their unemployment rate, provided the relative wage received by such workers were higher in the new equilibrium situation.

In the final paper, Nicholas Kiefer and George Neumann look for evidence that labor market transition probabilities, and hence equilibrium unemployment rates, are in fact sensitive to wage rates. This is of interest in itself and helps evaluate the validity of the Baily-Tobin model. The data set used is from the Denver Income Maintenance Experiment (DIME). The persons and families in the sample were low-income—less than $9,000 per year (or $11,000 for two earners)—and had family heads between the ages of 18 and 58. The Denver area has a lower rate of unemployment than the country as a whole, although the low-income sample has above-average unemployment. The experiment itself, of course, had an impact on the behavior of the people in the sample, but Kiefer and Neumann avoid this problem by working only with the control group. There are important differences between the way spells of unemployment and transitions into and out of the labor force are measured in DIME data and the usual methods of the Current Population Survey (CPS). In particular, the rate of transition from unemployment to nonparticipation is as much as one-fifth the

2. Martin Neil Baily and James Tobin, "Macroeconomic Effects of Selective Public Employment and Wage Subsidies," *Brookings Papers on Economic Activity, 2:1977,* pp. 511–41.

size in the DIME data as in the CPS data. But Kiefer and Neumann argue that many of the CPS transitions reflect classification error or are economically and behaviorally meaningless. They suggest that the implications of wage changes on equilibrium unemployment or employment rates can be estimated well from the DIME data.

Their empirical results indicate that indeed higher wage rates are associated with lower equilibrium unemployment rates for all four of their age-sex groups. This interesting finding is in accord with the assumption of the Baily-Tobin model. The authors note that the observed association could reflect unmeasured characteristics of the individuals—persons who tend to remain employed or leave unemployment quickly also earn higher wages. But they argue that this is not a valid interpretation of their results. Their estimates are not based on the actual wage received by a given individual, but rather on a predicted wage. The wage variable, therefore, does not contain information on unmeasured individual characteristics.

Although they support a key assumption of the Baily-Tobin model, Kiefer and Neumann are pessimistic about using a targeted wage subsidy to reduce the aggregate natural rate of unemployment. This is because they find that the labor force participation rate of teenagers tends to rise almost as fast as the employment rate. Many people may feel, however, that nonemployment of teenagers, with associated problems of crime and social discontent, may be at least as much of a problem as open unemployment. In that case a targeted subsidy might look better.

During a concluding panel discussion, two related questions were raised that are of particular relevance for policy. The first was whether a consensus had emerged from the conference on a suitable index to measure labor market performance. The second was whether, given some suitable measure, labor market equilibrium could be defined independently of inflation, so that achieving equilibrium would then be a policy target. This latter question grew out of a concern that the labor market was being blamed for the acceleration of inflation after 1978, whereas in many people's minds the sources of inflation acceleration were outside the labor market.

Several participants responded to these questions. It was argued that there was a broad consensus that structural problems had made unemployment worse in the 1970s. Some people felt that the adjusted unemployment rate developed by Perry corrected for this problem and, therefore, provided a valid measure of tightness. Other measures of labor market performance do not add information to a wage-determination equation. Many others felt that unemployment-based measures of the state of the labor market were inadequate. Information on turnover and help-wanted advertising should be considered. If the collection of job vacancy data could be resumed, this would provide the best complement to an unemployment measure, particularly if the skill level and geographical location of available vacancies could be estimated.

Thus, there was no consensus on a particular index of labor market performance. A rough consensus did emerge that policymakers should not restrict themselves to a single tightness measure but should try to evaluate several series, just as many monetary economists look at alternative monetary aggregates and at interest rates.

It was noted that Robert Gordon's paper had analyzed in detail precisely the question that had concerned policymakers, namely exogenous inflation shocks in the 1970s. His results demonstrated that most of the acceleration of inflation had come from these shocks, with unemployment being below the natural rate only in 1972–73 and 1979. Many people agreed that deviations of unemployment from its natural rate were a minor part of the inflation story in the late 1970s. But others argued that there was a widely held view that excess-demand inflation was a serious problem in the 1970s. It was suggested that this latter view may have been misunderstood. It could be argued that demand restraint was necessary to offset the price shocks, but that is not the same as saying excess demand caused the inflation increase.

The discussion of this point underlined how difficult it is to develop a policy target for the labor market independent of inflation. To offset accelerating inflation, one may wish for slack in the labor market and not for equilibrium. In addition, because of minimum wage laws, restrictive practices, and unemployment insurance, it could well be that the most desirable state of the labor market from the point of view of efficiency and job opportunities is not consistent with price stability, even with no further bad news about productivity or oil prices.

MARTIN NEIL BAILY

Labor Market Performance, Competition, and Inflation

HAS THE HIGH average unemployment rate of the 1970s indicated labor market slack? And if not, why has unemployment been high? Several of the papers at the conference have examined questions relevant to this issue, but it also turns out that the simple facts are quite instructive.

After looking at the key factual issues of the macro labor market, I examine the tensions between market forces and institutional and contractual arrangements. I then argue that a combination of contracts and bounded rationality provides the right mix to explain behavior and to use for policy analysis. Finally, I discuss possible policy strategies to reduce inflation by attempting to broaden the bounds of rationality or make the labor market more competitive and therefore more efficient.

Measuring Labor Market Tightness in the 1970s

Table 1 shows a variety of measures of labor market tightness over the postwar period. It also shows the size and significance of any time trend in each series and of the coefficient on a dummy variable equal to unity in 1970–79 and zero otherwise. The striking fact about these numbers is that they show no strong evidence that the labor market in the 1970s either had more slack or that it was tighter than during earlier periods. The overall unemployment rate certainly showed an upward trend and was substantially higher on average in the 1970s than in earlier periods. The demographically adjusted unemployment rate constructed by George Perry[1] also shows a worsening over time,

---

1. George L. Perry, "Changing Labor Markets and Inflation," *Brookings Papers on Economic Activity, 3:1970*, pp. 411–41. (Hereafter *BPEA*.)

15

Table 1. *Selected Measures of Labor Market Tightness, 1950–80*

Year or period and descriptive statistic	Unemployment rate (percent)	Perry unemployment rate (percent)[a]	Help-wanted index[b]	Layoff rate[c]	Quit rate[c]	New hire rate[c]
Year or period						
1950–54	4.0	3.3	112.8	1.3	2.4	3.5
1955–59	5.0	4.2	72.1	2.0	1.6	2.4
1960–64	5.7	4.6	69.1	2.0	1.4	2.4
1965–69	3.8	2.6	112.8	1.3	2.4	3.5
1970	5.0	3.6	94.6	1.8	2.1	2.8
1971	5.9	4.4	82.7	1.6	1.8	2.6
1972	5.6	4.0	100.0	1.1	2.3	3.4
1973	4.9	3.3	119.6	0.9	2.8	3.9
1974	5.6	3.9	101.9	1.5	2.4	3.1
1975	8.5	6.5	73.0	2.1	1.4	2.0
1976	7.7	5.8	84.7	1.3	1.7	2.6
1977	7.0	5.2	102.2	1.2	1.9	2.9
1978	6.0	4.3	125.3	0.9	2.1	3.1
1979	5.8	4.2	128.9	1.1	2.0	3.0
1980	7.1	5.7	103.6	1.8	1.5	2.2
Descriptive statistic						
Growth rate (percent)[d]	1.5	0.94	1.7	−1.5	0.15	0.21
	(3.0)	(1.5)	(14.1)	(−2.8)	(0.25)	(0.4)
Dummy 1970–79[d]	1.5	0.87	18.9	−0.36	0.08	0.02
	(3.4)	(2.1)	(2.3)	(−2.2)	(0.4)	(0.1)

Sources: U.S. Department of Labor, Bureau of Labor Statistics, establishment and household data in *Employment Situation* and *Employment and Earnings;* BLS Bulletin 1312; and U.S. Department of Commerce, Bureaus of the Census and of Economic Analysis, *Business Conditions Digest*, series 3 and 46.

a. George Perry's weighted unemployment rate as described in "Changing Labor Markets and Inflation," *Brookings Papers on Economic Activity, 3:1970*, pp. 411–41.

b. Help-wanted advertising in newspapers divided by the civilian labor force, indexed to 1972 equals 100.

c. All manufacturing, per 100 employees per month.

d. Numbers in parentheses are *t*-statistics.

although of a somewhat smaller magnitude, and by 1978–79 the Perry unemployment rate was back to a fairly "normal" level.

In contrast to the unemployment figures, however, the help-wanted index increased substantially relative to the labor force. The principal measures of turnover in manufacturing—layoffs, quits and new hires— all show no change or even a tighter labor market in the 1970s than in earlier periods. Of course, the restriction of this data to manufacturing is a limitation, but cyclical slack should show up in manufacturing.

Thus a key puzzle of the 1970s is that the unemployment rate has risen relative to other indicators of the state of the labor market, and there are three possible explanations of this divergence in the measurement signals.

1. High unemployment could be a structural problem resulting from such factors as demographic changes, rigid wages, or a change in industrial composition.

2. It may be that a *persistently* slack labor market reveals itself in high unemployment and not elsewhere. To some extent, help-wanted advertisements and layoffs are measures of *changes* in tightness, not the level. This could mean that the aggregate unemployment rate is the measure that gives the correct signal.

3. The opportunity cost of workers' time may have risen as a result of transfer payments, taxes, or the profitability of the underground economy.

The Structural Hypothesis

There is substantial support evident for the structural hypothesis. Table 2 shows the unemployment rates of males aged 35 to 44 and blacks aged 16 to 19. The former group has the lowest average unemployment rate of any age-sex category and its rate is very variable over the business cycle. This group also plays an important role in wage determination. There was no clear worsening of its unemployment rate in the 1970s. Certainly 1975 was a bad year, but compared with previous experience, 1973 was a rather low unemployment year and 1978 and 1979 were low to normal years. By comparison, blacks aged 16 to 19 form a group with a large fraction of hard-to-employ workers, and their unemployment rate is high throughout the business cycle. There has been a startling increase in the unemployment rate of this group over time.

Thus a breakdown of the overall unemployment rate into its constituent groups suggests that the chronically hard-to-employ have had adverse experience in the 1970s but other workers have not. This impression is reinforced by the series shown in table 2 of the fraction of the unemployed reporting uncompleted unemployment spells over fifteen weeks. This has also shown an increase over time, a particularly striking fact because young people, on average, have short spells. Thus it is likely that the percentage of the age-adjusted unemployed with long spells has actually been substantially higher in the 1970s than previously.

If it is true that structural unemployment has worsened, then the question is what has caused this phenomenon. Most studies find that the minimum wage has had a measurable negative impact on the employment of teenagers and a slight positive impact on their unemployment. It is clear from table 2 that increases in the level of the minimum wage itself do not appear to have been a contributory factor to the worsening of structural unemployment in the 1970s. But, of course, the existence of the minimum wage may well have interacted with the baby boom and the increase in female participation. Further, the escape valve provided by the uncovered sector has been seriously eroded (coverage figures are also shown in table 2). Most of the uncovered jobs available to urban workers today are jobs such as babysitting or household and yard work. Most of these jobs are unreported in the establishment data. It is unclear how they affect the Current Population Survey employment and unemployment numbers.

There are obstacles to the employment of low-skilled workers in addition to the legal wage minimum. High entry-level wages and direct restrictions on the numbers of trainees in many trades and professions also reduce opportunities. Table 2 shows the movement of some entry-level union wages and the relative level of wages in the key sectors—steel, coal, and automobiles—that are highly unionized with powerful leverage over industry wages. The figures show that these indicators of union wages rose in the 1970s. The final column of table 2 shows that employment in manufacturing, mining, and construction declined relative to total employment.

In a labor market with freely fluctuating relative wages, changes in the demographic or skill mix should show up primarily in changes in relative wages, not in unemployment. When wages fail to adjust, then a structural unemployment problem results. It seems that the increase over time in the number of young workers has coincided with slow growth in the number of manual jobs that are fairly well paid and have training and promotion prospects. Wage rigidities and even perverse wage movements have been partly a cause of the slow growth in the total number of such jobs. In addition, relative wage rigidity has reduced the fraction of these jobs given to the hard-to-employ by reducing the incentive for employers to hire and train workers with below-average skills or motivation.

The Persistent Slack Hypothesis

What happens when an economy experiences a prolonged period of slack? From 1958 to 1963 the average unemployment rate was about 6 percent, and there was considerable concern about the problem of structural unemployment. As recession was followed by rapid expansion, the unemployment rate fell very rapidly, dropping below 4 percent by 1966 and remaining there for four years. Firms that had argued in earlier years that it did not pay to train the unskilled were reported to be doing just that. Drawing on this example, and also the rapid decline of unemployment in the late 1930s and early 1940s, many economists have suggested that weak aggregate demand creates a labor market that looks as if it has structural problems. The "queue" model of Lester Thurow or the "two-tier" model of Arthur Okun are examples of this view.[2] Consider first some supporting evidence, and then the counterarguments.

EVIDENCE FOR THE QUEUE MODEL. Recent analysis of the distribution of lengths of unemployment spells has tended to reinforce the Thurow-Okun view. The data given in table 2 showed that there are sharp cyclical increases in the proportion of the unemployed with uncompleted spells over fifteen weeks. Clark and Summers estimated that 55 percent of the weeks of unemployment in 1975 were attributable to completed unemployment spells in excess of twenty-six weeks, compared to 35 percent in 1969.[3] Thus unemployment that is apparently structural seems to increase sharply during periods of slack.

Arthur Okun's model of a two-tier labor market suggested that a high-pressure economy could produce permanent benefits for disadvantaged workers. His empirical work showed that in an expansion (a) men over twenty-five leave low-paying jobs and their places are taken by young people, (b) adult men gain employment in high-paying manufacturing and transportation, but that other demographic groups are also able to enter these high-paying industries in substantial

2. Arthur M. Okun, "Upward Mobility in a High-Pressure Economy," *BPEA*, *1:1973*, pp. 207–52; Lester C. Thurow, *Poverty and Discrimination* (Brookings Institution, 1969), chap. 4; and Lester C. Thurow and Robert E. B. Lucas, "The American Distribution of Income: A Structural Problem," prepared for the Joint Economic Committee, 92 Cong. 2 sess. (Government Printing Office, 1972).

3. Kim B. Clark and Lawrence H. Summers, "Labor Market Dynamics and Unemployment: A Reconsideration," *BPEA*, *1:1979*, p. 37.

Table 2. *Selected Measures of Structural Factors, 1950–80*
Percent

Year or period and descriptive statistic	Unemployment rate, males 35–44	Unemployment rate, blacks 16–19	Unemployment over 15 weeks	Minimum wage[a]	Minimum wage coverage[b]	Entry wage[c]	High wage[d]	Industrial employment[e]
Year or period								
1950–54	2.7	n.a.	17.1	49.9	53.4	n.a.	135.4	44.1
1955–59	3.5	21.3	24.6	50.6	53.1	140.3	140.0	41.7
1960–64	3.7	27.0	27.7	50.2	62.3	143.7	140.3	38.0
1965–69	1.9	25.4	16.8	51.9	73.9	142.4	135.3	36.6
1970	2.4	29.1	16.2	49.5	78.4	145.8	131.0	34.4
1971	3.1	31.7	23.7	46.4	78.4	151.6	134.7	33.3
1972	2.7	33.5	23.9	43.2	78.4	149.1	138.7	33.2
1973	2.0	30.2	18.9	40.6	83.7	149.2	139.8	33.6
1974	2.6	32.9	18.5	45.8	83.3	148.5	143.0	32.9
1975	4.9	36.9	31.7	46.4	83.0	149.0	148.7	30.6

1976	4.1	37.1	32.1	47.3	83.8	148.2	151.3	30.5
1977	3.5	38.3	27.9	43.8	84.4	146.3	153.7	30.5
1978	2.8	36.3	22.8	46.6	85.1	n.a.	156.6	30.6
1979	2.9	33.5	20.1	47.1	85.5	n.a.	157.1	30.7
1980	4.1	35.8	24.6	46.5	86.1	n.a.	158.7	30.0

Descriptive statistic

Growth rate (percent)[f]	−0.6	2.7	0.66	−0.38	2.1	0.28	0.32	−1.4
	(−0.79)	(8.4)	(1.1)	(−2.5)	(17.7)	(7.6)	(3.8)	(−31.3)
Dummy 1970–79[f]	0.17	9.9	2.1	−5.0	21.7	6.8	7.7	−8.0
	(0.43)	(6.3)	(0.86)	(−4.1)	(7.2)	(8.6)	(3.4)	(−7.5)

Sources: BLS, establishment and household data in *Employment Situation and Employment and Earnings*; BLS Bulletins 2027, 2015, 2038; U.S. Department of Labor, Employment Standards Administration, Division of Evaluation and Research, *Fair Labor Standards Act Annual Report*; *Economic Report of the President, January 1980*; and *Employment and Training Report of the President, 1979*.

n.a. Not available.

a. As a percentage of the average gross hourly wage for the private nonagricultural sector.

b. Percentage of nonsupervisory workers covered by the minimum wage.

c. A weighted average of entry wages in the printing, local trucking, and building unions, weighted with 1977 membership estimates, as a percentage of the average gross hourly wage for the private nonagricultural sector.

d. A weighted average of wages of production workers in the steel, coal, and automobile unions, as a percentage of the average gross hourly wage for the private nonagricultural sector.

e. The employment in the manufacturing, mining, and construction industries, as a percentage of total employment.

f. Numbers in parentheses are *t*-statistics.

numbers, and (c) overall, these shift effects are substantial and can be viewed as movements up the ladder within demographic groups from low-wage to higher-wage industries.

Wayne Vroman has argued that "the evidence strongly supports the Okun-Thurow view of the benefits of a high-pressure economy." In particular, he noted substantial wage gains associated with the job shifts that occur in expansions. He also argued that there was "clear evidence of continuing benefits from the high-pressure economy" as "other" workers made continued gains during 1966–68 relative to white adult males.[4]

PROBLEMS WITH THE QUEUE MODEL. The contrasts recorded by these authors between the labor market of a slack economy and that of a tight economy are certainly striking. And the idea of labor market queues that are cyclical in length is plausible, and indeed is exactly what would be expected in a world where relative wages are sticky. However, the inferences to be drawn from this have to take account of the following: there is clear evidence of the stubbornness of structural problems in the labor market even when the economy is very tight, and the feasibility of using aggregate demand pressure to overcome structural problems has to be judged against an inflation constraint.

Consider the first issue. Even when the unemployment rate of adult males drops very low, the rates for blacks and teenagers remain stubbornly high. Martin Feldstein argued this point in his Joint Economic Committee report[5] and then examined the relation among the unemployment rates of various demographic groups in more detail in work with Brian Wright.[6] In addition, James Tobin and I tried numerous functional forms and tests in an unsuccessful attempt to shake the Feldstein conclusion.[7] It is not that the evidence conflicts with a queue model. Teenage unemployment rates do drop several percentage points when the adult male rate drops one point. And teenage employment is very variable over the cycle—more so than

4. Wayne Vroman, "Worker Upgrading and the Business Cycle," *BPEA*, *1:1977*, pp. 242, 249.

5. Martin S. Feldstein, "Lowering the Permanent Rate of Unemployment," prepared for the Joint Economic Committee, 93 Cong. 1 sess. (GPO, 1973).

6. Martin Feldstein and Brian Wright, "High Unemployment Groups in Tight Labor Markets," *Harvard Institute of Economic Research Discussion Paper no. 488* (June 1976).

7. This work was performed during research on our joint paper, "Macroeconomic Effects of Selective Public Employment and Wage Subsidies," *BPEA*, *2:1977*, pp. 511–41.

unemployment because of participation variations. But the Feldstein-Wright approach indicates that even if adult male unemployment had been as low and stable in the 1970s as it was in 1966–69, there would still have been high and rising unemployment for other groups.

On the side of the inflation constraint, one has to look back at the late 1960s with dismay. William Fellner made the following comments on Okun's 1973 paper:

This paper describes some important advantages of a 4 percent unemployment economy. . . . But the real question here is whether, in the contemporary United States, the attempt to maintain 4 percent unemployment would not result in a 4 percent interlude followed by a period with a rate of unemployment significantly higher than 5 percent.[8]

The answer to Fellner's question was evident even as he wrote. The rate of growth of hourly compensation in the private business sector of the economy accelerated from 3.9 percent in 1965 to 6.9 percent in 1970. This acceleration was not led by exogenous upward pressure on the consumer price index (CPI). The unemployment rate exceeded 5 percent by 1971 and has fallen below that level in only one year since then. There is, therefore, no doubt that within the range of unemployment rates that avoid accelerating wage inflation, there will remain a persistent problem of high unemployment among certain hard-to-employ workers, and this problem has worsened.

Finally, I would argue that there is some doubt as to the permanency of gains achieved by a very tight labor market. The economy went into a recession, or at least a downturn, in 1970–71. The unemployment rate reached 5.9 percent in 1971, and the rate for 20- to 24-year-olds reached 10.0 percent. This combination of unemployment rates is no better than the combinations that were observed in 1961 and 1963 before the long expansion of the late 1960s. The workers who had the advantage of entering the labor force as 16- to 19-year-olds during the late 1960s do not seem to have carried over any lasting benefit that was visible in their experience as 20- to 24-year-olds in the 1970–71 recession. Similarly, in 1978 the overall unemployment rate was 6.0 percent while the rate for 20- to 24-year-olds was 9.5 percent. Thus the workers who entered the labor force during the period of high unemployment from 1974 to 1977 do not seem to have carried over any lasting disadvantage once the overall unemployment rate returned to a normal level in 1978.

8. William Fellner, "Comments and Discussion," *BPEA*, 1:1973, p. 253.

The Opportunity Cost of Time

For most people, work is unpleasant, so that perhaps the pressure of financial necessity is required to encourage job acceptance and to discourage excessive turnover. The growth in importance of social insurance programs may have lessened the pressure to work and caused unemployment to grow.

Unemployment insurance (UI), as a direct subsidy to the unemployed, has obviously received the most attention. Table 3 shows the average weekly UI benefit over time relative to average weekly spendable earnings. There has been some uptrend in the series and in coverage. Transfer payments can also alter the incentive to accept employment even if there is no direct link to unemployment. Teenagers would be more likely to accept menial jobs if their families had no source of income at all. Middle-aged people would be more likely to accept an available but unattractive job if their parents had no social security check. Table 3 shows that transfer payments have skyrocketed in recent years and have become a significant source of disposable income. It is important to consider the possible consequences of income-support programs, but at the same time not to jump to the wrong policy conclusions. It has been noted that a heavy fine on all unemployed workers would surely reduce the measured unemployment rate, but would hardly be desirable. For good reasons, the prevailing view in most advanced countries of the world is that the threat of starvation should not be the principal force pushing people to accept jobs.

Transfer payments are not the only changing determinants of the opportunity cost of time. Underground and illegal activities are reportedly a matter of routine for a substantial number of unemployed people. By its very nature, this kind of activity is hard to measure, but in table 3 an index of property crime is shown. It is common wisdom that the crime rate has soared in the 1960s and 1970s. Unemployed young people question the rationale for working all week at a poor job for less money than could be made in a couple of hours "hustling" on the streets.

Conclusions on Labor Market Tightness

It was argued earlier that by inspecting a variety of measures one could conclude that the labor market did not show evidence of persistent

Table 3. *Selected Indicators of Nonwage Income Sources, 1950–80*

Year or period and descriptive statistic	Unemployment benefits as percent of spendable earnings[a]	Unemployment coverage as percent of labor force[b]	Transfer payments as percent of national income[c]	Property crime (offenses per 100,000)[d]
Year or period				
1950–54	39.4	56.0	4.8	1,047.2
1955–59	41.7	57.7	5.7	1,352.6
1960–64	44.8	58.1	6.9	1,968.6
1965–69	45.0	63.1	7.4	2,878.9
1970	48.0	63.0	9.5	3,782.5
1971	48.3	63.1	10.5	3,956.8
1972	45.9	70.8	10.4	3,741.1
1973	46.3	73.1	10.6	3,920.1
1974	47.7	73.5	11.8	4,598.7
1975	48.2	70.7	14.0	5,018.3
1976	48.2	71.8	13.5	5,002.5
1977	46.3	72.8	13.0	4,775.6
1978	46.3	82.9	12.6	4,813.6
1979	46.0	84.0	12.2	5,198.2
1980	47.9	83.1	13.4	n.a.
Descriptive statistic				
Growth rate (percent)[e]	0.71	1.3	3.9	6.5
	(10.1)	(11.9)	(16.5)	(42.0)
Dummy 1970–79[e]	4.4	13.8	5.6	2,668.9
	(5.1)	(7.7)	(11.1)	(9.8)

Sources: U.S. Department of Labor, Employment and Training Administration, *Handbook of Unemployment Insurance Financial Data;* BLS, establishment and household data in *Employment Situation* and *Employment and Earnings;* U.S. Department of Commerce, Bureau of Economic Analysis, recent issues of *Survey of Current Business;* Federal Bureau of Investigation, annual issues of *Uniform Crime Reports;* U.S. Bureau of the Census, *Historical Statistics of the United States, Colonial Times to 1970* (Government Printing Office, 1975).

n.a. Not available.

a. The average weekly unemployment benefit as a percentage of the average weekly spendable earnings of a married worker with three dependents, in current dollars.

b. Average number of workers covered by unemployment insurance in any month as a percentage of the civilian labor force. After 1970, covered workers includes those covered on a reimbursable basis.

c. Government transfer payments to persons as a percentage of national income in current dollars.

d. Includes larceny-theft, burglary, robbery and auto theft. Total crime rates were estimated from urban crime rates for the years 1952–55, and the series was adjusted for changes in the FBI's estimation techniques occurring in 1957, 1974, and 1977.

e. Numbers in parentheses are *t*-statistics.

slack during the 1970s despite the fact that the average rate of unemployment was 1.5 percentage points higher than in the 1960s. Certainly 1975–77 was a period of slack, but other years show signs of a fairly tight market.

Robert Gordon's paper for this volume confirms this view, using a detailed analysis of price behavior. He finds that the natural rate of unemployment was 5.9 percent during the 1970s, compared with the actual average rate of 6.2 percent. Slack in 1975–77 was largely offset by a tight market in 1970 and 1973. He finds that the labor market was almost exactly in equilibrium in 1978 and 1979 and was, therefore, not the source of the sharp inflationary pressure in 1979 and 1980.

Unemployment was worse in the 1970s than in the 1960s for two reasons. First, the labor market was in disequilibrium from 1965 through 1970, with excess demand for labor resulting in an acceleration of inflation. Thus some increase in unemployment in the 1970s was almost inevitable. Second, there has been an increase in structural unemployment.

The hard-to-employ enjoy substantial benefits if there is excess demand for labor, because the impact of wage and hiring restrictions is reduced. There is not much evidence that the benefits persist once equilibrium is restored. The increase in structural unemployment has occurred because of (a) the increased number of persons in unemployment-prone groups (young people especially); (b) the lack of adjustment of relative wages to accommodate the changing composition of the labor force as a result of legal and institutional restrictions; and (c) the unwillingness of some workers to accept available but menial employment.

The above description indicates that high unemployment among the hard-to-employ has both voluntary and involuntary components. The organization Reading Is Fundamental estimates informally that 23 million American adults cannot read well enough to understand a want ad. It is no wonder that most of the people in this group cannot obtain the kind of jobs that they aspire to. Should their unemployment be defined as voluntary because they are unwilling to accept the menial low-paying jobs that are available to them? Or should it be defined as involuntary because the educational system has not equipped them with the skills they need? It is not clear that the choice of labels matters for policymaking. Policy should aim to ensure that the labor market allows these people to compete for those jobs they can do, to ensure that they do have a clear financial incentive to work, and to improve the general level of skills and literacy.

Competition and Labor Market Problems

The unemployment rate in the 1970s averaged 6.2 percent. It follows that a conventional attack on inflation (by means of restrictive monetary and fiscal policy to create unemployment in excess of the natural rate in order to decelerate wage and price growth) would mean unemployment in the 7 to 8 percent range for a prolonged period.

It may be that unemployment in this range has become acceptable. In fact unemployment has been in this range since May 1980 and, as this is written, seems likely to stay above 7 percent for some time. And there are some signs of a slowing of inflation, as expected. But many economists rebel at the idea of fighting inflation with an unemployment rate as high as this, because they believe that it is either too costly or unnecessary. Proposals to reduce the cost in the labor market (and elsewhere) of the fight against inflation are based upon some concept of why wages respond so sluggishly to an excess supply of labor, or why they appear to respond this way. The nature of competition in the labor market and the role of expectations are generally seen as the crucial factors.

The Response of Wages to Excess Labor Supply

One of the most persistent and powerful tensions within the economy is between the force of competition and the desire for equity and stability. Short-run and long-run market forces place workers in competition with each other for jobs and create pressures for real and relative wage changes over time. But this conflicts with a desire for stability of real and relative wages and some form of job security— protection against being displaced by another worker and protection against layoffs as seniority is acquired. These are important attributes of the employment relation that are valued very highly by workers and influence union behavior.

Furthermore, limitations on competition do not all come out of the actions of employees. Employers will respond to their employees' preference for security even in a nonunion context because it is cheaper to do so in the long run, and because they too benefit from a stable work force. In a recent article Richard Freeman and James Medoff describe the two faces of unionism.[9] One face represents the role of unions in limiting competition and the second the role of unions as

9. The Freeman and Medoff approach draws on work by Albert Hirschman. See Albert O. Hirschman, *Exit, Voice and Loyalty: Responses to Decline in Firms, Organizations, and States* (Harvard University Press, 1970); and Richard B. Freeman and James L. Medoff, "The Two Faces of Unionism," *The Public Interest*, no. 57 (Fall 1979), pp. 69–93.

mediators of conflicts between workers and management. The argument here is a related one. If there were an auction market for labor, there would be a much easier adjustment to structural changes, such as a mix of demand changes or shifts in comparative advantage. There would be much easier accommodation to demographic changes, such as the baby boom and the increase in female labor force participation. There would be much easier adjustment to a shifting trend pattern of real wages in response to productivity and terms-of-trade changes. And it would be much easier to slow the upward movement of money wages in order to combat inflation. On the other hand, institutionalized wage and employment contracts, explicit or implicit, provide important real benefits. Several writers (of which I am one) have described these benefits in contract-theory models, and Arthur Okun's recent book makes an eloquent and forceful case stressing the many advantages of a labor market where wages are set by an invisible handshake, not by an invisible hand.[10]

Do Contracts Really Limit Market Forces?

There is an important efficient-market theorem that qualifies the argument given above. Fully informed, cooperative, rational economic agents will not agree or adhere to contracts that result in dead-weight losses or economic returns in certain states of nature. In particular, optimal income insurance can be provided separately from allocational decisions. The employment decision can be based upon a shadow wage that may differ from the actual wage paid.[11] And, of course, for the economy as a whole, the stability of real and relative wages could be achieved with arbitrary levels of nominal wage rates and prices, provided everything moved together. This theorem is fundamental and is in no way overturned by models such as those of Stanley Fischer, or Edmund Phelps and John Taylor, or by my own overlapping-contracts simulation model.[12] Neither is it overturned by Taylor's

10. Arthur M. Okun, *Prices and Quantities: A Macroeconomic Analysis* (Brookings Institution, 1981).

11. See Robert E. Hall, "Employment Fluctuations and Wage Rigidity," *BPEA, 1:1980*, pp. 91–123, and references.

12. Edmund S. Phelps and John B. Taylor, "Stabilizing Powers of Monetary Policy under Rational Expectations," *Journal of Political Economy*, vol. 85 (February 1977), pp. 163–90; Stanley Fischer, "Long-Term Contracts, Rational Expectations, and the Optimal Money Supply Rule," *Journal of Political Economy*, ibid., pp. 191–205; and Martin Neil Baily, "Contract Theory and the Moderation of Inflation by Recession and by Controls," *BPEA, 3:1976*, pp. 585–622.

models of contracts with rational expectations.[13] The inference has been drawn from this theorem that contracts—implicit or otherwise—need not impede the rapid adjustment of the labor market to changes in the rate of growth of the money supply, provided that such changes are anticipated or expected. But the fact that the theorem is true on its assumptions does not mean that it accurately reflects the way the real labor market operates. The kind of contracts assumed in the papers cited above are probably much more realistic than the ones that would have to hold to produce the fully efficient solution.

Why Does the Efficient-Market Theorem Fail in Practice?

Adam Smith's invisible hand required very little information on the part of individual economic agents. One of the key advantages that is claimed for a market system compared with a planned economy is precisely that no one need understand the system in order for it to work. Kenneth Arrow has argued that efficient information-gathering and decisionmaking agents will concentrate on the specific micro data most relevant to their own decisions and not on macro data.[14] The point is perhaps made better in terms of analysis of data rather than collection, however. Macro data is readily available and cheap. But it is very hard indeed to determine the *implications* of a given change in some aggregate series for the pricing decisions of a single firm. Milton Friedman has stressed that it is hard for anyone not trained as an economist to understand how a market system works.[15] Thomas Sargent found time-series data to be consistent with the natural-rate hypothesis only under the assumption that the full set of macro variables is not considered by micro agents. He suggests there may be "bounded" rationality, a concept developed by Herbert Simon.[16] Specifically, it seemed that monetary and fiscal policy instruments were not included

13. John B. Taylor, "Aggregate Dynamics and Staggered Contracts," *Journal of Political Economy*, vol. 88 (February 1980), pp. 1–23; and "Staggered Wage Setting in a Macro Model," *American Economic Review*, vol. 69 (May 1979, *Papers and Proceedings, 1978*), pp. 108–13.

14. Kenneth J. Arrow, "The Future and Present in Economic Life," *Economic Inquiry*, vol. 16 (April 1978), pp. 157–69.

15. Milton Friedman, "Blaming the Obstetrician," *Newsweek*, June 4, 1979, p. 70.

16. Herbert A. Simon, *Models of Man: Social and Rational* (Wiley, 1957), pp. 196–206.

in the information set relevant for unemployment outcomes.[17] Thus the first and central reason why the efficiency theorem does not hold is because the contracting parties simply do not fully and correctly incorporate all macroeconomic information into their own decisions.

The second difficulty occurs because in order to avoid the real cost of a nominal disturbance it is necessary to orchestrate a coordinated adjustment of all wages and prices. Exponents of market efficiency emphasize that goods and labor are traded for money and argue that a change in the supply of money will, therefore, directly alter the terms of trade between goods and money. That is to say the price level will change, with no need for a period of labor or product market slack. Because all prices and wages are quoted in dollars, their adjustment will automatically be coordinated.

Those who doubt the ability of markets to adjust in this way tend to see the role of money rather differently. Money is only the medium of exchange, allowing goods and labor to be traded for other goods and labor. Workers and firms see a wage of $5 an hour not as the rate of exchange between labor and money, but as reflecting the ten hours of labor it takes to buy a $50 bag of groceries. Alternatively, one group of workers compares their wage in dollars per hour with the wage of other workers in dollars per hour. This relative wage, of course, is a pure number and has no direct connection to the money supply. It is through this latter perception—in which the price level is determined by individual relative price-setting decisions—that the difficulty of achieving a coordinated decline in price and wage increases becomes apparent.

The third source of efficiency problems involves distributional questions and cartelization. The very same mechanisms and institutions that limit market forces in beneficial ways can be coopted to benefit one or more groups at the expense of others or of the general welfare. Some unions obtain the power to paralyze a city or even large parts of the national economy in order to achieve their wage demands. Major employers in a given city can agree not to compete with each other for workers. A majority of established union members can enforce rules that place all the costs of layoffs on low-seniority workers or prevent workers that might have had jobs from getting them. Some firms exploit changing economic circumstances to alter the terms of implicit or explicit contracts to their advantage.

17. Thomas J. Sargent, "Rational Expectations, the Real Rate of Interest, and the Natural Rate of Unemployment," *BPEA, 2:1973*, pp. 429–72.

Summing Up on Wage Adjustment

1. If there were a competitive auction market for labor, it would not be necessary to have rational expectations. A decline in money growth might create a temporary disequilibrium and high unemployment. But prices and wages would quickly adjust and inflation would be easily slowed. Relative wages would move smoothly from one equilibrium to another following structural change in the economy.[18]

2. In fact there is an institutional and/or contract labor market because of the real costs to workers of operating in an uncertain and perfectly competitive environment and the costly nature of turnover for firms.

3. The existence of a contract labor market *by itself* does not imply nominal wage stickiness or that wage inflation is costly to end. But it does when *combined* with the facts that economic agents have only bounded rationality, that a coordinated adjustment of money wages is hard to achieve, and that the labor market is not fully competitive. If money supply growth is slowed, this has only a limited effect on wage contracts in force or even those being negotiated. In general, only when the impact of aggregate demand has imposed real reductions in output and employment will behavior change. And even then a temporary downturn will be viewed as a change in the weather, not a change in the climate. The kind of insurance pledge that employers give is that there will be only a limited cutback in wage increases as a result of a temporary decline in labor demand.

4. But the efficiency theorem is still important because it highlights the possibility that in principle wage inflation could be reduced without disturbing real and relative wages and without prolonged labor market slack. It is this tantalizing prospect that has motivated rational-expectations theorists to suggest regime changes and has motivated others to suggest incomes policies.

Labor Market Problems

Relative Industry Wages

In most institutional or implicit contract situations, market forces seem strong enough to keep sectoral wage differences roughly in

18. There is a tricky issue of stability even with flexibility. But that is a hypothetical question for present purposes.

equilibrium in the long run. The salaries of engineers go up and down relative to other professions as supply and demand move. Teachers have seen salaries sink under the weight of excess supply. Employers provide a degree of wage insurance, but do not pledge to maintain real or relative wages at levels that are out of line with long-run market forces.

There is evidence of wages getting out of line over a long period when there is a strong union that can effectively control competition. The steel industry and the auto industry are the obvious examples. Any analysis of these industries will indict some bad management decisions and will point to the effects of the energy crisis and pollution control. But their most striking feature is that relative wages rose steadily relative to the manufacturing average.[19] The world economy has been a source of market discipline even in these industries, but it has generated political pressures for subsidies or tariffs.

Almost all economists oppose trade barriers and most of them oppose bailouts for failing companies. But the political pressure that is created when imports result in (or seem to result in) substantial unemployment and economic distress should not be underestimated. There is a kind of catch-22 here. The reason that the permanent closing of a steel or auto plant causes such distress is that the next best job for many of the laid-off workers would pay only half to two-thirds of their previous wage. But of course that is exactly why the plant closed to begin with.

There is much to be said for reducing intervention in this kind of situation. A great advantage of markets is that they are impersonal. Once the federal government accepts the responsibility for maintaining full employment in each industry or avoiding bankruptcy by large corporations, then incentives are reduced. There is a responsibility of the government to alleviate poverty by income redistribution. But long-run subsidizing of jobs for which wages have gone far above the average is not justifiable on those grounds. If everyone knew that trade barriers were never going to be introduced, perhaps the behavior of workers and firms in the high-wage industries would be different.

As a form of insurance, one can justify readjustment assistance to those affected by trade, but it would help if such assistance were designed to assist workers to retrain or relocate. It is not clear that such programs are very successful, but they would be better than

19. Robert W. Crandall, *The U.S. Steel Industry in Recurrent Crisis: Policy Options in a Competitive World* (Brookings Institution, 1981), pp. 34–38.

subsidies that prolong and worsen structural unemployment. And they would maintain the incentive to restrain costs before a firm or industry goes under.

Job Opportunities for Inexperienced Workers

This is not the place for a detailed discussion of ways to solve the structural unemployment problems of hard-to-employ workers. I have had my say elsewhere on the possible role for wage subsidies and public jobs.[20] There is surely a clear case for improving competition and job opportunities at the bottom end of the job market ladder. There is at present a climate favoring deregulation, and an application of this to the labor market would be welcome. Attempts to develop the skills of young people or those displaced by shifting trade or technology will fail if legal restrictions or the restrictive practices of professional organizations or unions prevent the expansion of employment in areas of growing demand. If curbing inflation is really an urgent priority, then so is reducing the amount of structural unemployment associated with a given amount of labor market slack.

Wage Inflation and Labor Market Slack

I will ignore for the present the proposals to change policy regimes and consider the old-fashioned unemployment-inflation trade-off. The standard view is that if there is enough labor market slack, then an entrenched inflation will unwind. The slope of the short-run trade-off is very flat, but the curve shifts down as inflationary expectations are reduced. Thus the long-run trade-off is steep.

There is no serious dispute about the validity of the above argument. Even the Okun-Perry wage norm will eventually be reduced.[21] But there is a serious question as to whether the steepening of the trade-off over time might be partly offset. Given the structure of the labor

20. Martin Neil Baily and James Tobin, "Macroeconomic Effects of Selective Public Employment and Wage Subsidies," *BPEA*, 2:*1977*, pp. 511–44; and Martin Neil Baily and Robert M. Solow, "Public Service Employment as Macroeconomic Policy," in *Job Creation Through Public Service Employment*, vol. 3, *Commissioned Papers*, an interim report to Congress of the National Commission for Manpower Policy (GPO, 1978).

21. Okun, *Prices and Quantities: A Macroeconomic Analysis;* and George L. Perry, "Inflation in Theory and Practice," *BPEA*, 1:*1980*, pp. 207–41.

market described earlier, it is layoffs of already employed workers that have the biggest impact on wage increases. The presence of a somewhat larger pool of unemployed has a smaller effect. If the economy goes into a downturn, bottoms out, and then starts to grow at the same rate as potential output (that is, it maintains persistent slack), then the layoff rate will rise during the downturn, but drop back again. In fact, even in a persistently slack labor market, most of the employees on temporary layoff can be rehired as attrition opens up jobs. This then leaves a larger pool of entrants, reentrants, and permanent layoffs looking for their first jobs or new jobs. The ability of this pool to compete against established workers is very limited. Its main impact is to allow those firms that are expanding to do so without bidding wages up. Thus the policy trade-off in the intermediate run may not be as steep as is sometimes claimed. Rational-expectations theorists stress that the Phillips curve gives an unreliable estimate of the long-run trade-off. True enough, but not everything goes in one direction. Persistent demand restraint has not been tried in recent times.

I have compared a standard wage equation (using the unemployment rate for adult males) with a wage equation using the layoff rate as the cyclical variable. The results, which are presented in the appendix, support the above argument. The layoff equation shows much greater stability than the unemployment equation. Parameter estimates from the period 1954–70 track the years 1971–79 well using layoffs but poorly using unemployment. A difference in timing is also evident. The layoff rate lagged one year works better than the contemporaneous value. The reverse is true for the unemployment rate. Increases in economywide unemployment and reductions in wage inflation tend to occur together as a result of prior declines in product demand and increases in layoffs in manufacturing. Robert Gordon's paper in this volume also gives partial confirmation of the importance of changes in unemployment. In his preferred equation, the change in the unemployment rate is a significant determinant of the rate of price inflation.

Summing Up on Labor Market Problems

1. As long as the line is held on trade barriers, market forces seem to work well enough in keeping sectoral relative wages in line.

2. Barriers to wage adjustment at the low end of the labor market

and direct restrictions on entry in some professions have limited competition and worsened structural unemployment. There is not enough competition even in the long run to allow hard-to-employ workers their best shot at getting jobs.

3. Various features of the labor market make wages particularly resistant to market pressures that are perceived to be temporary. This has suggested that a prolonged period of restraint is needed. No doubt if there were enough slack for long enough this would slow wage inflation. But the price of curbing inflation this way is very uncertain, because a downward shock and persistent slack may exert different amounts of market pressure on wages.

Labor Market Policy and Inflation

Despite the fact that the unemployment rate is currently over 7 percent, there is little pressure evident for expansionary policies. In fact the main political concern is whether or not tax cuts will be inflationary. If there are no adverse price shocks from energy, food or other commodities, then an unemployment rate of 7.5 percent could reduce wage inflation to about 5.5 percent a year within three years. If productivity growth recovers to about 2 percent a year, this would mean a core inflation rate of 3.5 percent a year. Thus it is quite possible for an orthodox anti-inflation, tight-money strategy to work. But the costs of this strategy are heavy and the risks of failure are high. As I noted earlier, a three-year spell of high but stable unemployment could have only a limited impact on wages. New price shocks may come along. Productivity growth may not do so well.

To improve the speed of the downward adjustment of inflation with lower costs of unemployment and output, there are two proposals that try to exploit the potential of the efficient-market theorem. The first proposal assumes the labor market is efficient, and that observed inertia in the response of wages to changes in money growth has come about because such variations in monetary policy were not anticipated. Thomas Sargent has argued that a "regime change" could halt inflation quickly and with little cost, and he offers as support economic events in the 1920s and 1930s in Europe. Hyperinflations in Poland, Germany, Austria, and Hungary were ended abruptly and (arguably) without major costs. A more gradual inflation was ended quickly in France.

Sargent argues that the United States should change its policy regime to bring its current inflation to an abrupt end.[22]

Changing the Policy Regime

The first issue is to make clear the nature of a regime change. Without a clear definition, the idea is an elusive proposition to test. In addition to the successful regime changes cited by Sargent, there have been examples of serious attempts to change price behavior that foundered. Britain went back on the gold standard after World War I at an exchange rate that did not match its price level. The result was widespread unemployment. Mrs. Thatcher's current experiment is hard to assess. Inflation has come down, but the costs have been high. As long as the definition of a regime change remains loose, one can always rule out the cases that did not work.

Sargent defines a regime as a "function or *rule* for repeatedly selecting the economic policy variable or variables." A regime change is then a "change in the rule for [a] pertinent variable [that is] widely understood, uncontroversial and unlikely to be reversed."[23] With this definition, Sargent's hypothesis that inflation can be ended quickly and without major costs is probably correct. The efficiency theorem shows that in principle real and relative wages and prices need not be altered by a lowering of inflation, or at least that dead-weight losses can be avoided. If by "widely understood" it is meant that everyone knows what to do in his own wage- and price-setting decisions to achieve this, and if by "uncontroversial" it is meant that everyone is willing to take the necessary actions, then almost as a tautology a regime change will work. To go even further, Sargent may be correct that there have been certain historical episodes in which something like a regime change has taken place.

But achieving these conditions in a fractious democracy is no easy task. A frequent proposal is that a constitutional amendment be passed to limit Federal Reserve power to expand the money supply and perhaps to impose some requirement for budget balance. This would

22. Thomas J. Sargent, "The Ends of Four Big Inflations," National Bureau of Economic Research Conference Paper 90 (Cambridge: NBER, January 1981); and "Stopping Moderate Inflations: The Methods of Poincaré and Thatcher" (University of Minnesota and Federal Reserve Bank of Minneapolis, 1981).

23. Sargent, "Stopping Moderate Inflations," p. 4.

be very hard to pass and would take many years, even assuming acceptable and workable limits on Federal Reserve action could be devised. And passage of an amendment is no guarantee that the new policy regime would be widely understood and uncontroversial. Was Prohibition widely understood and uncontroversial?

Sargent emphasizes irreversibility as a crucial element in a regime change, which is why an amendment is seen as the appropriate vehicle. Mrs. Thatcher's experiment has caused massive unemployment, he says, largely because it was expected that her policies would ultimately be reversed and that money growth would be increased in the future. If the big problem with controlling inflation is to persuade persons entering into multiyear price or wage contracts to build in to those contracts a low expected rate of inflation, then irreversibility may be important. But it is a strange argument for Sargent to make, since he disputes the importance of contracts in creating wage and price rigidity. Just because Mrs. Thatcher may be thrown out in the future does not mean her current monetarist policies were unanticipated. She campaigned on a monetarist platform. Anyone taken by surprise by the tight money that followed her election must not have been paying attention. According to Sargent's own model of the business cycle, it is only unanticipated monetary contractions that cause excess unemployment. The expectation of a policy reversal in the future should make no difference today. Thus there is no obvious way to reconcile the British experience with Sargent's business cycle model. This casts doubt on the model and hence on the likely success of a policy derived from it.

The difficulty with a regime change is that its restrictions on monetary and fiscal policy would limit the scope for countercyclical stabilization. That is one reason a constitutional amendment would be so hard to pass. Fighting inflation is not the only goal of policy. The U.S. economy was extremely unstable until the post–World War II period. Unemployment averaged 14.2 percent from 1893 to 1898 and 18.8 percent from 1931 to 1940.[24] It would be disastrous to return to such times as these.[25] This is the big danger of a rigid policy rule. It would be better to rely on the slow disinflation effects of 7.5 percent unemployment

24. U.S. Bureau of the Census, *Historical Statistics of the United States, Colonial Times to 1970*, pt. 1 (GPO, 1975), p. 135.

25. See also Martin Neil Baily, "Stabilization Policy and Private Economic Behavior," *BPEA, 1:1978*, pp. 12–50.

than to commit the economy to a rigid policy rule whatever the level of unemployment.

But nevertheless the credibility argument does have force if one abandons the assumption of freely flexible wages and prices and recognizes that multiyear contracts do play a part in inflation inertia. The slow process of unwinding wage inflation could well be speeded up by an attempt to broaden the "bounds of rationality." A firm commitment is needed to a program of gradual disinflation with clearly set goals and realistic monetary and fiscal policies to achieve those goals rather than the current conflicting combination of monetary and fiscal policies. The implications of the chosen policy strategy for individual decisions should be explained, and the consequences of not adjusting contracts should be stressed. But if the costs of deflation are really to be kept to a minimum, it is worth trying to come up with additional policies that may make the labor market act more efficiently.

Incomes Policies

There is a curious similarity between Sargent's description of the conditions for a successful regime change and the conditions that are cited for a successful incomes policy. Instead of mandating the growth of the money supply, the advocates of incomes policies suggest mandating the paths of wages and prices. In the former case the preconditions of understanding and agreement are to avoid the dead-weight losses due to recession; in the latter case they are to avoid strikes, evasion, and social unrest.

The problems with locking monetary and fiscal policy have been described. The problem with locking wages and prices is, of course, the distortion that is caused in relative wages and prices. Tax-based incomes policies (TIPs) are one way to limit the damage to relative wages. A firm wishing to raise its wages by more than the guideline amount can do so and forgo the tax-incentive payment. There has been much discussion of TIPs recently and so there is no need to go over the ground again.[26] If a workable and acceptable version could be found, my own view is that a TIP would be a valuable supplement to a program of coordinated monetary and fiscal policies to end inflation.

26. Arthur M. Okun and George L. Perry, eds., *Curing Chronic Inflation* (Brookings Institution, 1978).

But serious practical problems of implementation remain. In particular, wage controls can be administered by a bureaucracy, but tax law, it is argued, cannot be written with enough detail to cover every case. In addition, it is possible for a union to violate the spirit of the program by getting a very large wage increase in one year and smaller increases in the next two. This would give a three-year wage path that violated the guideline or average, but was technically in compliance two out of three years. These difficulties are enough to suggest looking for an alternative.

Stimulating a More Competitive Labor Market

Firms and workers enter into contractual arrangements partly to reduce the risks of fluctuating markets. They regard the overall macroeconomic environment as given exogenously, independent of any actions of their own. And, of course, on an individual basis they are correct. But the risk-reducing arrangements that may be optimal for a single firm create adjustment problems in the aggregate, partly because nominal disturbances, such as changes in the money supply, do not result in rapid revision of contracts. This means that the risk of recession and layoffs may be worsened by an economy with contract wages, even though this trade-off is not apparent to the individual decisionmakers.

Because of the side effects of a contract economy, the unemployed do not get an adequate opportunity to compete for jobs, and inflationary inertia becomes imbedded in wages. One approach to this problem is to impose more responsiveness to competition for jobs or a greater wage response to recessions. Such a policy would mean in practice that firms with workers on layoff or with substantially reduced employment (compared with some average of previous employment) would not be permitted to raise wages at all or by more than a token amount. Firms with no special hiring or firing activity could raise wages by a guideline amount. Firms that could demonstrate serious difficulty in retaining their work force or meeting their needs for new hires could raise wages by more than the guideline amount.

Such a proposal, if it could be made workable, would have the effect of making the short-run trade-off between inflation and unemployment steeper. It would be used only to decelerate inflation; nobody wants a steep trade-off when the economy might be edging into excess demand for labor. I am not sure whether such a proposal is feasible, but it is surely worth considering ways of making the labor market more responsive to excess unemployment. Unlike other wage controls, it could not be used to suppress inflation while excess demand expansion continued.

Concluding Comments

Some have argued that high unemployment in the 1970s has indicated chronic aggregate excess supply of labor, which should have lowered inflation. Others have argued that, on the contrary, the labor market was too tight in 1978–79, contributing to the surge of inflation. This paper has suggested that neither view is correct. The labor market has been neither a major restraint on inflation nor a major cause of its acceleration. Unemployment has worsened because of structural problems.

The slow response of wage inflation to excess labor supply is understandable within an economy where wages are set in contracts and monetary disturbances are not quickly and fully incorporated into the set of information used to set nominal wages. If it were possible to get widespread understanding of and agreement for a program of monetary and fiscal restraint, then such a program would be attractive. But the difficulties of achieving this and the possibility of limiting stabilization policy make such a strategy dangerous. If they could be made workable, direct measures to make wages more responsive to excess unemployment and to open up more competition for jobs would help to minimize the side effects of a contract economy.

Appendix

This appendix reports the findings of some earlier work in which I experimented with an equation to fit the annual rate of change of the adjusted hourly earnings index (*AHE*).[27] The purpose of this work was

27. Martin N. Baily, *Inflation and Social Security Financing*, prepared for the National Commission on Social Security, Washington, D.C., 1980.

to look at the relation between the unemployment rate and other cyclical variables—in particular the layoff rate—and to try to separate out wage and price feedback effects.

The following two equations (using terms defined below) performed well:

(1) $\quad \Delta \ln AHE = a_1 + a_2 LAYOFF(-1) + a_3 \Delta \ln AHE(-1)$
$\quad\quad\quad\quad + a_4 \Delta \ln AHE(-2) + a_5 RESCPI(-1);$

(2) $\quad \Delta \ln AHE = b_1 + b_2 \ln URAM + b_3 \Delta \ln AHE(-1)$
$\quad\quad\quad\quad + b_4 \Delta \ln AHE(-2) + b_5 RESCPI(-1).$

The *AHE* index is a fairly clean number, adjusted for overtime and interindustry shifts. It covers only production and nonsupervisory workers but excludes fringe benefits. The index for the nonfarm private economy was used. The dependent variable is the change from one year to the next in the natural logarithm of the index. Annual data were used.

The two cyclical variables used were the layoff rate (*LAYOFF*) and the unemployment rate of adult males (*URAM*). Originally I had hoped to construct an index of labor market tightness using turnover data and a vacancy measure, such as the help-wanted index, and then compare the performance of the index with that of the unemployment rate. But no index performed better than the layoff rate alone. The layoff rate covers only manufacturing.

I was persuaded by search theorists and by institutionally oriented, implicit-contract theorists like Okun that wage increases granted in a particular firm or industry are heavily influenced by wage increases granted to other firms and industries. This suggests that the wage-wage feedback process should be given as much scope as possible, with the feedback of prices on wages playing a secondary role. To achieve this, a variable, *RESCPI*, was constructed as follows:

(3) $\quad \Delta \ln CPI = c_1 + c_2 \Delta \ln AHE + c_3 \Delta \ln AHE(-1)$
$\quad\quad\quad\quad + c_4 \Delta \ln AHE(-2) + RESCPI.$

So *RESCPI* is defined as the residual of a least-squares regression of the rate of change of the CPI on current and lagged values of the rate of change of wages. Thus *RESCPI* consists of "wage-purged" changes in the cost of living. For the period including the 1970s, the *RESCPI* variable has considerable variance. Clearly the procedure does not

Table 4. *Estimated Wage Equation, Selected Periods*[a]

Variable and summary statistic	Equation 1 (LAYOFF)			Equation 2 (URAM)		
	1954–79	1954–70	1961–79	1954–79	1954–70	1961–79
Variable						
Constant	3.48	4.19	2.81	2.38	3.69	2.22
	(4.5)	(2.9)	(3.9)	(3.9)	(3.4)	(4.6)
LAYOFF(−1)	−1.39	−1.58	−1.18	. . .	. . .	. . .
	(−4.6)	(−2.9)	(−3.8)			
ln URAM	. . .	. . .	. . .	−1.87	−1.99	−2.16
				(−4.2)	(−3.7)	(−5.0)
ΔlnAHE(−1)	0.708	0.605	0.804	0.957	0.744	0.709
	(4.4)	(1.8)	(4.2)	(6.3)	(2.8)	(4.2)
ΔlnAHE(−2)	0.0834	0.0837	0.0450	0.106	0.00605	0.463
	(0.53)	(0.30)	(0.23)	(0.64)	(0.026)	(2.4)
RESCPI(−1)	0.297	0.235	0.239	0.371	0.131	0.523
	(3.2)	(1.1)	(2.1)	(3.6)	(0.69)	(4.4)
Summary statistic						
R^2	0.912	0.765	0.947	0.904	0.812	0.961
Standard error	0.586	0.692	0.487	0.611	0.619	0.418
Mean dependent variable	5.19	4.15	5.66	5.19	4.15	5.66
Mean cyclical variable	1.64	1.78	1.52	1.37	1.30	1.34

a. All changes in logarithms are multiplied by 100. Numbers in parentheses are *t*-statistics. Dependent variable is ΔlnAHE(100).

yield direct empirical identification of the relative importance of wage and price feedbacks. But it imposes an a priori ordering.

The results of estimating equations 1 and 2 for the periods 1954–79, 1954–70, and 1961–79 are shown in table 4. Estimated over the full period, both equations do well by standard tests. All variables except the two-year lagged dependent variable are significant, and the equation fits well. The subperiod estimates test the stability of the equations, and there equation 1 (with the lagged layoff rate) does noticeably better. Table 5 shows the actual and fitted values from the six equations in table 4. It is notable that the second column in table 4 tracks the 1970s remarkably well. Wage inflation is underpredicted, but by less than many wage equations fitted through 1970. The residuals from the full-period equations are negative during the mid-1960s, suggesting some impact of the guidelines policy. The residuals during the 1970s do not suggest that the Nixon controls had any impact on wages.

Table 5. *Actual and Fitted Values from Table 4, Multiplied by 100*

Year and summary statistic	Actual	With layoff rate			With unemployment rate		
		Esti-mated, 1954–79 (fitted)	Esti-mated, 1954–70 (fitted)	Esti-mated, 1961–79 (fitted)	Esti-mated, 1954–79 (fitted)	Esti-mated, 1954–70 (fitted)	Esti-mated, 1961–79 (fitted)
Year							
1954	3.46	4.66	4.70	4.89	4.08	4.27	3.37
1955	3.19	3.10	3.05	3.07	3.68	3.61	4.18
1956	5.05	3.76	3.90	3.63	3.28	3.58	3.11
1957	4.81	4.25	4.28	4.47	4.28	4.62	3.27
1958	4.04	4.39	4.22	4.45	4.12	3.68	4.04
1959	3.49	3.40	3.16	3.44	4.21	3.78	4.45
1960	3.37	3.48	3.47	3.43	3.22	3.23	3.17
1961	3.02	3.03	2.91	3.03	2.99	2.86	2.83
1962	3.29	3.02	2.97	2.95	3.00	3.01	2.94
1963	2.83	3.34	3.33	3.29	3.12	3.20	2.81
1964	2.64	3.56	3.58	3.36	3.27	3.25	3.34
1965	3.35	3.66	3.69	3.41	3.59	3.56	3.66
1966	4.40	4.30	4.37	4.11	4.37	4.46	4.14
1967	4.81	5.17	5.21	5.07	5.35	5.32	5.03
1968	6.02	5.12	5.12	5.10	5.76	5.66	5.64
1969	6.38	6.13	6.07	6.20	6.85	6.58	6.52
1970	6.42	6.67	6.54	6.69	6.60	5.92	6.55
1971	6.81	6.11	5.82	6.19	6.51	5.59	6.63
1972	6.23	6.04	5.87	6.26	6.28	5.79	6.02
1973	6.00	6.37	6.35	6.40	6.20	5.81	6.29
1974	7.58	7.40	7.24	7.18	6.80	5.72	7.19
1975	7.99	8.13	7.60	8.10	7.81	5.98	7.79
1976	7.02	7.01	6.48	7.24	7.73	6.23	7.85
1977	7.27	7.13	6.92	7.16	6.66	5.61	7.03
1978	7.86	7.45	7.22	7.50	7.30	6.26	7.37
1979	7.64	8.29	8.05	8.32	7.91	6.74	7.92
Summary statistic							
Mean absolute error		0.398	0.461	0.394	0.421	0.676	0.443
Root mean square error		0.527	0.562	0.543	0.549	0.889	0.637

Quarterly data do show an effect, so apparently this is lost in annual data. Many people have postulated that the Nixon controls may have altered the timing of wage adjustments but not the magnitude of the ultimate increases.

The equation was run with a correction for first-order serial correlation. The estimated rho was small, and the coefficients on the other variables were changed very little, so the results in table 4 are for ordinary least squares. Note that the preferred layoff equation uses explanatory variables, all of which are lagged by at least a full year. This avoids endogeneity problems. Wage increases appear to be largely predetermined.

Comments by Nancy S. Barrett

The first part of this paper looks at measures of labor market performance by which one can assess the state of the labor market in any given year. The measures that Baily considers are shown in table 1. One of the interesting things to be learned from this table is that it is only the unemployment rate measures that indicate that the labor market in the 1970s was more slack than in earlier periods. The table also has an answer to an important question that concerned us at the Labor Department. It indicates that the labor market was tighter in 1978 and 1979 than in 1972, although not necessarily tighter than in 1973, by all of the measures except the unemployment rate.

Having laid out the indicators and trends, Baily then goes on to suggest three possible sets of explanations for why the unemployment rate was higher than the other measures during the 1970s. The first set is structural explanations. The second is that persistent labor market slack might raise unemployment but not affect the level of help-wanted advertisements or other similar measures. The third set of explanations has to do with transfer payments, or work disincentives associated with them, such as unemployment insurance.

The next part of the paper goes on to examine these hypotheses, although none of them are given a rigorous test. Nevertheless, there is some evidence in table 2 regarding a number of structural factors that might have resulted in the divergence between the unemployment rate and the other measures of labor market tightness for the 1970s. I would say that, of all the evidence put forward, perhaps the strongest support for the view that demographic factors have played a role is that the Perry-weighted unemployment rate has not increased by as much as the overall unemployment rate in this period and in fact has behaved similarly to the other measures of labor market tightness.

Given the absence of any formal hypothesis testing, however, I think some of Baily's assertions are too strong. For instance, he says, "It is clear from table 2 that increases in the level of the minimum wage itself do not appear to have been a contributory factor to high unemployment in the 1970s." It is not clear to me, because, if you want to test this hypothesis, you need to develop a relationship between the minimum wage and the gap between the unemployment rate and the other measures. Ideally one wants a structural relationship that looks not only at the minimum wage and its relationship to average hourly earnings, but also at its relationship to welfare payments. Also, it is known that the relationship between the minimum wage level and unemployment varies among demographic groups, and hence labor force compositional changes will influence the aggregate relationship.

I would make a similar statement about other variables in table 2. For example, I would not be able to agree that changes in entry-level union wages have had an impact on the gap between the unemployment rate and other measures of labor market tightness without seeing a statistical test of the relationship.

The second set of explanations that Baily puts forward is based on the idea that prolonged unemployment may have long-term adverse effects on labor employability. If there is high unemployment among a demographic group in some period, this may affect the group's employability later on and hence result in more structural unemployment for the whole economy.

What Baily did to test this was rather ingenious, but I am not completely convinced. I think he could have done more. He looks at an age cohort for which the overall unemployment rate was very low when its members were teenagers. Then he examines the unemployment rate for that same cohort when it was somewhat older. He compares this with the unemployment rate of a similar age cohort that experienced high unemployment as teenagers. He found for a couple of different periods that the age group 20 to 24 was not any better off in a recession for having had low unemployment during its teenage years. I would be interested in a related question for this age group, namely, what happens to its labor force participation. It seems to me that one common explanation of low labor force participation rates among black youth is that they have experienced prolonged periods of high unemployment. Perhaps looking at employment-to-population ratios would have been instructive.

The next section of the paper is on contracts and the failure of markets to achieve efficiency. There is a very interesting and potentially valuable insight in this section. That is the notion that it is the layoff rate, and not unemployment, that has the biggest impact on the rate of wage increase. I think it is a very compelling argument, and I hope that he will pursue it further.

Baily reasons that the rehiring that goes on following a recession is mainly from the pool of people who have been laid off temporarily before the recession and that the size of the pool of other unemployed workers is not very important, or at least is not driving the system. He has some regression results to support this in the appendix. There are two wage equations of interest: one with the layoff rate as the principal measure of labor market tightness, and the other with the unemployment rate for adult males. In the equations are also some lagged values of the rate of change of earnings. He tested for the stability of the equations and found, using subperiods, that the layoff equations were considerably more stable than the equations using the unemployment rate.

I have one small problem. I think that it is probably right that the layoff rate is a better measure of labor market tightness for the 1970s, but Baily says that it is better because it underpredicts wage inflation for the 1970s less than the equation with the unemployment rate. The question is whether there may be an omitted-variable problem. Looking at the specification of that equation, I would expect it to underpredict inflation in the 1970s, because it minimizes the importance of the CPI. My view is that nominal wage increases, at least in the later part of the 1970s, were very much driven by the drop in real wages. The CPI is the relevant variable to look at because it is the index that escalates not only union wages but also social security payments. Workers who do not have CPI escalation start to become relatively worse off and then they want to catch up, either to social security recipients or to workers that have cost-of-living adjustments (COLAs).

In the final section, which discusses anti-inflation policy, Baily examines three approaches: change of regime, incomes policy, and labor market policies designed to stimulate competition. All have considerable merit. However, one questions whether regime changes are likely to be any less painful or prolonged in their effectiveness than restrictive demand measures. The change in monetary regime that occurred in 1978 is only just beginning (three years later) to have a perceptible negative effect on inflation, while high interest rates have escalated the CPI and the federal budget deficit. As for incomes policy, although administrative problems are overwhelming, changes in the way social security payments are indexed and restrictions on COLAs and multiyear contracts could be accomplished with little bureaucratic effort and minimal relative price distortions.

Comments by Arnold Packer

I enjoyed Baily's paper and agree with most of the conclusions, except for some of the policy questions. However, I do think some of Nancy Barrett's criticisms are correct.

Baily looks at alternative measures of labor market tightness in the 1970s. I am not sure that I would have used decades; instead, I would compare 1965 to 1979 in the first table. Whether all or only some of the variables are compared, the outcome of the comparison is ambiguous. For example, Perry's weighted unemployment rate, which Bob Gordon says gives an unambiguous measure of labor market tightness, shows a 20 percent tighter labor market in 1965 than in 1979, which I find surprising.

Baily examines the divergence in the 1970s between the unemployment rate and the other measures of labor market tightness. He discusses the structural problems and notes the fact that the unemployment rates for 35- to 44-year-old males remained constant, while the unemployment rate of blacks increased rapidly. That is consistent with other data.

I was impressed by Baily's observation that relative union wages rose, while employment in unionized sectors fell. These data suggest deterioration in the ability of relative wages to adjust, a phenomenon that presumably causes more structural unemployment.

Baily also notes that persistent slack may lead to structural unemployment. That makes sense. Persistent slack means there are no more layoffs, but it is tougher for new entrants to get jobs; therefore, a persistent-slack policy generates structural unemployment and does not reduce inflation. I think that is a very profound policy question. New entrants and other potential new employees do not compete for jobs with existing employees. This means that a slowdown in wage inflation is a function of the *decline* in the economy and resulting layoffs, more than the level of unemployment. This idea suggests that holding the unemployment rate high will not do very much toward lowering inflation.

Baily was surprised that structural unemployment of black youth never disappears no matter how tight the labor market gets. That is what I always expected. His discussion of opportunity costs was interesting. The point on which Baily just touches about the underground illegal economy is a very important and a very difficult question. It is the kind of question that I think economists ought to go at, but I frankly do not know how to do it.

Baily concludes that structural unemployment, not demand slack, caused high unemployment in the 1970s; that the labor market was tight, and that both voluntary and involuntary structural unemployment coexisted. He suggests that our institutional arrangements mean wages are set by the invisible handshake, not the invisible hand. The important thing here is expectations and bounded rationality. Do individual workers really understand what is going on in monetary and fiscal policy? Don Nichols suggests that the purpose of incomes policies is to get the labor market to behave as if it had rational expectations. Baily is saying something similar. That is really an important new way to look at the purpose of incomes policies, namely, to get people who are involved in wage negotiations to understand what people who do have rational expectations understand.

Baily concludes that the slowdown in wage inflation is a function of the decline in the economy and resulting layoffs; therefore, neither a recession and recovery nor persistent slack will do much good in reducing inflation.

JAMES L. MEDOFF *and* KATHARINE G. ABRAHAM

Unemployment, Unsatisfied Demand for Labor, and Compensation Growth, 1956–80

VIRTUALLY all empirical analyses of short-run aggregate wage growth have an unemployment rate at their heart.[1] What lies behind the expected inverse relationship between unemployment and the rate of growth in wages? The following quotation clearly presents the standard rationale for including an unemployment rate variable in wage-growth regressions: "In a given labor market, wages tend to rise under conditions of excess demand, fall with excess supply, and remain constant when excess demands are zero. Since the aggregate unemployment rate is a good indicator of the general state of labor markets, as unemployment decreases, more and more markets come into a state of excess demand and the general pace of wage inflation increases."[2]

For an unemployment rate to in fact be "a good indicator of the general state of labor markets," two conditions must be satisfied. First, the typical unemployed person must represent the same number of available units of labor at each point in time. Second, the relationship between the availability of labor and labor market tightness must

We have benefited greatly from discussions with a number of individuals, in particular Olivier Blanchard, Charles Brown, Gary Chamberlain, James Duesenberry, John Dunlop, Richard Freeman, Robert Hall, and Jeffrey Sachs. In addition, we gained much from the many helpful criticisms and suggestions offered by the participants in seminars held at Brookings, Harvard, and the National Bureau of Economic Research. We are also most grateful to Greg Bialecki, Jon Fay, Cliff Frazier, Susan Johnson, Martin Van Denburgh, and especially Lori Wilson for their very skilled assistance on various aspects of the research to be discussed.

1. The seminal work in this area was A. W. Phillips's article, "The Relation Between Unemployment and the Rate of Change of Money Wage Rates in the United Kingdom, 1861–1957," *Economica*, vol. 25 (November 1958), pp. 283–99.

2. William O. Nordhaus, "The Worldwide Wage Explosion," *Brookings Papers on Economic Activity*, 2:1972, p. 442. (Hereafter *BPEA*.)

49

remain constant, which implies that there must be stability in the relationship between labor availability and unsatisfied labor demand. Thus, if the unemployment rate does not mirror the number of available units of labor or if the importance of structural unemployment changes over time, the unemployment rate will not be a good indicator of wage pressure from labor market imbalance.

This paper presents evidence concerning the use of various unemployment rates as barometers of tightness in the labor market. We first demonstrate that proxies for the unsatisfied demand for labor (the help-wanted index and the manufacturing quit rate) perform at least as well as either the official or the prime-age male unemployment rate when entered alone in wage-growth regressions. Moreover, we find that in regressions that include both an unemployment rate and a measure of unsatisfied labor demand, the unemployment rate does not matter, while the unsatisfied demand proxy does. We next present evidence that strongly suggests that, at least for the United States, a substantial fraction of the growing instability in Phillips relationships (again defined in terms of either the official or prime-age male unemployment rates) can be linked to growing instability in the relationship between unsatisfied labor demand and the relevant rate of unemployment. Furthermore, the relationship between our unsatisfied demand proxies and the rate of compensation growth appears to have been more stable than the relationship between unemployment and the rate of compensation growth. In sum, measures of employers' unsatisfied labor demand dominate measured unemployment rates as indicators of wage pressure emanating from labor market conditions.

The third section discusses the interpretation of our empirical findings. The paper's concluding section discusses the main implication of our analysis for macroeconomic theory and policy: labor market pressure on wages can be more reliably assessed by looking at measures of unsatisfied demand than at unemployment rates, which have played the key role in earlier analyses. We also emphasize the need for new microdata if the reasons for this are to be fully understood.

Compensation Growth and Its Correlates

Most economists would think it important to consider the role of tight versus loose labor markets as part of any study of wage growth.

Since the appearance of Phillips's very influential 1958 article, most econometric analyses of wage growth have attempted to gauge the degree of labor market tightness with an unemployment rate variable. An alternative approach would be to use available proxies for the unsatisfied demand for labor to assess how tight labor markets are.

Model Specification

While the rationale for including an unemployment rate variable in wage-growth equations is not always clearly stated, the most prevalent notion seems to be that the unemployment rate should be highly correlated with the degree of excess demand in the labor market. A similar argument might be made regarding the inclusion of some measure of employers' unsatisfied demand for labor in place of an unemployment rate variable. A priori, such a measure should be at least as likely as any unemployment rate to be highly correlated with the excess demand for labor.

The labor market variable most common in wage-growth equations is the official unemployment rate. One important question is whether the official (total civilian labor force) unemployment rate adequately reflects the availability of qualified potential employees. Various researchers have argued that women and teenagers are less likely than prime-age males to possess requisite job skills and commitment. This line of reasoning has led many to believe that the prime-age male (25 to 54) unemployment rate might be a better variable to use in wage-growth equations than the official rate.

One measure of the unsatisfied demand for labor that could be substituted for the unemployment rate in wage-growth models is the job vacancy rate. Another is the fraction of the work force choosing to leave their jobs during a given time period. Some job vacancies arise because a new job has been created rather than because someone has quit, and the job vacancy rate reflects both the flow and the duration of job openings. Thus the quit rate and the seemingly better unsatisfied demand proxy, the vacancy rate, will not mirror each other perfectly, but the two rates should be highly correlated.

The first compensation-growth equations presented in this paper include either an unemployment rate:

(1) $$\dot{w}/w = \alpha + \beta(1/u) + \sum_{j=1}^{n} \lambda_j (\dot{p}/p)_{t-j},$$

or an unsatisfied demand variable:

(2) $$\dot{w}/w = \alpha + \gamma(1/d) + \sum_{j=1}^{n} \lambda_j (\dot{p}/p)_{t-j},$$

where $\dot{w}/w$ is the rate of growth of nominal hourly compensation, u is the chosen unemployment rate, d is the chosen unsatisfied demand proxy, $(\dot{p}/p)_{t-j}$ is the rate of inflation in period $t - j$, and α, β, γ and the λ_j are regression coefficients. The reasoning behind including labor market variables in these wage-growth equations implies that $\hat{\beta}$ should be positive (unemployment negatively related to the rate of wage growth) and that $\hat{\gamma}$ should be negative (unsatisfied demand positively related to the rate of wage growth).

One way to ascertain whether unemployment rates or our unsatisfied demand proxies represent better measures of labor market tightness might be to include both together in estimated Phillips-type equations. For this reason, perhaps the most interesting wage-growth regressions presented in this paper are those that include both an unemployment rate and a measure of unsatisfied demand. The relevant regression model can be written as:

(3) $$\dot{w}/w = \alpha + \beta(1/u) + \gamma(1/d) + \sum_{j=1}^{n} \lambda_j (\dot{p}/p)_{t-j},$$

where all the variables are defined as above.

The Role of Inflation

We have included either four or sixteen lagged inflation values—$(\dot{p}/p)_{t-j}$ terms—in the compensation-growth equations instead of a single variable intended to capture the expected rate of inflation in the current period, $(\dot{p}/p)_t^e$. There are several considerations that lead us to this course of action.

First, there is no generally accepted expected inflation series we could have used even had we wanted to. The usual approach to generating an expected inflation series is to assume that people anticipate a current rate of inflation equal to some distributed lag function of past inflation, with the distributed lag weights based on previous inflation history. This seems unrealistic insofar as many factors other than past rates of inflation will have an effect on current inflationary expectations. One way to construct a more realistic expected inflation series might be to survey a random sample of the population on a regular basis, asking those surveyed what they expect the average rate of inflation to be over the period until the next such survey. Unfortunately, a long enough series of the requisite data is not available.[3]

Suppose we could have obtained a time series that accurately captured expectations in each period regarding the rate of inflation in the immediately subsequent period. Even if the rate of wage growth reflected only labor market conditions and expectations regarding inflation, variables other than the single expected inflation variable just described should play an important role. For one thing, in a world where union wage contracts are typically set for three years, some period t wage changes may reflect period t price-change expectations generated up to three years earlier, rather than period t price-change expectations based on information through period $t - 1$. A similar situation will exist in nonunion establishments to the extent that across-the-board wage increases may occur only at annual intervals. Entering a large number of lagged inflation terms (we experiment with as many as sixteen) may allow us to capture the price-change expectations that should have existed at the time the oldest union contract still in force as of period t would have been negotiated, at least to the extent that price-change expectations are a function of past price changes. Including a single $(\dot{p}/p)_t^e$ variable based on a rolling autoregressive moving average or other mechanistic model using price data through period $t - 1$ would have been considerably more restrictive.

3. Since 1947, Joseph Livingston, a journalist, has conducted a small semiannual survey of economists. Among other questions, on each survey occasion he has asked these economists what they anticipate the level of the consumer price index and the wholesale price index will be roughly six and twelve months later. Given certain assumptions, these level forecasts can be converted into rate-of-inflation forecasts. There are a number of problems with these predicted rates of inflation, perhaps the most serious of which for our purposes is that economists are hardly a random sample of the population. See John A. Carlson, "A Study of Price Forecasts," in *Annals of Economic and Social Measurement,* vol. 6 (Winter 1977), pp. 27–56.

Since 1966:2, the Institute for Social Research at the University of Michigan has generated closed-end data on price changes expected by a random sample of economic actors. Starting in 1977:3, an open-ended, and hence better, version of the expected price-change question has been asked. See F. Thomas Juster and Robert Comment, "A Note on the Measurement of Price Expectations" (University of Michigan, Institute for Social Research, February 1978).

Perhaps more fundamentally, there is no clear reason why quarter *t* wage changes should reflect only quarter *t* expected price changes. Particularly where workers remain attached to the same employers over relatively long time periods,[4] money wages may reflect the expected pace of inflation over some longer horizon but not necessarily during a single quarter. One would expect the parties negotiating a wage bargain in period *t* to be concerned about the expected rates of inflation in periods *t*, *t* + 1, *t* + 2, and so on through period *t* + *n*, the end of the relevant time horizon. Again, entering lagged inflation terms rather than a single $(\dot{p}/p)_t^e$ term based on inflation through period *t* − 1 allows added flexibility; the coefficients on lagged price terms may reflect their influence on longer-term as well as on current-period inflationary expectations.

Finally, to the extent that inflation is not always perfectly foreseen, past rates of inflation may play an important role in their own right rather than solely because they influence expectations. Under many union contracts, cost-of-living adjustment (COLA) clauses provide for wage increases tied directly to the rate of inflation; union members covered by COLA clauses are thus at least partially protected against unforeseen price increases. Where prices have grown faster than wages, both union and nonunion workers may receive "catch-up" wage increases that are independent of what the rate of inflation is expected to be in the future. The existence of both COLA and catch-up wage increases provides an additional rationale for including lagged inflation terms in wage-growth equations.

Data Used

Throughout this study, we use both the official unemployment rate and the prime-age male unemployment rate. Two variables serve as unsatisfied demand proxies (the *d* variable in equations 2 and 3): the help-wanted index (HWI) and the manufacturing quit rate. The help-wanted index is used as a vacancy surrogate since no suitable vacancy series is available. This index is based on counts of help-wanted

4. Based on tenure data collected as part of the Current Population Survey, Robert Hall estimates that almost 60 percent of all currently employed workers hold jobs that will last five years or more and that nearly 30 percent hold jobs that will last twenty years or more. See Robert E. Hall, "The Importance of Lifetime Jobs in the U.S. Economy," working paper 560 (Cambridge, Mass.: National Bureau of Economic Research, 1980).

advertisements printed in the classified sections of leading newspapers in approximately fifty standard metropolitan statistical areas.[5] One potential problem with using the HWI rather than actual vacancy data is that affirmative action pressures may have led to greater advertising of available job openings, particularly after the American Telephone and Telegraph consent decree was signed in 1973,[6] so the HWI may have risen relative to the number of vacancies. Any decline in the price of newspaper advertisements relative to the price of other methods of recruiting employees would also have a similar effect. The fact that forces other than affirmative action can affect the amount of help-wanted advertising is consistent with the paths of the employment-deflated Canadian HWI and Canadian job vacancy rate during 1971–78; the HWI seems to have risen somewhat relative to the vacancy rate after 1974. Note that the HWI as reported by the Conference Board is a proxy for number of vacancies, not the vacancy rate; to create a variable that we could use as a rate proxy, we divided the published HWI by the number of employees on nonagricultural pay-rolls.[7] Monthly quit rate information exists only for the manufacturing sector; these data have been collected by the Bureau of Labor Statistics (BLS) in its "Monthly Report on Labor Turnover."[8]

Recall that our estimating equations are written with the rate of growth in nominal compensation as the dependent variable and lagged inflation terms on the right-hand side. The hourly compensation series we used for calculating $\dot{w}/w$, the rate of growth in nominal compensation, was generated by BLS; the bureau divided total compensation of nonfarm business sector employees as reported in the national income and product accounts by the total number of payroll hours in private nonagricultural establishments. The employee compensation

5. More details on the specifics of the procedure followed in creating the index can be found in Noreen L. Preston, *The Help Wanted Index: Technical Descriptions and Behavioral Trends*, report no. 716 (New York: The Conference Board, 1977).

6. Phyllis A. Wallace, "The Consent Decree," in Phyllis A. Wallace, ed., *Equal Employment Opportunity and the AT&T Case* (MIT Press, 1976), pp. 269–76.

7. The need for normalization is discussed in Malcolm S. Cohen and Robert M. Solow, "The Behaviour of Help-Wanted Advertising," *Review of Economics and Statistics*, vol. 49 (February 1967), pp. 108–10. They normalized with the civilian labor force rather than employment. Our results are quite insensitive to the choice between these two deflators.

8. See U.S. Department of Labor, Bureau of Labor Statistics, *Handbook of Methods for Surveys and Studies*, Bulletin 1910 (Government Printing Office, 1976), pp. 43–48, for a discussion of the "Monthly Report on Labor Turnover."

Table 1. *Compensation-Growth Equations with Either an Unemployment Variable or an Unsatisfied Demand Variable*[a]

| Independent variable and summary statistic | Percentage change in average hourly compensation during quarter/100[b] | | | | | | | | Mean[e] |
| | Models with four lagged inflation values[c] | | | | Models with sixteen lagged inflation values[c] | | | | |
	(1)	(2)	(3)	(4)	(5)	(6)	(7)	(8)	(9)
Independent variable									
Inverse of official unemployment rate	0.012 (0.009)	...	...	...	...	...	...	...	0.193 (0.047)
Inverse of prime-age male unemployment rate[d]	...	0.005 (0.003)	...	...	0.025 (0.011)	0.008 (0.004)	...	...	0.323 (0.122)
Inverse of normalized help-wanted index	...	...	−0.007 (0.002)	...	...	...	−0.008 (0.003)	...	0.796 (0.177)
Inverse of manufacturing quit rate	...	...	...	−0.008 (0.003)	...	...	...	−0.009 (0.003)	0.572 (0.157)
Summary statistic									
Total effect of lagged inflation	0.780 (0.071)	0.760 (0.067)	0.667 (0.069)	0.685 (0.067)	0.926 (0.095)	0.858 (0.082)	0.702 (0.080)	0.737 (0.076)	...
ρ	−0.089 (0.115)	−0.097 (0.114)	−0.128 (0.112)	−0.134 (0.112)	−0.112 (0.121)	−0.113 (0.121)	−0.142 (0.119)	−0.149 (0.119)	...
$\bar{R}^2$	0.520	0.524	0.554	0.555	0.543	0.541	0.565	0.570	...

a. All regressions were fitted with seasonally adjusted quarterly data for 1956:1 through 1980:3 ($N = 99$) and were estimated using a maximum likelihood correction for first-order serial correlation. The numbers in parentheses below the coefficient estimates are standard errors.
b. The mean (standard deviation) of the dependent variable is 0.015 (0.006).
c. The lagged inflation values are based on the gross national product deflator.
d. The prime-age male unemployment rate is for men aged 25 through 54.
e. The numbers in parentheses in this column are standard deviations.

figure in the national accounts includes wages and salaries, employer contributions to social insurance programs such as social security and unemployment insurance, and other labor income such as employer contributions to private pension and welfare funds.[9]

As noted above, we entered either four or sixteen lagged inflation variables into all our regression models. In considering an appropriate price deflator series to use for constructing these lagged inflation terms, it is important to note that in a world with more than one commodity, the price series that is relevant for suppliers of labor will very likely differ from that for demanders of labor. One would expect labor suppliers to be concerned about their earnings relative to the price of the bundle of commodities they consume, whereas labor demanders should be concerned about the wages they pay relative to their product prices. Using lagged inflation terms based on the gross national product (GNP) deflator thus seemed like a reasonable compromise between the prices relevant to these two groups.[10]

Compensation-Growth Equations

Table 1 presents compensation-growth equations that include a single labor market variable and either four or sixteen lagged inflation terms based on the GNP deflator. The official unemployment rate, the prime-age male unemployment rate, the HWI and the manufacturing

9. The construction of the employee compensation figures we used is not at the time of this writing described in print, although the Department of Commerce will soon publish a volume describing the derivation of each element in the national accounts. Discussion with individuals at Commerce indicated that the series was produced with wage and supplements information from various tax forms, censuses, records of some private-sector vendors, and files of some professional and trade associations. The total payroll hours data used in converting these figures to hourly rates came from the "Monthly Report on Employment, Payroll and Hours," which is discussed in Bureau of Labor Statistics, *Handbook of Methods*, pp. 26–42.

10. The Data Resources, Inc., (DRI) computer system was the source of all of the data and programs used in conducting the analyses under discussion. All of the reported regressions were fit on the DRI system with seasonally adjusted quarterly data for 1956:1 through 1980:3 and were estimated using a maximum likelihood correction for first-order serial correlation. We did estimate all of the models reported in the tables of this paper without any serial correlation correction. The Durbin-Watson statistics for these equations were often such that we could not readily determine whether or not the presence of an autoregressive error process was indicated; to be on the safe side, we chose to present models incorporating a serial correlation correction. The parameter estimates in the corrected models were very similar to those in the ordinary least squares models.

Table 2. *Compensation-Growth Equations with Both an Unemployment Variable and an Unsatisfied Demand Variable*[a]

Independent variable and summary statistic	Percentage change in average hourly compensation during quarter/100[b]								Mean[e]
	Models with four lagged inflation values[c]				Models with sixteen lagged inflation values[c]				
	(1)	(2)	(3)	(4)	(5)	(6)	(7)	(8)	(9)
Independent variable									
Inverse of official unemployment rate	-0.011 (0.012)	-0.019 (0.013)	...	...	-0.010 (0.019)	-0.018 (0.020)	...	...	0.193 (0.047)
Inverse of prime-age male unemployment rate[d]	...	...	-0.004 (0.005)	-0.008 (0.005)	...	...	-0.004 (0.006)	-0.007 (0.007)	0.323 (0.122)
Inverse of normalized help-wanted index	-0.010 (0.003)	...	-0.010 (0.004)	...	-0.010 (0.005)	...	-0.010 (0.005)	...	0.796 (0.177)
Inverse of manufacturing quit rate	...	-0.013 (0.004)	...	-0.013 (0.005)	...	-0.013 (0.005)	...	-0.013 (0.005)	0.572 (0.157)
Summary statistic									
Total effect of lagged inflation	0.615 (0.089)	0.600 (0.087)	0.632 (0.081)	0.626 (0.077)	0.624 (0.169)	0.617 (0.155)	0.649 (0.123)	0.657 (0.110)	...
ρ	-0.134 (0.112)	-0.152 (0.112)	-0.131 (0.112)	-0.148 (0.112)	-0.146 (0.120)	-0.158 (0.120)	-0.145 (0.120)	-0.159 (0.120)	...
$\bar{R}^2$	0.553	0.560	0.552	0.560	0.561	0.568	0.562	0.570	...

a. See footnotes a, b, c, d, and e for table 1.

quit rate are each entered in inverse form as alternative measures of labor market conditions. The unemployment rate variables consistently assume the expected positive sign and the unsatisfied demand variables uniformly take on the expected negative sign. The official unemployment rate coefficient is not statistically significant in the model with four lagged inflation terms; it achieves statistical significance in the model with sixteen lagged inflation terms.[11] All of the prime-age male unemployment rate, HWI and manufacturing quit rate coefficients are statistically significant. The $\bar{R}^2$s for the unsatisfied demand variable models are consistently larger than the $\bar{R}^2$s for the unemployment rate models. This would seem to suggest that the unsatisfied demand variables work better than the unemployment rates we have used; however, the magnitude of the differences in $\bar{R}$s between the two sets of models are small, so no strong conclusion regarding the relative strength of the various labor market variables seems warranted on this basis alone.[12]

Table 2 presents compensation-growth equations that include both an unemployment rate variable and the inverse of either the HWI or the manufacturing quit rate. Once either of the unsatisfied demand variables has been controlled for, the inverse unemployment rate variables no longer retain their expected positive association with the rate of wage growth. In fact, the point estimates of the unemployment rate variable coefficients are uniformly negative, though never significant. The prime-age male unemployment rate performs just as poorly as the official unemployment rate, even though some have argued that it is a better indicator of unutilized labor supply. In contrast, all of the coefficients on the two variables we have chosen as proxies for the

11. Throughout this paper, when we say a variable is statistically significant, we mean that it has passed at least a .05 level one-tailed test.

12. Earlier papers in which variables such as the manufacturing quit rate, the manufacturing layoff rate or the help-wanted index have been substituted for the unemployment rate in wage-growth models include Sara Behman, "Wage Determination Process in U.S. Manufacturing," *Quarterly Journal of Economics*, vol. 82 (February 1968), pp. 117–42; Charles L. Schultze, "Has the Phillips Curve Shifted? Some Additional Evidence," *BPEA*, 2:1971, pp. 452–67; and Martin Neil Baily and James Tobin, "Macroeconomic Effects of Selective Public Employment and Wage Subsidies," *BPEA*, 2:1977, pp. 511–41. Each of the cited articles concludes that the demand side variables experimented with perform as well as or better than the unemployment rate in manufacturing-sector (Behman) or aggregate (Schultze, Baily and Tobin) wage-growth equations. Although Baily and Tobin also present results for different sectors of the economy, these findings seem irrelevant for the present discussion since information on help-wanted advertising does not exist at the sectoral level.

level of unsatisfied demand (the inverse of the HWI and of the manufacturing quit rate) are of the expected negative sign and statistically significant.[13]

Sensitivity to Alternative Specifications

Thus far we have explicitly or implicitly made a number of assumptions about the "proper" specification of the compensation-growth models we have estimated. Fortunately, our central conclusions appear to be quite robust with respect to alternative plausible specifications.

The key compensation-growth ($\dot{w}/w$) models presented in the text included an unsatisfied demand variable (either the HWI or the quit rate) in inverse form ($1/d$). We chose this functional form because it matched the way the unemployment rate is usually entered in this sort of regression (as $1/u$) and because regressions with both d and d^2 as independent variables indicated that $\dot{w}/w$ increases with d at a decreasing rate. We did replicate all of the relevant table 1 and table 2 models with d or log d replacing $1/d$; our qualitative results were completely unaffected by this substitution.

Another question that might be raised concerning the results presented is whether the Perry-weighted unemployment rate might not be a better variable to use than either the official or the prime-age male rate.[14] Through 1978:4, the last quarter for which we could calculate the Perry-weighted unemployment rate, the correlation for the Perry-weighted and the prime-age male unemployment rates was .991. Not surprisingly, substituting the Perry-weighted rate for the prime-age male rate did not alter the message of our results.

13. The results presented in table 2 are consistent with earlier findings reported by Martin Neil Baily and James Tobin. They estimated several aggregate wage growth equations using quarterly data for 1958:1 through 1976:4 that included both an inverse unemployment rate variable and the help-wanted index deflated by total employment; while their model specification is otherwise rather different from ours, they also obtain generally insignificant wrong-signed unemployment coefficients and strongly significant right-signed help-wanted index coefficients. Baily and Tobin also present similar equations for different sectors of the economy; again, we would argue that these findings are not relevant for the present discussion since information on help-wanted advertising does not exist at the sectoral level. See Baily and Tobin, "Macroeconomic Effects of Selective Public Employment and Wage Subsidies."

14. See George L. Perry, "Changing Labor Markets and Inflation," *BPEA, 3:1970*, pp. 411–41.

A third possibility we considered was that unemployment and/or our unsatisfied demand variables might affect $\dot{w}/w$ with some lag rather than concurrently. To determine whether allowing for delayed impacts would alter our central conclusions, we reestimated each of the models in table 1 and table 2 with four lagged values of $1/u$ or four lagged values of $1/d$ added wherever a current value of $1/u$ or $1/d$ appeared. The sums of the coefficients on the $1/u$ variables and $1/d$ variables were uniformly very similar to the $1/u$ and $1/d$ coefficients in our original models.

A fourth specification issue that seemed potentially important was that (as has been suggested by Robert J. Gordon and George Perry) certain periods during the past two decades are likely to have had below- or above-average wage growth because of events that would not make their way into a normal wage-growth model.[15] We estimated respecified models that included dummy variables for each of three periods: 1964:1 to 1966:2, when the Johnson guideposts were in effect; 1971:3 to 1972:4, the Nixon controls period; and 1974:2 to 1975:1, a period of very sharp increases in oil prices. These produced conclusions no different than those based on the original regressions.

Another question that might be raised is whether the higher rate of growth in hourly compensation associated with increases in either the HWI or the quit rate actually reflects higher base wage rates, or simply greater use of overtime hours and thus more time worked for premium pay. In determining what factors lie behind inflation, the answer to this question may not be particularly important. Nevertheless, we did try adding a measure of average weekly overtime hours in manufacturing to each model that included an unsatisfied demand variable. The overtime hours variable was always completely insignificant and none of the affected $1/u$ or $1/d$ coefficients increased or decreased appreciably. It should also be noted that the inverse of this overtime hours variable performed in very much the same way as the inverse of the HWI or of the quit rate when used alone as a proxy for unsatisfied demand in models like those in table 1 and table 2.

A sixth issue that deserves mention is our choice of an inflation series to appear on the right-hand side of our compensation-growth

15. See George L. Perry, "Inflation in Theory and Practice," *BPEA*, *1:1980*, pp. 207–41; and Robert J. Gordon, "Can the Inflation of the 1970s Be Explained?" *BPEA*, *1:1977*, pp. 253–77.

models. We picked the GNP deflator in an attempt to strike a compromise between the prices most relevant to labor suppliers and those most relevant to labor demanders. Redoing the table 1 and table 2 analyses with a more "supplier-oriented" price index (the implicit consumption deflator, considered vastly superior to the consumer price index because of its treatment of housing expenditures) and then again with a more "demander-oriented" price index (the wholesale price index) changed none of our conclusions.

Thus, the central implications of the compensation-growth equations reported in table 1 and table 2 appear to be quite robust with respect to the precise model specification used. When entered separately, both unemployment and our unsatisfied demand variables perform in the expected fashion, with unemployment negatively and unsatisfied demand positively related to the rate of compensation growth (although in every instance but one the $\bar{R}^2$s in the unsatisfied demand models were larger than the $\bar{R}^2$s in the comparable unemployment models). However, in equations that include both an unemployment rate variable and an unsatisfied demand proxy, only the unsatisfied demand variable matters.

One might be tempted to interpret these results as implying that wages are flexible upward but not downward. While perhaps true, this conclusion cannot be drawn from the evidence presented; the coefficient on the vacancy rate could reflect wages falling when the vacancy rate goes down, rather than wages rising when the vacancy rate goes up. Nor do the results demonstrate that only employers, and not the unemployed, can directly affect the rate of wage growth. While the unemployed may in fact have no direct effect on wage growth, a legitimate test of this hypothesis cannot be based on the crude aggregate data we employ. A discussion of what interpretation can legitimately be given to the results that have been presented appears later in this paper.

Observed Instability in the Phillips Curve Relationship

One empirical phenomenon that has received considerable attention during the past decade has been the breakdown in the Phillips relationship.[16] This breakdown is consistent with the hypothesis of Milton Friedman and Edmund Phelps that revisions in inflationary expectations will cause outward shifts in the short-run Phillips curve.[17] While inflation is clearly important, we believe that a substantial fraction of the outward shift in the Phillips curve may be linked to an outward shift in the inverse relationship between unemployment and the unsatisfied demand for labor. Furthermore, the relationship between unsatisfied demand and compensation growth appears to have been more stable than the relationship between unemployment and compensation growth.

Plots of the Shifting Phillips Curve

The top panel of figure 1 documents a fact that should be familiar to most readers: the rate of growth in compensation associated with any given value of the official unemployment rate has been substantially higher since 1970 than before that date. The curve linking the percentage change in average hourly compensation to the official unemployment rate appears to have shifted outward first in 1970 and then again in 1974; a smaller backward shift seems to have occurred after 1976.

As demonstrated in the bottom panel of figure 1, the relationship between the rate of growth in compensation and the prime-age male unemployment rate has exhibited a similar shift pattern. Sharp outward shifts in 1970 and 1974 appear to have been followed by a smaller backward shift after 1976.

The question we are interested in answering is whether the observed shifts in both the official unemployment rate and prime-age male unemployment rate Phillips relationships are somehow related to

16. Instability in the Phillips curve may take the form of shifts in the intercept or changes in the slope. Here we consider shifts in the intercept. For analyses suggesting that the United States' Phillips curve has been much flatter since World War II than earlier, see Philip Cagan, "Changes in the Recession Behaviour of Wholesale Prices in the 1920's and Post–World War II," *Explorations in Economic Research*, vol. 2 (Winter 1975), pp. 54–104; and Jeffrey Sachs, "The Changing Cyclical Behavior of Wages and Prices: 1890–1976," *American Economic Review*, vol. 70 (March 1980), pp. 78–90. Any flattening in the Phillips curve that may have occurred during the postwar period appears to have been substantially less pronounced.

17. See Milton Friedman, "The Role of Monetary Policy," *American Economic Review*, vol. 58 (March 1968), pp. 1–17; and Edmund S. Phelps, "Phillips Curves, Expectations of Inflation and Optimal Unemployment Over Time," *Economica*, vol. 34 (August 1967), pp. 254–81.

Figure 1. *Wage Growth versus Official and Prime-Age Male Unemployment Rates, 1956–79*[a]

Change in average hourly compensation (percent)[b]

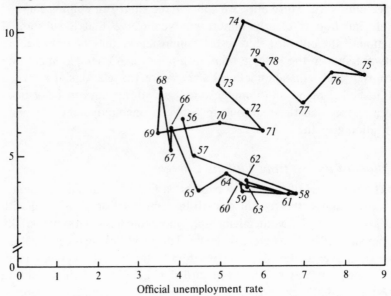

Official unemployment rate

Change in average hourly compensation (percent)[b]

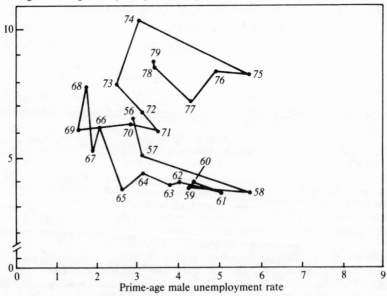

Prime-age male unemployment rate

a. Annual averages of seasonally adjusted monthly rates.
b. The percentage change in fourth-quarter hourly compensation between the given year and the preceding year.

changes in the relationship between unemployment and unsatisfied demand. There is at least good circumstantial evidence suggesting that this is the case.

The Shifting Relationship between Unsatisfied Demand and Unemployment

Figure 2 presents plots relating each of our two unsatisfied demand proxies, the normalized HWI and the manufacturing quit rate, to the official U.S. unemployment rate. In both plots, the points from 1958 through 1969 seem to lie more or less along a single curve. Both plots exhibit a dramatic shift outward in 1970, which is when the first obvious outward shift in the official unemployment rate Phillips relation occurred.[18] The plot relating the HWI to the official unemployment rate shifts sharply outward again after 1974, but the plot relating the quit rate to the official unemployment rate does not. As was mentioned earlier, the volume of help-wanted advertising may have increased during the middle and late 1970s because of increased affirmative action pressures; this could have caused the post-1974 shift in the second plot even if there were no shift in the underlying vacancy versus unemployment relationship. The outward shift in the official unemployment rate Phillips curve that occurred in 1974 thus might better be linked to the sharp increase in the price of oil around the same date than to labor market changes. The plot relating the quit rate to the official unemployment rate may have shifted slightly backward after 1977; no backward shift appears in the plot relating the HWI to the official unemployment rate. As noted earlier, the official unemployment rate Phillips relation appeared to shift backward after 1976.

Figure 3 presents plots like those in figure 2, substituting the prime-age male unemployment rate for the official unemployment rate. While the shifts in the figure 3 plots are somewhat less pronounced than those in figure 2, their timing is very similar. The same connections

18. Schultze, "Has the Phillips Curve Shifted? Some Additional Evidence," looks at quit rate and official unemployment rate data for the period 1952–71. The article reports that the curve linking these two rates seems to shift outward in about 1966 and argues that a shift in the Phillips relationship must have occurred. This late 1960s shift is not obvious in our quit rate/official unemployment rate plot in part because we omit the data points for 1952–55 so as to be consistent with the time period covered by our regression analysis, and in part because the shift in the quit rate/official unemployment rate relationship that occurred after 1969 was much larger than any shift occurring during the late 1960s.

Figure 2. *Unsatisfied Demand Variables versus Official Unemployment Rate, 1956–79*

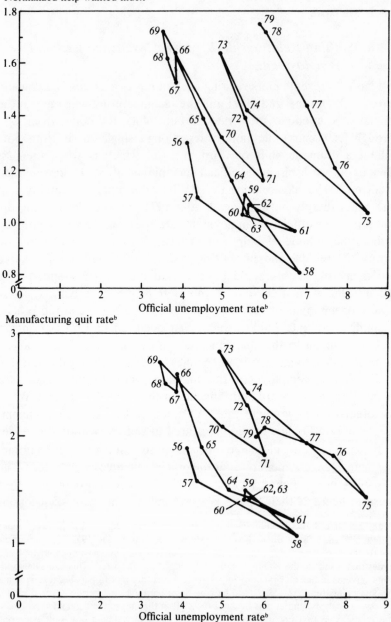

Normalized help-wanted index[a]

Manufacturing quit rate[b]

Official unemployment rate[b]

a. The average of the monthly seasonally adjusted help-wanted index figures for each year, divided by the seasonally adjusted number of employees on nonagricultural payrolls.
b. The annual average of seasonally adjusted monthly rates.

Figure 3. *Unsatisfied Demand Variables versus Prime-Age Male Unemployment Rate, 1956–79*

Normalized help-wanted index[a]

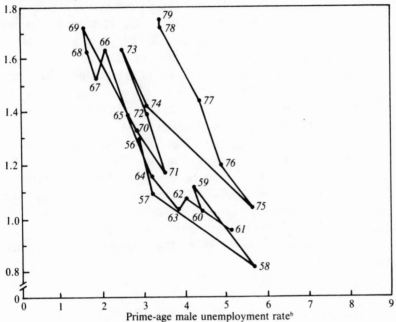

Prime-age male unemployment rate[b]

Manufacturing quit rate[b]

Prime-age male unemployment rate[b]

a. The average of the monthly seasonally adjusted help-wanted index figures for each year, divided by the seasonally adjusted number of employees on nonagricultural payrolls.
b. The annual average of seasonally adjusted monthly rates.

can be drawn between each of these two plots and the prime-age male unemployment rate Phillips curve plot as were drawn between the relevant pairs of official unemployment rate plots.

It is interesting to note that the relationship between unsatisfied demand and unemployment seems also to have been quite unstable in a large number of other developed countries. Beveridge curve (job vacancy rate versus overall unemployment rate) plots for Canada, the United Kingdom, Japan, France, Norway, Finland, and Australia all clearly exhibit sharp outward shifts during the late 1960s and early 1970s.[19] It would be of considerable interest to conduct a careful exploration of whether these Beveridge curve shifts might also be linked to movements in the relevant countries' Phillips curves.

While looking at pictures is interesting, quantifying the extent to which shifts in the United States' official unemployment rate and prime-age male unemployment rate Phillips relationships might be linked to the shifting relationship between these unemployment variables and unsatisfied demand can perhaps better be accomplished econometrically.

Econometric Evidence on the Shifting Phillips Curve

To summarize the magnitude of the overall shift in the Phillips relations shown in figure 1, we estimated equations of the following form:

$$(4) \qquad\qquad \dot{w}/w = \alpha + \beta(1/u) + \delta t,$$

where u is either the official or the prime-age male unemployment rate and t is a time trend. The estimate of δ from the official rate regression indicates that the annual rate of wage growth associated with any given level of unemployment grew by approximately 6.1 percentage points between 1956 and 1980. Over the same period, the similarly estimated shift in the prime-age male relationship was approximately 5.7 percentage points.

Adding an unsatisfied demand variable to equation 4 is one approach to estimating the extent to which these upward shifts can be linked to

19. See Organisation for Economic Co-Operation and Development, *Medium-Term Strategy for Employment and Manpower Policies* (Paris: OECD, 1978), pp. 104–05.

the changing relationship between unemployment and unsatisfied demand. The relevant regression is:

$$(5) \qquad \dot{w}/w = \alpha + \beta(1/u) + \delta t + \gamma(1/d),$$

where d may be either the normalized HWI or the manufacturing quit rate and the other variables are as before. To the extent that the outward shifting of the relationship between $\dot{w}/w$ and $1/u$, indicated by $\delta > 0$ in equation 4, can be linked to the shifting relationship between $1/u$ and $1/d$, the estimate of δ in equation 5 should fall toward zero. Introducing the normalized HWI variable into the official rate equation reduced the magnitude of the estimated time trend by 20 percent; adding the manufacturing quit rate variable reduced the official rate equation time trend by 29 percent. In the prime-age male models, the introduction of the inverse of the HWI knocked the estimated time trend down by 23 percent and adding the inverse of the manufacturing quit rate lowered the estimated time trend by 25 percent. Thus, this approach suggests that between 20 percent and 30 percent of the observed upward shift in these Phillips relationships may be linked to the shifting relationship between unemployment and unsatisfied demand.

Econometrically estimated Phillips curves more typically include variables intended to capture the impact of the rate of inflation. In this paper we have focused primarily on augmented Phillips curve equations containing either four or sixteen lagged inflation terms. An alternative approach to assessing the role of the shifting relationship between unemployment and unsatisfied demand would be to look at the time trend remaining after lagged inflation terms have been introduced into the wage-growth model, and then to add an unsatisfied demand variable to see whether it can knock out the residual time trend in the augmented model.

The first and fourth columns of table 3 contain regressions of the following form, estimated using the official unemployment rate and either four or sixteen lagged inflation terms:

$$(6) \qquad \dot{w}/w = \alpha + \beta(1/u) + \sum_{j=1}^{n} \gamma_j \, (\dot{p}/p)_{t-j} + \delta t.$$

The point estimate of the time trend coefficient in the model with four lagged inflation terms (column 1) implies that the annual rate of wage growth associated with any given level of the official unemployment rate would have been approximately 2.1 percentage points higher in

Table 3. *The Positive Time Trend in Phillips Curve Equations with the Official Unemployment Rate*[a]

Independent variable and summary statistic	Percentage change in average hourly compensation during quarter/100[b]						Mean[e] (7)
	Models with four lagged inflation values[c]			Models with sixteen lagged inflation values[c]			
	(1)	(2)	(3)	(4)	(5)	(6)	(7)
Independent variable							
Time/100	0.005	0.000	0.001	0.003	-0.003	-0.001	0.500
	(0.002)	(0.004)	(0.003)	(0.003)	(0.004)	(0.003)	(0.286)
Inverse of official unemployment rate	0.016	-0.011	-0.017	0.022	-0.020	-0.019	0.193
	(0.009)	(0.018)	(0.018)	(0.011)	(0.023)	(0.021)	(0.047)
Inverse of normalized help-wanted index	...	-0.010	...	...	-0.014	...	0.796
		(0.006)			(0.007)		(0.177)
Inverse of manufacturing quit rate	...	...	-0.012	...	...	-0.014	0.572
			(0.006)			(0.006)	(0.157)
Summary statistic							
Total effect of lagged inflation	0.582	0.616	0.588	0.764	0.700	0.649	...
	(0.114)	(0.113)	(0.109)	(0.202)	(0.195)	(0.197)	
ρ	-0.116	-0.134	-0.151	-0.117	-0.153	-0.160	...
	(0.113)	(0.113)	(0.112)	(0.121)	(0.121)	(0.121)	
$\overline{R}^2$	0.539	0.548	0.556	0.542	0.559	0.563	...

a. See footnotes a, b, c, and e for table 1.

1980 than in 1956, even if the four previous quarters' inflation rates had been the same. The point estimate of the time trend coefficient in the model with sixteen lagged inflation terms (column 4) implies that the annual rate of wage growth would have been approximately 1.2 percentage points higher in 1980 than in 1956, again holding the official unemployment rate and the relevant inflation rate history constant. The coefficient in the model with four lagged inflation values is strongly significant, but when sixteen lagged inflation values are included in the model, the time trend coefficient loses its significance. The point estimates of these time trends are 66 percent and 80 percent smaller than the time trend in the crude Phillips curve with no lagged inflation terms based on the official unemployment rate, which means that a residual shift between 20 and 34 percent of the total remains to be explained.

If this residual shift is related to the outward shift in the relationship between unemployment and unsatisfied demand, then adding $1/d$ to equation 6, which gives:

$$(7) \qquad \dot{w}/w = \alpha + \beta(1/u) + \sum_{j=1}^{n} \gamma_j \, (\dot{p}/p)_{t-j} + \delta t + \gamma(1/d),$$

should drive $\hat{\delta}$ to zero. Columns 2, 3, 5, and 6 of table 3 report coefficient estimates for equations with the inverse of either the normalized HWI or the manufacturing quit rate added to our augmented Phillips equations based on the official unemployment rate. The point estimate of the time trend coefficient remaining after either of these unsatisfied demand variables has been introduced is either very close to zero or negative (in the model with sixteen lagged inflation values to which the HWI has been added); none of these estimated time trend coefficients is statistically significant. The negative time trend in the model that includes sixteen lagged inflation terms and the normalized HWI might reflect the spurious increase in the level of the index relative to the vacancy rate that we suspect may have occurred after 1973 or 1974. In any event, the positive time trend in the augmented compensation-growth models with just the inverse of the official unemployment rate but no unsatisfied demand variable does seem to disappear once some control for the level of unsatisfied demand has been introduced.

Qualitatively similar results were obtained from augmented Phillips curve equations estimated based on the prime-age male unemployment

Table 4. The Positive Time Trend in Phillips Curve Equations with the Prime-Age Male Unemployment Rate[a]

Independent variable and summary statistic	Models with four lagged inflation values[c]			Models with sixteen lagged inflation values[c]			Mean[e]
	(1)	(2)	(3)	(4)	(5)	(6)	(7)
Independent variable							
Time/100	0.004	0.001	0.002	0.002	−0.001	0.001	0.500
	(0.002)	(0.003)	(0.002)	(0.004)	(0.004)	(0.003)	(0.286)
Inverse of prime-age male unemployment rate[d]	0.005	−0.003	−0.007	0.007	−0.004	−0.007	0.323
	(0.003)	(0.005)	(0.006)	(0.004)	(0.006)	(0.007)	(0.122)
Inverse of normalized help-wanted index	...	−0.009	...	...	−0.011	...	0.796
		(0.005)			(0.005)		(0.177)
Inverse of manufacturing quit rate	...	...	−0.012	...	...	−0.013	0.572
			(0.005)			(0.005)	(0.157)
Summary statistic							
Total effect of lagged inflation	0.594	0.604	0.570	0.766	0.711	0.623	...
	(0.115)	(0.112)	(0.110)	(0.211)	(0.203)	(0.206)	
ρ	−0.115	−0.131	−0.149	−0.114	−0.147	−0.158	...
	(0.114)	(0.113)	(0.112)	(0.121)	(0.121)	(0.121)	
$\bar{R}^2$	0.535	0.548	0.558	0.536	0.557	0.564	...

a. See footnotes a, b, c, d, and e for table 1.

rate. The augmented Phillips curve equation with four lagged inflation terms presented in column 1 of table 4 implies an upward shift between 1956 and 1980 of 1.7 percentage points in the annual rate of wage growth associated with any given unemployment rate (coefficient statistically significant). The comparable model with sixteen lagged inflation terms presented in column 4 implies an upward shift of 0.7 percentage point (coefficient estimate not significant). Thus, changes in the pattern of inflation would appear to account for between 70 and 88 percent of the total shift in the Phillips curve relation based on the prime-age male rate of unemployment, leaving an unexplained residual of between 12 and 30 percent of the total.

As was true with the official rate equations, adding an unsatisfied demand variable to the augmented prime-age male Phillips curve equations seems to knock out the positive residual time trend. When the HWI variable is introduced, the point estimates of the time trend coefficients fall very near zero; adding the quit variable brings the point estimates of the time trend coefficients down by roughly 60 percent. None of the time trend coefficients in the equations that include an unsatisfied demand variable is statistically significant.

Taken as a whole, our econometric results seem supportive of the proposition that a substantial fraction of the total observed instability in the Phillips curve relations based on both the official and the prime-age male unemployment rates can be linked to shifts in the relationships between those two variables and the level of unsatisfied demand.

The Relationship between Unsatisfied Demand and Compensation Growth

At this point the question might be asked whether the relationship between unsatisfied demand (proxied by the HWI or the quit rate) and the rate of growth in compensation has been more stable than the relationship between unemployment and compensation growth. To answer this question, we first estimated equations of the following form:

$$(8) \qquad \dot{w}/w = \alpha + \gamma(1/d) + \delta t,$$

which is just like equation 4 except with an unsatisfied demand variable $(1/d)$ based on either the HWI or the manufacturing quit rate substituted for the unemployment rate variable $(1/u)$. The estimate of δ from the

HWI regression indicates that the annual rate of wage growth associated with any given value of that variable increased by approximately 4.9 percentage points between 1956 and 1980; the estimate of δ from the quit rate regression implies a comparable upward shift of approximately 5.0 percentage points. These shifts are appreciably smaller than the 6.1 percentage-point shift estimated for the official unemployment rate Phillips curve equation with no lagged inflation terms and the 5.7 percentage-point shift estimated for the prime-age male unemployment rate Phillips curve equation with no lagged inflation terms.

Throughout this paper, we have focused primarily on compensation-growth equations that include a string of lagged inflation terms on the right-hand side. Models with an unsatisfied demand variable, a time trend and lagged inflation terms:

$$(9) \qquad \dot{w}/w = \alpha + \beta(1/d) + \sum_{j=1}^{n} \gamma_j \, (\dot{p}/p)_{t-j} + \delta t,$$

are presented in table 5. In both the HWI and the quit rate models with four lagged inflation values, the time trend coefficient has a positive point estimate but is not significant. Where the significant time trend coefficients in the comparable official and prime-age male unemployment rate equations implied upward shifts of 2.1 and 1.7 percentage points, respectively, in the annual rate of inflation associated with given values of those variables, the insignificant time trend coefficients in these HWI and quit rate equations imply smaller upward shifts of 0.7 and 1.1 percentage points, respectively. In models that include sixteen lagged inflation values, the time trend coefficient in the HWI equation is slightly negative but not significant, and the time trend coefficient in the quit rate equation is extremely close to, and not significantly different from, zero. The slightly negative or zero implied shifts in the HWI and quit rate equations with sixteen lagged inflation terms compare to upward shifts of 1.2 and 0.7 percentage points in the analogous official and prime-age male unemployment rate equations respectively, as discussed above. In spite of the problems with our measures of unsatisfied demand, the Phillips-type compensation-growth equations in table 5 that contain an unsatisfied demand proxy rather than an unemployment rate do appear to be relatively more stable than the comparable equations in table 3 and table 4.

We noted earlier that the HWI and the manufacturing quit rate are most certainly flawed measures of the level of unsatisfied demand for labor in the economy as a whole. It seems plausible that compensation-

Table 5. *The Relationship between Unsatisfied Demand Variables and the Rate of Compensation Growth*[a]

Independent variable and summary statistic	Percentage change in average hourly compensation during quarter/100[b]				Mean[e]
	Models with four lagged inflation values[c]		Models with sixteen lagged inflation values[c]		
	(1)	*(2)*	*(3)*	*(4)*	*(5)*
Independent variable					
Time/100	0.002	0.003	−0.001	0.000	0.500
	(0.003)	(0.002)	(0.004)	(0.003)	(0.286)
Inverse of normalized help-wanted index	−0.006	. . .	−0.009	. . .	0.796
	(0.003)		(0.003)		(0.177)
Inverse of manufacturing quit rate	. . .	−0.007	. . .	−0.009	0.572
		(0.003)		(0.003)	(0.157)
Summary statistic					
Total effect of lagged inflation	0.606	0.588	0.762	0.732	. . .
	(0.112)	(0.110)	(0.182)	(0.176)	
ρ	−0.130	−0.140	−0.144	−0.149	. . .
	(0.112)	(0.112)	(0.120)	(0.120)	
$\bar{R}^2$	0.551	0.556	0.561	0.564	. . .

a. See footnotes a, b, c, and e for table 1.

growth equations estimated with a better unsatisfied demand variable, in particular a well-measured job vacancy rate, might exhibit even greater stability. Unfortunately, we cannot test this hypothesis at present.

Sensitivity to Alternative Specifications

To determine whether the conclusions just reached were robust with respect to alternative specifications, we reestimated the equations in tables 3, 4, and 5 in each of the various ways we had previously reestimated the table 1 and 2 equations, as described at the end of the first section of the paper: with d or log d replacing $1/d$; with the Perry-weighted unemployment rate rather than the prime-age male unemployment rate; with the current and four lagged values of $1/u$ and $1/d$ instead of just the current value of each; with the three special-period dummy variables added to the original models; with overtime hours added to all equations containing either the HWI or the quit rate; with overtime hours used instead of the HWI or the quit rate as our unsatisfied demand variable; and with lagged values of either the implicit consumption deflator or the wholesale price index replacing lagged values of the GNP deflator. The conclusions implied by these alternative sets of models were quite similar to the conclusions implied by the results we originally presented: in all of the models with four lagged inflation values and in all but one set with sixteen lagged inflation values, the standard augmented Phillips curve seemed to have shifted upward over time, sometimes by substantially more than in the models discussed in the text; introducing an unsatisfied demand proxy into the standard Phillips equations always reduced the point estimate of the time trend coefficient; and the equations with only unsatisfied demand variables seemed for the most part to have been more stable than those with only unemployment rates.

Interpretation of Findings

Thus far, we have presented empirical results without seriously addressing the issue of their proper interpretation. In this section, we first lay out two plausible interpretations, one built on the premise that the unemployment rate does not provide a consistent measure of the true unutilized labor supply and the other resting on the notion that there has been growing structural imbalance in the labor market. Knowing more about why the Beveridge curve has shifted outward could allow one of these interpretations to be selected over the other. However, at this point we are able to do no more than speculate about the factors associated with the observed movement in the Beveridge curve, so that both must be considered viable hypotheses.

Two Possible Explanations

Suppose the unsatisfied demand for labor and the true unutilized supply of labor to have been stably correlated with one another. If the rate of growth in wages were a stable function of unsatisfied demand and/or unutilized supply (for example, the rate of wage growth might depend on $d - s$, $\alpha d - \beta s$, d alone or s alone, where d represents unsatisfied demand and s unutilized supply), then good measures of either variable should serve equally well in wage-growth regressions. As stated above, one potential explanation of our findings can be built on the premise that available unemployment rates do not provide consistent measures of the unutilized labor supply. In particular, it might be hypothesized that the true unutilized labor supply associated with any given unemployment rate has fallen over time.

Why might the unemployment rate not provide a consistent measure of the true unutilized labor supply? One possibility would be a decline in the number of hours per week the typical unemployed person wishes to work relative to the number of hours per week put in by the typical employed person. Another might be reduced eagerness of the unemployed to secure employment, which would decrease the effective availability of unutilized labor. Such changes would be expected to lead to an increase in the amount of unsatisfied demand associated with any given unemployment rate.

For this sort of divergence between the unemployment rate and the effective unutilized supply of labor to explain our results, we must further suppose that the normalized HWI and the manufacturing quit rate measure the effective unsatisfied demand for labor more consistently than the unemployment rate measures the effective unutilized supply of labor. The existence of greater total measurement error in the unemployment rates than in the unsatisfied demand proxies would be consistent with our result that in wage-growth equations including both, unsatisfied demand variables matter but unemployment rates do not. A positive time trend in the error with which unemployment rates capture the effective unutilized labor supply, that is, a decline in the effective unutilized labor supply associated with any given level of unemployment, could explain the positive time trend in estimated Phillips relationships. Furthermore, if the trend in the measurement error in unemployment rates is greater than the comparable trend in our unsatisfied demand proxies, then a measurement-error story could be used to explain the somewhat greater stability of Phillips curves defined in terms of unsatisfied demand proxies instead of unemployment rates. Most of our results can thus be explained in terms of a simple time trend measurement error in unemployment rates.

It should be noted, though, that a simple trend-related error could not explain our finding that, even after a time trend is entered into wage-growth models, unsatisfied demand proxies still dominate unemployment rates when both are present. To explain this result, one must further suppose there to be some non-trend-related measurement error in unemployment rates that is greater than the comparable error in our unsatisfied demand measures. However, any non-trend-related error would not have to be just noise. For example, a one-time shift in the meaning of the unemployment rate as a measure of the effective unutilized labor supply would be imperfectly captured by a simple time trend, leaving a non-trend-related error component.

While the story we have just told seems plausible, a measurement-error interpretation of our results may be suspect insofar as it is easy to believe that our unsatisfied demand proxies might be at least as inconsistent in their meaning as our indicators of unutilized labor supply, the official and prime-age male unemployment rates. As stated above, affirmative action considerations and other factors are likely to have caused some upward trend in the ratio of help-wanted advertising to effective unsatisfied labor demand. The quit rate can be expected to diverge from the vacancy rate. In addition, neither of our unsatisfied demand proxies fully reflects all sectors of the economy. The HWI is based on newspaper advertising and some types of job vacancies may be more likely to be advertised than others; the quit rate we have used is based on data for only the manufacturing sector. Any divergence between the degree of effective unsatisfied demand for labor in the sectors covered by our surrogates and that in the economy as a whole would cause measurement-error problems with our proxies. For these reasons, we are reluctant to assert that the story given above offers the best possible explanation of our findings.

Alternatively, our empirical results might be explained as the natural outcome of greater structural imbalance. One might suppose that the perceived availability of workers qualified to fill existing jobs should be reflected in the difficulty employers experience in filling those jobs. To the extent that the piece of the unemployment rate that captures what employers know about the potentially usable unutilized labor supply is reflected in measures of unsatisfied demand, the residual piece of the unemployment rate that is uncorrelated with unsatisfied demand would tell us only about the amount of irrelevant unutilized labor supply.

The formal exposition of how this sort of change could produce the empirical results laid out earlier would be virtually identical to that just presented for the measurement-error story. Instead of the unemployment rate being viewed as comprising the true unutilized labor supply plus an error component, it would be viewed as comprising a relevant component (reflecting the known availability of persons qualified to fill vacant jobs) plus an irrelevant component; the logic from that point forward would be as given above. This story could explain our results if the irrelevant component of the unemployment rate had grown in importance over time in some nonsimple trend fashion, provided that measurement error in the vacancy rate proxies did not outweigh the change in relevance of the unemployment figures.

The Shifting Relationship between Unsatisfied Demand and Unemployment

The first story sketched out above implies that the outward shift in the U.S. Beveridge curve reflects a divergence between measured unemployment and the true unutilized supply of labor; the second implies that this outward shift reflects growing structural imbalance in the labor market. Unfortunately, available evidence does not permit us to say which of these causes of shift has been more important. Thus, neither explanation can be ruled out.

Readily available data can document that significant demographic and unemployment insurance program changes have occurred in the United States during the period we are studying.[20] The proportion of the labor force between the ages of 25 and 54 fell from an average of 66 percent in 1955–60 to an average of 61 percent in 1976–80. Female representation in the labor force grew from an average of 33 percent of the total during 1956–60 to an average of 42 percent during 1976–80. If the 1956–60 period is compared to the 1976–80 period, we observe that employment covered under state unemployment insurance (UI) programs grew from an average of 78 percent of nonfederal civilian wage and salary workers to an average of 95 percent. The average potential duration of benefits for all UI claimants was substantially higher during the latter period, since many claimants were eligible for extended benefits. The ratio of average weekly UI benefits to average weekly wages of covered employees increased slightly from

20. Perry, "Changing Labor Markets and Inflation," was the first to emphasize the importance of the growing proportion of women and teenagers in the labor force in the context of understanding the relationship between unemployment and wage growth.

0.34 to 0.37.[21] Unfortunately, hard data on other potentially important changes are not so readily accessible.

Changes in the demographic composition of the labor force do seem to have played an important role in shifting the relationship between our unsatisfied demand variables and the official unemployment rate. As noted before, the shifts in the plots of the unsatisfied demand proxies against the prime-age male unemployment rate appear to be less pronounced than the shifts in the comparable official unemployment rate plots. To summarize the magnitude of the shifts in these relationships, we estimated equations of the following form:

$$(10) \qquad\qquad d = \gamma + \phi u + \psi t,$$

where d represents either the normalized HWI or the manufacturing quit rate, u represents either the official or the prime-age male unemployment rate and t is a time trend. The time trend coefficients imply that the shift of the normalized HWI was approximately 32 percent smaller against the prime-age male unemployment rate than against the official unemployment rate and that the shift of the manufacturing quit rate was approximately 40 percent smaller against the prime-age male unemployment rate than against the official unemployment rate. This would seem to suggest that the changing age and sex structure of the labor force may account for a substantial fraction of the shift in the official rate curves.

We also estimated a more complete set of models of the same form as equation 10, except with u equal in turn to the official unemployment rate, the prime-age unemployment rate, the male unemployment rate, and the prime-age male unemployment rate. The time trend coefficients from the male (prime-age male) unemployment rate curves were compared with those from the official (prime-age) unemployment rate curves to assess the effect of changes in the sex structure of the labor force; the time trend coefficients from the prime-age (prime-age male)

21. The figures pertaining to the participation rates of teens and women come from the relevant Data Resources, Inc. data bank. Early unemployment insurance program statistics are from U.S. Department of Labor, Employment and Training Administration, *Handbook of Unemployment Insurance Financial Data, 1936–1976* (ETA, 1979). The various pieces of legislation passed during the 1970s that provided for extended unemployment insurance benefits are described in National Commission on Unemployment Compensation, *Unemployment Compensation: Final Report* (Arlington, Va.: National Commission on Unemployment Compensation, 1980).

unemployment rate curves were held up against those from the official (male) unemployment rate curves to gauge the impact of changes in the age structure of the labor force. On the basis of these comparisons, it would appear that changes in age structure are associated with factors that can explain most of the difference between the magnitude of the outward shifts in the unsatisfied demand proxy/official unemployment rate curves and the magnitude of the less pronounced outward shifts in the unsatisfied demand proxy/prime-age male unemployment rate curves; changes in sex structure appear to have been less important.[22]

It is perhaps worth noting that shifts in the relationship between unsatisfied demand and unemployment occurring because of changes in demographic structure might reflect either a change in the number of available units of labor represented by the typical unemployed individual or increased structural imbalance. On the one hand, women, youth or older persons might desire to work fewer hours per week or be less committed to finding and keeping a job than others. On the other hand, these people might simply be less likely to possess requisite job skills (or be perceived as such by employers). To say the same thing in a slightly different way, the elasticity of substitution between prime-age male workers and other workers might be infinite but with a prime-age male worker equivalent on average to a larger number of effective labor units; or, alternatively, the elasticity of substitution between prime-age males and others might be less than infinite.

It seems likely that changes in UI coverage and benefits may have played a substantial role in shifting the relationship between unsatisfied demand and measured unemployment. While an investigation for the United States has not yet been completed, research for Canada and Great Britain has linked outward shifts in those countries' Beveridge curves to changes in the relevant UI laws.[23] Increased generosity of UI benefits is commonly supposed to affect the eagerness of the typical unemployed worker to secure new employment.

22. Katharine Abraham is currently exploring a cross-section/time-series data set that may shed additional light on the role played by demographic changes in shifting the relationship between unsatisfied demand and unemployment. Preliminary results seem supportive of the proposition that changes in age structure have been more important than changes in sex structure.

23. For a discussion of the shifts in the Canadian and British Beveridge curves, see, for example, Frank Reid and Noah M. Meltz, "Causes of Shifts in the Unemployment-Vacancy Relationship: An Empirical Analysis for Canada," *Review of Economics and*

Other factors, such as a growing mismatch between the requirements and location of vacant jobs and the skills and location of the unemployed (even beyond what might have been expected given observed demographic changes), appear likely to have also played important roles in the phenomenon under discussion.[24] Unfortunately, at this point we cannot document how large the role of each of the potentially important factors might be.

Conclusions and Directions

This paper has presented two key facts that call into question the value of unemployment rates as barometers of labor market tightness. First, both unemployment rates and unsatisfied labor demand proxies perform reasonably well on their own in compensation-growth equations, but in models that include both, only the unsatisfied demand variable appears to matter. Second, the past decade's outward shifts in Phillips plots can to a substantial degree be tied to outward shifts in plots pairing the relevant unemployment rate and unsatisfied demand proxies. We also found that Phillips relationships defined in terms of unsatisfied demand variables appear to be somewhat more stable than those using unemployment rates.

Taken together, our findings have a clear message for those concerned with macroeconomic theory and policy: measures of employers' unsatisfied demand dominate unemployment rates as indicators of how labor market conditions are likely to affect wage growth.

Before the 1970s, the choice between various indicators of labor market tightness had little practical consequence, since the relationship

---

Statistics, vol. 61 (August 1979), pp. 470–75; and United Kingdom Department of Employment, "The Changed Relationship Between Unemployment and Vacancies," *British Labour Statistics: Yearbook, 1976* (Her Majesty's Stationery Office, 1977), app. H, pp. 356–62. The cross-section/time series data set currently being explored by Katharine Abraham may yield insight into the role of changes in the unemployment insurance system in explaining shifts in the relationship between unsatisfied demand and unemployment in the United States. Preliminary results seem to support the proposition that these changes have played an important role.

24. For relevant discussion, see, for instance, William W. Winpisinger, "Correcting the Shortage of Skilled Workers," *AFL-CIO American Federationist,* vol. 87 (June 1980), pp. 21–25; W. H. Weiss, "Help Wanted: The Skill Shortage—What Can Be Done About It?" *Supervision,* vol. 41 (July 1979), pp. 4–5; and Richard B. Freeman, *The Overeducated American* (New York: Academic Press, 1976), pp. 51–73.

between unsatisfied demand proxies and unemployment rates was stable. Moreover, without some independent variation in the potential tightness indicators, it was not possible to determine which was "best." This has all changed in the past ten years, when relationships between unsatisfied demand proxies and unemployment rates have broken down in many countries throughout the world. We have been allowed to peek inside the black box that links unemployment rates and compensation growth. This glimpse has revealed that unemployment rates affect wage growth only to the extent that they are correlated with unsatisfied labor demand and has raised very basic questions about the whole wage-growth process.

To fully understand the determinants of wage growth in our country, it would seem that the following queries must be addressed: How exactly does a wage-setting unit determine the rate of wage growth? Which factors are central and which are tangential in this process? What information is available to those determining wages? Does the shifting during the past decade of the curves that link unsatisfied demand proxies and unemployment rates reflect a diminished desire to work or growing structural unemployment? It appears to us that an analysis of the issues at hand requires the collection of new micro data.

This paper has demonstrated that labor market pressure on wages can be more reliably assessed by looking at measures of unsatisfied labor demand than by looking at the unemployment rates that have played the key role in most earlier analyses. Our understanding of the reasons for this finding must for now remain incomplete. Nevertheless, we are confident that the collection and analysis of micro data can lead to a solution of this macro puzzle.

Comments by James Tobin

This paper can be summarized in three propositions, which I may state a little more baldly than the authors themselves do.

First, the Beveridge curve relating vacancy rates to employment rates has shifted outward in the United States in the postwar period and become somewhat flatter.

Second, the outward shift in the Beveridge curve in the United States is the main reason that the short-run Phillips curve has drifted

outward and upward and become flatter over these years, particularly
in the last ten or fifteen years.

Third, the vacancy rate has all the punch that there is in measures
of unemployment and vacancies—labor market variables—in the short-
run Phillips curve.

The evidence in the paper for the first proposition consists of the
Beveridge scatters of figures 2 and 3. In the absence of a long time
series of vacancy rates, the authors plot a normalized help-wanted
index against the overall and the adult male unemployment rates, and
then use the manufacturing quit rate as an alternative unsatisfied
demand or vacancy measure.

Shown below is another Beveridge curve of my own, which gives
quarterly vacancy rates against unemployment for the period in which
vacancy statistics were collected by the Labor Department. (I never
did understand why that experiment was ended. I always had the
suspicion it was because they could not find enough vacancies to
support the view that all those unemployed were out there turning
down jobs all the time, though that may be unfounded.) In their plots
and in mine you can see the evidence of the outward shift and the
flattening.

The second proposition—that the Phillips curve shift reflects the
Beveridge curve shift—is defended in a series of regressions shown in
tables 3 to 5. Adding a trend to alternative specifications, the authors
find that the Phillips curve shift as measured by the coefficient of time
is much reduced when the unsatisfied demand variables are substituted
for unemployment in the regressions.

The third proposition also is supported by regression analysis. Table
2 shows that unsatisfied demand variables added to a Phillips curve
cause a reversal of sign and a collapse of significance of the coefficients
on the unemployment variables.

I think those are the main points and the main evidence of the
paper. Let me comment on two things the paper does not do. First, it
does not explain *why* the Beveridge curve has shifted out or why it
has flattened. The authors speculate about possible explanations, but
they do not investigate how important their candidates could have
been in the period of time they are studying.

Second, the paper does not tell us whether or not there is a natural
rate of vacancies—I guess it would be a NAIRV. Indeed their general
approach runs counter to natural-rate concepts. In their view, wage

Figure 4. *U.S. Beveridge Curve, 1969–73*

Vacancy rate

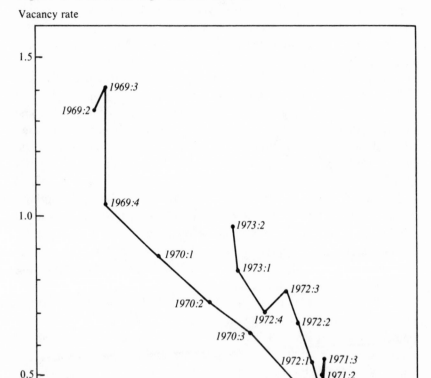

Source: U.S. Department of Labor, Bureau of Labor Statistics, *Employment and Earnings*, February 1974, pp. 129 and 166.

inflation occurs for lots of reasons, among them labor force tightness and inflation itself, but they do not subscribe to a theory that would lead them to compute a natural rate.

Next I offer some comments on what they did do. First of all, I am in principle sympathetic to the use of demand-side variables of labor market tightness. The vacancy rate certainly is one, possibly a very good one for that purpose. The Phillips curve has always been neither a supply nor a demand curve but a quasi-reduced form of disequilibrium in labor markets. Therefore one would expect that it should contain demand-side variables as well as, maybe more importantly than, labor supply-side variables. I am also sympathetic to the authors' notion that one should expect asymmetrical wage adjustment—stronger response to excess demand measured by vacancies than to excess supply measured by unemployment.

In fact, in a paper published in *Brookings Papers on Economic Activity* in 1977, Martin Baily and I used the help-wanted index in estimating various aggregate Phillips wage relationships and some disaggregated ones.[25] We concluded then that a help-wanted index (normalized to total employment) did better than unemployment rates, both in our aggregate relationships and in some of our disaggregated equations.

My second comment is that, in spite of the reluctance of the authors to say anything about natural rates, there seems to have been a big rise in the unemployment rate corresponding to any vacancy rate. According to their charts, it amounts to two or three points of unemployment for any given vacancy rate. This is rather depressing news to anyone who takes a NAIRU or NAIRV approach.

Incidentally, the shift is not confined to the last decade or to the period subsequent to the halcyon days before 1965. It occurred at two points at least between 1952 and 1965. The trend has been adverse for a long time, according to the evidence in the top panel of figure 2, which plots the help-wanted index against the official unemployment rate.

These implications may mean that the authors have proved a little too much. The U.S. Phillips curve troubles began to be really serious and to accelerate around the end of the 1960s. But this timing is not consistent with the steady trend that the authors use in their regressions, which is also evident in the plot. Why didn't the steady trend in the help-wanted index since the early 1950s cause trouble during the first fifteen years? Why was there so much trouble in the second fifteen years of the period? Maybe those questions are not well studied by models that use a steady time-trend variable in the regressions. Anyway the regressions are not compelling. The best ones explain about half the variance of wage change over the period.

Third, I am not sure that the price variable the authors introduce as the feedback term in their regressions is the one, or the only one, consistent with their general hypothesis. They have used the implicit

25. "Macroeconomic Effects of Selective Public Employment and Wage Subsidies."

GNP deflator. It also might be desirable to use a price series related to the demand side of the labor market rather than the supply side, perhaps the deflator for nonfarm business product in the national income accounts.

Beyond that, I have always believed more in the wage-wage hypothesis than the price-wage dynamic, although there is room in the world for both. I think using past wages instead of or in addition to past prices is consistent with a general model of labor markets in which vacancies are an important measure of labor force tightness. In that model, it is employers' bids for workers that are moving the market rather than unemployed workers' bids for work at lower wages than the going pattern.

It is important to formulate wage and price relationships in ways that distinguish price or inflation shocks external to the sector in which wages are being studied from movements in the prices of the products that the workers are making. These two have rather different effects on the demand side of the labor market. For example, an energy price shock would not cause employers other than energy producers to bid more for workers and might cause them to bid less. On the other hand, increases in the prices of the products that the employees are making increases their dollar marginal product and could lead to employers' bidding up wages.

Finally, I would like to say more about the help-wanted index and vacancy statistics in general. As I mentioned before, it is rather extraordinary how small the count of vacancies in the United States was when vacancy data were collected by the Labor Department. The numbers average in the neighborhood of 1 percent and vary by 0.5 or 0.6 of 1 percent over a business cycle. Those are large relative variations, but they are not large variations in absolute numbers of people or vacancies.

The variation may be important nevertheless. The variable may be a proxy for something else. But the small absolute numbers are bound to lead to some general skepticism, even among people like me who think that vacancies should be in the equations, about what is being measured. I suspect that there are some other trends involved in the relationship between the measure and the real phenomenon, about which not very much is known. I would have a lot more faith if the vacancy figures, from whatever source they came, were comparable in magnitude with the unemployment figures, as they are in some of the other countries that collect data of this kind.

Fortune magazine reported an interesting piece of economic research, not by an economist but by a reporter who made a case study of all the help-wanted ads in a county in New York State.[26] In fact, he tracked the ads down to see whether the jobs were there and what they were. What came out of his study is that there is a tremendous amount of fluff in help-wanted ads. Lots of those jobs actually evaporate when you follow them up and go and apply for them.

For example, many firms routinely keep ads in the papers for highly skilled workers. Yale could well have an ad in the *Job Opportunities for Economists* for an economist with the specifications of Kenneth Arrow; any time Kenneth Arrow comes along we will make the job. But how much of a vacancy is that really? *Fortune* found that of about 1,000 advertised vacancies only 100 were genuine positions open to people without special skills. Although one case study does not prove a point, this one suggests caution in using vacancy and help-wanted measures. Trends in the help-wanted index may or may not correspond to trends in a true measure of labor demand.

26. Herbert E. Meyer, "Jobs and Want Ads," *Fortune*, November 20, 1978, pp. 88–96.

ROBERT J. GORDON

Inflation, Flexible Exchange Rates, and the Natural Rate of Unemployment

"The supply response of the economy to monetary impulses" is still the central issue, for both theory and policy.
—James Tobin (*Economic Journal*, March 1981)

THE PREREQUISITES for an informed discussion of anti-inflationary demand-management policy are a quantitative assessment of the response of inflation to alternative degrees of demand restraint, and an estimate of the real output loss associated with each hypothetical policy. Central to the planning of an anti-inflationary strategy is the concept of the "constant inflation" or "natural" rate of unemployment, below which inflation accelerates and above which inflation decelerates. Policymakers planning to stop inflation by restrictive demand-management policy must know how high the unemployment rate must be maintained to induce slower inflation and how rapidly inflation will adjust per unit of time for a given excess of unemployment above the natural rate.

The traditional quantitative tool to address these issues has been the econometric Phillips curve equation, which explains the current inflation rate as depending on the unemployment rate and lagged inflation, that is, on labor market tightness and on inertia that delays the adjustment of inflation to changes in labor market conditions. Econometric Phillips curves have been under attack for most of the past decade, partly because the relation between inflation and unem-

This project was funded under contract no. B9M02667 from the Office of the Assistant Secretary for Policy Evaluation and Research, U.S. Department of Labor. Points of view stated in this document do not necessarily represent the official position or policy of the Department of Labor. Substantial additional research support was provided by the National Science Foundation. The research reported here is part of the research program in economic fluctuations of the National Bureau of Economic Research. Any opinions expressed are those of the author and not those of the NBER. I am grateful to Stephen R. King for his ingenious research assistance, and to Martin Baily, Herschel Grossman, Don Nichols, and George Perry for helpful comments on an earlier draft.

ployment has been positive rather than negative over much of that time. Although the consensus view of a decade ago estimated the natural unemployment rate to be about 5 percent, the actual recorded unemployment rate between early 1971 and late 1980—6.4 percent— was accompanied not by a deceleration of inflation, but a doubling of inflation (in the gross national product deflator) from about 5 percent to almost 10 percent. The juxtaposition of the unemployment and inflation figures seems to imply, as Robert Hall and others have argued, that the natural unemployment rate in the United States in the late 1970s reached close to 7 percent.[1] This conflict between high unemployment and accelerating inflation led commentators like Robert Lucas and Thomas Sargent to announce the demise of the Phillips curve and, with it, the collapse of Keynesian economics.[2]

This paper finds that the Phillips curve has been prematurely buried. The Phillips curve specification—that inflation depends on inertia and real aggregate demand in the form of a labor-market tightness variable— is less wrong than incomplete. Just as today's undergraduate students learn that accelerations of inflation depend on a Marshallian scissors of demand and supply shifts, so the econometric explanation of inflation requires the inclusion not just of inertia and aggregate demand variables, but also of variables to represent the impact of external supply shocks and government intervention in the price-setting process. This paper, which is the fourth in a series on the U.S. inflation process,[3] provides new estimates of the natural unemployment rate and the responsiveness of inflation to demand-management policy that are neither as pessimistic

1. Robert E. Hall, "Labor Markets in Recession and Recovery," in *NBER 1979 Research Conference: A Summary* (National Bureau of Economic Research, 1979), pp. 5–8.

2. See Robert E. Lucas, Jr., and Thomas J. Sargent, "After Keynesian Macroeconomics," in Federal Reserve Bank of Boston, *After the Phillips Curve: Persistence of High Inflation and High Unemployment,* Conference Series No. 19 (Federal Reserve Bank of Boston, 1978), pp. 49–72.

3. This series of papers began with an attempt to explain U.S. inflation in annual data with a single equation covering the entire period between 1892 and 1978: Robert J. Gordon, "A Consistent Characterization of a Near-Century of Price Behavior," *American Economic Review,* vol. 70 (May 1980, *Papers and Proceedings, 1979*), pp. 243–49. A second paper used the same specification to examine the impact of episodes of government intervention in the postwar U.S. inflation process: Jon Frye and Robert J. Gordon, "Government Intervention in the Inflation Process: The Econometrics of 'Self-Inflicted Wounds'," *American Economic Review,* vol. 71 (May 1981, *Papers and Proceedings, 1980*), pp. 288–94. The third paper provided a direct test of the Lucas-Sargent "policy ineffectiveness proposition" in quarterly data extending back to 1892: Robert J. Gordon, "Price Inertia and Policy Ineffectiveness," NBER working paper 708 (Cambridge: NBER, July 1981).

as those based on traditional Phillips curves nor as optimistic as those incorporating the Lucas-Sargent assumption of instantaneous price responsiveness to anticipated nominal demand disturbances.

There are four distinguishing features of this study:

1. Inflation is found to depend upon inertia and on both demand and supply shifts. A careful treatment of supply factors, especially the relative prices of food and energy and the impact of the 1971–74 Nixon price controls program, helps to explain why inflation and unemployment were positively related in the early 1970s and leads to improved estimates of the impact of demand variables on inflation.

2. Demand effects are shown to include the influence of exchange rates. Traditional Phillips curve equations allow the impact of aggregate demand to enter only through a single real variable, the unemployment rate (usually its inverse, and often weighted to correct for demographic shifts). The specification adopted here allows demand policy to enter through two additional channels, the rate of change of real or nominal demand and the change in the effective exchange rate of the dollar (which in turn depends on monetary and fiscal policy). The exchange rate variable makes a critical contribution to the explanation of inflation behavior in the 1970s, particularly the low inflation rate in 1976 and its acceleration in 1978. Further, the exchange rate variable, when combined with an equation that links exchange rate behavior to monetary policy, substantially increases the responsiveness of inflation to monetary restriction and leads to a lower estimate of the associated loss of real gross national product (GNP).

3. Inflation is explained without explicit reference to wage behavior. Some past studies of inflation, including those of George Perry, have estimated only wage equations, without presenting separate estimates of the responsiveness of the price-wage markup to aggregate demand conditions.[4] Since the wage equation captures only part of the impact of demand on inflation, it implies an overly pessimistic verdict on the outcome of restrictive demand-management policy. By concentrating on the relation of inflation to past inflation and both demand and supply factors, this paper circumvents the need to estimate separate wage equations. Sensitivity tests indicate that the omission of a wage equation actually improves the ability to explain historical inflation data.

4. Among others, see three papers by George L. Perry, "Changing Labor Markets and Inflation," *Brookings Papers on Economic Activity*, 3:1970, pp. 411–41 (hereafter *BPEA*); "Slowing the Wage-Price Spiral: The Macroeconomic View," *BPEA*, 2:1978, pp. 259–91; and "Inflation in Theory and Practice," *BPEA*, 1:1980, pp. 207–41.

4. The direct impact of money on prices is tested explicitly. Some critics of the Phillips curve approach state, usually without explicit empirical proof, that past changes in the money supply are the dominant influence on inflation. If the reaction of inflation is sufficiently prompt, a monetary disturbance can change the inflation rate without any response in the real variables (like unemployment or real output) that typically play the key explanatory role in Phillips curve equations, causing such equations to be fundamentally misspecified. In a contest with traditional specifications, short lags on past monetary changes are found to be a good substitute for changes in unemployment, and long lags a good substitute for the level of unemployment. A dynamic simulation of an equation including long lags on money can explain inflation data for the 1970s as well as, although no better than, a similar equation excluding money. The major drawback of the equation with money is the long-run instability of its estimated form and its implausible long-run behavior in simulations of alternative policy regimes.

Two types of quantitative analysis of the impact of aggregate demand on inflation are presented. First, the robustness of the basic inflation equation is tested by comparing it with alternative specifications. What difference is made by specifying the growth of aggregate demand to operate through nominal monetary changes rather than a real variable like unemployment? Is there any evidence of shifts in the importance of the demand variables between the first and last halves of the 1954–80 interval? Is a separate wage equation necessary to track the inflation process, or can the process be adequately summarized in a single equation that ignores wages? The second task of the paper is more directly related to the present concerns of policymakers. What would have been the effects of alternative demand-management policies on inflation during the 1975–80 period? What is the implied natural rate of unemployment during the 1970s and at present? And what would be the outcome for inflation and real GNP of alternative monetary growth rates over the next decade?

Basic Data on Inflation, Aggregate Demand, and Unemployment

Although regression equations are the basic tool of analysis in this paper, some basic features of the postwar inflation process can be identified in a simple summary of the raw data, as shown in table 1. The first outstanding fact shown in the first section of the table is

Table 1. *Inflation, Nominal Demand Growth, Money Supply, Output Ratio, and Unemployment, 1954:2–1980:4*
Percent

Measurement by time period	Inflation[a]	Demand growth[b]	Money supply[c]	Perloff-Wachter output ratio[d]	Official unemployment rate	Perry-weighted unemployment rate
Average over interval						
1954:2–1959:3	2.20	5.44	2.09	−0.70	5.08	4.24
1959:3–1964:4	1.28	5.39	2.37	−1.87	5.71	4.58
1965:1–1970:2	3.80	7.61	4.75	3.24	3.89	2.68
1970:3–1975:4	6.33	9.04	5.85	−0.84	6.04	4.40
1976:1–1980:4	7.52	10.42	7.14	−2.16	6.73	4.97
Standard deviations over interval						
1954:1–1959:3	1.31	5.27	2.03	2.36	1.08	1.04
1959:3–1964:4	0.59	3.25	2.34	1.65	0.58	0.61
1965:1–1970:2	1.34	2.71	2.60	1.27	0.43	0.38
1970:3–1975:4	2.46	4.06	2.09	2.91	1.27	1.12
1976:1–1980:4	1.87	4.14	3.26	1.64	0.80	0.69
Average over four quarters ending in inflation peaks and troughs[e]						
Trough, 1954:3	0.84	−0.46	1.54	−0.82	5.19	4.32
Peak, 1957:1	3.96	6.42	0.95	0.75	4.10	3.28
Trough, 1958:4	1.04	5.05	3.25	−4.57	6.84	5.93
Peak, 1959:4	1.89	5.82	2.05	−1.43	5.45	4.51
Trough, 1961:4	0.70	7.22	2.71	−3.93	6.69	5.56
Peak, 1970:1	5.47	5.37	2.90	2.46	3.68	2.50
Trough, 1972:2	3.69	9.18	6.12	−0.29	5.85	4.27
Peak, 1974:3	10.31	6.82	4.58	−1.10	5.59	3.93
Trough, 1976:4	5.05	8.89	5.83	−3.99	7.68	5.85
Peak, 1980:4	9.29	8.97	6.88	−3.40	7.17	5.33

a. Quarterly rate of change in fixed-weight GNP deflator at annual rate.
b. Quarterly rate of change in nominal GNP at annual rate.
c. Quarterly rate of change in M1B at annual rate.
d. Computed from QPOT$_1$ series estimated by Jeffrey Perloff and Michael Wachter, extrapolated after 1978 at a growth rate corresponding to the official Council of Economic Advisers potential GNP series (2.8 percent in 1979 and 1980), and adjusted for the 1980 revisions in the national income and product accounts.
e. Peaks and troughs are those of the four-quarter percentage change in the fixed-weight GNP deflator.

the simultaneous increase in both inflation and unemployment during 1970–80 as compared to 1954–65. Inflation rose from an average of 1.7 percent in the first two subperiods to 6.9 percent in the last two subperiods, while official unemployment rose from 5.4 to 6.4 percent, and the weighted unemployment rate rose from 4.4 to 4.7 percent. The output ratio duplicates the story told by the weighted unemployment rate, as would be expected, since a demographic correction was used by Perloff and Wachter in creating their natural output series. The following "Okun's law" regression shows the close connection between the weighted unemployment rate U^W and the output ratio $\hat{Q}$, the latter measured as a deviation from 100 percent (the numbers in parentheses are t-statistics):

(1) $U_t^W = 3.96 - 0.243\hat{Q}_t - 0.142\hat{Q}_{t-1} - 0.040\hat{Q}_{t-2}.$
            $(46.2)\quad (-12.0)\qquad (-6.39)\qquad\quad (-1.78)$

$R^2 = 0.976$; Durbin-Watson $= 1.55$, standard error $= 0.178$,

where the coefficient of first-order serial correlation $= 0.79$.

Thus the output ratio is 100 percent when the weighted unemployment rate is 3.96 percent, and this corresponds to an official unemployment rate in 1980 of 5.8 percent. The Perloff-Wachter output ratio and the associated values of the weighted and official unemployment rates are used only as a point of departure for this investigation, which will attempt to determine whether the Perloff-Wachter output ratio overstates natural real GNP and understates the corresponding natural rate of unemployment. Stated another way, this paper seeks to determine whether the acceleration of inflation in the 1970s can be explained when on average the Perloff-Wachter output ratio was negative throughout the decade.

Between the first and last subperiods, the acceleration of inflation of 5.3 percentage points was accompanied by similar accelerations in nominal GNP and monetary growth of 5.0 and 5.1 percentage points. (It is interesting that velocity growth was so stable across the five subperiods, ranging only from 2.9 to 3.4 percent.) But within each subperiod the relationship between inflation, nominal GNP, and money was not nearly so close. The second section of the table shows the standard deviations within each of the five intervals of each variable. The variance of inflation and the output ratio was greatest in the early 1970s, whereas the variance of adjusted nominal GNP growth was greatest in the 1950s, and the variance of monetary growth was greatest in the late 1970s. In fact, the variance of monetary growth was relatively low in the early 1970s, just when the variance of inflation, the output ratio, and unemployment was highest. These summary statistics reflect my finding that postwar inflation cannot be adequately characterized simply as a lagged adjustment to one or more of the other variables included in table 1, but rather that its explanation requires an explicit quantitative treatment of supply shocks and of government intervention in the inflation process.

A different subdivision of the data is presented in the bottom section of table 1. The dates shown are those of the trough and peak inflation rates (measured as four-quarter changes) corresponding to each of the five National Bureau of Economic Research (NBER) business cycles. The upward ratcheting of the peaks and troughs after 1961 is clearly evident, although the 1980 inflation peak fell short of that reached in 1974 (another clue that supply shocks played a special role in the highly variable inflation of the early 1970s). The correlation of inflation and either demand or monetary growth is extremely weak across inflation peaks and troughs, and is negative between 1970 and 1976. The negative Phillips curve relation between inflation and unemployment is evident before but not after 1970.

Methodology

Two Equations or One?

Just as the Phillips curve econometricians and the Lucas-Sargent classicists hold different views about the impact of aggregate demand on inflation, so they also set up their empirical studies differently. The traditional procedure has been to specify a wage equation and then to assume that the price level is marked up over standard unit labor cost, that is, the wage rate divided by a productivity trend. Some traditional studies, which do not provide estimates of the markup equation, imply that their estimated coefficient on the level of unemployment in the wage equation is the only channel through which aggregate demand can alter the inflation rate.[5]

In contrast, proponents of the Lucas-Sargent approach focus directly on an equation in which the inflation rate rather than wage change is the dependent variable.[6] The effect of demand is entered through

5. The three papers by Perry cited in the previous footnote contain the terms *inflation* or *wage-price spiral* in their title, yet contain only wage equations. They were influential in leading to the low estimates of inflation responsiveness popularized by Arthur M. Okun in "Efficient Disinflationary Policies," *American Economic Review,* vol. 68 (May 1978, *Papers and Proceedings, 1977*), pp. 348–52.

6. Actually the most cited "new classical" empirical work by Barro, for example, Robert J. Barro and Mark Rush, "Unanticipated Money and Economic Activity," in Stanley Fischer, ed., *Rational Expectations and Economic Policy* (University of Chicago Press, 1980), pp. 23–48, fits an equation in which the dependent variable is the price *level* rather than its rate of change. The failure to difference the price level leads to serial correlation in the residuals and severely biased coefficients, a classic example of

changes in nominal money or nominal GNP, and there is no attention to variables representing labor market tightness. This single-equation approach has several advantages over the traditional two-equation mainline framework that emphasizes wages.

First, wage and price markup equations cannot be distinguished as truly structural equations applying to behavior in particular markets. The behavior of wages, for instance, can be explained just as well by real GNP as by labor market variables like unemployment, suggesting that the wage equation does not provide us with any special insight about the working of labor markets. Indeed, if the Okun's law relationship linking the output ratio and the unemployment rate works well, as in equation 1 above, then output variables can mimic the behavior of labor market variables over the business cycle.[7] Second, traditional wage and price equations may be particularly prone to simultaneous equations bias. If current prices explain wages and current wages explain prices, then the coefficient on a variable that influences both simultaneously—whether a demand proxy like real GNP or a supply variable like price-control effects—may be biased downward if it is measured with error and part of its true effect is "soaked up" by the right-hand wage or price variable.

A third problem is that the use of separate wage and price markup equations leads to an artificial separation of the variables that "belong" in each equation. Thus the inflationary impact of the payroll tax or Kennedy-Johnson wage guidelines depends not just on their coefficient in the wage equation, but also on the response of prices to that particular source of wage variation. Finally, the two-equation approach is inconvenient and clumsy. The full impact of a variable on the inflation rate cannot be learned from the simple inspection of a table; it requires multiplying and adding coefficients.

On all of these counts a single inflation equation, which relates the rate of price change to its own lagged values, seems superior. The equation is openly a convenient characterization of the data rather

---

spurious regression examined in the work of C. W. J. Granger and P. Newbold, "Spurious Regressions in Econometrics," *Journal of Econometrics*, vol. 2 (July 1974), pp. 111–20; and Charles I. Plosser and G. William Schwert, "Money, Income, and Sunspots: Measuring Economic Relationships and the Effects of Differencing," *Journal of Monetary Economics*, vol. 4 (November 1978), pp. 637–60.

7. The level and change of the output ratio were first introduced into a wage equation in Robert J. Gordon, "Can the Inflation of the 1970s Be Explained?" *BPEA, 1:1977*, pp. 253–77. See table 3 on pp. 266–67 and the discussion on p. 279.

than an attempt to describe structural behavior. Because the underlying structure may shift, the coefficients in the estimated equation may shift, so that any such single-equation approach should pay special attention to tests of the stability of coefficients across subintervals within the sample period.

Details of the Specification

My single inflation equation is derived from separate wage and price markup equations. Because economic theory gives no guidance as to the exact form of the impact of aggregate demand on inflation, I shall postulate that the level and rate of change of a real-utilization variable— either the output ratio or weighted unemployment—enters both the wage and price markup equations. The level of the real-demand variable is denoted below by X_t, and its rate of change as x_t. An important restriction on the wage equation is that we rule out a wage-wage spiral, that is, the dependence of the rate of wage change on the inherited norm of lagged wage change due to the attention paid by workers to wage differentials.[8] Instead, the influence of inertia on wage change, w_t, is assumed to enter through a single term, defined as lagged price change p_{t-1} plus the equilibrium growth rate of the real wage, λ_t. While the wage-wage view is plausible, any role of lagged wages must be purged from the wage equation to allow the development of a single inflation equation free from the need to explain wage behavior. The section below on the role of wage equations demonstrates that lagged price changes perform much better than lagged wages in a wage equation.

In addition to the real-demand and inertia variables, wage change is allowed to depend on a vector of supply variables, z_{wt}, that shift the rate of wage change for any given values of lagged prices and the demand variables. Among the supply shifts that might enter the wage equation are the impacts of wage controls and changes in the payroll tax and minimum wage. When an error term, ϵ_{wt}, is included, the wage equation becomes:

$$(2) \qquad w_t = \alpha_0 + \alpha_1(p_{t-1} + \lambda_t) + \alpha_2 X_t + \alpha_3 x_t + \alpha_4 z_{wt} + \epsilon_{wt}.$$

8. The wage-wage mechanism is stressed by Robert E. Hall, "The Process of Inflation in the Labor Market," *BPEA*, 2:1974, pp. 343–93; Arthur M. Okun, *Prices and Quantities: A Macroeconomic Analysis* (Brookings Institution, 1981); and Perry, "Inflation in Theory and Practice," and in fact dates back to Keynes's view that workers care about relative wage rates.

In the steady state the actual growth in the real wage, $w_t - p_t$, will be at the equilibrium rate, λ_t, only if $\alpha_1 = 1$, the level of the real-demand variable is constant at $X_t^* = -(\alpha_0/\alpha_2)$, and the supply and error terms have realizations equal to zero. Thus the term *equilibrium* to describe λ_t is used in the highly restricted sense of a "no shock" equilibrium. In exactly the same sense, the natural rate of output or unemployment, X_t^*, is compatible with steady wage growth only if the same set of restrictive conditions is satisfied.

In the long run, the λ_t term plays no role in the inflation process *if* the productivity variable in the price equation below, σ_t, equals λ_t. But some have argued that a decline in productivity growth can cause an acceleration of inflation if firms and workers try to maintain the old path of real wages, rather than instantly allowing the growth rate of real wages to decelerate in proportion to the productivity slowdown, $\lambda_t > \sigma_t$. A distinction between the real wage and productivity is introduced to test empirically whether productivity behavior has been a separate determinant of the observed rate of inflation. An independent channel is introduced in appendix A, which contains equations that translate monetary growth into unemployment. Slower growth in productivity—and thus in potential output—reduces the unemployment rate relative to the natural unemployment rate for any given growth rate of money, and thus in the basic equation in table 2 causes the inflation rate to accelerate.

The price markup equation relates current price change p_t to the current change in standard unit labor cost $w_t - \sigma_t$, the same demand variables as in equation 2, a vector of supply-shift variables z_{pt} that influence the level of prices relative to wages, and an error term ϵ_{pt}:

$$(3) \qquad p_t = \beta_0 + \beta_1(w_t - \sigma_t) + \beta_2 X_t + \beta_3 x_t + \beta_4 z_{pt} + \epsilon_{pt}.$$

The fact that the current wage enters the price equation, but only lagged price change enters the wage equation, is an expositional convenience that does not restrict the empirical work presented below.[9] Among the supply-shift variables z_{pt} that could enter into the price equation are government price controls, changes in foreign exchange rates and in the relative prices of food and energy, and shifts in indirect tax rates.

9. If lagged wage change also enters the price equation, then lagged values of the right-hand variables in the wage equation enter the reduced form equation 4. In fact the empirical work below allows flexible lags on all variables.

When equation 2 is substituted into equation 3, a single inflation equation is obtained:

(4) $\quad p_t = \beta_0 + B_1\alpha_0 + \beta_1\alpha_1 p_{t-1} + \beta_1(\alpha_1\lambda_t - \sigma_t) + (\beta_2 + \beta_1\alpha_2)X_t$
$\quad\quad + (\beta_3 + \beta_1\alpha_3)x_t + \beta_4 z_{pt} + \beta_1\alpha_4 z_{wt} + \epsilon_{pt} + \beta_1\epsilon_{wt}.$

The long-run equilibrium properties of equation 4 can be seen more easily if the separate z variables, error terms, and coefficients from the wage and price equations are combined:

(5) $\quad\quad p_t = \gamma_0 + \gamma_1 p_{t-1} + \gamma_1(\lambda_t - \sigma_t)$
$\quad\quad\quad + (\gamma_1 - \beta_1)\sigma_t + \gamma_2 X_t + \gamma_3 x_t + \gamma_4 z_t + \epsilon_t,$

where

$\gamma_0 = \beta_0 + \beta_1\alpha_0;$
$\gamma_1 = \beta_1\alpha_1;$
$\gamma_2 = \beta_2 + \beta_1\alpha_2;$
$\gamma_3 = \beta_3 + \beta_1\alpha_3;$
$\gamma_4 z_t = \beta_4 z_{pt} + \beta_1\alpha_4 z_{wt};$
$\epsilon_t = \epsilon_{pt} + \beta_1\epsilon_{wt}.$

What are the conditions necessary for equation 5 to generate a constant equilibrium rate of inflation? First, the coefficient on lagged price change γ_1 must be unity. Second, the equilibrium real-wage term in the wage equation and standard productivity growth in the price equation must be equal ($\lambda_t - \sigma_t = 0$). Third, the coefficient on standard unit labor cost in the price equation must be unity ($\beta_1 = 1$).[10] Fourth, the rate of change in the real-demand variable, as well as every supply-shift variable, must also be equal to zero ($x_t = z_t = 0$). Finally, the level of the real-demand variable must be at its "natural rate," $X_t^* = -(\gamma_0/\gamma_2)$. Correspondingly, equation 5 lays out those events that can cause the inflation rate to accelerate, including an excess of λ_t over σ_t, a level of real demand above the natural rate ($X_t > X_t^*$), a positive rate of growth of the real-demand variable, and any adverse supply shock.

10. This does not deny a role for the prices of other inputs, for example, capital or raw materials, since these variables can be entered as relative prices. See the more complete specification of the price markup equation in Robert J. Gordon, "The Impact of Aggregate Demand on Prices," *BPEA*, 3:1975, p. 620.

Clearly X_t^* represents the natural rate of output only if all of the other conditions stated in the previous paragraph are valid. If there is, for instance, an adverse supply shift ($z_t > 0$), inflation can accelerate even if $X_t = X_t^*$. An excess of λ_t over σ_t, or a positive realization of any z_t variable, pushes the constant-inflation level of real demand below the value of X_t^*. Thus the framework of equation 5 has the potential of explaining why inflation accelerated during the 1970s, despite the fact that the Perloff-Wachter output-ratio measure summarized in table 1 was negative on average during the decade.

Endogeneity Problems

Leaving aside the possible endogeneity of elements in the z_t supply vector (discussed below) a weakness of equation 5 is the appearance of two endogenous variables, the level and rate of change of real demand (X_t and x_t, respectively). A bias in the coefficient on both demand variables, and particularly on the rate of change effect, x_t, may be introduced from two sources. First, if x_t is represented by the change in real GNP, measurement error may introduce a spurious negative correlation between the dependent variable, p_t, and x_t, the output change variable, thus biasing downward the parameter γ_3, since in the United States the national accounts nominal GNP and prices are measured independently, with real GNP as a residual.[11] Thus any error that exaggerates the rate of price increase in a given quarter would depress the official growth rate of real GNP by an equal amount, since data for nominal GNP are collected independently. This type of measurement error can be avoided by using a real-demand variable collected from an independent data source, such as Perry's weighted unemployment rate, to measure both X_t and x_t.

Second, for any given growth rate of nominal GNP, a supply shock ($z_t > 0$) raises the inflation rate and reduces real GNP growth. In principle, the impact of any supply shock that shifts the inflation rate for given values of the output variables is supposed to be captured by the vector of z_t variables included in the equation. But errors in the

---

11. Nominal GNP is estimated from sources such as retail sales, investment surveys, and government expenditure data. The price data used for the deflation of individual components of GNP come primarily from the two major Bureau of Labor Statistics price indexes, the consumer and producer price indexes.

measurement of the z_t variables may introduce a spurious negative correlation between the inflation rate and the change in either output or unemployment. For instance, with fixed nominal GNP growth, imagine that an oil price increase raises the inflation rate and reduces output growth by 1 percentage point in the initial quarter, and that the oil shock variable times its coefficient erroneously indicates only a 0.5 percent upward shift in the inflation schedule. The explanation of the other 0.5 percentage point acceleration of inflation would be captured by a coefficient of -0.5 on the output-change variable if there were no other observations; more generally when the true coefficient on output growth γ_3 is positive, the estimated coefficient would be biased toward zero. Given the close negative association between real output and unemployment in equation 1, the same bias would apply (with the opposite sign) to unemployment variables. To test the possibility that this supply shock bias might affect the estimated equation, an alternative version is estimated below in which the real rate-of-change variable is replaced by the lagged growth rate of the nominal money supply.

The GNP deflator seems the natural choice as dependent variable in a study of the basic U.S. inflation process. Given any specified path of nominal GNP and natural (or potential) real GNP, determination of the path of the GNP deflator automatically yields as residual the output ratio $\hat{Q}_t$, and, through equation 1, the unemployment rate. A pitfall introduced by the GNP deflator stems from the use of shifting current-period expenditure weights in its construction, leading to a confounding of price changes with changes in the mix of output. In a quarter in which there is a sharp change in a particular category of nominal spending, as in the case of an auto strike or oil embargo, the value of the deflator may rise or fall due to shifting weights, even if there were no effect of nominal GNP on any individual price change. Fortunately this problem can be avoided through the use of the published fixed-weight GNP deflator that insulates true price changes from expenditure shifts, just as studies of wage inflation during the past decade have adopted the practice of employing a dependent variable that is corrected for changes in the interindustry employment mix.[12]

---

12. The fixed-weight wage index was first constructed and used for quarterly research in Robert J. Gordon, "Inflation in Recession and Recovery," *BPEA, 1:1971*, pp. 105–58.

The Basic Inflation Equation

The Point of Departure: A Naive Phillips Curve

My starting place is the simple Phillips curve, which incorporates only the effects of real demand and inertia. Although most Phillips curve research has stressed the relationship between wage change and the level of the unemployment rate, a quasi-Phillips curve equation can be estimated within my framework by regressing the rate of inflation on its own lagged values and the current level of the Perry-weighted unemployment rate, U_t^W. This is equivalent to the estimation of equation 5 with the omission of the demand-growth, productivity, and supply-shift terms. As in all of the equations presented in this paper, the level of the unemployment rate appears in its linear rather than its inverse form (used in most previous studies). Since the inverse form improves the fit by only a trivial amount, less than 1 percent, I prefer the linear form, which makes the coefficients on the constant and unemployment terms easier to interpret.[13] Also in common with the other equations in this paper, the role of the lagged dependent variable may be to represent either the adaptive formation of the expected rate of inflation or simply the inertia in the inflation process through the influence of three-year wage contracts and other similar institutional phenomena. Since these two interpretations cannot be distinguished empirically, there is no point in trying to decide which is valid.[14]

To standardize the equations in the paper and economize on the number of permutations of equations that must be estimated, the lagged dependent variable is entered into every equation as a fourth-degree polynomial extended over twenty-four lagged values with a zero end-point constraint. In table 2, column 1 illustrates an equation in which the quarterly rate of change of the fixed-weight GNP deflator (expressed as an annual rate) is regressed on this polynomial distributed lag, on the level of the weighted unemployment rate, and on a constant term.

---

13. The 5 percent F value for the significance of the inverse as compared to the linear form in table 2, column 1, is only 1.19, compared to a critical value of 3.98.

14. The distinction between backward- and forward-looking expectations is discussed by Perry, "Slowing the Wage-Price Spiral," pp. 268–70.

Table 2. *Alternative Equations for the Estimation of the Weighted Natural Unemployment Rate, 1954:2–1980:4*[a]

Independent variable and summary statistic	Unconstrained equations			Constrained equations[b]		
	(1)	(2)	(3)	(4)	(5)	(6)
Independent variable						
1. Constant	2.14	3.04	2.45	2.72	3.35	2.45
	(4.69)	(7.37)	(3.52)	(6.68)	(9.68)	(6.51)
2. Lagged inflation[c]	1.22	1.17	. . .	1.00	1.00	. . .
	(19.6)	(20.3)		. . .	. . .	
3. Lagged inflation, first half[c]	. . .	. . .	1.01	. . .	. . .	1.00
			(3.10)			. . .
4. Lagged inflation, last half[c]	. . .	. . .	1.03	. . .	. . .	1.00
			(10.5)			. . .
5. Weighted unemployment rate	−0.62	−0.78	−0.59	−0.65	−0.76	−0.58
	(−5.17)	(−7.35)	(−4.30)	(−6.42)	(−8.84)	(−6.51)
6. Change in weighted unemployment	. . .	. . .	−0.64	. . .	. . .	−0.66
			(−1.92)			(−2.61)
7. Productivity deviation	. . .	. . .	−0.08	. . .	. . .	−0.09
			(−2.03)			(−2.66)
8. Food and energy prices[d]	. . .	0.46	0.74	. . .	0.48	0.73
		(3.12)	(3.31)		(3.51)	(5.21)
9. Foreign exchange rate[e]	. . .	. . .	−0.11	. . .	. . .	−0.12
			(−1.70)			(−3.61)
10. Effective minimum wage[d]	. . .	. . .	0.02	. . .	. . .	0.02
			(1.17)			(1.87)
11. Social security tax[d]	. . .	. . .	0.27	. . .	. . .	0.21
			(1.00)			(0.91)

Table 2 *(continued)*

Independent variable and summary statistic	Unconstrained equations			Constrained equations[b]		
	(1)	*(2)*	*(3)*	*(4)*	*(5)*	*(6)*
12. Nixon controls "on"[f]	. . .	−1.60 (−3.07)	−1.45 (−2.61)	. . .	−2.04 (−3.41)	−1.76 (−3.21)
13. Nixon controls "off"[f]	. . .	2.92 (5.52)	2.67 (3.86)	. . .	2.78 (5.35)	2.36 (4.07)
14. Shift, 1970:3– 1975:4	. . .	. . .	. . .	1.05 (3.88)	0.76 (2.47)	0.41 (1.38)
15. Shift, 1976:1– 1980:4	. . .	. . .	. . .	0.94 (3.19)	0.68 (2.54)	0.05 (0.19)
Summary statistic						
R^2	0.867	0.916	0.942	0.317	0.682	0.837
Sum of squared residuals	115.2	72.0	50.2	118.1	73.8	49.2
Standard error	1.068	0.875	0.823	1.071	0.877	0.785

a. Dependent variable is quarterly change in GNP fixed-weight deflator. The numbers in parentheses are *t*-statistics.

b. In columns 4 through 6, the constraint is imposed by subtracting from the quarterly change in the GNP fixed-weight deflator the twenty-four lagged inflation variables times their respective coefficients from columns 1 through 3, divided by the sum of coefficients. This difference is the dependent variable in a regression in which all of the other indicated variables appear on the right-hand side.

c. In columns 1 to 3 the indicated figures are sums of coefficients (and their *t*-statistics) when the lagged dependent variable is entered as a fourth-degree polynomial distributed lag on twenty-four lagged values, with a zero end-point constraint. In lines 3 and 4 the lagged inflation variable is entered twice in the same form, with the first distributed lag fitted to values for 1948:2 through 1966:4, and the second fitted to values for 1967:1 through 1980:4.

d. For each of these variables both the current and four lagged values are entered into the equation, with the listed coefficient indicating the sum of all five coefficients and associated *t* ratio on the sum.

e. Same as above, except that the current and three lagged values are entered.

f. The Nixon controls "on" dummy variable is entered as a variable equal to 0.8 for the five quarters 1971:3–1972:3. The "off" variable is equal to 0.4 in 1974:2 and 1975:1, and 1.6 in 1974:3 and 1974:4. The respective dummy variables sum to 4.0 rather than 1.0 because the dependent variable in each equation is a quarterly change expressed as an annual rate, that is, multiplied by 4.0.

The estimated coefficients in column 1 seem satisfactory at first glance. The Phillips curve slope—the coefficient on U_t^w—is strongly significant and indicates that a permanent 1 percentage point reduction of the unemployment rate is accompanied by 0.6 percentage point of extra inflation for any given contribution of the lagged inflation variable. But there is a problem in the sum of coefficients on lagged inflation, which lies significantly above unity. Maintenance of the weighted unemployment rate at $-\gamma_0/\gamma_2 = 3.45$ would be associated with an acceleration of inflation. Thus the natural unemployment rate cannot be calculated directly in column 1.

A central focus of this study is the extent to which the natural unemployment rate has increased during the 1970s. A measure of the upward shift implied by column 1 can be provided if one constrains the sum of coefficients on lagged inflation to be unity and includes two dummy variables for the first and last half of the 1970s to measure the shift in the constant term as compared to the sample period as a whole. The constraint is imposed in column 4 by subtracting from the dependent variables the twenty-four lagged inflation variables times their respective coefficients in column 1, all divided by the sum of coefficients (1.22). The results in column 4 imply that the natural weighted unemployment rate rose about 1 percentage point after 1970:

	Weighted	Official
1956	4.18	5.00
1972	5.23	6.81
1978	5.12	6.80

The conversion from the weighted to the official rate is accomplished simply by adding in the actual difference between the two rates in the listed year. The resulting estimate of an official natural unemployment rate in the 1970s of 6.8 percent corresponds to the back-of-the-envelope estimate of Hall.[15]

Introducing the Supply-Shift Variables

The basic equation 5 contains several variables in addition to those shown in the first column of table 2, including a vector of supply shifts, a productivity term, and an additional demand variable, the rate of change of real demand. These additional variables are introduced in two stages in table 2. First, in the second column, two key supply-shift variables are included—the Nixon controls and changes in the relative prices of food and energy. Then in column 3, the complete set of additional variables is included. Because the exact specification of the supply-shift variables was examined in detail in a previous

15. Hall, "Labor Markets in Recession and Recovery," pp. 5–8.

paper, here every equation enters each component of the z_t vector with the same definition and lag distribution.[16]

FOOD AND ENERGY EFFECT. The most readily available measure of the impact of changes in the relative price of food and energy is the difference between the respective rates of change of the national accounts deflators for personal consumption expenditures and for personal consumption net of expenditures on food and energy. The advantages of this measure are that it incorporates food and energy products with weights reflecting their importance in final spending (as opposed, for instance, to the producer price index for energy, which applies multiple weights to crude oil); and it assumes a value of zero when the relative prices of food and energy are constant, thus allowing the "no shock" natural rate of unemployment to be calculated directly in table 2.[17]

NIXON CONTROLS. The impact of the price controls during the Nixon administration is assessed with a pair of dummy variables, specified to show the cumulative displacement of the price level by the controls and the extent of its subsequent postcontrols rebound. Previous econometric evaluations of control effects have been based both on dummy variables and on postsample dynamic simulations of equations. Blinder and Newton contributed a third method, based on a time series of the fraction of prices actually controlled. In a detailed comparison, Frye and Gordon concluded that when the dummy variable and Blinder techniques are used in conjunction with the same specification of other variables, they give identical fits and measures of the displacement of the price level by controls.[18] The postsample simulation technique is

16. See Jon Frye and Robert J. Gordon, "The Variance and Acceleration of Inflation in the 1970s: Alternative Explanatory Models and Methods," NBER working paper 551 (Cambridge: NBER, September 1980).

17. This is not the conceptually correct variable to include in the equations that explain the GNP deflator, since no allowance is made for the price of food and energy exports and imports. The conceptually correct measure was used in Gordon, "The Impact of Aggregate Demand," pp. 613–20. There was insufficient time in the preparation of the present paper to allow the 1975 variable to be reconstructed and updated from the revised national accounts, but reestimation of the basic inflation equation for the 1954–75 period using the 1975 variable indicates virtually no change in results.

18. The analysis of Alan Blinder and William J. Newton is contained in Alan S. Blinder and William J. Newton, "The 1971–1974 Controls Program and the Price Level: An Econometric Post-Mortem," *Journal of Monetary Economics*, vol. 8 (July 1981), pp. 1–23. The comparison of the Blinder-Newton technique is contained in the paper by Frye and Gordon, "Variance and Acceleration of Inflation," fig. 1, p. 52. In this

judged inferior, because it is unable to incorporate information on variables that were unimportant before 1971 but were important thereafter (especially flexible exchange rates). The coefficients displayed in lines 12 and 13 of table 2 show a substantially greater "off" effect than "on" effect, a result attributed below to the impact of the foreign exchange rate.

The estimates in column 2, and the corresponding constrained equation in column 5, add to the "naive Phillips curve" only the impact of Nixon controls and the current change in the relative prices of food and energy. In my research I have found that a number of other variables are useful in explaining postwar inflation. The following list describes the additional variables in the order in which they are entered in column 3, and the corresponding constrained equation in column 6.

SPLIT LAGGED DEPENDENT VARIABLE. The fit of the equation improves markedly when the single distributed lag on past inflation in columns 1 and 2 is replaced by two separate distributed lags in column 3 applied respectively to lagged price data before and after 1967:1—chosen because it is the midpoint of the sample period. The improvement in fit occurs because the shape of the lag distribution shortens substantially in the last half of the sample period, from 11.2 to 6.8 quarters. The F value for the significance of the additional lag distribution is 2.06, close to the 5 percent critical value of 2.49. Two factors may have speeded up the responsiveness of the inflation process. First, higher inflation rates have brought increased awareness of inflation behavior, and, second, the share of wage contracts containing escalator clauses increased substantially in the 1970s, compared to the 1960s.[19]

CHANGE IN UNEMPLOYMENT. A significant contribution is made by the change in unemployment, entered as a simple first difference of

---

paper the timing of the dummies has been adjusted to reflect the December 1980 revisions in the national income and product accounts, which concentrates more of the 1974 inflation upsurge in the third and fourth quarters.

19. Historical data on escalator coverage in major union contracts is found in the following sources: 1958–73—H. M. Douty, *Cost-of-Living Escalator Clauses and Inflation,* Council on Wage and Price Stability (Government Printing Office, 1975); 1974—*Monthly Labor Review,* vol. 97 (July 1974), pp. 12–13; 1975–80—January issues of the *Monthly Labor Review,* and *BLS Bargaining Calendar 1980,* Bureau of Labor Statistics Bulletin 2059 (GPO, 1980).

the Perry-weighted unemployment rate. An equation that omits the unemployment-change variable exhibits a jump in the coefficient on the level of the unemployment rate from -0.59 to -0.72. The F value for the additional rate-of-change variable is 3.76, compared to a 5 percent critical value of 3.98.

PRODUCTIVITY DEVIATION. If the equilibrium real-wage growth variable in the wage equation, λ_t, and the standard productivity variable in the price markup equation, σ_t, were identical, then the behavior of actual productivity changes would have no influence on the actual inflation rate in equation 5. However, in general there is no reason for these two variables to be identical, and thus there is room for tests of the direct influence of actual productivity changes on inflation. Imagine that the productivity variable in the wage equation, λ_t, is a constant representing a straight time trend, t_w, whereas the "standard" productivity variable in the price equation, σ_t, is a weighted average of the actual growth rate of productivity, ρ_t, and another constant trend, t_p:[20]

(6) $$\lambda_t = t_w,$$

(7) $$\sigma_t = \mu(\rho_t) + (1 - \mu)t_p,$$

so that the productivity variable that appears in equation 5 becomes:

(8) $$\lambda_t - \sigma_t = t_w - t_p - \mu(\rho_t - t_p).$$

The $(t_w - t_p)$ term becomes absorbed in the constant of the inflation equation and, if it is not zero, becomes part of the estimated natural unemployment rate. Table 2 measures the "productivity deviation," $\rho_t - t_p$, by specifying t_p as a variable time trend.[21] The productivity-deviation variable—the difference between the quarterly growth rate of nonfarm output per hour and this variable trend—enters significantly

---

20. For previous uses of the specification in equation 7, see Gordon, "Inflation in Recession and Recovery," pp. 128–29; and Gordon, "The Impact of Aggregate Demand," pp. 619–20.

21. The time trends run between actual levels of nonfarm output per hour achieved in the first quarter of the sample period (1954:2) and three succeeding quarters when the Perloff-Wachter output ratio was approximately 100 percent: 1964:3, 1972:1, and 1978:4. The extrapolation after 1978:4 was computed to correspond to the slowdown in the growth of potential GNP assumed in the *Economic Report of the President, January 1980*. The computed trend lines are: 1954:2–1964:3, 2.56 percent; 1964:3–1972:2, 2.11 percent; 1972:2–1978:4, 1.22 percent, and after 1978:4, 0.5 percent.

on line 7 of the equation in column 3. Experimentation with lags indicates that its entire impact occurs in the current quarter. The F value on its inclusion is 4.22, compared to the 5 percent critical value of 3.98.

FOREIGN EXCHANGE RATE. Changes in the effective exchange rate of the dollar have not been included as an explanatory variable in previous studies of inflation, mainly because it has been difficult to find a statistically significant impact. The previous insignificance of the exchange rate appears to have been caused by the impact of the Nixon controls in delaying the adjustment of U.S. domestic prices to the dollar depreciation that occurred in two stages between 1971 and 1973. My variable is the quarterly change in the effective exchange rate of the dollar, starting in 1975:2, the quarter when the postcontrols rebound is assumed to terminate. This variable, entered as a current and three lagged values, makes a significant contribution to the equation (with an F value of 2.55 compared to a 5 percent critical value of 2.49) and helps to explain why inflation was so low in 1976 and accelerated so rapidly in 1978. The policy implications of this variable are important, since movements in the exchange rate introduce a direct impact of monetary policy (and the monetary-fiscal mix) on the inflation rate. I believe that the artificial device of setting the exchange rate change equal to zero before 1975 accounts for the fact that the Nixon controls "off" coefficient is larger than the "on" coefficient. The cumulative depreciation of the dollar between 1970:1 and 1975:1 was 17 percent, contributing 1.94 percent to the inflation rate when multiplied by the 1975–80 coefficient of -0.11. Of this 1.94 points of extra inflation, 1.2 points are captured by the excess positive coefficient on the controls "off" variable, and the remainder is presumably soaked up by other variables.

A question may be raised about the possible endogeneity of the foreign exchange rate variable. Fortunately, there is strong evidence against contemporaneous feedback from inflation to the exchange rate. First, the exchange rate variable enters in the form of the current and three lagged values, but all of its explanatory power comes from the lags; the coefficient on the current variable is insignificant. Second, a regression of the foreign exchange rate on current and four lagged changes in money, nominal GNP, and the GNP deflator yields coefficients on current and lagged inflation that are jointly and individually insignificant. Thus all of the short-run interaction between the exchange rate and inflation is due to the effect of the former on the latter, and any impact in the reverse direction is both imperfect and long delayed.[22]

EFFECTIVE MINIMUM WAGE AND SOCIAL SECURITY TAX. In previous studies I have found the effective minimum wage variable and the social security tax variable to be significant self-inflicted wounds, that is, changes in government policy variables that had a direct adverse impact on the inflation rate. The effective minimum wage rate is defined as changes in the ratio of the statutory minimum wage to average hourly earnings in the nonfarm economy, and the effective payroll tax rate as the ratio of total contributions for social security (employee and employer shares) divided by wages and salaries. Neither variable is statistically significant in column 3, but both are included to maintain comparability with previous studies. In addition, their effect in separate wage and price markup equations is of interest and is estimated in table 5 below.

Sensitivity of Natural Unemployment Rate to Form of Equation

The specification of the equations in columns 1 through 3 is repeated on the right-hand side of table 2, with a unity constraint imposed on the sum of the coefficients on lagged inflation in each equation in columns 4 through 6. The latter equations also insert two additional constant terms for the first and last half of the 1970s in order to test for shifts in the natural rate of unemployment. The inclusion of the food-energy and price-control effects in column 5 eliminates roughly one-third of the increase in the weighted unemployment rate between 1956 and 1978, while the complete specification in column 6 eliminates most of the remaining increase in the natural rate of unemployment:

	Weighted			Official		
	(4)	*(5)*	*(6)*	*(4)*	*(5)*	*(6)*
1956	4.18	4.41	4.15	5.00	5.21	4.97
1972	5.23	5.17	4.56	6.81	6.75	6.14
1978	5.12	5.09	4.20	6.80	6.77	5.88
Change, 1956–78	0.94	0.68	0.05	1.80	1.56	0.91

22. The weak long-run relation between inflation differentials and exchange rate movements is examined in Jacob Frenkel, "The Collapse of Purchasing Power Parities during the 1970s," *European Economic Review*, vol. 16 (May 1981), pp. 145–65.

The insignificance of the dummy shift variable for 1976–80 in column 6 (line 15) indicates that there was no upward shift in the natural weighted unemployment rate between the 1950s and late 1970s (the same result occurs when five dummies are included for each five-year subperiod). The marginal significance of the 1970–75 dummy shift variable in column 6 (line 14) may reflect the treatment of the foreign exchange rate variable, which is set equal to zero before 1975 because the Nixon controls contaminate the timing of its impact on inflation. It was calculated above that 1.9 points of extra inflation during 1970–75 would be accounted for by the depreciation of the dollar if the 1975–80 coefficient on that variable were applied to the cumulative 1970–75 depreciation. After deducting 0.6 percentage point for the excess of the Nixon "off" dummy coefficient over the Nixon "on" coefficient, there remain 1.3 points to be accounted for, or 0.24 point of inflation per year. Subtraction of 0.24 from the estimated 1970–75 dummy shift variable of 0.41 would reduce the estimated shift to 0.17.

Overall, the figures for the official unemployment rate indicate an upward shift in the natural rate of 1.8 percentage points in column 4, 1.6 points in column 5, and only 0.9 point in column 6. Since all of this shift in column 6 is accounted for by the upward drift of the difference between the official and weighted unemployment rates, caused by the increasing demographic importance of teenagers and women and a worsening of their relative unemployment rates, column 6 carries the implication that there has been no upward shift in the natural rate for other than demographic reasons. Less-inclusive Phillips curves, like those displayed in columns 4 and 5, incorrectly interpret as a shift in the natural rate the impact of the productivity slowdown and exchange rate depreciation, particularly in the 1977–80 period. If U.S. productivity behavior and exchange rate performance continue to be unfavorable during the 1980s, then column 5 is relevant in estimating the natural rate, but a "neutral" behavior of productivity and the exchange rate (that is, trend productivity growth and a constant exchange rate) would imply that the natural unemployment rate in 1980 was 5.9 percent. An annual time series of the natural rate is presented in table 11 in the appendix.

Sensitivity to Changes in Sample Period

Did the process of price adjustment in the United States become less sensitive to demand in the 1970s? George Perry's recent analysis

Robert J. Gordon

Table 3. *Sensitivity to Sample Splits of Equations Explaining the Acceleration of Inflation*[a]

| | | | | Sample period | |
| | Basic con-strained equation (1) | Split U_t^w (2) | Split U_t^w and ΔU_t^w (3) | 1954:2–1969:4 (4) | 1964:1–1980:4 (5) |
Independent variable and summary statistic					
Independent variable					
Constant	2.42	2.44	2.34	5.69	2.67
	(6.86)	(6.93)	(6.49)	(13.7)	(6.79)
Weighted unemployment rate	−0.57	...	...	−1.34	−0.75
	(−7.51)			(−13.8)	(−8.32)
Weighted unemployment, 1954–66	...	−0.60	−0.58	...	...
		(−7.56)	(−7.20)		
Weighted unemployment, 1967–80	...	−0.55	−0.53	...	...
		(−7.06)	(−6.51)		
Change in weighted unemployment	−0.67	−0.64	...	0.14	−0.30
	(−2.74)	(−2.64)		(0.34)	(−0.63)
Change in weighted unemployment, 1954–66	...	...	−0.88	...	...
			(−2.77)		
Change in weighted unemployment, 1967–80	...	...	−0.23	...	...
			(−0.53)		

of wage change found a significant shift in the coefficient on unemployment in 1970, with the implication that the Phillips curve had become virtually flat during the past decade.[23] My basic equation already allows the lag distribution on past inflation to shift between the first and last halves of the sample period. The first three columns of table 3 examine shifts in the coefficients on the level and change in the unemployment rate, holding constant the influence of lagged inflation and constraining the sum of coefficients on lagged inflation to be unity. Thus column 1 in table 3 repeats the constrained basic equation from column 6 of table 2, differing only in the omission of the insignificant constant shift terms. Because the dependent variable in table 3 is price change minus the constrained effect of lagged

23. Perry, "Inflation in Theory and Practice."

Table 3 *(continued)*

Independent variable and summary statistic	Basic constrained equation (1)	Split U_t^w (2)	Split U_t^w and ΔU_t^w (3)	Sample period 1954:2– 1969:4 (4)	1964:1– 1980:4 (5)
Productivity deviation	−0.08	−0.08	−0.08	−0.07	−0.01
	(−2.47)	(−2.46)	(−2.55)	(−1.56)	(−0.63)
Food and energy prices[b]	0.80	0.74	0.70	0.99	1.10
	(6.74)	(5.80)	(5.29)	(3.37)	(6.87)
Foreign exchange rate[c]	−0.12	−0.11	−0.11	. . .	−0.36
	(−3.54)	(−3.60)	(−3.53)		(−10.4)
Effective minimum wage[b]	0.02	0.02	0.02	0.04	−0.02
	(1.68)	(1.69)	(1.52)	(2.90)	(−0.88)
Social security tax[b]	0.25	0.27	0.29	0.19	0.11
	(1.09)	(1.18)	(1.26)	(0.71)	(0.43)
Nixon controls "on"[d]	−1.38	−1.55	−1.54	. . .	−1.91
	(−2.90)	(−3.12)	(−3.14)		(−3.73)
Nixon controls "off"[d]	2.69	2.63	2.63	. . .	4.09
	(5.15)	(5.04)	(5.04)		(7.02)
Summary statistic					
R^2	0.815	0.818	0.821	0.880	0.937
Sum of squared residuals	50.5	49.6	48.8	22.7	26.5
Standard error	0.785	0.783	0.781	0.718	0.785

a. Columns 1 through 3 share the same dependent variable, which is used in column 6 of table 2 and explained in notes a and b to table 2. In columns 4 and 5, the lagged dependent variable is constrained by the same technique used in table 2, columns 4 and 5, that is, without a split in the lag distribution on past inflation. The numbers in parentheses are *t*-statistics.

b, c, and d. See notes d through f to table 2.

inflation, the displayed equations explain the *change* in the rate of inflation (that is, the second derivative of the price level).[24]

The coefficient estimates in columns 1 and 2 are virtually identical, indicating no shift in the coefficient on the level of unemployment in explaining accelerations and decelerations of inflation. The F ratio for the significance of the additional unemployment variable is 1.40, compared to the 5 percent critical value of 3.98. In column 3 the level effect of unemployment is unchanged, but a split in the coefficient on the unemployment-change effect results in a low and insignificant coefficient after 1966. However, this shift is insignificant, with a

24. The constraint on the lagged dependent variable is imposed to simplify the interpretation of the shift in coefficients on the unemployment variables. Comparisons in unconstrained equations mix together the impact of shifts in the coefficients on unemployment and on the lagged inflation variables.

comparison of columns 2 and 3 yielding an F ratio of only 1.25, compared to the 5 percent critical value of 3.98. Comparing columns 1 and 3, the F ratio is 1.33, versus a 5 percent critical value of 3.11. The downward shift in the unemployment-change variable may be partially explained by a bias predicted in the earlier discussion of endogeneity problems. Errors in the measurement of supply shocks tend to create a positive correlation between inflation and the change in unemployment (as unmeasured supply shifts raise inflation, reduce output, and raise the unemployment rate), thus causing a bias toward zero in the coefficient on the change in unemployment.

A greater degree of doubt about the robustness of the unemployment-change effect is suggested by columns 4 and 5, which display constrained regression equations fitted to the portion of the sample period ending in 1969 and to the portion beginning in 1964. Each of these equations includes only a single distribution on lagged inflation. The results for the earlier subperiod indicate that all of the impact of demand operated through the level of the unemployment rate, and none through the rate of change, but that the level effect was more than double the coefficient in the basic full-period equation in column 1. The results for the later subperiod also indicate a stronger level effect than in the full-period equation, and a weaker change effect. It is interesting that the sum of the coefficients on the level and change effects varies much less across sample periods than the individual coefficients—the respective sums of the level and change coefficients in columns 1, 4, and 5 are -1.24, -1.20, and -1.05.

There are other interesting aspects of the short-sample results in columns 4 and 5. First, the productivity deviation and minimum wage coefficients are much larger in the early period and insignificant in the later period. Second, the impact of food and energy prices was actually stronger in the early period (column 4) than in the full period (column 1). These aspects of the equations are confirmed in several other experiments, which (a) estimate unconstrained versions of columns 4 and 5, and (b) split the sample period roughly in half between an early 1954–66 subperiod and a late 1967–80 subperiod. A formal Chow test on the equations run in the second experiment fails by a wide margin to reject the null hypothesis that the first half of the observations obeys the same relation as the subperiod relation for the last half of the sample period. The conclusion is the same, but by a narrower margin, when the Chow test is conducted in reverse in a comparison of the last half of the observations with the subperiod relation for the first half of the sample period.[25] Thus, despite shifts in individual coefficients over time, conventional statistical tests confirm that the basic equation describes a stable relation between inflation and its determinants.

Comparing Direct and Indirect Channels of Monetary Influence

Introducing Monetary Variables into the Basic Inflation Equation

Interest in the direct effect that changes in the nominal money supply have on inflation is motivated by three considerations. First, the discussion of endogeneity problems above suggested that if nominal demand were exogenous, errors in the measurement of supply shifts would bias toward zero the coefficient on the change in real demand in the basic equation 5. Second, by forcing the impact of demand to operate entirely through real variables, the basic equation may under-state the short-run responsiveness of inflation to changes in monetary policy. Finally, and perhaps most important, a substantial segment of the economics profession considers inflation to be a monetary phe-nomenon not only in the long run, but also in the short run. Regarding changes in the money supply as basically exogenous, this group views real variables like real GNP and unemployment as contemporaneously determined, and therefore is likely to suspect that my basic equation is plagued by simultaneity problems.

The relationship between the money supply and the unemployment variable appearing in the basic equation can be described concisely in three equations. First, the rate of growth of nominal GNP, y_t, by definition equals the sum of the growth rates of money, m_t, and velocity, v_t:

$$(9) \qquad y_t \equiv m_t + v_t.$$

---

25. In each case listed below, the F ratio is below the 5 percent critical value, indicating failure to reject the null hypothesis that the additional observations obey the same relation as the shorter period.

	F ratio	5 percent critical value
Full compared to late, unconstrained	1.02	1.81
Full compared to late, constrained	0.69	1.75
Full compared to early, unconstrained	1.65	1.79
Full compared to early, constrained	1.72	1.74

To simplify the subsequent exposition, the change in velocity will be treated as a serially independent random variable with mean zero and constant variance, but the impact of other assumptions will be considered in the discussion of the empirical results presented below. A second identity links the growth rate of real output, q_t, to the growth of nominal GNP and prices, and, by substitution of equation 9, to the growth rate of the money supply:

$$(10) \qquad q_t \equiv y_t - p_t \equiv m_t + v_t - p_t.$$

The third equation is an Okun's law relation between the weighted unemployment rate, U_t^W and the ratio of actual to natural real GNP, $\hat{Q}_t$. Equation 1 is rewritten here, neglecting the lagged terms:

$$(11) \qquad U_t^W = \psi_0 + \psi_1 \hat{Q}_t + e_t,$$

where e_t is an error term. Taking first differences, equation 11 can be converted into a relationship between the change in the unemployment rate and the deviation of actual from natural real GNP growth:[26]

$$(12) \qquad \Delta U_t^W = \psi_1(q_t - q_t^*) + \Delta e_t.$$

In the basic inflation equation 5, the real-demand variable was given the general designation X, which could stand for the real GNP ratio $\hat{Q}$, the weighted unemployment rate U^W, or some other proxy. The empirical version of the equation as estimated in tables 2 and 3 uses the weighted unemployment rate to represent X and can be written in its general form by substituting U^W for X in equation 5 (the term $(\gamma_1 - \beta_1)\sigma_t$ has been dropped because γ_1 and β_1 are both assumed to equal unity):

$$(13) \quad p_t = \gamma_0 + \gamma_1(p_{t-1} + \lambda_t - \sigma_t) + \gamma_2 U_t^W + \gamma_3 \Delta U_t^W + \gamma_4 z_t + \epsilon_t.$$

To replace the unemployment-change variable by the change in the nominal money supply, equation 10 is substituted into 12, and 12 into 13. After rearranging, the new inflation equation becomes:

$$(14) \qquad p_t = \frac{1}{1+\gamma_3\psi_1}[\gamma_0 + \gamma_1(p_{t-1} + \lambda_t - \sigma_t) + \gamma_2 U_t^W \\ + \gamma_3\psi_1(m_t - q_t^*) + \gamma_4 z_t + v_t],$$

26. Equation 12 follows from equation 11 if one makes the approximation that $\hat{Q}_t - \hat{Q}_{t-1} = q_t - q_t^*$. The conditions under which this approximation holds are set out in Robert J. Gordon, *Macroeconomics*, 2d ed. (Little, Brown, 1981), footnote 1, p. 291.

where v_t is a composite error term ($= \gamma_3 \psi_1 v_t + \gamma_3 \Delta e_t + \epsilon_t$). It is important to note that the condition for monetary neutrality in equation 14 is no longer a unitary coefficient on lagged inflation; instead, the coefficients on lagged inflation and on monetary growth sum to unity.[27]

The consequences of inserting a monetary growth rate variable into the basic inflation equation are illustrated in table 4. To simplify the presentation, the table displays only the coefficients on the level and change of unemployment and the rate of change of the money supply. The M1B definition of the money supply is used throughout. The results hinge on the length of the lag allowed on the monetary variable. When only the current and four lagged values are allowed to be entered, as in the section on short-run effects, the impact of the monetary variable is minor. But when the lag distribution is extended to include twenty-four past monetary values, there is a substantial improvement in the fit of the equation. No results are shown for intermediate lag lengths, as a result of experiments that indicate a deterioration in fit when the lag distribution is truncated in the range between eight and twenty lagged values.

Line 2 adds the current and four lagged values of M1B growth to the basic unconstrained inflation equation displayed in line 1. There is an insignificant sum of coefficients on money, and the F ratio on the joint significance of the monetary variables in line 2 is only 0.70, compared to the 5 percent critical value of 2.33. When the unemployment change variable is omitted in line 3, the sum of coefficients on the money change variable becomes significant, but the F ratio (comparing lines 3 and 4) is still only 1.00, indicating that a higher coefficient on unemployment in line 4 substitutes for part of the contribution of the monetary variable in line 3. Thus a monetary-change variable in the form of the current and four lagged values does not add any significant explanatory power and appears mainly to be a substitute for the unemployment-change variable.

The results are more favorable to a monetary explanation of inflation, however, when the lag distribution is stretched out to twenty-four quarters. All of the lag distributions displayed in the second section of table 4 share two common features. First, they are highly bimodal, with a peak in the current quarter, than a trough, and a second peak

27. Again ignoring any trend in velocity, inflation in the long run must be equal to the excess of monetary growth over natural output growth, $p_t = m_t - q_t^*$. Thus the condition for steady inflation becomes $(\gamma_1 + \gamma_3 \psi_1)/(1 + \gamma_3 \psi_1) = 1$.

Table 4. *Effect of the Inclusion of Monetary Growth Rate Variables in the Basic Unconstrained Inflation Equation, 1954:2–1980:4*[a]

Alternative specification	Sum of squared residuals	Independent variable		
		Level of unemployment (U_t^w)	Change in level of unemployment (ΔU_t^w)	Rate of change of money supply
Short-run effects				
1. Basic equation[b]	51.25	−0.60	−0.62	. . .
		(−4.45)	(−1.88)	
2. Add growth of M1B[c]	48.99	−0.47	−0.48	0.17
		(−2.90)	(−1.37)	(1.42)
3. Omit ΔU_t^w	50.25	−0.53	. . .	0.21
		(−3.31)		(1.86)
4. Omit ΔU_t^w and M1B	53.58	−0.72	. . .	. . .
		(−6.07)		
Long-run effects				
5. Basic equation plus growth of M1B[d]	43.47	−0.14	−0.83	0.91
		(−0.56)	(−2.30)	(2.73)
6. Omit ΔU_t^w	46.57	−0.40	. . .	0.67
		(−1.80)		(2.06)
7. Omit ΔU_t^w and U_t^w	48.59	. . .	. . .	1.15
				(6.10)
8. Omit ΔU_t^w, U_t^w and lagged price values	60.81	. . .	. . .	1.34
				(21.6)

a. The numbers in parentheses are *t*-statistics.

b. The basic equation is unconstrained and is identical to that estimated in table 2, column 3, with the single exception that the change in the social security tax rate is entered only as a current value, not as a current and four lagged values. This deletion of the insignificant lagged social security tax variables is required by space limitations in the regression package and is carried out uniformly in table 4.

c. In this section, the monetary growth variable is entered in the form of the current and four lagged values, with no contraints on the lag distribution.

d. In this section, the monetary growth variable is entered in the form of the current and twenty-four lagged values, with the lag distribution estimated to lie along a fourth-degree polynomial with a zero end-point constraint.

in quarters 14–18. Second, their mean lag lengths are quite long (counting the current quarter as zero, and the first quarter as one, the mean lags in lines 5–8 are, respectively, 9.6, 10.2, 8.4, and 10.4 quarters). The addition of the long-lag monetary variable not only improves the fit of the equation, but also substantially reduces the size and significance of the coefficient on the level of unemployment. Comparing lines 1 and 5, the *F* ratio on the joint significance of the monetary variables is 3.31, compared to a 5 percent critical value of 2.50. Omission of both unemployment variables in line 7 results in a significant loss of explanatory power; the F ratio that compares lines 1 and 3 is 4.36, compared to the critical value of 3.13. Thus it appears that the long-lag money-growth variable and at least one unemployment variable (level or rate of change) do better in explaining inflation than either variable alone.

Finally, line 8 shows the marked deterioration in fit when the lagged inflation variables are removed, resulting in an F ratio of 2.28 compared to a critical value of 2.03. Thus an adequate description of the inertia in the inflation process appears to require inclusion of both lagged money and lagged inflation variables, rather than either lagged variable alone. An extra experiment, not shown in table 4, was to fit separate lag distributions on money for the first and last halves of the sample period. The F ratio on the inclusion of the extra lag distribution on money is 0.33, compared to a critical value of 2.50.

How do the implications of the best-fitting equation in line 5 of table 4 differ from those of the basic unconstrained equation (column 3 of table 2 and line 1 of table 4)? The main difference is that the equation including money exhibits long-run instability, with a sum of coefficients on the money and lagged inflation variables summing to 1.80 in the first half of the sample period and to 1.35 in the last half. In contrast, the sums of coefficients on lagged inflation in the basic unconstrained equation are 1.01 and 1.03, respectively. The estimated effects of the supply-shift variables are similar, with almost identical coefficients on the productivity deviation and the food-energy effect in the monetary version, and a smaller coefficient on the minimum wage and social security taxes. It is somewhat surprising that the inclusion of the monetary variable does not reduce the impact of the foreign exchange rate; instead that coefficient increases from -0.11 to -0.15.

The interpretation of the monetary equation in line 5 is influenced by the unrealistic assumption in equation 9 above that changes in velocity could be treated as a serially uncorrelated variable with mean zero and constant variance. In fact, the change in velocity over the sample period has been about 3 percent per year (table 1), and this trend is absorbed in the constant term of the equation. The relation between nominal GNP and money may also explain why the coefficients in line 5 exhibit long-run instability. This comes primarily from the high elasticity of nominal GNP changes to changes in the money supply, rather than from instability in the basic inflation process. In the vector autoregressive equation explaining nominal GNP changes (presented in table 5), the sum of coefficients on lagged money in the nominal GNP equation is 1.68 (this finding is parallel to the income elasticity of the demand for M1 of 0.6–0.7 found in studies by Goldfeld and others).[28] A version of line 5 with nominal GNP changes replacing the money supply exhibits less long-run instability; the sum of coefficients in the last half of the sample period on nominal GNP plus the lagged inflation variables is 1.10, in contrast to 1.35 when the money supply is included.[29]

Despite the modest improvement in fit in the equations that include money or nominal GNP, there is no change in the conclusion that inertia plays a major role in the inflation process, due to the long mean lags in the influence of both money and past inflation. A complete analysis of the policy implications of the alternative equations, including their predictions regarding the output loss that would accompany a policy of steadily decelerating monetary growth, is contained in the section on simulations below.

Granger Causality Results

Considerable attention has been given recently to the concept of Granger causality as a useful way of describing relations among time series. A series X is said to cause another series Y if the inclusion of lagged values of X significantly improves the fit of regression equations explaining Y that also include lagged values of Y and other available past information. In a recent survey of this literature, John Geweke has found that tests in autoregressive models are as good as or superior to other methods for testing causal orderings in time series.[30]

It is interesting to compare the results of Geweke's tests to mine, and to replicate his findings for my data and sample period. Geweke's major conclusion supports my results that inertia plays a major role

28. Stephen M. Goldfeld, "The Demand for Money Revisited," *BPEA, 3:1973*, pp. 577–638.

29. Several other versions of these equations have been estimated. There is little change in the results, other than a minor deterioration in fit, when current values of nominal GNP or money are omitted, and only the twenty-four lagged values are included.

30. John Geweke, "Causality, Exogeneity, and Inference," working paper 8025 (University of Wisconsin–Madison, Social Systems Research Institute, December 1980), to be published in Werner Hildenbrand, ed., *Advances in Econometrics* (Cambridge University Press, forthcoming).

Table 5. *Granger Causality Results, 1954:2–1980:4*

	Endogenous variable[a]			
Dependent variable	Inflation	Weighted unemployment rate	M1B change	Nominal GNP change[b]
Inflation	8.65***	1.21	2.15*	. . .
Weighted unemployment rate	1.21	152.40***	2.55**	. . .
M1B change	1.52	1.31	2.03*	1.37
Nominal GNP change	1.73	3.37***	4.51***	. . .

* Significant at 10 percent level.
** Significant at 5 percent level.
*** Significant at 1 percent level.
a. The numbers are *F* ratios on the significance of the six lagged values of the endogenous variables.
b. Lagged nominal GNP change is included only in the equations explaining changes in M1B.

in the postwar U.S. inflation process. He finds that feedback from M1 to nominal GNP "seems to arise mostly from the relationship between money and real GNP. The hypothesis that M1 and the GNP deflator are uncorrelated at all leads and lags cannot be rejected at the 10 percent level when seasonally adjusted data are used." This, however, is a result characterizing business cycle frequencies. In the long run, feedback from M1 to real GNP nearly vanishes, and almost all of the long-run variance in prices is attributed to innovations in M1. Finally, there is some evidence of feedback from nominal and real GNP to M1 at "those frequencies where transactions demand would lead us to expect it."[31]

Table 5 reports on tests similar to those of Geweke for the same 1954–80 sample period as my basic inflation equation, in contrast to his study of the earlier 1949–69 interval. The endogenous variables included are the same inflation, unemployment level, and money-change variables used in table 4. To minimize multicollinearity, nominal GNP change is not included in the inflation or unemployment equations. All data are seasonally adjusted, and all equations include a constant and trend term, six unconstrained distributed lags on the other endogenous variables, and (unlike Geweke's test) the set of exogenous supply variables that appear in the basic inflation equation.[32]

31. Ibid., pp. 32, 34.
32. These are the dummy variables for the Nixon controls; the current productivity deviation; the current and four lagged values for the changes in the relative price of food and energy; the effective social security tax and the effective minimum wage; and the current and three lagged values for the foreign exchange rate.

The results appear basically consistent with those of Geweke, despite the inclusion of eleven years of data after the end of his sample period. Lagged inflation is the main variable driving inflation, reflecting inertia. Short-run feedback from M1B change to inflation is marginally significant, whereas short-run feedback from unemployment to inflation is surprisingly insignificant. The short-run feedback from money change to unemployment is stronger than that from money to prices, as in Geweke's study, while I also confirm that feedback between money and nominal GNP runs almost entirely from the former to the latter. Because all equations exclude current endogenous variables, these results do not rule out contemporaneous feedback between money and nominal GNP.

Taken together, the results in tables 4 and 5 tell a consistent story in which monetary innovations cause changes in nominal GNP, real GNP, unemployment in the short run, and the inflation rate in the long run. The price level is neither perfectly flexible nor perfectly inflexible in response to monetary innovations. There is a substantial short-run response, channeled entirely through unemployment variables in conventional Phillips curves and in my basic inflation equation, and through a combination of unemployment and money variables in tables 4 and 5. As this initial effect feeds back through the lagged inflation variables, the responsiveness of inflation to monetary innovations becomes larger and that of real GNP and unemployment becomes smaller. It is the task of the simulation experiments in a later section to quantify the short-run and long-run responsiveness of inflation to monetary innovations and to test whether the simulation results are sensitive to the direct inclusion of monetary variables in the inflation equation.

The Role of Wage Equations and Wage-Wage Feedback

The explanation of the U.S. postwar inflation process in this paper differs from most previous studies, not only in its stress on supply-shift variables, but also in its omission of an equation explaining the behavior of wages. Any inertia in the wage-setting process is captured by the patterns of coefficients on the lagged inflation variables in the inflation equation itself. Several considerations call for an examination of wage determination and parallel equations that explain price change relative to wage change. First, a dynamic simulation of the basic single-equation explanation as compared to a two-equation wage-price model can help to determine which approach provides the best fit to inflation data within the sample period. Second, simulations for future periods under different monetary regimes can compare the dynamic responsiveness of one-equation and two-equation systems. Third, estimation of wage equations is required to test a maintained hypothesis in the original specification in equation 2 that wage change depends on past price change, not past wage change. Fourth, the hypothesis of wage-wage inertia, which has played a major role in recent empirical research and in theoretical analyses of the inflation process by Hall and Okun, needs to be tested directly.[33]

Table 6 is an extension of table 2. Column 1 in table 6 is the basic unconstrained inflation equation, exactly the same equation as in column 3 of table 2. All the unemployment and supply-shift variables are entered identically in every equation in table 6, and the only difference is in the choice of current wage or price change as the dependent variable, and in the choice of lagged wages or prices (or both) as an explanatory variable.

Columns 2 and 3 report price markup and wage equations that correspond to the original specification in equations 2 and 3. Because it is difficult to determine a priori which of the supply-shift variables influences the price markup and which influences wages, all of those variables are entered in each column. The implications of the two-equation system can be compared to the single equation in column 1 by summing coefficients across columns 2 and 3. Such a summation yields roughly consistent results for the inertia variables, the productivity deviation, food and energy prices, and the social security tax. But in the two-equation system, the combined impact of the unemployment variables and the Nixon controls appears to be greater, while the influence of the minimum wage rate vanishes. A surprise in the two-equation system is the fact that both the level and rate-of-change effects for unemployment are significant in both the price markup and

33. The hypothesis that the U.S. inflation process is characterized by "nominal wage inertia," while that in other countries is characterized by "real wage inertia," is central to the papers of Jeffrey D. Sachs, "Wages, Profits, and Macroeconomic Adjustment: A Comparative Study," *BPEA*, 2:1979, pp. 269–319; and William H. Branson and Julio J. Rotemberg, "International Adjustment with Wage Rigidity," *European Economic Review*, vol. 13 (May 1980), pp. 309–32.

Table 6. *The Relation between Price and Wage Change,*
1954:2–1980:4[a]

Independent variable and summary statistic	Price change		Wage change		
	Basic equation (1)	Markup version (2)	Lagged prices (3)	Lagged wages (4)	Lagged both (5)
Independent variable					
Constant	2.45	2.63	−0.16	2.08	2.00
	(3.52)	(4.24)	(−0.13)	(2.01)	(2.20)
Lagged inflation[b]	. . .	. . .	. . .	. . .	0.91
					(1.96)
Lagged inflation, first half[b]	1.01	. . .	1.31[c]	. . .	. . .
	(3.10)		(4.30)		
Lagged inflation, last half[b]	1.03	. . .	1.17[c]	. . .	. . .
	(10.5)		(6.92)		
Lagged wage change[b]	. . .	. . .	. . .	. . .	−0.08
					(−0.16)
Lagged wage change, first half[b]	. . .	0.72[c]	. . .	0.79	. . .
		(3.03)		(3.23)	
Lagged wage change, last half[b]	. . .	1.03[c]	. . .	1.00	. . .
		(1.33)		(7.47)	
Weighted unemployment rate	−0.59	−0.41	−0.42	−0.36	−0.40
	(−4.30)	(−3.18)	(−2.92)	(−2.51)	(−2.56)
Change in weighted unemployment	−0.64	−0.64	−0.81	−0.67	−0.81
	(−1.92)	(−1.95)	(−2.42)	(−1.86)	(−2.33)
Productivity deviation	−0.08	−0.10	0.02	0.00	0.01
	(−2.03)	(−2.75)	(0.49)	(0.00)	(0.33)
Food and energy prices[d]	0.74	0.55	0.37	0.13	0.50
	(3.31)	(2.60)	(1.81)	(0.59)	(2.42)
Foreign exchange rate[e]	−0.11	−0.06	−0.04	−0.04	−0.18
	(−1.70)	(−1.00)	(−0.62)	(−0.73)	(−2.95)
Effective minimum wage[e]	0.02	0.02	−0.02	−0.02	0.01
	(1.17)	(0.86)	(−0.86)	(−1.04)	(0.47)
Social security tax[d]	0.27	0.13	−0.32	−0.35	−0.27
	(1.00)	(0.48)	(−1.18)	(−1.16)	(−1.03)

Table 6 *(continued)*

Independent variable and summary statistic	Price change		Wage change		
	Basic equation (1)	Markup version (2)	Lagged prices (3)	Lagged wages (4)	Lagged both (5)
Nixon controls "on"[f]	−1.45	−1.61	−0.83	−1.15	−0.86
	(−2.61)	(−2.93)	(−1.48)	(−1.85)	(−1.51)
Nixon controls "off"[f]	2.61	2.25	1.61	1.92	1.47
	(3.86)	(3.33)	(2.39)	(2.65)	(2.20)
Summary statistic					
R^2	0.942	0.942	0.898	0.874	0.900
Sum of squared residuals	50.2	50.7	48.7	59.9	47.8
Standard error	0.823	0.827	0.811	0.899	0.803

a. Numbers in parentheses are *t*-statistics.
b. See note b to table 4.
c. The lagged wage variable in column 2 is the quarterly change in the fixed-weight average hourly earnings index minus the change in the productivity trend (see footnote 21). The lagged price variable in column 3 is the inflation rate plus the same productivity trend.
d, e, and f. See corresponding notes to table 2.

wage equations. This differs from past studies, including my own, which have typically included only a level term in the wage equation and only a rate-of-change term in the price markup equation.[34] Another unexpected result is that current and lagged increases in food and energy prices significantly boost the rate of wage change, even when lagged changes in the GNP deflator are included in the wage equation. This tends to argue against the simple wage-wage view stressed by Hall and Okun.

Two direct tests of wage-wage inertia are provided in columns 4 and 5 of table 6. Column 4 replaces the lagged inflation variables of column 3 with lagged wage-change variables, resulting in a 23 percent increase in the unexplained variance. The statistical weakness of the wage-wage explanation is surprising, since feedback is allowed from food and energy prices to wages. Another test in column 5 enters both lagged inflation and wage change in the wage equation. The result is a sum of coefficients on lagged inflation that is close to unity, and on

34. Although I have never previously included the level of unemployment or output in a price-change equation, one previous paper of mine found that the rate of change of real output was more significant than the output ratio in a wage equation that included both. See Gordon, "Can the Inflation of the 1970s be Explained?" table 3, columns 5 and 6, p. 266.

lagged wage change is of the incorrect sign and is insignificantly different from zero.[35] When column 5 is reestimated with the *difference* between lagged wage and price change entered instead of lagged wage change itself, the resulting sum of coefficients is -0.55, rather than the coefficient of 1.0 that would be required to validate pure wage-wage inertia.[36] Overall, lagged inflation contributes significant explanatory power in wage equations and seems superior to the alternative hypothesis of wage-wage inertia. Simultaneity problems do not influence these results, since current inflation is not included as a right-hand variable in any of the wage equations in table 6. I have previously attributed the influence of lagged prices in wage equations to the importance of shifts in labor demand along a relatively inelastic supply curve for labor.[37]

Additional hypotheses can be tested with the structure of wage and price equations displayed in table 6, but most of these are outside of the scope of this paper. One issue that has received much recent attention is the inflationary impact of the treatment of home ownership in the consumer price index.[38] When the difference between the change in the CPI and in the fixed-weight GNP deflator is entered into the basic wage equation in table 6, column 3, in the form of eight lagged values, the resulting sum of coefficients is 0.35 with a *t*-statistic of 2.1. When the same variable is entered into the basic inflation equation in column 1, the sum of coefficients is 0.35 with a *t*-statistic of 1.7. The *F* ratio on the inclusion of this extra lag distribution in the inflation equation is 1.44, compared to the 5 percent critical value of 2.50. Thus it appears that differences in measurement procedures between the CPI and GNP deflator affect the overall inflation process and that this effect is channeled through the use of the CPI as an escalator in wage contracts. This additional variable is not included in the basic inflation

35. The lag distributions on past inflation or wage change are estimated separately in columns 1 through 4 for the first and last halves of the sample period. A single distribution, without a sample split, is estimated for both past inflation and wage change in column 5, due to space limitations in the regression package.

36. If one estimates $w_t = \delta_1 p_{t-1} + \delta_2(w_{t-1} - p_{t-1}) + \beta X$, coefficients of $\delta_1 = \delta_2 = 1.0$ would be required to validate the view that "only lagged wages matter."

37. Robert J. Gordon, discussion of Hall, "The Process of Inflation in the Labor Market," pp. 394–99.

38. Alan S. Blinder, "The Consumer Price Index and the Measurement of Recent Inflation," *BPEA*, 2:1980, pp. 539–65; and Robert J. Gordon, "The Consumer Price Index: Measuring Inflation and Causing It," *The Public Interest*, no. 62 (Spring 1981), pp. 112–34.

equation used in the simulations described in the next two sections because it is clearly endogenous (depending on interest rates) and an adequate treatment would require going beyond the scope of this paper by building a model of interest rate behavior. Fortunately this omission is not a serious one, since the significance level of the CPI variable is marginal and its inclusion causes only minor changes in other coefficients.

Counterfactual Simulations within the Sample Period

The inflation equation can be used to measure the quantitative impact of specific supply shifts and of alternative demand policies. Every simulation illustrated in this section is dynamic, that is, they all apply the fitted coefficients on the lagged dependent variable to those generated within the simulation rather than to the actual historical values. I first present simulations in which the actual values of the unemployment and productivity variables are entered. Next, equations are added that explain unemployment, productivity, and the foreign exchange rate, in order to be able to examine the responsiveness of inflation to alternative counterfactual demand policies.

Tracking Ability in Dynamic Simulations

The inflation equation included in all simulations in this section and the next is the constrained version listed in table 2, column 6. This equation was estimated in a form that constrains the sum of coefficients on the lagged dependent variable to be unity, so that the equation can track a steady-state relation between money growth and inflation in the simulations of hypothetical future demand-management policies. The equation, as in table 2, also includes small coefficients on dummy variables for the first and last halves of the 1970s (these were the dummy variables used to compute the shifts in the natural rate of unemployment, as listed earlier).

The first pair of columns in table 7 compares four-quarter averages of the actual inflation rate with those fitted in a dynamic single-equation simulation of the 1971–80 period, that is, a simulation in which fitted values of the lagged dependent variable are fed back into the equation

Table 7. *Actual and Fitted Values in Dynamic Simulations
of the 1971–80 and 1978–80 Intervals*
Percent

	Inflation rate			Unemployment rate	
		Simulated with unemployment			Simulated with un-employment: endogenous
Time period[a]	Actual (1)	Exogenous (2)	Endogenous (3)	Actual (4)	(5)
1971–80					
1971	4.40	4.20	4.52	5.95	5.97
1972	4.12	4.15	4.44	5.58	5.29
1973	6.75	7.16	7.51	4.85	4.57
1974	10.31	10.43	10.14	5.59	6.08
1975	7.05	6.78	6.57	8.48	8.88
1976	5.05	5.73	5.17	7.68	8.27
1977	6.41	6.07	5.64	7.03	7.24
1978	8.33	8.43	8.08	6.00	6.06
1979	8.51	9.37	9.11	5.79	5.62
1980	9.29	8.82	8.52	7.17	6.84
Cumulative error	. . .	−1.06	0.20	. . .	−0.87
1978–80					
1978	8.33	8.37	8.24	6.00	6.02
1979	8.51	9.37	9.54	5.79	5.74
1980	9.29	8.83	8.82	7.17	7.01
Cumulative error	. . .	−0.58	−0.76	. . .	0.05

a. Including all four quarters of each year, ending in the fourth quarter.

but all other variables are taken as exogenous. The cumulative error
is − 1.06 percent, meaning that the actual price level is about 1 percent
less than the simulated price level after ten years, so that the mean
error in tracking the inflation rate is only − 0.10 percent per year. The
standard error of the simulation (not shown in the table) is 0.751, close
to the 0.785 standard error listed in table 2 for the estimated equation
over the entire 1954–80 period. For purposes of comparison, an identical
simulation was computed for a two-equation model containing the
wage and price markup equations listed in table 6, columns 2 and 3.
The resulting standard error for the inflation rate over the same period
was 0.833, indicating an increase in the unexplained variance of about
20 percent. This confirms that wage equations, while interesting in

their own right, are not necessary for a historical understanding of the U.S. inflation process. By way of contrast, a dynamic simulation of the best-fitting equation that directly enters lagged changes in the money supply (table 4, line 5) has a standard error of 0.751, exactly the same as the basic equation.

A more challenging task is to track historical inflation rates in a three-equation model in which the unemployment rate and productivity deviation are made endogenous. The inflation equation is the same as before, but equations are added that explain changes in the unemployment rate and the productivity deviation as a function of current and lagged changes in the output ratio (that is, ratio of real to natural real GNP). The unemployment equation is a first-difference version of the "Okun's law" equation 1, and the productivity equation reflects the lagged adjustment of hours to changes in output. Detailed listings of coefficients and further comments on these "auxiliary" equations are contained in appendix A. The purpose of the three-equation model is to allow changes in both the inflation and unemployment rates to be calculated for changes in the exogenous supply-shift variables and for specified time paths of nominal GNP. When nominal GNP is specified, an identity can be used to calculate the change in the output ratio corresponding to any inflation rate, and then the auxiliary equations can be used to compute the unemployment rate and productivity deviation. An iterative procedure is used to make the initial given inflation rate converge to that predicted by the inflation equation.

The third column of table 7 shows the fitted values of the inflation rate in a dynamic simulation of the three-equation model. The cumulative and mean errors are actually smaller than those in the simulations of the one-equation model. Columns 4 and 5 show how closely the unemployment rate can be tracked in this simple model, which takes nominal GNP and the supply-shift variables as exogenous and uses coefficients estimated from the full 1954–80 period, but uses no information on the actual values of inflation, unemployment, or the productivity deviation after 1970 in the calculations of the fitted values.

The bottom section of the table repeats the simulations for the last three years of the sample period. The results are very close to those from the decade-long sample period. The most interesting, and potentially serious, error in all the inflation simulations is the tendency to predict too high an inflation rate in 1979 and too low a rate in 1980.

Table 8. Change in the Inflation Rate When Sources of Inflation Are Suppressed, 1971–80

	Simulated inflation rate		Supply-shift variable				
Time period[a]	All supply shifts exogenous (1)	Suppress all supply shifts (2)	Productivity deviation (3)	Foreign exchange (4)	Minimum wage and social security (5)	Food and energy (6)	Nixon controls (7)
1971	4.20	5.34	-0.17	0.04	-0.07	-0.22	-0.72
1972	4.15	5.58	-0.35	0.41	-0.09	0.05	-1.45
1973	7.16	6.07	-0.11	0.56	0.07	1.41	-0.84
1974	10.43	5.76	0.19	1.33	0.09	2.32	0.72
1975	6.78	4.15	-0.24	0.70	0.41	1.84	-0.08
1976	5.73	4.26	-0.21	0.09	0.31	1.25	0.03
1977	6.07	4.28	-0.27	0.64	0.27	1.15	0.00
1978	8.43	4.59	-0.04	1.79	0.39	1.73	-0.03
1979	9.37	3.74	0.05	1.33	0.49	2.94	-0.01
1980	8.82	3.74	0.04	1.38	0.49	3.24	0.03
Cumulative difference[b]	-1.06	19.77	-1.12	7.71	2.17	14.44	-2.37

a. Including all four quarters of each year, ending in the fourth one.
b. The cumulative difference in columns 1 and 2 is the difference between actual and predicted inflation. In columns 3 through 7 the difference refers to the change in the fitted inflation rate when the coefficients on the supply-shift terms are successfully set to zero. The sum of the differences in columns 3 through 7 equals the difference between column 2 and column 1.

Decomposing the Impact of Supply Shifts

The estimated impact of the various supply-shift variables in the inflation equation can be calculated by successively setting each to zero in dynamic simulations like those of table 7. Should the unemployment rate or nominal GNP be chosen as the exogenous variable in these counterfactual simulations? Either choice is unsatisfactory. This can be seen in table 8, where column 1 repeats the fitted values from the single-equation simulation that treats unemployment as exogenous (table 7, column 2), and where column 2 computes an artificial inflation series by setting equal to zero the coefficients on changes in the relative prices of food and energy, the foreign exchange rate, productivity deviation, effective minimum wage rate and social security tax, and on the Nixon control dummy variables. The result in column 2 is an estimated increase in the inflation rate from 5.3 in 1971 to 6.1 percent in 1973, followed by a decline to 3.7 percent in 1980. This time path reflects, of course, the historical fact that the unemployment rate dipped below my estimate of the natural unemployment rate in 1972–73 and again in 1979, but was above the natural rate during the rest of the decade. This is an unrealistic simulation of a world without supply shocks, because much of the high unemployment experienced during 1974–77 and in 1980 was a direct result of the supply shocks themselves, so it is doubtful that the low simulated 1980 inflation rate would have been achieved.

On the other hand, additional simulations (not shown in table 7) with the growth of nominal GNP or the money supply treated as exogenous and with supply shifts suppressed lead to a predicted 1980 inflation rate of 8.1 percent and an unemployment rate of 4.5 percent. This is equally unrealistic, because much of the acceleration in nominal GNP and money growth after 1975 occurred as policymakers partially accommodated the supply shifts in order to prevent a larger increase in unemployment than actually occurred. The growth in nominal GNP, money, and prices would all have been lower in the late 1970s in the absence of supply shifts. The fact that 1980 inflation without supply shifts and with nominal GNP exogenous is predicted at 8.1 percent, only slightly less than the predicted 8.8 percent with supply variables included, illustrates the neutrality property displayed by the estimated inflation equation: over a period as long as a decade, inflation depends almost entirely on the growth of nominal demand, and supply shifts serve mainly to influence the unemployment rate.

The right-hand section of table 8 illustrates the estimated effects of the separate right-hand variables when unemployment is exogenous. The figures show the extra inflation in each year contributed when the estimated coefficients of the listed variable are included in the equation, as compared to the inflation that occurs when the coefficients are set at zero. It is not surprising to find that the most important of the supply-shift variables in contributing to inflation was the change in the relative price of food and energy, followed by the change in the foreign exchange rate.[39] The lack of importance of the productivity deviation is explained not just by the small size of its coefficient, but also by the fact that the steplike slowing of the productivity trend is estimated from the entire sample period, so that the mean of the productivity deviation is zero (see footnote 21 above). The impact of the minimum wage rate and social security tax is minor, enough to contribute about half a point of inflation in 1980 and a 2 percent higher price level in that year. Finally, the cumulative effect of the Nixon controls is negative despite the fact that the "on" and "off" coefficients are equal; this result is an artifact of the dynamic simulation, which allows any variable having an early impact a longer chance to be built into the lagged dependent variable than variables having a later impact.[40]

To Accommodate or Not?

After the first OPEC oil shock in 1973–74, economists debated the merits of accommodating the shock by allowing a one-time jump in the money supply to pay for the jump in oil prices. Other economists argued that in this circumstance, as in all other circumstances, the best policy was a constant growth rate rule for the money supply. In this section I present the verdict of my inflation equation regarding

39. Recall that exchange rate variable is set to zero before 1975:2. How is the impact of the 1971–73 depreciation to be included? Following the argument presented earlier, I attribute to changes in the foreign exchange rate both the excess of the Nixon "off" coefficient over the Nixon "on" coefficient and half of the coefficient on the dummy variable for 1970–75.

40. The effect of the controls is based on "on" and "off" coefficients that are set equal to each other, because the estimated excess of the "off" over the "on" coefficient is attributed to the effects of the exchange rate rather than the controls (see the previous footnote).

the costs and benefits of alternative monetary policies after the first OPEC shock.

The previous section described the auxiliary equations that generated paths for the unemployment rate and productivity deviation with nominal GNP treated as exogenous. This section goes further and allows for the impact of monetary policy on inflation through the channel of changes in the foreign exchange rate. Although a complete treatment of exchange rate determination requires a consideration of differentials between domestic and foreign interest rates, an exchange rate equation is presented in appendix A that provides a surprisingly good fit to data for 1972–80, including as exogenous variables only the growth rates of money, nominal GNP, and the relative price of food and energy. When this equation is joined by a simple vector autoregressive equation that explains nominal GNP changes by its own lagged values and by current and lagged changes in the money supply, it is possible to generate alternative scenarios corresponding to different monetary growth rates. The basic inflation equation plus the four auxiliary equations allow five variables to be treated as endogenous: inflation, unemployment, the productivity deviation, and the growth rates of nominal GNP and the effective exchange rate.

Table 9 shows the impact of two counterfactual monetary growth paths. The first is a constant growth-rate rule (CGRR) path that sets M1B growth each year exactly 2.0 points above the growth rate of natural real GNP. Because the latter declines between 1975 and 1980, the CGRR path for M1B growth in table 9 also displays a deceleration. The second is an accommodative jump path designed to generate the same cumulative growth in M1B that actually occurred between 1975:1 and 1980:4, but in a different time configuration, with an initial jump followed by a CGRR policy that sets the rate 1 percentage point faster than the pure CGRR policy. This hypothetical policy is displayed only to show the mechanical properties of the model, since it is unlikely that the Federal Reserve could actually achieve such precise control of the money supply.

The results show the expected reduction of inflation and increase in unemployment under the pure CGRR path. But the trade-off is more favorable than in the typical simulation of large-scale econometric models. By the end of 1980 the inflation rate is 3 percentage points lower with CGRR, while the unemployment rate is about 1 percentage point higher. The cumulative loss in output over the six-year simulation

Table 9. *Impact of Alternative Monetary Policies, 1975–80*

Time period[b]	M1B growth			Inflation rate[a]			Unemployment rate[a]		
	Actual (1)	CGRR path[c] (2)	Jump path (3)	Actual (4)	CGRR path (5)	Jump path (6)	Actual (7)	CGRR path (8)	Jump path (9)
1975	5.21	5.87	10.28	7.05	0.00	0.25	8.48	0.00	-0.33
1976	5.82	5.57	6.57	5.05	0.06	2.33	7.68	-0.06	-1.78
1977	7.77	5.28	6.28	6.41	-0.24	1.77	7.03	0.11	-1.15
1978	7.86	5.28	6.28	8.33	-1.50	0.75	6.00	0.86	0.25
1979	7.36	4.74	5.74	8.51	-2.35	-0.25	5.79	1.19	1.26
1980	6.87	4.74	5.74	9.29	-2.93	-1.08	7.17	0.97	1.61

a. The inflation and unemployment figures shown for the simulated paths refer to the difference when the indicated money growth rates are entered, compared to a control solution that enters the actual growth rate of money.

b. Including all four quarters of each year, ending in the fourth one.

c. Constant growth-rate rule.

is only 5.7 percent of real GNP. The alternative accommodative jump path, as would be expected, initially generates more inflation and a reduction in the unemployment rate, but then generates the reverse as money growth rates fall below those that actually occurred. The cumulative loss in output relative to the actual path taken by the money supply is negligible, only 0.4 percent of real GNP. In both cases, however, the cumulative output loss figure is an understatement because it ignores the further losses that would occur if the simulation were allowed to run after 1980.

Simulations of Hypothetical Future Policies

Limitations of Simulations across Policy Regimes

Simulations of the basic inflation equation are of interest only if the parameters will remain invariant to alternative hypothetical policy regimes.[41] Is there reason to believe that key parameters would shift between a world of 7 percent monetary growth and a world of 2 percent monetary growth? Such a policy change, although it seems drastic from the perspective of 1981, would simply throw into reverse the policy shift that allowed the growth rate of M1B to accelerate from 2 percent in 1954–64 to 7 percent in 1976–80 (see table 1).[42] Confidence in the relevance of policy simulations is bolstered by the earlier finding that a Chow test fails to reject the null hypothesis that the first half of the sample period obeys the same inflation equation as the last half.

Two sets of parameters are allowed to shift in the basic inflation equation. First, the lag distribution on past inflation is fitted separately to the first and last halves of the sample period, shortening the mean lag from about eleven to about seven quarters. Would a reversal to an earlier monetary policy regime cause the lag to lengthen? This would occur if agents became less concerned about inflation and were willing

41. The general point that parameters depend on policy regimes is stated in Robert E. Lucas, Jr., "Econometric Policy Evaluation: A Critique," in Karl Brunner and Allan H. Meltzer, eds., *The Phillips Curve and Labor Markets* (Amsterdam: North-Holland, 1976), pp. 19–46.

42. The hypothesis that the feedback from lagged values of real GNP and money to the current money supply was constant across the subperiods 1949–63 and 1964–74 was rejected at high confidence levels in Salih Neftci and Thomas J. Sargent, "A Little Bit of Evidence on the Natural Rate Hypothesis from the U.S.," *Journal of Monetary Economics*, vol. 4 (April 1978), pp. 315–19.

to accept a greater fraction of nominal contracts in preference to escalated contracts. I doubt that such a shift is likely in the near future, because agents will want to experience a substantial period of stable prices before abandoning indexed contracts. Another consequence of rapid monetary growth has been the advent of the flexible exchange rate system, which in my inflation equation makes the inflation rate more responsive to variations in money growth. While a stable inflation rate in the United States is unlikely to cause a return from flexible exchange rates to the Bretton Woods agreements, nevertheless the likely impact of U.S. monetary policy on other nations needs to be considered explicitly in any simulation of future events.

As is illustrated below, the inclusion of the foreign exchange rate variable allows the model to generate a sharp slowdown in the inflation rate in a relatively short time with a relatively low cost in terms of lost output. This occurs because a slowdown in the rate of monetary growth relative to nominal GNP growth, as occurs during a transition period before nominal GNP growth responds, is estimated to cause an appreciation of the exchange rate. (The 15 percent appreciation in the effective exchange rate of the dollar that occurred between 1980:4 and 1981:4 demonstrates the responsiveness of the exchange rate to changes in interest rates and the growth of velocity.) In addition, the subsequent slowdown in nominal GNP growth is estimated to cause an additional appreciation.

If it were interpreted literally, the foreign exchange rate equation would predict a continuous and permanent appreciation following a return to low rates of growth in money and nominal GNP, with continuous downward pressure on the inflation rate. This would be unrealistic, however, because the exchange rate equation contains no variables for other nations, and they would surely respond to a new monetary regime in the United States. All these simulations assume a response by other nations after two years, which is implemented by making the exchange rate respond not to nominal GNP growth itself, but rather to the difference between current nominal GNP growth and a four-quarter moving average of nominal GNP growth two years earlier. Following the arrival of money at its new lower steady state, this treatment causes the exchange rate appreciation to disappear after roughly two years.

The inflation equation implies that the impact of high interest rates caused by monetary restriction is to dampen inflation through the exchange rate effect. This impact might be mitigated by two other effects of high interest rates that are ignored, those operating through capital costs and through the CPI measurement error. In previous research I was unable to find an effect of interest rates on inflation through the capital-cost channel.[43] As for the CPI channel, its omission is a defect of the simulations, but there may be two offsetting implications. Initially a restrictive monetary policy raises both nominal and real interest rates, boosting the CPI and adding to inflation. But then as other variables, particularly the unemployment rate and the exchange rate, cause inflation to decelerate, the nominal interest rate will fall relative to the real rate, and this will reduce the growth of the CPI relative to the GNP deflator and help to decelerate the GNP deflator further.

These simulations are all based on specified growth paths for the growth of the money supply (M1B). Some "cold turkey" simulations are based on an instantaneous 5 percent drop in the rate of monetary growth. Like the accommodative jump simulation described in the previous section, the cold turkey experiments assume an unrealistic degree of control by the Federal Reserve over the money supply. They are presented not because they are plausible, but to allow the characteristics of the model simulations to be clearly perceived in the figures. A final qualification is that the relation between nominal GNP growth and M1B growth is determined by an equation estimated to the entire 1954–80 sample period. If financial innovations or the flexible exchange rate system have altered the relationship between nominal GNP and money in the last few years, the simulations may contain an error. For instance, I may have understated the growth in the velocity of M1B if financial innovations have accelerated the movement into other assets. In addition, I have ignored the impact of an exchange rate appreciation in reducing the foreign trade surplus, thus creating a channel of negative feedback from exchange rates to velocity.

The Control Solution and the Arithmetic of Disinflation

The U.S. economy was not in long-run equilibrium in early 1981, thus posing a problem in the choice of a benchmark for policy

43. Robert J. Gordon, "The Impact of Aggregate Demand," pp. 643–45.

Figure 1. *Alternative Simulations, 1981:1–1991:4*

Inflation rate

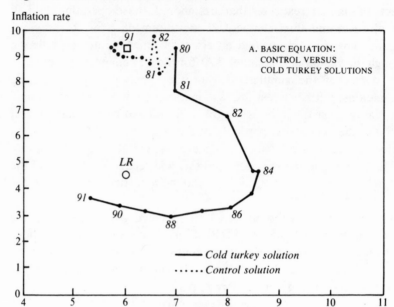

A. BASIC EQUATION:
CONTROL VERSUS
COLD TURKEY SOLUTIONS

LR

——— Cold turkey solution
······ Control solution

Unemployment rate

Inflation rate

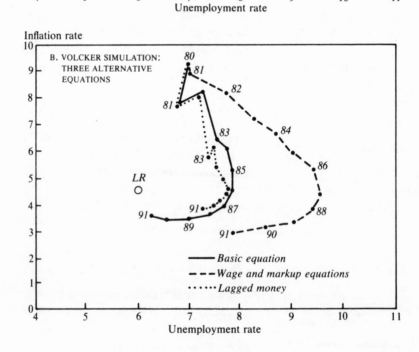

B. VOLCKER SIMULATION:
THREE ALTERNATIVE
EQUATIONS

LR

——— Basic equation
– – – Wage and markup equations
······ Lagged money

Unemployment rate

simulations. In the eight quarters ending in 1980:4, the growth of M1B averaged 7.1 percent at an annual rate. My nominal GNP equation predicts that maintenance of that money growth rate permanently would be associated with a 10.3 percent growth rate of nominal GNP, reflecting the historical behavior of velocity. Since the excess of nominal GNP growth over natural real GNP growth, roughly 7.5 percent in this case, must be equal to the inflation rate in the long run, the U.S. inflation rate of 9.3 percent in 1980 was almost 2 percentage points above the long-run equilibrium rate.[44] Turning the arithmetic around, if one ignores the possibility of faster growth in velocity or slower growth in natural real GNP than I have assumed, a steady state with 9.3 percent inflation would require M1B growth of 9 percent.

The situation of the U.S. economy in early 1981 is explained by the supply shocks and exchange rate changes of 1977–80, which pushed the inflation rate above the long-run equilibrium level, together with overshooting in response to the acceleration of nominal demand growth in the late 1970s. Because my dynamic simulations set all of the supply-shift variables equal to zero after 1981:1, they exhibit the property that continuation of 7 percent growth in M1B will cause the inflation rate to fall to 7.3 percent while the unemployment rate is declining to its natural rate of 6.0 percent. The elimination of adverse supply shifts itself creates a beneficial supply shift, allowing policymakers to achieve a simultaneous reduction in inflation and unemployment, just as occurred in the United States between 1975 and 1976. The relatively optimistic set of simulations presented here reflects the assumed absence of further increases in the relative price of food and energy or in the effective social security tax and effective minimum wage.[45]

To avoid confusing the deceleration of the inflation rate that would occur with continued 7 percent M1B growth with the further deceleration that would accompany a slower monetary growth, the control solution displayed as the dotted line in figure 1A sets the monetary growth rate at 9 percent in order to generate a long-run inflation rate

44. Nominal GNP growth, y, is equal by definition to the sum of the growth rates of real GNP and the GNP deflator $(q + p)$. This implies $y - q^* \equiv q - q^* + p$. Since actual and natural real GNP growth must be equal in the long run, in that situation $y - q^*$ must be equal to p.

45. A small dash of realism is introduced by allowing the food-energy, minimum wage, and social security tax variables to assume their actual values for 1981:1.

equal to the 1980 rate of 9.3 percent.[46] As is the case in all of the
dynamic simulations in this part of the paper, the simulation extends
from 1981:1 to 1991:4, and uses the four auxiliary equations of appendix
A to translate specified patterns of monetary growth into the unemployment, productivity deviation, and exchange rate variables that
appear on the right-hand side of the basic inflation equation from table
2, column 6. The zig-zag pattern displayed in figure 1A by the control
solution in 1981 and 1982 reflects the response of the foreign exchange
rate to the deceleration of monetary growth to 9 percent from an
extremely rapid 12 percent annual rate in the last half of 1980. This
exchange rate effect soon dies out, and the control solution thereafter
smoothly approaches the long-run values of 9.3 percent inflation and
6.0 percent unemployment indicated by the open square in figure 1A.

Two Approaches to Disinflation

A dramatic contrast to the control solution is provided by the cold
turkey solution, which would suddenly and permanently reduce M1B
growth to 4.0 percent in 1981:1, implying a long-run equilibrium inflation
rate of 4.4 percent, shown by the open circle labeled *LR* in figure 1A.
The economy's adjustment to this monetary shock is surprisingly rapid,
with inflation falling to 4.4 percent by 1984, and then overshooting for
the rest of the decade as a result of the high unemployment rates
reached during the process of adjustment.

The cold turkey simulation presents a more optimistic view regarding
the possibility of achieving a permanent reduction in the inflation rate
than is implied by the consensus of existing large-scale econometric
models. Arthur Okun popularized the view that the cost of a permanent
reduction in the inflation rate by 1 percentage point is 10 percent of a
year's GNP, or a 50 percent output loss to cut inflation by 5 percentage
points.[47] In contrast, the cumulative loss of output in the cold turkey
simulation, as opposed to the control solution, is 29 percent, as shown

46. In this part of the paper, all figures refer to four-quarter changes ending in the
fourth quarter of the given year. If the 1980 inflation rate of 9.3 percent seems low, this
results from the practice of expressing quarterly growth rates as annual rates by
multiplying the quarterly rate by 4.0 (thus ignoring compounding) and then computing
four-quarter growth rates by adding successive quarterly rates. Compounding (as in
table 8.1 of the national income and product accounts) yields an inflation rate of 9.6
percent for the four quarters ending in 1980:4, in contrast to our 9.3 percent.

47. Arthur M. Okun, "Efficient Disinflationary Policies," p. 348.

on line 4 of table 10. As shown on the same line, contributing to the relative degree of optimism in this simulation is the behavior of the foreign exchange rate, which in 1991 is 35 percent higher with the cold turkey policy than with the control solution policy.

The effect of an alternative and more realistic monetary policy is illustrated in figure 1B. Corresponding to the stated intention of the Federal Reserve Board to achieve a deceleration in M1B growth of 0.5 percentage point per year, the "Volcker path" slows money growth at that pace from 6.9 percent in 1980:4 to 4.0 percent in 1985:4. Corresponding to the gradualist nature of this policy, the inflation rate decelerates more slowly and the peak unemployment rate is 7.8 percent, compared to 8.5 percent under cold turkey. The period of high unemployment lasts longer, however, which accounts for the fact that the cumulative output loss under the two disinflationary policies is almost identical, as is the cumulative appreciation of the dollar (as shown in table 10).

Sensitivity of Simulation Results to Specification Changes

The earlier analysis of historical dynamic simulations reported that data for 1971–80 could be tracked equally well by my basic equation and by an alternative equation that added a long distributed lag of past changes in the money supply (equivalent to table 4, line 5). I also tested the tracking ability of a wage equation combined with a price markup equation (table 6, columns 2 and 3) and found a substantial deterioration in tracking ability. The behavior of the economy in response to a Volcker path of monetary deceleration is simulated with the money and wage-price equations and compared with the basic equation in figure 1B. Each of these simulations shares in common the same auxiliary equations, and thus identical time paths of money, nominal GNP, and exchange rates. The less responsive the inflation rate, of course, the greater will be the transitional unemployment rate experienced during the period of adjustment.[48]

The equation that includes lagged money behaves almost identically to the basic equation through 1985, as shown by the dotted line in figure 1B. But then the economy seems to get stuck at a relatively high

48. To allow the money and wage-price equations to generate a long-run steady state, the relevant sum of coefficients on lagged nominal variables has been constrained to sum to unity, as in the basic equation.

Table 10. *Summary of Policy Simulations, 1981–91*
Percent

Equation	Infla-tion in 1991	Un-employ-ment in 1991	Peak unemployment rate[a]	Cumula-tive ex-change rate appre-ciation	Cumula-tive per-centage output loss
Basic inflation equation					
1. Control solution	9.4	5.9	6.7 (1981)	− 12.1	8.7
2. Cold turkey	3.7	5.4	8.6 (1984)	22.8	37.7
3. Volcker path	3.6	6.2	7.8 (1985)	20.8	37.2
4. Impact of cold turkey (2 − 1)	− 5.7	− 0.5	. . .	34.9	29.0
5. Impact of Volcker path (3 − 1)	− 5.8	0.3	. . .	32.9	28.5
Equation with lagged money					
6. Control solution	9.0	5.1	6.7 (1981)	− 12.1	1.2
7. Cold turkey	3.8	7.1	8.4 (1985)	22.8	50.0
8. Volcker path	3.9	7.3	7.8 (1987)	20.8	42.1
9. Impact of cold turkey (7 − 6)	− 5.2	2.0	. . .	34.9	48.8
10. Impact of Volcker path (8 − 6)	− 5.1	2.2	. . .	32.9	40.9
Wage and price mark-up equations					
11. Control solution	9.4	6.7	6.9 (1981)	− 12.1	24.0
12. Cold turkey	2.8	6.6	10.2 (1985)	22.8	73.0
13. Volcker path	2.9	7.8	9.6 (1987)	20.8	70.0
14. Impact of cold turkey (12 − 11)	− 5.6	− 0.1	. . .	34.9	49.0
15. Impact of Volcker path (13 − 11)	− 5.5	1.1	. . .	32.9	46.0

a. The peak unemployment rate is calculated on a four-quarter average basis, beginning in the four quarters ending in 1981:4.

rate of unemployment, leading this simulation to generate a higher cumulative output loss than the basic equation (table 10, line 10). This occurs because the lagged money terms reduce the coefficient on the level of unemployment rate almost to zero, thereby eliminating the mechanism by which the basic equation gravitates to the natural unemployment rate. The pattern of coefficients on lagged inflation and lagged monetary changes does not generate the substantial overshooting required to reduce the unemployment rate to the natural unemployment rate, so in 1991 the unemployment rate is still 7.3 percent. The control solution displays a tendency to drift in the opposite direction and yields a 5.1 percent unemployment rate in 1991 (figure 1A).

The wage and price markup equations produce an adjustment path that exhibits more sluggish behavior than the basic equation and thus implies higher unemployment rates and a higher cumulative output loss during the period of adjustment. The cumulative output loss is 46 percent along the Volcker path (table 10, line 15), similar to Okun's estimate of a 50 percent loss, and this is an understatement because the economy still has not arrived at the natural unemployment rate in 1991. The sluggish behavior of the wage and price markup system reflects the longer implicit adjustment lags introduced by the interaction of two lag distributions, one in each equation. Thus the impact of the higher unemployment and foreign exchange rates in the wage equation cannot affect inflation until it feeds into the price markup equation through a lag distribution that has a mean lag of six quarters.

Further evidence on the characteristics of the different equations is provided in figure 2, where the top panel illustrates the difference between the cold turkey and control solutions. As shown by the circle marked *LR*, in the long run the difference should be −5 percent for the inflation rate and zero for the unemployment rate. By 1991 both the basic equation and the wage-price markup equations have completed most of their adjustment, with the latter displaying a more sluggish response and a greater degree of overshooting. The equation that includes lagged money displays the same tendency to get stuck and in 1991 generates an unemployment rate with the cold turkey policy 2 percentage points higher than with the control solution policy. The bottom panel of figure 2 shows that the response of the basic equation becomes much more sluggish if the foreign exchange effect is artificially suppressed while the other coefficients remain the same. The cumulative output loss along the cold turkey path rises from 29 percent to 48 percent.

The degree of response of the inflation rate can be stated alternatively as the percentage of the deceleration in nominal GNP along the cold turkey path, as opposed to the control path, taking the form of a deceleration of inflation. The more rapid responses of the basic equation and the one including lagged money are clear here in comparison with the wage-price markup equations (each line shows the inflation percentage for four-quarter changes ending in the fourth quarter of the listed year):

Figure 2. *Deviation of Cold Turkey Simulation from Control Solution, 1981:1–1991:4*

Deviation from control inflation rate

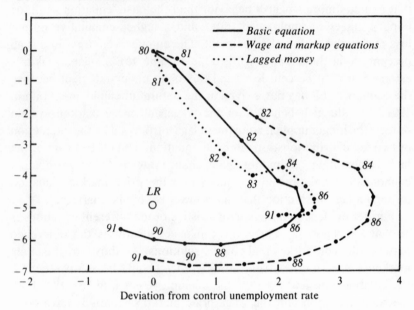

Deviation from control unemployment rate

Deviation from control inflation rate

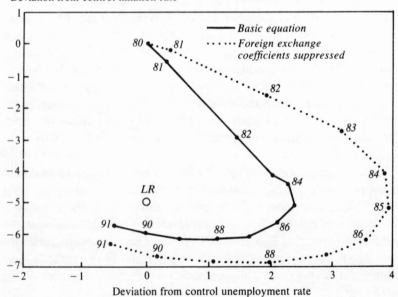

Deviation from control unemployment rate

	Basic equation	Equation including lagged money	Wage-price markup equations
1981	22	39	13
1982	58	66	42
1983	88	85	70
1984	87	73	77
1985	100	86	92

Summary and Conclusions

This paper has explored a number of central issues in the relations among inflation, unemployment, the foreign exchange rate of the dollar, and the growth rates of wages and the money supply. The conclusions should be of equal interest to econometricians attempting to understand the behavior of the postwar U.S. economy and to policymakers attempting to devise a strategy for achieving lower rates of inflation and unemployment. The main conclusions can be described in the following way.

ALTERNATIVE CONCEPTS OF THE NATURAL RATE OF UNEMPLOY-MENT. The natural rate of unemployment, that is, the unemployment rate consistent with a constant rate of inflation, can be defined either for an existing set of conditions or for a hypothetical state in which there are no supply shocks. My estimate of the no-shock natural unemployment rate is 5.9 percent for 1980. The increase in this rate from 5.1 percent in 1954 is attributed entirely to the shifting demographic composition of the labor force and of relative unemployment rates. A striking finding is that the natural rate never fell below 5 percent throughout the 1954–80 period, which implies that the 4 percent unemployment goal of the Kennedy and Johnson administrations was incompatible with a constant inflation rate.

INFLATION VARIANCE IN THE SEVENTIES. The behavior of inflation during the decade between 1971 and 1980 cannot be explained by the simple inertia and labor-market-tightness variables included in traditional Phillips curve equations. Critical additional contributions are made by changes in the relative prices of food and energy, changes in the effective exchange rate of the dollar, and government intervention in the form of the Nixon price controls and their termination. Much of the acceleration of inflation in the 1970s is attributed to changes in the relative prices of food and oil and in the exchange rate rather than to a shortfall of the actual unemployment rate below the natural rate. My preferred inflation equation exhibits neutrality with respect to changes in the nominal money supply: after a decade such nominal disturbances alter only the inflation rate and have no impact on the unemployment rate.

EFFECT OF THE FOREIGN EXCHANGE RATE IN THE PAST AND FUTURE. The demise of the Bretton Woods system and the advent of floating exchange rates have increased the responsiveness of the U.S. inflation rate to monetary policy. Changes in the effective exchange rate of the dollar, through their influence on the prices of exports and import substitutes, help to explain why inflation was so low in 1976 and why it accelerated so rapidly between late 1977 and early 1979. Granger causality tests indicate that lagged exchange rate changes influence inflation, but lagged inflation does not cause exchange rate changes. Most important, my basic equation, which includes the foreign exchange rate, predicts that a policy of ending inflation through restrictive monetary policy would have a much smaller cost in the form of lost output than an alternative equation that sets the exchange rate coefficient to zero.

In the late 1970s it was a commonplace that exchange rate movements helped to account for the low inflation rates experienced by Switzerland, West Germany, and Japan. It has been less widely recognized that a monetary deceleration in the United States in the 1980s could cause the dollar to appreciate and reverse the inflation differentials among nations from those of the 1970s. The counterpart to slower inflation in the United States, at least initially, would be faster inflation and lower real GNP in foreign countries experiencing depreciations. Policies of exchange rate stabilization by these countries would require that they duplicate the monetary restriction initiated by the United States, thus allowing the United States to achieve a worldwide slowdown in the growth rates of money and prices.

SENSITIVITY TO SPECIFICATION CHANGES. The major shifts in the U.S. inflation process in the last decade have been a faster response time, measured as a reduction in the mean lag in an inflation equation on past values of the inflation rate, and the shift to floating exchange rates. Splits in the sample period indicate that my basic equation is stable across the first and last halves of the 1954–80 period, but there is a tendency for the coefficients on the change in unemployment and in the effective minimum wage to be lower after 1966.

DIRECT IMPACT OF MONEY IN THE INFLATION PROCESS. In the inflation equation, short lags on past changes in the money supply are a substitute for current changes in the unemployment rate, and long lags are a substitute for the current level of the unemployment rate. Although they are capable of fitting the historical data as well as the basic equation, versions that include lagged changes in the money supply display implausible behavior in long-run simulations.

EVIDENCE AGAINST WAGE-WAGE INERTIA. Several dynamic models of the inflation process—including that of the late Arthur Okun—are based on the assumption of feedback from lagged wages to current wages, rather than from lagged prices to current wages, as in my model. Several alternative specifications reject the hypothesis of wage-wage inertia. When lagged price and wage variables are allowed to compete on equal terms, the contest is decisively won by lagged price changes.

THE COST OF DISINFLATION. My basic equation implies that inflation can be reduced by 5 percentage points at the cost of 29 percent of GNP, or about $760 billion in 1980 prices. This contrasts to the traditional consensus estimate of a 50 percent output loss (about $1,310 billion). The major factor explaining my more optimistic verdict is the channel of influence from restrictive monetary policy to inflation through the appreciation of the exchange rate. Nevertheless, I support the conclusion of the traditional Phillips curve literature that stopping inflation is not costless; my inflation equation predicts that a continuation of current Federal Reserve policy will achieve a 4 percent inflation rate by 1987 at the cost of an unemployment rate that remains modestly above the levels of early 1981 at least until 1988. The costs of disinflation warrant a continued search for beneficial supply shocks, such as reductions in taxes and regulations that directly raise business costs and reduce productivity.

Directions for Future Research

The analysis of the past and likely future behavior of inflation is inevitably a complex undertaking. Every possible explanatory variable—both those included in this paper and those excluded from

consideration—can be specified in several alternative ways and allowed
to enter with alternative lag lengths. While this paper and others in
this series have exhaustively examined a number of variables, questions
still remain.

How sensitive to different specifications of the productivity trend
is the impact of the productivity slowdown on inflation? What accounts
for the weak estimated impact of the social security tax on inflation,
that is, which economic sectors bear the burden of the tax and why?
Can evidence be found for a robust effect on inflation of the user cost
of capital, or capital taxes, or personal taxes? Much experimentation
not reported in this paper has convinced me that direct supply-side
effects of tax rate changes on the inflation rate are so weak as to be
invisible. But there remain numerous unanswered questions that require
both an improved specification of tax changes and other supply-side
effects and can be answered with added assurance only after the
passage of time allows the accumulation of further evidence on the
effects of foreign exchange rates and other central determinants of the
U.S. inflation process.

Appendix A: Auxiliary Equations Used in Simulations

The primary purpose of the inflation equations estimated in this
paper is to determine the time path of the economy's adjustment to
demand disturbances and supply shocks. Following a change in the
growth rate of the money supply, which is assumed to be under perfect
control by the Federal Reserve, changes occur in four explanatory
variables in the basic inflation equation: the level and change of the
unemployment rate, the deviation of productivity growth from its
trend, and the change in the foreign exchange rate. This appendix
presents the equations used to compute the responses of these variables
to changes in monetary growth.

The primary objective in specifying each equation is to exclude
endogenous variables that would require equations of their own, such
as the interest rate. An additional objective is to make each equation
neutral in the long run with respect to the growth rate of money; after
an initial transition period, the model forces productivity to grow at
its trend rate and the unemployment rate to be constant. Long-run
constancy is also imposed on the foreign exchange rate. Unless

otherwise stated, each equation is estimated over the same sample period as the basic inflation equation, 1954:2 to 1980:4.

From Money to Nominal GNP

The only endogenous variable that enters the model without appearing in the inflation equation is the difference between nominal GNP growth and natural real GNP growth, $\hat{y}_t$. This is explained entirely by its own lagged values and current and lagged changes in the money supply relative to natural real GNP growth, $\hat{m}_t$. This specification does away with the need to guess the growth rate of natural real GNP in the future; historical values are from Perloff and Wachter, updated by the author, as described in table 1. (Numbers in parentheses are t-statistics.)

(15)
$$\hat{y}_t = 4.10 + \sum_{i=1}^{4} b_i \hat{y}_{t-i} + \sum_{i=0}^{3} c_i \hat{m}_{t-i}$$
$$(6.16)$$

$R^2 = 0.373$; standard error $= 3.47$; Durbin-Watson $= 2.03$

$b_1 =$	0.138 (1.27)		$c_0 =$	0.332 (2.49)
$b_2 =$	$-0.082\ (-0.77)$		$c_1 =$	0.479 (3.22)
$b_3 =$	$-0.100\ (-0.94)$		$c_2 =$	0.079 (0.47)
$b_4 =$	$-0.195\ (-1.91)$		$c_3 =$	0.221 (1.42)
Sum $=$	$-0.237\ (-1.27)$		Sum $=$	1.111 (4.60)

From Nominal GNP to Unemployment and Productivity

An identity allows the deviation of real GNP from natural real GNP growth, $\hat{q}_t$, to be calculated from an initial guess for the inflation rate, $\tilde{p}_t$:

(16)
$$\hat{q}_t = \hat{y}_t - \tilde{p}_t + DIF_t.$$

Iterative solution allows $\tilde{p}_t$ to converge to the inflation rate, p_t, calculated in the basic inflation equation. DIF_t, included in the historical but not in the future simulations, is the difference between the growth rates of the implicit and fixed-weight GNP deflators.

The weighted unemployment rate, U_t^W, is related to real GNP growth and the lagged deviation of productivity growth from trend (θ_{t-1}) by the following Okun's law relationship:

(17)
$$U_t^W - U_{t-1}^W = 0.021\,\theta_{t-1} + \sum_{i=0}^{2} d_i \hat{q}_{t-i}$$
$$\quad\quad\quad (2.42)$$

$R^2 = 0.787$; standard error $= 0.18$; Durbin-Watson $= 1.81$

$d_0 = -0.260\,(-13.0)$ $\quad\quad d_2 = -0.011\,(-0.50)$
$d_1 = -0.197\,(-6.67)$ $\quad\quad$ Sum $= -0.467\,(-16.9)$

In the long run, when inflation is equal to $\hat{y}_t$, actual and natural real GNP growth are equal, productivity grows at its trend rate (see equation 18), and the weighted unemployment rate is constant.

The productivity deviation variable is explained by current and lagged changes in output, unemployment, and the relative price of food and energy, p^{FE}:

(18)
$$\theta_t = 0.933\,\hat{q}_t + \sum_{i=0}^{2} f_i p_{t-i}^{FE} + 2.71\,(\Delta U_{t-1}^W - 0.468\,\hat{q}_{t-1})$$
$$\quad (7.24)\quad\quad\quad\quad\quad\quad\quad (2.74)$$

$R^2 = 0.623$; standard error $= 1.94$; Durbin-Watson $= 1.87$

$$f_1 = -0.179\,(-0.84)$$
$$f_2 = -0.332\,(-1.33)$$
$$f_3 = -0.006\,(-0.02)$$
$$\text{Sum} = -0.517\,(-2.73)$$

The device of explaining unemployment by lagged productivity and productivity by lagged unemployment helps the model stay on track during historical simulations when productivity behavior experiences shocks that cannot be explained simply by the lagged adjustment of employment to changes in output. The constant term (0.468) used to adjust output growth is the sum of coefficients on output in the unemployment equation, so that in the long run $\theta_t = \hat{q}_t = \Delta U_t^W = 0$.

The Foreign Exchange Rate

The experience of 1980–81 has dramatized the sensitivity of the exchange rate of the dollar to changes in the interest rate differential between dollar-denominated and foreign assets. However, entering domestic and foreign interest rates into a foreign exchange rate equation here would require numerous additional equations to explain interest rate movements. To avoid this additional complexity, I take advantage of the short-run relation between changes in velocity and interest rate movements, and explain changes in the effective foreign exchange rate of the dollar (x_t, as represented by the series *amx* from *International Financial Statistics*) as depending on changes in velocity and nominal GNP (the sample period is 1972:2–1980:4):

$$(19) \qquad x_t = 14.2 - 21.4 \, D73 + 2.66 \, p_t^{FE}$$
$$ (2.10) \ (-3.45) \qquad (2.25)$$

$$+ \sum_{i=0}^{4} g_i(\hat{m}_{t-i} - \hat{y}_{t-i} - 3.2) + \sum_{i=0}^{4} h_i \hat{y}_{t-i}.$$

$R^2 = 0.708$; standard error = 7.58; Durbin-Watson = 1.63

$g_0 =$	0.046	(0.07)	$h_0 =$	0.425	(0.87)
$g_1 =$	-1.929	(-3.26)	$h_1 =$	-0.790	(-1.48)
$g_2 =$	-0.504	(-0.71)	$h_2 =$	-1.173	(-1.86)
$g_3 =$	-1.177	(-1.66)	$h_3 =$	-0.555	(-0.76)
$g_4 =$	-1.055	(-1.51)	$h_4 =$	-0.741	(-0.81)
Sum $=$	-4.620	(-2.65)	Sum $=$	-2.834	(-2.54)

Here $D73$ is a dummy variable for 1973:1–1973:2. The numbers in parentheses are *t*-statistics. The constant term 3.2 is the long-run trend of velocity growth implicit in equation 15. Equation 19 states that when velocity is growing at its trend rate, the dollar appreciates with $\hat{y}_t < 5.02$ and depreciates with $\hat{y}_t > 5.02$. To avoid the implication of a permanent appreciation in future simulations following a restrictive monetary policy that brings $\hat{y}_t$ below 5 percent, it is assumed that foreign nominal GNP growth responds with a two-year lag. This assumption is implemented in future simulations by subtracting from equation 19 the following:

$$14.2 + 0.25 \left(\sum_{i-1}^{4} \hat{y}_{t-6-i} \right) \left(\sum_{i=0}^{4} h_i \right).$$

As a result, the exchange rate is constant in the long run in all future simulations.

Appendix B: Annual Time Series of Natural Rate of Unemployment

Table 11. *Annual Estimates of the Natural Rate of Unemployment and Natural Real GNP, 1954–80*[a]

Year	Actual unemployment rate (percent)	Natural rate of unemployment (percent)	Natural real GNP (1972 dollars)	Ratio of actual to natural real GNP (percent)
1954	5.5	5.1	620.2	99.3
1955	4.4	5.1	639.3	102.8
1956	4.1	5.1	659.0	102.0
1957	4.3	5.1	680.2	100.5
1958	6.8	5.0	705.0	96.5
1959	5.5	5.1	724.2	99.7
1960	5.5	5.2	749.6	98.3
1961	6.7	5.2	778.4	97.1
1962	5.5	5.3	806.6	99.2
1963	5.7	5.4	834.1	99.8
1964	5.2	5.5	865.7	101.2
1965	4.5	5.6	895.5	103.8
1966	3.8	5.6	936.5	105.1
1967	3.8	5.6	977.8	103.4
1968	3.6	5.6	1,012.6	104.5
1969	3.5	5.6	1,048.4	103.7
1970	4.9	5.6	1,087.6	99.8
1971	5.9	5.8	1,131.8	99.2
1972	5.6	5.8	1,173.6	101.0
1973	4.9	5.8	1,217.2	103.1
1974	5.6	5.9	1,257.1	99.8
1975	8.5	6.0	1,298.0	95.0
1976	7.7	5.9	1,345.0	96.7
1977	7.0	6.0	1,391.4	98.6
1978	6.0	5.9	1,436.6	100.0
1979	5.8	5.9	1,479.5	100.2
1980	7.2	5.9	1,520.7	97.4

a. The natural weighted unemployment rate is estimated to be a constant 4.25 percent, from the constrained equation presented in column 1 of table 3. This is converted into the natural unweighted unemployment rate by adding to 4.25 a four-quarter moving average of $0.9\,(U_t - U_t^W)$, where U_t is the actual unweighted rate, U_t^W is the actual weighted rate, and where the coefficient of 0.9 (rather than 1.0) eliminates the estimated cyclical component in $U_t - U_t^W$. The natural real GNP series is calculated by reestimating equation 1 in the text in the form

$$(U_t^W - 4.25) = \sum_{j=1}^{5} C_j + \sum_{i=0}^{2} \hat{Q}_{t-i},$$

where the C_j are five constants corresponding to the five subperiod divisions of table 1, and $\hat{Q}_t$ is the Perloff-Wachter output ratio. The resulting constants are interpolated linearly to create a smooth series for the percentage adjustment that is subtracted from the Perloff-Wachter QPOT$_1$ series to make it consistent with my estimate of the natural weighted unemployment rate.

Comments by Donald A. Nichols

This paper continues Bob Gordon's quest for an empirical explanation of the process of inflation in the United States. New in this paper are (1) an important role for the exchange rate as a channel of influence of monetary policy on the price level; (2) a direct role for money to affect prices independent of its effect on unemployment; and (3) the use of a single equation to explain price inflation rather than separate equations for wages and prices.

The exchange rate effect is sensible enough on a priori grounds. Monetary stringency raises the value of the domestic currency, thereby reducing the cost of imported goods. Indeed, for smaller, more open, economies this is generally conceded to be one of the major ways that monetary policy affects prices. Analyses of U.S. inflation by American economists often surprise European observers by their lack of any attention to international issues. Gordon shows that this issue should not be ignored in an explanation of U.S. inflation.

Gordon's dependent price variable is the fixed-weight GNP deflator. Since imports are systematically excluded from GNP, their prices can have no direct effect on this index. The index is a measure of inflation in domestic value added, and not in the domestic price level. The substantial exchange rate effects Gordon finds must be due to indirect effects such as those caused by the law of one price—except for transportation costs, traded commodities must sell for the same price within the United States as outside. When the dollar is devalued, the price of these goods must rise within the United States or fall outside in order to preserve the law of one price.

The exchange rate itself does not capture all the price changes of foreign goods. Foreign inflation matters as well. Perhaps the import price deflator would be a better measure of the foreign price level than the exchange rate, despite the fact that import prices have no direct effect on the price level being explained. In any event, substantial fluctuations in foreign inflation have taken place and these are ignored by Gordon's use of the exchange rate as a determinant of domestic inflation.

Gordon argues that because of this exchange rate effect, the costs of disinflation are far smaller than previously reported. Although he notes in several places the possibility that foreign governments might take action to prevent a substantial exchange rate change, nowhere does he point out that this effect is simply a transfer of inflation from one country to another. If all countries use monetary stringency to reduce inflation together in such a way that exchange rates are not disturbed from their original path, then disinflation remains as painful as it was thought to be before this paper. Only if one country is permitted to export half of its desired inflation reduction to its trading partners do we get the lower estimates Gordon emphasizes. Exchange rate appreciation cannot be used as a disinflationary policy by all countries at once.

Monetary policy or, more generally, demand policies, can affect inflation several ways. First, by reducing demand, a tight monetary policy could lead to unemployment, excess capacity, and idle resources, forces that could be expected to bid prices down. Second, these forces could affect expectations of future policies and bring prices down directly without any intervening effect on production. By estimating simultaneously the effects of money growth and unemployment on inflation, Gordon attempts to estimate the second independent effect of money on inflation. I do not find the estimates convincing, however, for several reasons.

The treatment of money as an exogenous variable is implausible. If one asks how the rate of growth of the money supply ever got so large as to permit the current high inflation rates, the answer would have to be that the monetary authorities responded to economic conditions. They tried to prevent recessions that would otherwise have taken place, and in doing so they ratified inflationary wage and price behavior. The Geweke paper in this volume presents plausible estimates of the joint dependence of wage inflation and money growth. Gordon's description of this as a one-sided dependence is questionable.

Another indication of flaws in Gordon's argument is the peculiar lag pattern he reports. The tables report estimates of the effect of five quarters and twenty-four quarters of money growth on inflation. In the text Gordon states that the fit deteriorates for lag lengths between eight and twenty quarters. If the independent effect of money on inflation cannot be found with twenty quarters of lags, one must question its nature. Those who argue that money growth can affect inflation directly, without necessarily first affecting economic activity, generally rely on the influence of expectations, a force that is supposed to work quickly. If expectations cannot be changed significantly by twenty quarters of money growth, it is hard to believe that twenty-four quarters will do the job. That five quarters of money growth have no significant effect on inflation—in addition to any possible effects on unemployment—indicates that the channel of influence through expectations has been quite weak in the past.

The use of one equation to explain price inflation has the advantages Gordon ascribes to it, but it has the disadvantage that it is hard to get the dimensions of all the variables straight if some of the effects one tries to capture are price-level effects and some are rate-of-change effects. For example, the food and energy price effects and the exchange rate effect are thought to change relative prices and therefore to affect the price level as they change, but are not thought to change the rate of inflation permanently. Wage change, on the other hand, is thought to be affected by past wage and price changes, so an increase in wage inflation has a permanence to it that demands that attention be paid to the causes of wage acceleration.

The single equation Gordon estimates displays coefficients of lagged price increases that sum to at least one. This means that a one-time change in any of the independent variables will lead to a permanent increase in inflation. Whether a one-time increase in energy inflation leads to a permanent increase in overall inflation is a hypothesis that should be tested, rather than a constraint that should be imposed on the model. The standard model permits an estimate of this acceleration effect in the wage equation and then captures the full one-time price-level effect in the price equation. Where the two-equation model is estimated in this paper, it can be seen that the permanent acceleration effect of food and energy inflation is 0.13 (in the wage equation), while its one-time effect is 0.55 (in the price equation). It should also be noted that the substantial effect on inflation that Gordon attributes to money working through the exchange rate is due to the fact that his specification requires that a change in exchange rates affect the permanent rate of price inflation. Where wages and prices are estimated separately, its effect is found to be far smaller.

Comments by Herschel I. Grossman

Gordon's paper presents a suggestive new empirical study of the Phillips curve relation for the United States from 1954 through 1980.

The main innovation is the inclusion of the effective exchange rate of the dollar and of various supply shocks among the determinants of inflation, in addition to the usual measures of unemployment and past inflation. The introduction of the exchange rate is especially useful because it provides a more complete picture of the channels of effect of aggregate demand on price inflation. Measures of price inflation include the prices of internationally traded goods, but unemployment variables can at best capture well only the causal link that involves the excess demand for nontraded goods and services. In his treatment of the exchange rate variable, Gordon cleverly makes allowance for presumed mitigation by the Nixon wage and price controls of the effect of exchange rate changes on measured inflation.

For the general reader, probably the most interesting conclusion from this study is that inflation in the 1980s would decline readily in response to a reduction in money growth, with an accompanying recession that would be much milder than either casual reference to past experience or other econometric studies suggest. This optimistic projection results from incorporating an estimated causal link running from reduced money growth to exchange rate appreciation to reduced inflation and from eliminating the estimated effects of past supply shocks on inflation on the supposition that further adverse supply shocks will not occur. Actually, with regard to traded goods, the outlook seems even brighter than Gordon's simulations suggest because, although he speculates that the appreciation of the dollar would induce reductions in foreign money growth, he does not take account of the favorable effect that this foreign response would have on U.S. inflation. Another interesting aspect of this study is the calculation of the separate effects of supply shocks and demographic changes on the unemployment rate consistent with constant inflation.

These and other results of this paper warrant careful study and further elaboration. Gordon displays an impressive command of U.S. macroeconomic data, and his manipulations of the relevant time series are imaginative and exotic. Nevertheless, I doubt that the quantitative conclusions from this study are much more reliable than what has been learned from previous unsuccessful attempts to quantify short-run causal relations about macroeconomic variables.

One serious problem is the apparent sensitivity of the estimated Phillips curve to small changes in specification. For example, the statistical significance of some variables, such as the foreign exchange rate, apparently depends on including just the "right" number of lagged values of the variable and on constraining the coefficients of lagged inflation appropriately. In addition, measures of the effective minimum wage and of social security taxes, which Gordon had found in earlier studies to have important effects on inflation, now turn out to be insignificant. Perhaps most important, the wage-inflation version of the Phillips curve, which is not obviously inferior in fitting the data, generates radically different, and less optimistic, simulation results.

In addition to the estimated Phillips curve, the simulations also involve a set of estimated "auxiliary" equations that relate unemployment, the exchange rate, and productivity growth either directly or indirectly to money growth. Another serious problem is that these specifications have no apparent rationale beyond their ability to fit the data, and they substantially blur the critical distinction between exogenous and endogenous variables. For example, the step of calculating the deviation of real GNP from natural GNP growth implicitly treats the growth rate of nominal GNP as exogenous with respect to inflation.

A fundamental question about the research strategy used in this paper concerns the reality of the version of the Phillips curve employed here, in which the primary causal chain runs from exogenous disturbances through excess demand to changes in inflation rates. Gordon gives some attention to this question by considering an alternative model in which monetary growth is a direct determinant of inflation. He dismisses this alternative model because the estimated regression coefficients do not imply long-run monetary neutrality. This result, however, seems to me hardly conclusive, because Gordon treats velocity as an exogenous random variable. The problem is not merely that velocity has actually increased over time, which Gordon recognizes, but rather that velocity is surely an endogenous variable that depends on the money growth and inflation through the development of inflationary expectations. Estimates of the direct effect of money growth on inflation presumably would be much smaller if the indirect effects through increased velocity were properly modeled.

Another fundamental question concerns the relevance of the Lucas critique about policy invariance to this study. The basic problem here is that Gordon's simulations attempt to predict the effects of sustained deceleration of money growth by using equations estimated from data generated under a policy regime that evidences no capability to produce such a monetary policy. Gordon points out that his estimated Phillips curve is stable over the sample period, and his reasons for believing in the relevance of his simulations are plausible. Nevertheless, it would be more convincing to see an explicit analysis of policy regimes and some direct evidence that the estimated coefficients would be invariant to the drastic change in monetary policy that the simulations envisage.

Gordon properly reminds us that over periods of five years and longer, inflation is closely related to money growth. This paper, of course, reflects an interest in understanding and, presumably, managing the course of inflation and other macroeconomic variables over much shorter intervals. It seems to me that in recent years this focus on short-run policy, together with the sort of research reported in this paper, has been the source of substantial mischief. This paper, despite Gordon's considerable ingenuity, does not encourage me to think that we are now close to being able to quantify the magnitude and timing of macroeconomic relations on a quarterly basis with any confidence. My conclusion is that we would be better off with a long-run policy perspective and the resulting prescription of stable money growth.

JOHN GEWEKE

Feedback between Monetary Policy, Labor Market Activity, and Wage Inflation, 1955–78

ASSUMPTIONS about the relationships between policy tools and macroeconomic aggregates form the core of the economic evaluation of alternative policies. To greater or lesser degree, these assumptions are buttressed by the interpretation of observed behavior in the context of macroeconomic theory. To those charged with the formulation of policy, directions of causation, signs and magnitudes of effects, and the distribution of these effects over time are all important considerations. Given assumptions about directions of causation, macroeconomic theory often yields determinate conclusions about the signs of effects. The magnitudes of these effects are sometimes also determinate, but are often conceded to be an empirical matter.

However, theory has almost nothing to say about the distribution of effects over time. In comparative statics, the only temporal dimension is the elusive "long run" over which factors are sufficiently mobile for aggregation theorems to be sensible. In dynamic models, time exists formally but artificially: time periods are of unspecified and possible varying length, and by happy coincidence the duration of the theorist's time period often turns out to be the empirical investigator's observation interval. If there were well-established stable empirical relationships among the relevant variables to be interpreted, then policymakers would not be inconvenienced by these limitations of

Research assistance from Luke Froeb and Suk Kang, and financial support from the Department of Labor and National Science Foundation grant SES8005606, are gratefully acknowledged. This paper reflects many of the suggestions of the conference participants, and in particular the written comments of Robert Hall and Christopher Sims. The usual disclaimers regarding the author's final responsibility apply.

macroeconomic theory, but such does not seem to be the case. In this environment, alternative models providing often disparate evaluations can flourish, but none speak systematically to the matters of strength and timing on which the success of policy hinges to a large degree. Consider some of the hypothesized interactions among monetary growth, labor market activity, and wage inflation.

The simplest textbook model illustrates these strengths and limitations. If labor markets are regarded as perfectly competitive in the long run, then long swings in the monetary growth rate affect the nominal wage but produce no long swings in the growth rate of real wages. Monetary policy does not affect real behavior in the labor market, and there is no systematic relationship between this behavior and the growth rate of nominal wages.[1] If fluctuations in the monetary growth rate are the chief source of disturbances, then in the long run the growth rate of nominal wages is primarily a monetary phenomenon. Over the short run none of these results need hold, and casual observation suggests that none of them do. The classical static model can be embedded in various ways in dynamic models in which the monetary growth rate is exogenous, and they all share its long-run characteristics. The empirical counterpart (if any) of the long run is not considered in the static model, and in dynamic models its form and often its scope are assumed. Neither approach indicates whether the theoretical long run is relevant for practical policy purposes.

A second extreme example is provided by the wage-standard model, in which nominal wages are set by contractors with little regard for market conditions. Movements in the nominal wage are the outcome of attempts, inherent in the contracting process, to redistribute income between sectors. If this process is not to bring about secular change in employment, and monetary velocity cannot be sustained at arbitrarily high or low levels by financial institutions, the central bank must confirm a wage standard by allowing monetary growth rates to respond appropriately to wage growth.[2] Over the long run, the monetary growth rate is passive and explained entirely by the growth rate of wages. To the extent that the central bank fails to confirm the wage standard, shocks to the nominal wage may have consequences for aggregate real activity.

1. Martin J. Bailey, *National Income and the Price Level,* 2d ed. (New York: McGraw-Hill, 1971), chap. 2.
2. John Maynard Keynes, *The General Theory of Employment, Interest, and Money* (New York: Harcourt, Brace, 1936), chap. 21.

A third class of models emphasizes real activity in the labor market as a source of macroeconomic disturbances. In conventional Phillips curve models,[3] unemployment or closely related variables are interpreted as indicators of labor market disequilibrium, which is hypothesized to have the effect on wages that one would expect in a single-market, static model. In simple formulations prices are assumed to be sticky and statistically exogenous, so that unemployment explains nominal wage changes. In more elaborate expectations-augmented Phillips curve models, prices and lagged prices are introduced, which may in turn be affected by nominal wage movements. The latter models allow for the possibility that in the long run exogenous movements in unemployment will affect nominal wage movements but not the real wage. All models in this class share the implication that short-run nominal wage movements are due substantially to variations in unemployment.

Natural-rate theories[4] offer an alternative interpretation of the Phillips curve in which the order of causation is reversed. Unemployment is interpreted as reflecting primarily shifts in labor supply. In the long run, workers have no money illusion, but in the short run, information constraints or prior contractual arrangements produce an association between nominal wage or price movements and unemployment. Classical demand and supply produce an equilibrium natural rate of unemployment: deviations from this rate are the consequence of a divergence between the real wage rates perceived on opposite sides of the market. Whether or not wage rates will appear to drive unemployment in the econometrician's data depends on whether marginal economic agents can receive, process, and act on information in a period of time shorter than, equal to, or longer than the econometrician's interval of data collection. If the relevant reactions occur within the data collection interval, then the effect of nominal wage shocks on unemployment will emerge as a contemporaneous association, and the whole relationship bears the statistical interpretation of unemployment leading the rate of wage inflation, as in the conventional Phillips curve models. Given the institutional and informational constraints of the labor market and the use of quarterly data, this

3. George L. Perry, *Unemployment, Money, Wage Rates, and Inflation* (MIT Press, 1966), chap. 2.
4. Milton Friedman, "The Role of Monetary Policy," *American Economic Review*, vol. 58 (March 1963), pp. 1–17.

assumption seems unreasonable. If the natural-rate explanation is relevant, one should expect to see an effect of nominal wage growth on unemployment, at least in the short run.

These hypothesized interactions among monetary growth, labor market activity, and wage inflation have varying implications about directions of causation, and they distinguish between long- and short-run effects. Each hypothesis can be illustrated by explicit dynamic models that introduce explicit ad hoc assumptions about timing left unspecified in the original formulation. Conditional on the assumptions about timing, the terms *long run* and *short run* then have exact definitions. These definitions are achieved at the price of constructing a model that is much more specific than is required for the hypothesis to be true. When dynamic models formulated in this way are used as the basis of empirical work, then at best the interpretation of the data in the context of the particular hypothesis is colored by an array of technically convenient but essentially superfluous assumptions. At worst, these further assumptions can lead to rejection of a meritorious idea.

This paper is an attempt to obviate these problems in investigating some aspects of the hypotheses just outlined. The macroeconomic aggregates of interest are indicated by policy problems and the hypothesized interactions: the money supply, unemployment and other measures of labor market activity, wage rates, and prices. Rather than impose a dynamic model directly on the data, I first summarize historical relations between these aggregates, using estimated vector autoregressions. These estimates are then interpreted in terms of the implied association among variables, using methodological innovations developed in full elsewhere.[5] The effect of one group of variables on another is quantified, and then decomposed into a range of frequencies providing operational definitions of the terms *long run* and *short run*. It is thus possible to interpret the observed association between a group of variables X and another group of variables Y as (say) primarily being due to Y affecting X in the short run and a long-run effect of X on Y. This methodology is summarized and its relevance to the economic interpretation of time series is discussed in the next section.

5. John Geweke, "The Measurement of Linear Dependence and Feedback Between Multiple Times Series," *Journal of the American Statistical Association* (forthcoming, 1982).

Methodology

Causality and Feedback

To develop the specific technical foundation for the empirical work reported in this paper,[6] suppose that the considerations just discussed lead one to focus attention on a multiple time series $Z = \{z_t, t \text{ integer}\}$. To simplify the exposition, assume that Z is wide sense stationary, that is, the mean of z_t exists and does not depend on t, and for all t and s, $\text{cov}(z_t, z_{t+s})$ exists and depends on s but not t. It is also convenient to assume that the series is purely nondeterministic: the correlation of z_{t+p} and z_t vanishes as p increases in such a way that in the limit the best linear forecast of z_{t+p} conditional on $\{z_{t-s}, s \geqslant 0\}$ is the unconditional mean of z_{t+p}, which for convenience we take to be **0**. Suppose finally that Z has an autoregressive representation:

$$(1) \qquad z_t = \sum_{s=1}^{\infty} \mathbf{B}_s\, z_{t-s} + \boldsymbol{\epsilon}_t \text{ or } \mathbf{B}(L)z_t = \boldsymbol{\epsilon}_t, E(\boldsymbol{\epsilon}_t) = \mathbf{0}, \text{var}(\boldsymbol{\epsilon}_t) = \mathbf{Y}.$$

The polynomial $\mathbf{B}(L) = I - \sum_{s=1}^{\infty} \mathbf{B}_s\, L^s$ is a function of the conventional lag operator L, whose defining property is $L^s \mathbf{w}_t = \mathbf{w}_{t-s}$ for any time series $W = \{\mathbf{w}_t, t \text{ integer}\}$. The disturbance $\boldsymbol{\epsilon}_t$ is serially uncorrelated and uncorrelated with lagged values of z_t, so equation 1 indicates the linear projection of z_t on its own past. The operator $\mathbf{B}(L)$ is invertible, and consequently there also exists a moving average representation for Z:

$$(2) \qquad z_t = \sum_{s=0}^{\infty} \mathbf{A}_s\, \boldsymbol{\epsilon}_{t-s} = \mathbf{A}(L)\boldsymbol{\epsilon}_t.$$

These technically convenient assumptions about time series are similar to those that are made in the derivation of estimators for simultaneous equation models. In most cases where the assumptions are not met for the time series in question themselves, suitable transformations and adjustments will render them reasonable. For example, they do not pertain to macroeconomic time series that exhibit stochastic

---

6. These thoughts are developed more elaborately and rigorously in ibid. In particular, all assertions made in this subsection are proved in that paper.

exponential growth, but the first differences of logarithms of those series often can be plausibly regarded as stationary. Seasonal movement that appears deterministic can be accounted for by the incorporation of seasonal dummies in equation 1, and an intercept term will accommodate a nonzero mean.

Suppose now that z_t: $m \times 1$ has been partitioned into $k \times 1$ and $l \times 1$ subvectors x_t and y_t, $z_t' = (x_t', y_t')$, reflecting an interest in relationships between $X = \{x_t, t \text{ integer}\}$ and $Y = \{y_t, t \text{ integer}\}$. Denote the autoregressive representations of X and Y,

$$(3) \qquad x_t = \sum_{s=1}^{\infty} E_{1s} x_{t-s} + u_{1t}, \text{var}(u_{1t}) = \Sigma_1$$

and

$$(4) \qquad y_t = \sum_{s=1}^{\infty} G_{1s} x_{t-s} + v_{1t}, \text{var}(v_{1t}) = T_1,$$

respectively. The disturbance u_{1t} is the one-step-ahead error when x_t is forecast from its own past alone, and similarly for v_{1t} and y_t. These disturbance vectors are each serially uncorrelated, but may be correlated with each other contemporaneously and at various leads and lags. Since u_{1t} is uncorrelated with lagged values of x_t, equation 3 denotes the linear projection of x_t on its own past, and likewise equation 4 denotes the linear projection of y_t on its own past. Through the obvious partition of equation 1 is obtained the linear projection of x_t and y_t on past values of themselves and each other,

$$(5) \qquad x_t = \sum_{s=1}^{\infty} E_{2s} x_{t-s} + \sum_{s=1}^{\infty} F_{2s} y_{t-s} + u_{2t}, \text{var}(u_{2t}) = \Sigma_2;$$

$$(6) \qquad y_t = \sum_{s=1}^{\infty} G_{2s} y_{t-s} + \sum_{s=1}^{\infty} H_{2s} x_{t-s} + v_{2t}, \text{var}(v_{2t}) = T_2.$$

The disturbance vectors u_{2t} and v_{2t} are serially uncorrelated, but since each is uncorrelated with lagged values of both x_t and y_t, they can be correlated with each other only contemporaneously; denote $\text{cov}(u_{2t}, v_{2t}) = C$. Also useful is the linear projection of x_t on its own past and current and lagged values of y_t,

(7) $\qquad \mathbf{x}_t = \displaystyle\sum_{s=1}^{\infty} \mathbf{E}_{3s}\, \mathbf{x}_{t-s} + \sum_{s=0}^{\infty} \mathbf{F}_{3s}\, \mathbf{y}_{t-s} + \mathbf{u}_{3t}, \; \mathrm{var}(\mathbf{u}_{3t}) = \mathbf{\Sigma}_3,$

and symmetrically for $\mathbf{y}_t$,

(8) $\qquad \mathbf{y}_t = \displaystyle\sum_{s=1}^{\infty} \mathbf{G}_{3s}\, \mathbf{y}_{t-s} + \sum_{s=0}^{\infty} \mathbf{H}_{3s}\, \mathbf{x}_{t-s} + \mathbf{v}_{3t}, \; \mathrm{var}(\mathbf{v}_{3t}) = \mathbf{T}_3.$

Clearly $\mathbf{\Sigma}_1 \ominus \mathbf{\Sigma}_2 \ominus \mathbf{\Sigma}_3$ and $\mathbf{T}_1 \ominus \mathbf{T}_2 \ominus \mathbf{T}_3$, where $\ominus$ denotes the usual ordering among positive definite matrices; hence $|\mathbf{\Sigma}_1| \geq |\mathbf{\Sigma}_2| \geq |\mathbf{\Sigma}_3| > 0$ and $|\mathbf{T}_1| \geq |\mathbf{T}_2| \geq |\mathbf{T}_3| > 0$ where $|\cdot|$ denotes determinant. Define the measure of linear feedback from Y to X, $F_{Y \to X} = \ln(|\mathbf{\Sigma}_1|/|\mathbf{\Sigma}_2|)$ and the measure of linear feedback from X to Y, $F_{X \to Y} = \ln(|\mathbf{T}_1|/|\mathbf{T}_2|)$. These measures are nonnegative, and have direct interpretation in terms of the proportionate increase in the variance of the one-step-ahead population forecast errors: for example, if X and Y are univariate and X is forecast only from its own past, then the variance of the one-step-ahead forecast error is $\exp(F_{Y \to X})$ times that which would result if past Y were also used. The series Y fails to cause the series X in the sense of Granger and Sims[7] if and only if $F_{Y \to X} = 0$. Furthermore, if the exogenous variables in a simultaneous equation model are X and the endogenous variables are Y, then $F_{Y \to X} = 0$.

Define the measure of instantaneous linear feedback $F_{X \cdot Y} = \ln(|\mathbf{\Sigma}_2|/|\mathbf{\Sigma}_3|)$; this is a monotonic function of the proportionate reduction in "forecast" error that results when one employs current values of Y in addition to lagged values of X and Y in forecasts of the current value of X, in the population. It can be shown that $\ln(|\mathbf{\Sigma}_2|/|\mathbf{\Sigma}_3|) = \ln(|\mathbf{T}_2|/|\mathbf{T}_3|)$, as is suggested by the fact that whether x_t improves forecasts of y_t or vice versa, both reduce to a question about the partial correlation between these two vectors. It can further be shown that both expressions are equivalent to $\ln(|\mathbf{T}_2| \cdot |\mathbf{\Sigma}_2|/|\mathbf{Y}|)$. The series Y fails to cause the series X instantaneously (and vice versa) in the sense of Granger and Sims if and only if $F_{X \cdot Y} = 0$. As a practical matter, instantaneous feedback is usually the consequence of the fact that time series are observed only averaged over periods of time or sampled

7. C. W. J. Granger, "Investigating Causal Relations by Econometric Models and Cross Spectral Methods," *Econometrica*, vol. 37 (July 1969), pp. 424–38; and Christopher A. Sims, "Money, Income and Causality," *American Economic Review*, vol. 62 (September 1972), pp. 540–52.

at regular intervals. What would appear as directional feedback if the time series were observed at very frequent intervals or continuously through time is subsumed in instantaneous feedback in the relationship between the series as recorded.

The relationship between these measures of three kinds of feedback can be better understood by introducing a fourth measure, that of linear dependence, $F_{X,Y} = \ln(|\Sigma_1|\cdot|\mathbf{T}_1|/|\mathbf{Y}|)$. It can be shown that $F_{X,Y} = 0$ if and only if the time series X and Y are uncorrelated at all leads and lags, and that $F_{X,Y} = \ln(|\Sigma_1|/|\Sigma_4|) = \ln(|\mathbf{T}_1|/|\mathbf{T}_4|)$, where Σ_4 is the variance of X conditional on its own past and all values (past, current, and future) of Y and $\mathbf{T}_4$ is the variance of Y conditional on its own past and all values of X. From these definitions,

$$F_{X,Y} = F_{Y \to X} + F_{X \to Y} + F_{X \cdot Y}.$$

Linear relationships between any two stationary vector time series may be additively decomposed into linear feedback from the first to the second, linear feedback from the second to the first, and instantaneous linear feedback.

These measures of feedback generalize the taxonomy of relationships between time series due to Granger and Sims: unidirectional causality from X to Y is the special case $F_{Y \to X} = 0$, $F_{X \to Y} > 0$, and conversely for unidirectional causality from Y to X. Moreover, the taxonomy is complete for purely nondeterministic stationary time series with autoregressive representation, since the measures of feedback always exist for such series. More important for the questions to which this paper is addressed, measures of feedback are more naturally linked to propositions about macroeconomic behavior than are assertions about causal orderings. The proposition that "Y causes X, but X does not cause Y" may be true of a macroeconometric model, but it is difficult to find an X and a Y for which one would literally entertain the proposition. The notion that X influences Y a great deal more than Y influences X is more common and usually more tenable, and such notions may be quantified by $F_{X \to Y}$ and $F_{Y \to X}$.

Decomposing Feedback by Frequency

Important propositions about the fundamental nature of macroeconomic behavior nearly always assert more than directions of influence or their absence. No one interprets the neutrality of money to mean that money influences prices but not real activity. What is usually meant is that in the long run money will affect prices but not real activity, whereas in the short run money may affect prices or real activity or both. Whether prices and real activity affect money is irrelevant to questions about the neutrality of money, although if they do not do so, then investigation of the proposition of interest may be simplified somewhat. Framed this way, the proposition that money is neutral has no implications for feedback measured in the way suggested, and a fortiori does not imply a unidirectional causal ordering between any of the three variables—money, prices, and real activity.

This use of the concepts of *long run* and *short run* is characteristic of the way propositions about macroeconomic behavior tend to be stated. The distinction arises sometimes because there really are specific theories about short-run adjustments on the one hand and some kind of long-run equilibrium on the other, but more often the probable reason is that theory speaks more to comparative statics than it does to monthly or quarterly dynamics. Inference about the long-run propositions of comparative statics is treacherous, for long-run equilibrium is a moving target that macroeconomic systems hit only coincidentally, and they move toward it in ways not well understood. Propositions about the long run can be tested definitively only in conjunction with theories about dynamics. In the absence of such theories, it is necessary to be ad hoc in tests of the interesting propositions, but some ways of doing this are more reasonable than others. In most cases, a reasonable way to construe the long run is as "that which is permanent" relative to the short run, which is more temporary. For stationary time series, there are natural classifications of what is more and less permanent in the frequency domain, and these classifications may be used to decompose measures of feedback to provide one way of making the distinction between the long and short run.

Consider the system

(9)
$$\mathbf{x}_t = \sum_{s=1}^{\infty} \mathbf{E}_{2s}\mathbf{x}_{t-s} + \sum_{s=1}^{\infty} \mathbf{F}_{2s}\mathbf{y}_{t-s} + \mathbf{u}_{2t}$$

$$\mathbf{y}_t = \sum_{s=0}^{\infty} \mathbf{H}_{3s}\mathbf{x}_{t-s} + \sum_{s=1}^{\infty} \mathbf{G}_{3s}\mathbf{y}_{t-s} + \mathbf{v}_{3t},$$

which is formed by appending equations 5 and 8. It is the case that $\text{cov}(\mathbf{u}_{2t}, \mathbf{v}_{3t}) = 0$. One might think of these equations as a block-recursive system in which all instantaneous feedback has been combined with feedback from X to Y, so that the equations in X represent only that part of the X-Y relationship that can unambiguously be called feedback from Y to X. Since the bivariate representation (equation 1) is invertible, the system in equation 9 can also be inverted, to yield expressions for $\mathbf{x}_t$ and $\mathbf{y}_t$ in terms of $\mathbf{u}_{2t}$ and $\mathbf{v}_{3t}$:

(10)
$$\begin{pmatrix} \mathbf{x}_t \\ \mathbf{y}_t \end{pmatrix} = \begin{bmatrix} \mathbf{P}(L) & \mathbf{Q}(L) \\ \mathbf{R}(L) & \mathbf{S}(L) \end{bmatrix} \begin{pmatrix} \mathbf{u}_{2t} \\ \mathbf{v}_{3t} \end{pmatrix}.$$

The first k equations of equation 10,

(11)
$$\mathbf{x}_t = \mathbf{P}(L)\mathbf{u}_{2t} + \mathbf{Q}(L)\mathbf{v}_{3t},$$

provide a decomposition of X into distributed lags on the orthogonal innovations $\mathbf{u}_{2t}$ and $\mathbf{v}_{3t}$. These innovations have been constructed so that $\mathbf{v}_{3t}$ may be interpreted unambiguously as new information entering the system at time t arising from Y rather than from X. At any point in time, $\mathbf{x}_t$ is a linear combination of current and past innovations, one of which is innovations in Y in the X-Y system, and one of which is a mixture of innovations in X and new information that cannot be attributed unambiguously to X or Y alone.

Equation 11 has an interesting interpretation in the frequency domain. The Cramér representation for stationary time series states that such series can be decomposed additively in a continuum of sine and cosine waves, for example,

$$\mathbf{x}_t = \frac{1}{2\pi} \int_{-\pi}^{\pi} e^{it\lambda} \mathbf{dZx}(\lambda), \quad \mathbf{u}_{2t} = \frac{1}{2\pi} \int_{-\pi}^{\pi} e^{it\lambda} \mathbf{dZu}_2(\lambda).$$

For series that are serially correlated, like X, the random term $\mathbf{dZx}(\lambda)$ has variance that varies with λ, but for series that are serially uncorrelated, like $\mathbf{u}_{2t}$, $\mathbf{dZu}_2(\lambda)$ has the same variance at all frequencies. In terms of the Cramér representations of the variables involved, equation 11 is

(12)
$$\mathbf{dZx}(\lambda) = \tilde{\mathbf{P}}(\lambda)\mathbf{dZu}_2(\lambda) + \tilde{\mathbf{Q}}(\lambda)\mathbf{dZv}_3(\lambda),$$

where $\tilde{\mathbf{P}}(\lambda)$ and $\tilde{\mathbf{Q}}(\lambda)$ denote the Fourier transforms of the respective lag operators $\mathbf{P}(L)$ and $\mathbf{Q}(L)$. The vector $\mathbf{x}_t$ may be regarded as a mixture of sine and cosine waves. At each frequency, these waves are a linear combination of two other sets of such waves, those associated with the serially uncorrelated vector innovations $\mathbf{u}_{2t}$ and $\mathbf{v}_{3t}$, respectively. The unambiguous innovation in $\mathbf{y}_t$, which is $\mathbf{v}_{3t}$, is a mixture of waves that are reflected to greater or lesser degree in the mixture of waves that comprise $\mathbf{x}_t$. The relative importance of these waves depends on $\boldsymbol{\Sigma}_2$ and $\mathbf{T}_3$ and on the relative magnitudes of $\tilde{\mathbf{P}}(\lambda)$ and $\tilde{\mathbf{Q}}(\lambda)$ at the frequency in question.

To measure this relative importance in an exact way, notice that (from either equation 11 or 12) the spectral density matrix $\mathbf{S}_x(\lambda)$ of X at frequency λ is the sum of two matrices, the first of which is positive definite provided $I - \boldsymbol{\Sigma}_{s=0}^{\infty} \mathbf{G}_{3s}L^s$ has no roots on the unit circle, and the second of which is at least positive semidefinite:

(13) $$\mathbf{S}_x(\lambda) = \tilde{\mathbf{P}}(\lambda)\boldsymbol{\Sigma}_2 \tilde{\mathbf{P}}(\lambda)' + \tilde{\mathbf{Q}}(\lambda)\mathbf{T}_3 \tilde{\mathbf{Q}}(\lambda)'.$$

When X is univariate, $|\tilde{\mathbf{P}}(\lambda)|^2\boldsymbol{\Sigma}_2/\mathbf{S}_x(\lambda)$ is the fraction of $\mathbf{S}_x(\lambda)$ attributed to $\mathbf{u}_{2t}$. When X is not univariate, the corresponding generalized variance ratio is $|\tilde{\mathbf{P}}(\lambda)\boldsymbol{\Sigma}_2\tilde{\mathbf{P}}(\lambda)'|/|\mathbf{S}_x(\lambda)|$. The measure of feedback from Y to X at frequency λ can be taken to be $f_{Y \to X}(\lambda) = \ln(|\mathbf{S}_x(\lambda)|/|\tilde{\mathbf{P}}(\lambda)\boldsymbol{\Sigma}_2\tilde{\mathbf{P}}(\lambda)'|)$. This measure reflects the relative importance of the contributions of $\mathbf{u}_{2t}$ and $\mathbf{v}_{3t}$ to variance in X at frequency λ: it is always nonnegative, zero when $\mathbf{dZ}v_3(\lambda)$ is not reflected at all in $\mathbf{dZ}x(\lambda)$, and approaches infinity as the contribution of the variance in $\mathbf{dZ}u_2(\lambda)$ to $\mathbf{dZ}x(\lambda)$ approaches zero relative to that of $\mathbf{dZ}v_3(\lambda)$. Furthermore, it may be shown that

$$F_{Y \to X} = \frac{1}{2\pi} \int\limits_{-\pi}^{\pi} f_{Y \to X}(\lambda)d\lambda,$$

so long as

$$I - \sum_{s=0}^{\infty} \mathbf{G}_{3s}L^s$$

is invertible, a condition usually met by point estimates in empirical work. The measure $f_{Y \to X}(\lambda)$ therefore provides a decomposition of feedback by frequency, and indicates the relative importance of variance at different frequencies in explaining feedback from Y to X. Symmetric remarks apply to feedback from X to Y and lead to corresponding measure $f_{X \to Y}(\lambda)$ of feedback from X to Y at frequency λ.

In the empirical work that follows, these measures will be estimated for several time series. In interpreting the estimates, I shall identify feedback at lower frequencies with longer runs relative to feedback at higher frequencies. One advantage of this approach is that it enables an immediate identification of feedback associated with seasonal effects, that associated with the business cycle frequencies, that associated with runs longer than the business cycle, and so on. It is possible to confine attention to secular movements alone, to feedback associated with the business cycle, and to relations of a more transitory nature. When this identification is made, macroeconomic theory, which tends to be vague about chronological time, is linked in a nonparametric way with the characteristics of multivariate stationary time series. It is probably not the only way that such a link could be forged, and presumably identification of what is short or long run would be different for different methods. When a specific dynamic theory is available that affords an exact parameterization, then parametric inference is preferable; in such cases long and short run often have an exact interpretation that is not exactly the same as that proposed here but is generally consistent with it.[8] Specific dynamic theories that are not uncomfortably ad hoc are rare; hence direct estimation of the measures proposed here seems fruitful.

Inference

All the measures of linear feedback, and their decomposition by frequency, may be constructed from the parameters of equations 5

---

8. For example, consider the simplest variant of the version of the permanent-income consumption model, presented in Thomas J. Sargent, "Rational Expectations, Economic Exogeneity, and Consumption," *Journal of Political Economy*, vol. 86 (August 1978), pp. 673–700:

$$C_t = \beta Y_{pt} + u_t$$

$$Y_{pt} = (1 - \alpha) \sum_{j=0}^{\infty} \alpha^j E_t Y_{t+j}.$$

If Y_t is uncaused in the sense of Granger and Sims and follows a first-order autoregressive process with parameter δ, and if U_t is independent of Y_s for all t and s, then equation 9 for this system is

$$C_t = [\beta(1 - \alpha)/1 - \alpha\delta]Y_t + u_t$$
$$Y_t = \delta Y_{t-1} + \epsilon_t.$$

Pursuing the manipulations that follow equation 9, it may be verified that

$$f_{Y \to C}(\lambda) = \ln \left[a + \frac{b}{1 + \delta^2 - 2\delta\cos(\lambda)} \right],$$

where $a = (1 - \alpha\delta)^2/(1 - \alpha\delta - \beta + \beta\alpha)^2$, $b = \beta^2(1 - \alpha)^2/(1 - \alpha\delta - \beta + \beta\alpha)^2 \sigma_u^2$. For realistic values of δ, $f_{Y \to C}(0) >> f_{Y \to C}(\pi)$.

and 6, including the variance matrix $\mathbf{Y}$ of the vector of innovations in those equations. All inference about these measures in the empirical work reported here is based on estimates of those two equations with lag length truncated at six or ten quarters. Extensive experimentation showed that coefficients on lags seven through ten were nearly always insignificant as a group. The longer lag was employed because it was thought more likely to permit discrimination among competing hypotheses, and in many cases the economic interpretation of the results indeed turns out to be sensitive to the choice of lag length.

In the estimation procedure employed, equations 5 and 6 were first estimated by ordinary least squares, which provides maximum likelihood estimates conditional on presample values and the truncation of lags at six quarters. The estimation algorithm used a Householder decomposition, which affords very cheap and accurate computation even for the largest systems considered, and has as one by-product the inner product of the residuals of equations 3 and 4. Wald tests of the hypotheses of no feedback are then constructed in the obvious way, and the outcomes of these tests provide the reported indication of whether the measure of feedback is significantly different from zero. The estimate of $\mathbf{Y}$ was formed by taking the inner product of the residuals from all m equations, and dividing by the number of observations less the number of parameters estimated in each equation.

Estimates of equation 9 were constructed using the relationships $\mathbf{G}_{3s} = \mathbf{G}_{2s} - \mathbf{C}'\mathbf{\Sigma}_2^{-1}\mathbf{F}_{2s}$, $\mathbf{H}_{3s} = \mathbf{H}_{2s} - \mathbf{C}'\mathbf{\Sigma}_2^{-1}\mathbf{E}_{2s}$, $\mathbf{T}_3 = \mathbf{T}_2 - \mathbf{C}'\mathbf{\Sigma}_2^{-1}\mathbf{C}$. The Fourier transforms of the lag operators in equation 9 were evaluated at 1,024 equally spaced ordinates in the interval $[-\pi, \pi]$, and the matrix of Fourier-transformed lag operators was inverted, which yields an estimate of the Fourier transform of lag operators in equation 10. Replacing estimates with unknown parameters in equation 13 provides an estimate of $\mathbf{S}_x(\lambda)$ at each of the 1,024 ordinates, and these estimates used in the expression for $f_{X \to Y}(\lambda)$ yield an estimate of that measure. By using the method of Fourier transforms to obtain equation 10 by inversion of equation 9, it may be seen that $\bar{\mathbf{Q}}(\lambda) = \mathbf{0}$ if and only if

$$(14) \qquad \sum_{s=1}^{\infty} \mathbf{F}_{2s} \cos(\lambda s) = \mathbf{0}, \; \sum_{s=1}^{\infty} \mathbf{F}_{2s} \sin(\lambda s) = \mathbf{0}.$$

Since $\bar{\mathbf{Q}}(\lambda) = \mathbf{0}$ is equivalent to $f_{Y \to X}(\lambda) = 0$, a test of the hypothesis $f_{Y \to X}(\lambda) = 0$ is equivalent to a test of the $2kl$ linear restrictions (equation

14) on the $6kl$ coefficients F_{2s}, $s = 1, \ldots, 6$, which were estimated by ordinary least squares. Wald tests of these joint hypotheses provide the reported indication of whether the measure of feedback is significantly different from zero at specific frequencies.

Empirical Results

Time Series Variables and Estimation Periods

The estimates reported here are functions of five quarterly macro-economic time series, from the period 1955:1 to 1978:4. Monetary policy is represented by the growth rate in M1. Two measures of labor market activity are used. The inverse of the civilian unemployment rate (Un^{-1}) is the most popular such measure in empirical wage equations. The other is the quit rate $(Quit)$ among production workers in manufacturing. This measure is employed because there is substantial evidence that most nonseasonal variation in the quit rate among production workers in manufacturing is accounted for by workers who leave jobs after having found alternative employment,[9] and the quit rate therefore provides a proxy for excess demand in one important labor market. Since the unemployment rate is based on household surveys and the quit rate on establishment surveys, much of the measurement error in one ought not to be reflected in the other. The wage rate used for the reported results (W) is average hourly earnings among production workers in manufacturing, corrected for overtime. The consumer price index (CPI) is employed as a representative of the nominal price measure typically employed in wage equations.

At various stages of empirical work, alternatives to some of these five time series were used. Virtually all of the results reported here that incorporate Un^{-1} or $Quit$ were replicated using the inverse of the unemployment rate among prime-age white males, and manufacturing average hourly earnings were used in lieu of W. In no cases did these substitutions affect the estimates in any way that would suggest a change in the interpretation of the results. Occasional differences near seasonal frequencies occurred for the alternative unemployment rate measure, and the statistical significance associated with the substan-

9. John Geweke, "Employment, Turnover and Wage Dynamics in U.S. Manufacturing, 1932–1972" (Ph.D. dissertation, University of Minnesota, 1975), chap. 2.

tially unchanged estimates at low frequencies was affected in a few cases. In cases in which overall measures of feedback were substantially affected, differences in feedback at seasonal frequencies accounted for the differences in the overall measures.

All variables except Un^{-1} and *Quit* are used in logarithmic form. In all equations, centered first differences of logarithms, denoted $\triangle\ln(\;\;)$, are employed rather than conventional first differences of logarithms. A centered first difference of logarithms is the logarithm of the ratio of the last monthly observation in the quarter to the first. This method of differencing assures that in systems that incorporate both Un^{-1} or *Quit* and the first difference of a logarithm, there will be virtually no systematic shifting forward or backward, as would be the case if conventional first differences of quarterly logarithms were used. Measures of feedback and their decomposition by frequency can in principle be affected substantially by systematic shifting backward or forward: as a series is successively shifted backward, for example, it will show increasingly greater feedback to the other, until in the limit all linear dependence in the two series is attributed to feedback from the shifted series.

Experimentation showed that the relationship between Un^{-1} or *Quit* and other variables was affected in the expected way, in a few cases substantially, by use of conventional first differences of quarterly logarithms instead of centered first differences. In comparison with conventional first differences, centered first differences accentuate high frequencies relative to low ones. To the extent that high-frequency variations in economic variables tend to be independent of one another or incorporate a greater proportion of measurement error, measures of feedback are thereby diminished. Since the problem arises mainly at high frequencies and this study is primarily interested in low frequencies, it was decided that the systematic shifting inherent in conventional differences, which affects all frequencies, should be avoided at the expense of possibly introducing some noise.

All series are seasonally unadjusted, and all estimates are based on equations that include an intercept and three seasonal dummies. When seasonal dummies were not incorporated, there was virtually no substantive change in the behavior of directional feedback at frequencies corresponding to periods greater than five quarters. The magnitude of feedback at seasonal frequencies and of instantaneous linear feedback was often much greater and increased the estimated overall measures of directional feedback. In about half the cases, short-run directional feedback—that at frequencies corresponding to periods less than a year but well away from seasonal frequencies—was affected by the removal of seasonal dummies, more in some cases and less in others. There is no reason why feedback at seasonal frequencies should simply be ignored, and the fact that directional feedback at those frequencies tends to be reduced by the incorporation of seasonal dummies is a reflection of the dynamics of macroeconomic seasonal fluctuations, not analytical characteristics of the measures introduced above in the discussion of methodology. The use of data that has undergone official seasonal adjustment procedures was not explored systematically. For the series employed here the official seasonal adjustment filters are not at all the same, and useful analytical characterization of their effect on measures of feedback is difficult. Empirical results for a handful of seasonally adjusted series showed little effect on overall measures of feedback, but there was some shifting of the decomposition of feedback by frequency.

A few characteristics of the five time series variables used in the empirical work are reported in table 1. Two estimation periods were used. The first, 1955:1–1971:2, begins well after the end of Korean War price controls and stops just short of the wage and price freeze of August 1971. The second, 1971:3–1978:4, embraces a period of varied wage and price controls and higher and more volatile rates of inflation than occurred in the first period. During 1955:1–1971:2 the univariate innovations in $\Delta\ln(M1)$, $\Delta\ln(W)$, and $\Delta\ln(CPI)$ exhibited variances of about the same order of magnitude. In the second period all innovations in the rates of change of nominal variables were more volatile, except for $\Delta\ln(W)$, which was only slightly more volatile. Most striking is the behavior of $\Delta\ln(M1)$, whose innovation variance increased by a factor of six, more than twice that of any other variable. Innovation variances for the two "real" series, Un^{-1} and *Quit*, show no increases of the same magnitude; if anything, that for Un^{-1} declined. In table 1, and those that follow, the results of tests of the hypothesis that both coefficients and innovation variances remained stable are frequently reported, because both enter measures of feedback. Given the finding that for two and perhaps three of the five series the autoregressive representations (equations 5 and 6) were not the same in the two periods, attention is focused on measures of feedback in the respective periods, rather than the entire period 1955:1–1978:4.

Table 1. *Time Series Variables Used in Empirical Work*

Variable[a]	Standard deviation of innovation[b]		Tests for stability[c]		
	1955:1–1971:2	1971:3–1978:4	Coefficient [F(10,76)]	Variance [F(20,56)]	Overall [χ²(11)]
$\triangle$ln(M1)	5.30×10^{-3}	1.35×10^{-2}	2.01**	6.47***	40.09***
Un^{-1}	1.64	1.01	0.93	0.38***	18.02*
Quit	1.60	2.03	0.91	1.62	8.82
$\triangle$ln(W)	4.64×10^{-3}	5.01×10^{-3}	1.56	1.16	13.91
$\triangle$ln(CPI)	2.79×10^{-3}	4.58×10^{-3}	2.41**	2.70***	25.29***

* Rejection of the hypothesis indicated, or of the hypothesis that the estimated magnitude is zero, at the 10 percent significance level.
** 5 percent significance level.
*** 1 percent significance level.
a. $\triangle$ln(Ml) = within-quarter first difference of natural logarithm of M1.
Un^{-1} = inverse of civilian unemployment rate.
Quit = quit rate per 100 production workers, all manufacturing.
$\triangle$ln(W) = within-quarter first difference of natural logarithm of production worker average hourly earnings adjusted for overtime, all manufacturing.
$\triangle$ln(CPI) = within-quarter first difference of natural logarithm of consumer price index.
b. Square root of sum of squared residuals divided by degrees of freedom in regression on intercept, three seasonal dummies, and six lagged values.
c. Here, and in the tables that follow, coefficient test is standard stability test, assuming homoskedasticity 1955:1–1978:4; variance test statistic is ratio of sums of squared residuals deflated by degrees of freedom, 1955:1–1971:2 in numerator and 1971:3–1978:4 in denominator; overall test is likelihood ratio statistic, scaled by ratio of degrees of freedom to number of observations in unconstrained model.

Presentation and Interpretation of Results

Measures of feedback between several of these series were estimated for the two periods; numerical results are shown in tables 2 through 7. In these tables, estimated measures of linear dependence and instantaneous and directional linear feedback are presented, along with estimates of the decomposition of directional linear feedback at the zero frequency (the infinitely long run) and frequencies corresponding to periods of 42.67 quarters (in the neighborhood of the secular long run), 12.80 quarters (the business cycle), 4.00 quarters (the seasonal frequency), 2.67 quarters (a short run, perhaps), and 2.00 quarters (also a seasonal frequency). In addition, estimates of the decomposition of directional feedback by frequency are portrayed graphically in selected cases.

In interpreting the results it is important to take account of some of the effects that changes in lag length, both absolute and relative to sample size, have on the estimated measures of feedback. Increasing the lag length increases the range of possible shapes for the estimated $f_{X \to Y}(\lambda)$ and $f_{Y \to X}(\lambda)$ functions. A longer lag length permits more local

Table 2. *Estimated Measures of Feedback between Monetary Growth Rate and Labor Market Activity*[a]

	X and Y vectors,[b] by sample periods and lag lengths					
Measure of feedback, overall and specific frequencies (quarters)	*1955:1–1971:2*				*1971:3–1978:4*	
	Six lags		*Ten lags*		*Six lags*	
	$\Delta ln(M1)$ Un^{-1}	$\Delta ln(M1)$ *Quit*	$\Delta ln(M1)$ Un^{-1}	$\Delta ln(M1)$ *Quit*	$\Delta ln(M1)$ Un^{-1}	$\Delta ln(M1)$ *Quit*
$F_{X,Y}$	0.613***	0.444***	0.917***	0.749***	0.720	0.362
$F_{X \cdot Y}$	0.184***	0.004	0.375***	0.000	0.056	0.007
$F_{X \to Y}$	0.199*	0.333***	0.238	0.472***	0.464	0.236
∞	0.234**	0.471**	0.112	0.247**	7.087	1.370
42.67	0.255**	0.543***	0.139**	0.283**	1.162	0.099
12.80	0.475**	1.196***	1.192**	1.240**	0.243	0.042
4.00	0.118	0.032	0.081	0.146	0.120	0.076
2.67	0.139*	0.017	0.043	0.166	0.151	0.329
2.00	0.163	0.317	0.076	0.001	0.000	0.010
Coefficient stability [$F(16,64)$]	. . .	. . .	. . .	. . .	1.12	0.88
Variance stability [$F(14,50)$]	. . .	. . .	. . .	. . .	0.57	2.68***
Overall stability [$\chi^2(17)$]	. . .	. . .	. . .	. . .	22.34	19.19
$F_{Y \to X}$	0.230***	0.107*	0.304***	0.277**	0.200	0.119
∞	0.172	0.494**	0.276**	0.942***	0.082	0.015
42.67	0.470***	0.768***	0.579***	2.050***	0.226	0.023
12.80	0.411**	0.131	0.121	0.099	0.165	0.060
4.00	0.206	0.046	0.697*	0.384	0.082	0.110
2.67	0.174	0.016	0.084	0.047	0.194	0.039
2.00	0.093	0.123	0.152	0.349	0.432	0.325
Coefficient stability [$F(16,64)$]	. . .	. . .	. . .	. . .	1.79*	3.07***
Variance stability [$F(14,50)$]	. . .	. . .	. . .	. . .	9.26***	8.98***
Overall stability [$\chi^2(17)$]	. . .	. . .	. . .	. . .	46.75***	39.92***

a. For variable definitions, notational conventions, and significance levels, see table 1. All stability tests are based on regression equations with six lags. Small-sample biases are indicated in tables 3, 4, and 5.
b. X vector (first row) = monetary variable: Y vector (second row) = labor market variable.

maxima and minima and functional forms that can change rapidly over a small interval. Estimates of feedback at neighboring frequencies are positively correlated, but correlation diminishes with the distance between frequencies. When the distance becomes $\pi/3$ in the case of six lags or $\pi/5$ in the case of ten, the estimates are asymptotically independent, and the same is true of integer multiples of these distances.[10] Estimates with other separations are weakly correlated. Consequently, estimates of feedback in the secular long run are positively correlated with those in the business cycle frequencies and those at the infinitely long run, but when lag length is ten, estimates in the business cycle frequencies and at the infinitely long run are probably only weakly correlated.

Little is known about the small sample properties of the estimates presented here, but some features that assist in interpretation can reasonably be surmised. The estimates are maximum likelihood (conditional on presample values and truncation), which implies a probable downward bias in variance estimates and a corresponding upward bias in feedback estimates in finite sample. By analogy with linear regression with nonstochastic regressors, a rough approximation to this upward bias is $\ln[(T-k_2)/(T-k_1)]$, where T is sample size, k_1 is the number of regressors per equation, and k_2 is the number of regressors with nonzero coefficients if there is no feedback of the type in question. Biases so estimated are indicated parenthetically in all tables (except table 2, because of space constraints); the estimated bias at each frequency is the same as the bias for the estimate of overall directional feedback. Biases are often substantial relative to estimates of overall feedback, but usually small relative to estimated measures of feedback at low frequencies in those cases in which estimated feedback is substantively large in the estimation period 1955:1–1971:2.

Monetary Policy and Labor Market Activity

Measures of feedback between the monetary growth rate and two measures of labor market activity, Un^{-1} and $Quit$, were estimated for the two sample periods. Numerical results are shown in table 2, and

10. John Geweke, "Causality, Exogeneity, and Inference," in Werner Hildenbrand, ed., *Advances in Econometrics* (Cambridge University Press, forthcoming).

figures 1 and 2 provide a graphical presentation. There is unambiguous evidence of bidirectional feedback during 1955:1–1971:2, and with the exception of instantaneous feedback, there is little difference in the results using Un^{-1} and those using *Quit*. In all cases, directional feedback is concentrated in the lower frequencies. In the case of feedback from the monetary growth rate to the measures of labor market activity, feedback is strongest at business cycle frequencies. Referring to estimates based on ten lags shown in figures 1 and 2, for Un^{-1} the peak is 1.258 at 12 quarters (point *A* in figure 1), which after bias correction indicates that $\triangle\ln(M1)$ innovations account for 65 percent of the variance in Un^{-1} at this frequency. For *Quit* there are two peaks of roughly equal magnitude at 6 and 14 quarters (points *A* and *B* in figure 2) where $\triangle\ln(M1)$ innovations again account for about 65 percent of the variance in the labor market variable; the double peak, and the fact that the contribution of the $\triangle\ln(M1)$ innovation to variance in *Quit* is at least 35 percent at any business cycle frequency, account for the fact that feedback to *Quit* is estimated to be greater than feedback to Un^{-1}. The greater flexibility of functional form afforded by ten lags (relative to six) is indicated by the estimated decomposition of feedback from $\triangle\ln(M1)$ to Un^{-1} and *Quit*. In particular, note the greater difference in estimates at 12.80 quarters and the infinitely long run for 10 lags.

In the case of feedback from either labor market activity variable to the monetary growth rate, feedback is concentrated in the secular long run, rather than in the business cycle frequencies. The nature of feedback from $\triangle\ln(M1)$ is very similar for both labor market variables. The top panels of figures 1 and 2 show a sharp peak in the six- to eight-year range, with negligible feedback at immediately higher frequencies (the business cycle), and strong tapering toward the zero frequency. In both cases the innovation in the labor market activity variable accounts for over 90 percent of the variation in the monetary growth rate at the long-run peak. Feedback at the infinitely long run is statistically significant, except when six lags are used with Un^{-1}. Given the magnitude of feedback in the secular long run and the positive correlation of estimates over all of these frequencies even with ten lags, this may be an artifact of parameterization. The introduction of yet more lags might resolve this point.

Thus, the monetary growth rate and labor market activity were related over the period 1955:1–1971:2. This association was due

Figure 1. *Feedback between Monetary Growth Rate and Inverse of Civilian Unemployment Rate, 1955:1–1971:2, Ten Lags*

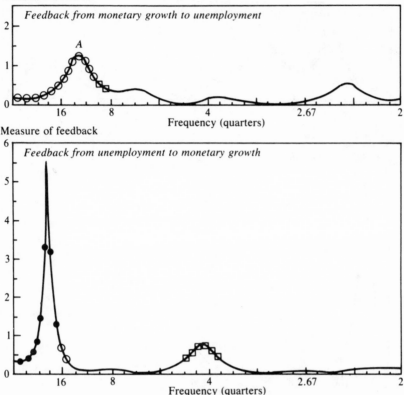

Measure of feedback

Measure of feedback

Frequency (quarters)

Frequency (quarters)

● Significantly different from zero at the 1 percent significance level.
○ 5 percent level.
□ 10 percent level.

primarily to the effect on labor market activity of variations in M1 growth over the business cycle, and to a dependence of M1 growth on labor market activity in the long run. These results speak to two of the polar cases discussed in the preceding section. The proposition that money is neutral in its long-run effect on labor market activity does not fare badly. Some statistical ambiguity arises because of the difficulty of sorting out feedback at business cycles from that in the long run. When six lags are used, point estimates of feedback from $\Delta\ln(M1)$ to Un^{-1} or *Quit* at frequency zero are statistically significant,

Figure 2. *Feedback between Monetary Growth Rate
and Manufacturing Quit Rate, 1955:1–1971:2, Ten Lags*

Measure of feedback

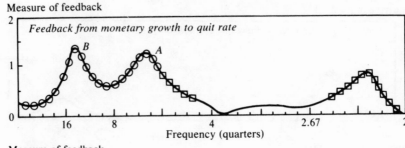

Measure of feedback

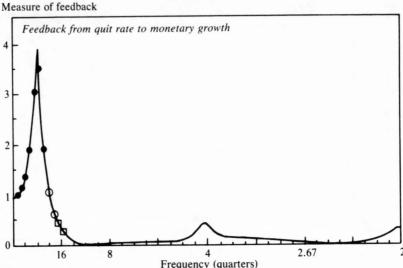

● Significantly different from zero at the 1 percent significance level.
○ 5 percent level.
□ 10 percent level.

but could result from the positive correlation of this estimate with the
large estimates of feedback at business cycle frequencies. Support for
this interpretation is provided by the changes in the point estimates
that result when ten lags are used. Point estimates are reduced, to the
point of statistical insignificance in the case of Un^{-1}, and to the point
of little economic consequence in either case: after the bias correction
described above, $\triangle\ln(M1)$ innovations account for less than 4 percent
of the variance in *Quit* in the infinitely long run.

Strong feedback at business cycle frequencies again arises as a complicating factor when one attempts to answer the question "How long is the long run?" for classical neutrality propositions, but it seems plausible on the basis of these results that it is not much more than ten years. A statistical test for no feedback at frequencies corresponding to ten years fails, but that is clearly a consequence of the fact that even with ten lags it is impossible to have no feedback at these frequencies without having implausibly small feedback at the business cycle frequencies: point estimates are about the same size as the conjectured small-sample bias in the estimates.

The most obvious feature of figures 1 and 2 is the very large estimate of feedback from either measure of labor market activity to the monetary growth rate at a frequency corresponding to a period of about seven years (twenty-eight quarters). The estimates imply that well over 90 percent of the variance in the monetary growth rate is ascribed to variance in labor market activity variables at this frequency. Over the whole range of frequencies corresponding to periods exceeding five years, the estimates of feedback from labor market activity variables to the monetary growth rate are large and statistically significant, but as before it is difficult to discriminate finely within this interval. In natural-rate models these phenomena are consistent with an interpretation of changes in the monetary growth rate as attempts to sustain an unnatural rate of unemployment. This interpretation is reinforced by the coefficient estimates themselves in the autoregression, which imply that a 1 percent standard deviation increase in the innovation of Un^{-1} leads eventually to an addition of 4.2 percent to the annualized rate of growth of the money stock.[11]

Virtually no statement can be made about the 1970s with any degree of statistical confidence, except that the nature of feedback to $\triangle\ln(M1)$ was not the same as in the earlier period. To a large extent these results may simply reflect the greater volatility of $\triangle\ln(M1)$ in the period 1971:3–1978:4 noted in table 1.

Monetary Policy, Labor Market Activity, and Wage Inflation

Measures of feedback between monetary policy and labor market activity, taken together as a vector, and wage inflation are now

11. More explicitly, let x_t be monetary growth and y_t be Un^{-1} in equation 10. Let v_{3t} have mean 0 and variance τ^2. If the mean of v_{3t} were increased to 0.01τ, then the mean of the monetary growth rate (x_t) would increase by 4.2 percent.

examined. In addition to the monetary policy and labor market activity variables already introduced, the rate of consumer price inflation, $\Delta\ln(\text{CPI})$, is also employed, as a substitute for $\Delta\ln(\text{M1})$. This is done because of the importance of the consumer price index or very similar variables in the theory of wage adjustment and wage equations, and because it is plausible that the monetary growth rate may affect wage inflation primarily through its effect on the prices of goods and services. In order to render the dynamics more easily understood and to emphasize the marginal contribution of individual constituents to feedback from a vector of time series to the rate of wage inflation at various frequencies, first estimates of feedback between $\Delta\ln(W)$ and individual variables are considered, and then estimates of feedback between $\Delta\ln(W)$ and the vector.

Estimates of measures of feedback between Un^{-1}, *Quit*, $\Delta\ln(\text{M1})$, and $\Delta\ln(\text{CPI})$, respectively, and $\Delta\ln(W)$ for the period 1955:1–1971:2 are provided in tables 3 and 4. It is evident that feedback is essentially unidirectional; there is little evidence of feedback of likely economic consequence from the rate of wage inflation to any of the other variables. On statistical grounds one can reject the hypothesis of no feedback from $\Delta\ln(W)$ to Un^{-1} with six lags, but the feedback responsible occurs at the seasonal harmonic. This suggests least squares bias for behavioral wage equations in which wages are not constrained to respond smoothly to movements in unemployment, but from a macroeconomic perspective the important point is that feedback from $\Delta\ln(W)$ to Un^{-1} is small and statistically insignificant at frequencies corresponding to the business cycle and the secular long run. The most important source of feedback from $\Delta\ln(W)$ to any of these variables is that to $\Delta\ln(\text{CPI})$ at business cycle frequencies.

The magnitude of feedback from labor market activity series and consumer price growth rates appears to be large, and estimates are significantly nonzero at the lower frequencies corresponding to periods longer than those of a typical business cycle. With six lags feedback appears to diminish slowly as frequencies increase; feedback at business cycle frequencies is still important. The incorporation of ten lags, which removes most correlation between estimates at the very long run and in the business cycle frequencies, shows that feedback to the rate of wage inflation is a long-run phenomenon. With ten lags, feedback is strongest at or very near (thirty years or more) the zero frequency, accounting for 80 percent to 90 percent of the long-run variation in the rate of wage inflation.

Table 3. *Estimated Measures of Feedback between Wage Inflation and Univariate Indicators of Labor Market Activity and Monetary Policy, 1955:1–1971:2, Six Lags*[a]

Measure of feedback, overall and specific frequencies (quarters)	X and Y vectors[b]			
	Un^{-1} $\Delta ln(W)$	$\Delta ln(CPI)$ $\Delta ln(W)$	$\Delta ln(M1)$ $\Delta ln(W)$	Quit $\Delta ln(W)$
$F_{X,Y}$ (.246)	0.487***	0.392**	0.339**	0.293*
$F_{X \cdot Y}$ (.020)	0.001	0.016	0.085**	0.007
$F_{X \to Y}$ (.113)	0.240*	0.235**	0.154	0.281**
∞	1.500**	0.500**	0.026	2.278***
42.67	1.192**	0.503*	0.029	1.361***
12.80	0.652**	0.461***	0.100	0.568**
4.00	0.073	0.174	0.272	0.167
2.67	0.069	0.163	0.243**	0.027
2.00	0.007	0.002	0.214	0.432
$F_{Y \to X}$ (.113)	0.246**	0.141*	0.100	0.005
∞	0.001	0.276*	0.240	0.084
42.67	0.028	0.031	0.230	0.086
12.80	0.319	0.568*	0.107	0.061
4.00	0.270	0.009	0.068	0.135
2.67	0.084	0.049	0.072	0.035
2.00	0.756***	0.124	0.114	0.003

a. For variable definitions, notational conventions, and significance levels, see table 1. Small-sample biases are shown parenthetically here and in following tables.
b. X vector shown in first row, Y vector shown in second row.

In principle, interpretation of the bivariate results shown in tables 3 and 4 could be confounded by the bidirectional feedback between monetary growth rates and labor market activity variables, but the results are not affected drastically when measures of linear feedback between monetary growth rates or consumer price inflation and labor market activity, taken jointly on the one hand, and the rate of wage inflation, on the other, are estimated. Estimates are shown numerically in tables 5 and 6 and some are presented graphically in figures 3 and 4. Feedback from wage inflation to consumer price inflation at business cycle frequencies is once again evident; comparison of the relevant estimates in table 5 with those in table 6 indicates that feedback is probably confined to business cycle frequencies. Estimated feedback from wage inflation to other variables tends to be greatest in these frequencies even when it is not statistically significant. Interestingly, the sole case in which the hypothesis of no feedback from wage

Table 4. *Estimated Measures of Feedback between Wage Inflation and Univariate Indicators of Labor Market Activity and Monetary Policy, 1955:1–1977:2, Ten Lags*[a]

Measure of feedback, overall and specific frequencies (quarters)	X and Y vectors[b]			
	Un^{-1} $\triangle ln(W)$	$\triangle ln(CPI)$ $\triangle ln(W)$	$\triangle ln(M1)$ $\triangle ln(W)$	Quit $\triangle ln(W)$
$F_{X,Y}$ (.450)	0.623***	0.609***	0.523**	0.617***
$F_{X \cdot Y}$ (.024)	0.000	0.011	0.083*	0.088*
$F_{X \to Y}$ (.213)	0.316	0.333*	0.259	0.423**
∞	3.674***	1.548**	0.112	2.133***
42.67	1.060**	1.140*	0.151	1.897***
12.80	0.292	0.110	0.578	0.346
4.00	0.095	0.542*	0.432	0.535
2.67	0.290	0.403*	0.118	0.249
2.00	0.076	0.019	0.093	0.108
$F_{Y \to X}$ (.213)	0.307	0.265	0.181	0.106
∞	0.202	0.001	0.772*	0.146
42.67	0.426	0.119**	0.579	0.159
12.80	0.626	1.469**	0.001	0.083
4.00	0.304	0.198	0.201	0.303
2.67	0.163	0.174	0.081	0.207
2.00	0.495	0.259	0.314	0.068

a. For variable definitions, notational conventions, and significance levels, see table 1.
b. X vector shown in first row, Y vector shown in second row.

inflation can be rejected formally at the 5 percent level is that in which the nonwage variables are Un^{-1} and $\triangle ln(CPI)$, the two most common constituents of wage equations. In this case feedback from wage inflation peaks at about sixteen quarters, where its innovation accounts for over 95 percent of the generalized variance in Un^{-1} and $\triangle ln(CPI)$.

Feedback to $\triangle ln(W)$ is primarily a low-frequency phenomenon, but there is evidence of short-run feedback, too. To discriminate between business cycle and long-run frequencies, consider the results in table 6 and in figures 3 and 4. Estimated feedback at business cycle frequencies is never statistically significant, and except for Un^{-1} and $\triangle ln(M1)$, is of about the same size as conjectured bias. When the quit rate is included, statistically significant feedback for periods of five to eight quarters is evident. In every case feedback to $\triangle ln(W)$ is strongest at very low frequencies, where innovations in the other two variables account for between 90 percent [in the case of Un^{-1} and $\triangle ln(M1)$] and

Table 5. *Estimated Measures of Feedback between Wage Inflation and Bivariate Indicators of Labor Market Activity and Monetary Policy, 1955:1–1971:2, Six Lags*[a]

Measure of feedback, overall and specific frequencies (quarters)	X and Y vectors[b]			
	Un^{-1}, $\Delta ln(M1)$ $\Delta ln(W)$	Quit, $\Delta ln(CPI)$ $\Delta ln(W)$	Un^{-1}, $\Delta ln(CPI)$ $\Delta ln(W)$	Quit, $\Delta ln(M1)$ $\Delta ln(W)$
$F_{X,Y}$ (.505)	0.741***	0.741***	0.715***	0.709***
$F_{X \cdot Y}$ (.023)	0.018	0.109**	0.018	0.162***
$F_{X \to Y}$ (.241)	0.500**	0.395**	0.344*	0.418**
∞	1.976**	2.574**	0.988	2.604***
42.67	1.099***	1.151**	1.105	1.361***
12.80	0.819*	0.625**	0.613***	0.751*
4.00	0.405	0.392	0.351	0.351
2.67	0.456***	0.255	0.306	0.221*
2.00	0.627*	0.225	0.005	0.745
Significance test of $X1$ $[F(6,44)]$[c]	2.86**	1.31	0.77	2.20*
Significance test of $X2$ $[F(6,44)]$[d]	2.42**	1.27	1.34	1.14
$F_{Y \to X}$ (.241)	0.223	0.237*	0.353**	0.129
∞	0.039	0.448*	0.316	0.227
42.67	0.060	0.490	0.368	0.244
12.80	0.325	0.793	0.912	0.280
4.00	0.225	0.148	0.203	0.218
2.67	0.093	0.105	0.164	0.032
2.00	0.597**	0.095	0.724**	0.082

a. For variable definitions, notational conventions, and significance levels, see table 1.
b. *X* vector shown in first row, *Y* vector shown in second row.
c. *X*1 represents labor market activity variable.
d. *X*2 represents monetary or price variables.

99.9 percent [Un^{-1} and $\Delta ln(CPI)$] of the variance in the rate of wage inflation. Feedback at higher frequencies, corresponding to periods of a year or less, is sometimes statistically significant and sometimes not, but never nonnegligible, accounting for anywhere between 20 percent and 70 percent of the variance in wage inflation, depending on frequency and series.

Thus there is a very strong and statistically significant relationship between the rate of wage inflation on the one hand, and measures of labor market activity and monetary policy on the other. The association is due almost entirely to the long-run effect of labor market activity and monetary policy on wage inflation, and the marginal contribution

Table 6. *Estimated Measures of Feedback between Wage Inflation and Bivariate Indicators of Labor Market Activity and Monetary Policy, 1955:1–1971:2, Ten Lags*[a]

Measure of feedback, overall and specific frequencies (quarters)	X and Y vectors[b]			
	Un^{-1}, $\triangle ln(M1)$ $\triangle ln(W)$	Quit, $\triangle ln(CPI)$ $\triangle ln(W)$	Un^{-1}, $\triangle ln(CPI)$ $\triangle ln(W)$	Quit, $\triangle ln(M1)$ $\triangle ln(W)$
$F_{X,Y}$ (.764)	1.335***	1.452***	1.170***	1.096***
$F_{X·Y}$ (.028)	0.020	0.186**	0.001	0.134*
$F_{X \to Y}$ (.368)	0.858**	0.844***	0.617	0.656*
∞	2.672***	3.844***	7.358***	4.366***
42.67	2.061***	1.638***	2.331**	1.559
12.80	2.084	0.473	0.424	0.183
4.00	1.229***	1.650**	0.552	0.783
2.67	0.867*	0.895**	0.805	0.350
2.00	0.577*	0.066	0.012	0.316
Significance test of $X1$ $[F(10,32)]$[c]	2.23**	2.38**	0.96	1.69
Significance test of $X2$ $[F(10,32)]$[d]	2.08*	1.93*	1.30	0.85
$F_{Y \to X}$ (.368)	0.457*	0.423	0.552**	0.306
∞	0.128	0.240	0.037	0.149
42.67	0.217	0.326	0.097	0.189
12.80	0.841	1.688***	1.650*	0.670
4.00	0.644	0.265	0.366	0.678
2.67	0.072	0.352	0.663	0.200
2.00	0.354	0.686	0.688	0.081

a. For variable definitions, notational conventions, and significance levels, see table 1.
b. X vector shown in first row, Y vector shown in second row.
c. X1 represents labor market activity variable.
d. X2 represents monetary or price variables.

of labor market activity to this effect is greater than that of monetary policy. In terms of goodness of fit, Un^{-1} and $\triangle ln(M1)$ provide the best explanation of $\triangle ln(W)$.

These results can be given an economic interpretation within the framework set forth in the introduction. The results for the bivariate system incorporating the monetary growth rate and labor market activity variables supported the implication of the long-run competitive labor market cum monetary growth hypothesis, that innovations in the monetary growth rate should have no effect on labor market activity in the long run. The results for the three variable systems are less favorable for two other implications of this hypothesis: that wage growth is a monetary phenomenon, and that in the long run wage

Figure 3. *Feedback between Inverse of Civilian Unemployment Rate and Monetary Growth Rate, and Rate of Wage Inflation, 1955:1–1971:2, Ten Lags*

Measure of feedback

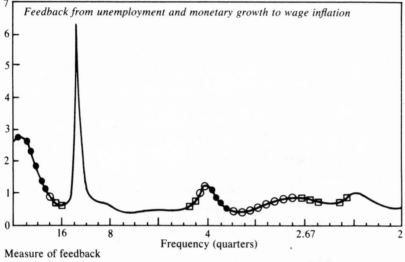

Feedback from unemployment and monetary growth to wage inflation

Frequency (quarters)

Measure of feedback

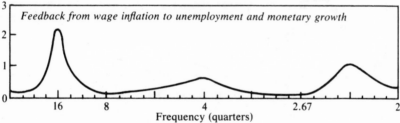

Feedback from wage inflation to unemployment and monetary growth

Frequency (quarters)

● Significantly different from zero at the 1 percent significance level.
○ 5 percent level.
□ 10 percent level.

inflation and measures of labor market activity are independent. There simply is no evidence that nominal wages are primarily a monetary phenomenon. In the long run, innovations in the monetary growth rate are estimated to account for about 10 percent of the variation in the wage growth rate, and this estimate is not significantly different from zero.[12] The implication that wage inflation and labor market activity

12. By contrast, when the same methodology is applied to the rates of growth of the money supply and gross national product deflator and the same sample period, the innovations in the former explain over 98 percent of the variation in the latter in the long run. See Geweke, "Causality, Exogeneity, and Inference."

Figure 4. *Feedback between Manufacturing Quit Rate and Consumer Price Inflation, and Rate of Wage Inflation, 1955:1–1971:2, Ten Lags*

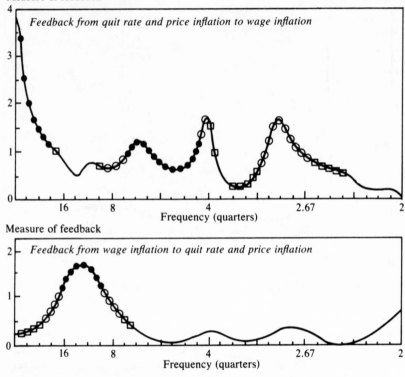

Measure of feedback

Feedback from quit rate and price inflation to wage inflation

Frequency (quarters)

Measure of feedback

Feedback from wage inflation to quit rate and price inflation

Frequency (quarters)

● Significantly different from zero at the 1 percent significance level.
○ 5 percent level.
□ 10 percent level.

are independent in the long run is clearly incompatible with these data. There are effects of labor market activity on wage inflation in the long run, and in the presence of measures of labor market activity there is no marginal contribution of innovations in the monetary growth rate to long-run variation in wage inflation.

The wage-standard hypothesis is rejected by these findings only in an extreme form, which asserts that movements in the nominal wage reflect a bargaining process on which labor market activity has no bearing in the long run. Labor market activity has an influence on wage inflation in the long run, but the wage standard can incorporate such an influence. Perhaps the most important implication of this hypothesis is that the monetary growth rate passively follows the wage growth rate. Conventional statistical methods focusing on overall feedback from wage inflation to the monetary growth rate would find no evidence of this effect, but after decomposition by frequency, long-run variations in the innovation of wage inflation are estimated to explain over half the variation in monetary growth rate. Considering the influence of secular change in other (omitted) variables like technical progress and labor supply, this estimate would seem to be very consistent with the wage-standard hypothesis. Unfortunately, the point estimate is significantly different from zero only at the 10 percent level: the data are weak, not the hypothesis.

These findings are most consistent with a strong version of the conventional Phillips curve model in which long-run movements in the rate of wage inflation and the monetary growth rate are the consequences of persistent movements in unemployment. Over the very long run (operationally, at frequency zero), labor market activity measured in any of the ways mentioned here accounts for at least 80 percent of the variation in wage inflation, a fraction significantly different from zero at the 1 percent level. This observation is not affected when the labor market activity variable is used in conjunction with either the monetary growth rate or the rate of growth of consumer prices, whose marginal contribution to long-run variations in the rate of wage inflation is quite small. Since no evidence is found of an effect of wage inflation on labor market activity at any frequency, the natural-rate interpretation of the Phillips curve is not supported. As emphasized in the introduction, this conclusion must rest on the assumption that reaction times of marginal agents are longer than a quarter; if not, the finding of no feedback from wage inflation to the unemployment rate is consistent with the natural-rate interpretation. Monthly data might prove useful in resolving this point.

When similar estimates are made for the period 1971:3–1978:4, very little is statistically significantly different from zero. Results for the bivariate systems using six lags are shown in table 7. In those equations whose dependent variable was one of the series for which there was evidence of change in the univariate autoregressive representation in table 1, stability over the entire period 1955:1–1978:4 is again rejected. Feedback from $\triangle \ln(W)$ to the other four variables once again appears much less important than directional feedback from these to $\triangle \ln(W)$, but the hypothesis that the pertinent equations remained unchanged

Table 7. *Estimated Measures of Feedback between Wage Inflation and Univariate Indicators of Labor Market Activity and Monetary Policy, 1971:3–1978:4, Six Lags*[a]

Measure of feedback, overall and specific frequencies (quarters)	X and Y vectors[b]			
	Un^{-1}, $\triangle ln(W)$	$\triangle ln(CPI)$ $\triangle ln(W)$	$\triangle ln(M1)$ $\triangle ln(W)$	Quit $\triangle ln(W)$
$F_{X,Y}$ (.788)	1.050	0.546	0.684	0.994
$F_{X \cdot Y}$ (.074)	0.103	0.033	0.007	0.050
$F_{X \to Y}$ (.357)	0.356	0.305	0.481	0.739
∞	0.032	4.072***	4.099	0.164
42.55	0.066	1.816**	1.249	0.221
12.82	0.025	0.293	0.265	0.002
4.00	1.090	0.043	0.156	0.087
2.67	0.343	0.068	0.339	0.199
2.00	0.087	0.038	0.026	1.297
Coefficient stability [$F(16,64)$]	1.45	1.35	1.12	1.53
Variance stability [$F(14,56)$]	2.18**	1.29	1.54	2.58***
Overall stability [$\chi^2(17)$]	20.36	18.98	15.86	22.27
$F_{Y \to X}$ (.357)	0.591	0.208	0.194	0.205
∞	1.204	0.208	0.078	0.589
42.55	1.715	0.218	0.081	0.248*
12.82	1.101	0.404	0.103	0.162*
4.00	0.192	0.153	0.249	0.099
2.67	0.160	0.076	0.373	1.018
2.00	0.127	0.000	0.003	0.063
Coefficient stability [$F(16,64)$]	1.30	2.15**	1.54	1.15
Variance stability [$F(14,50)$]	0.43	3.06***	7.15***	1.18
Overall stability [$\chi^2(17)$]	28.06**	30.45**	37.57***	16.88

a. For variable definitions, notational conventions, and significance levels, see table 1.
b. X vector shown in first row, Y vector shown in second row.

is rejected in three out of four cases. Although interpretation is confounded by statistical insignificance resulting from only thirty observations, the structure of feedback from monetary and labor market activity variables indicated in table 7 seems drastically different from that which seems to have prevailed in the earlier period. Estimated feedback from monetary and consumer price growth rates to wage

inflation is now very strong at long-run frequencies, accounting for 60
to 98 percent of the variation in wage inflation as one moves from the
secular to the very long run. Feedback from the labor market activity
variables is unimportant at all but seasonal frequencies. Feedback of
this type appears more consistent with the monetary growth–competitive labor market hypothesis than that found for the earlier period;
but until means for coping with short samples are devised, one can
infer with confidence very little about periods like the 1970s.

Summary and Conclusion

In this paper, measures of feedback between time series (introduced
elsewhere by the author)[13] were used to describe some relationships
between the monetary growth rate, measures of labor market activity,
and wage and price inflation in the United States during the period
1955:1–1978:4. In this methodology, linear dependence between two
vector time series is additively decomposed into linear feedback from
the first to the second, feedback from the second to the first, and
instantaneous linear feedback. The two measures of directional feedback may in turn be additively decomposed into measures of linear
feedback by frequencies. It was argued that this decomposition by
frequency corresponds well to the notions of the short run and long
run employed in the comparative statics analysis of economic theory.
(This analysis varies in how specific it is about dynamics but is always
vague about chronological time.) The decomposition also permits
identification of those aspects of the relationships between time series
that reflect or account for the business cycle.

Estimates of measures of feedback were presented for two kinds of
relationships: those between monetary growth rates and labor market
disturbances; and those between these two groups of variables and
nominal wage inflation. Strong evidence was found that most of these
relationships were different in the subperiods 1955:1–1971:2 and 1971:3–
1978:4, and so the two subperiods were treated separately. Estimated
measures of feedback for the former period were in many cases large
and often statistically significant, whereas those for the latter were
never statistically significantly different from zero, although point
estimates were sometimes large.

13. Geweke, "Measurement of Linear Dependence."

Empirical findings for the first subperiod can be summarized as follows:

1. Strong bidirectional feedback was found between the monetary growth rate (the rate of growth of M1 within each quarter) and labor market activity (whether measured by the inverse of the civilian unemployment rate or the manufacturing quit rate). Feedback from the monetary growth rate to the labor market variables was concentrated in frequencies corresponding to a period of three to five years. Feedback in the other direction was concentrated about frequencies corresponding to periods of eight years or more, somewhat longer than a typical business cycle.

2. With one exception, little evidence of feedback from nominal wage inflation to the other variables was found. The exception was the monetary growth rate: in the very long run—frequencies corresponding to periods of ten years or longer—feedback from wage inflation to money growth accounts for over half the variance in the latter in a bivariate relationship.

3. There is strong feedback from the measures of labor market activity to the rate of wage growth, and it is concentrated in the long run—frequencies corresponding to periods ten years or longer. Either measure of labor market activity employed here accounts for over 80 percent of the variance in the rate of wage inflation at these frequencies.

4. When the monetary growth rate is introduced by estimating measures of feedback between wage inflation and a vector consisting of one of the labor market variables and money growth, its marginal contribution is at most small. When this exercise is repeated with the rate of growth of the consumer price index in lieu of M1 growth, the marginal contribution of CPI growth is larger, but the measures of labor market activity are still the predominant source of feedback into wage inflation.

The implications of these findings were considered for specific relationships among macroeconomic policy variables, labor market activity, and wage inflation that have arisen in the macroeconomic theory of the long run. The theory of the long run is that which assumes perfect factor mobility and thereby the validity of aggregation and which abstracts from phenomena associated with the business cycle. The contribution of the present paper is that it defines and abstracts long-run relationships between time series from those associated with the business cycle and does so in a way that preserves orderings among variables. Implications of alternative theories of the long run may then be compared with estimates of feedback at frequencies corresponding to long periods.

The simple classical model in which wage inflation is driven by monetary growth and labor markets are regarded as competitive is supported by the finding of no long-run feedback from the monetary growth rate to labor market activity. On the other hand, the evidence strongly suggests that in the long run wage growth is a function of labor market activity, rather than a monetary phenomenon. The wage-standard model, whose main implication is that monetary growth passively follows wage inflation, receives support from the finding of long-run feedback from wage inflation into monetary growth. The findings provide strong support for the hypothesis that long-run variations in monetary policy, labor market activity, and wage inflation are the consequence of persistent deviations in the unemployment rate from its natural rate.

A tentative description of long-run dynamics for monetary growth, labor market activity, and wage inflation for the period 1955:1–1971:2 emerges from these results. Labor market activity (as measured by the inverse of the civilian unemployment rate or the manufacturing quit rate) was responsible for most wage inflation during this period. There is strong evidence that long-run variations in the monetary growth rate can be ascribed to this same source. Other evidence, more suggestive because point estimates are not so precise, is consistent with the idea that this influence occurred in part through the nominal wage: as in the wage-standard model, monetary authorities over the years have confirmed wage trends by appropriate responses in the money supply.

Given this interpretation, it would be unwise to regard wage inflation as a monetary phenomenon. A policy regime in which monetary growth does not respond to wage inflation might be possible, but reliable quantitative knowledge of how such a regime would function is not likely to be gleaned from the postwar period. The data may tell us more about the functioning of a wage-standard regime, which appears to be more viable politically. The findings reported here point to variations in labor market activity as a very important source of wage inflation. It is primarily long-run variations in labor market activity that influence long-run variations in wages; the influence is uncovered in a clear way by the frequency decomposition methodology employed in this paper, but overall is obscured by business cycle variations and would at most surely be unnoticed by myopic policymakers. This influence is consistent with natural-rate theories of unemployment, but this interpretation has not been examined critically here. From a policy perspective, it clearly would be desirable to sort out policy-induced variations in labor market activity from endogenous ones in order to study their respective long-run influences on wage inflation.

Comments by Christopher A. Sims

Geweke has applied a valuable new statistical tool to the analysis of wage determination. The conclusions I find most interesting are: (1) a conventional reduced-form Phillips curve approach—ignoring the possibility that feedback from errors in the wage equation to the consumer price index and unemployment might bias estimates—is incompatible with the data; and (2) wages and labor market conditions are strongly related even at very low frequencies, that is, in the "long run." Each of these results runs counter to a simple but influential view of how the economy functions. Geweke's work is a good example of the value of serious attention to the data in conditioning substantive debate.

Geweke's results would be even more helpful had he not focused exclusively on the one descriptive measure he employs in this paper—the decomposition of variance in a variable by "source of shock" and by frequency. There are certain kinds of questions about the data that cannot be answered by these measures. For example, conclusion 2 above might be interpreted as implying that demand-management policy is set off on wide swings by temporary oscillations of the labor market. The same descriptive result, however, could also have been generated by a strong association of long swings in labor market variables with long swings in the wage. This latter result might emerge in a classical model with inelastic aggregate demand producing inverse simultaneous movements of employment and the wage level. Or finally it might have emerged from a situation in which long swings in wages about the trend line are very small, so that the allocation of percentages of long-run variance to various sources is a pointless exercise. These ambiguities could have been resolved by display of parts of the moving average representations of the systems Geweke estimated, along with the variance decompositions. The moving average representation gives the shape of the response of each variable to each shock.

A paradox emerges in footnote 12. We are told that feedback from money to the GNP deflator at low frequencies has been found to be strong in previous work, while this paper concludes that feedback from money to wage growth is weak in low frequencies. Does this mean that monetary expansions lead to declines in real wages in the long run? One cannot tell without seeing the moving average representation. Furthermore, one suspects that this paradox might disappear or change in form if a system containing wages, prices, money, and real variables were jointly estimated. There is no reason Geweke's methods could not be applied to larger systems, and future work with such systems ought to be on the research agenda.

The paper makes a major point of the absence of feedback from nominal wages to unemployment as a strike against the natural-rate hypothesis. This is somewhat surprising. The main advocates of the natural-rate hypothesis as an econometric specification have ordinarily maintained that information delays are on the order of one quarter or less, so that it becomes a prediction of the theory that there is no feedback from the wage variable (or any other single nominal variable) into the real variables of the model as a block. Sargent has even presented a test of Granger causal priority of unemployment (that is, of absence of feedback from other variables into unemployment) as a test of the natural-rate hypothesis. Geweke could be right that it is natural to suppose that information delays exceed a quarter. (It is hard for me to see why delays based on information availability should be that long—or even why they should be taken seriously as a source of cyclical variability.) Nonetheless it appears to be a mistake to claim that his statistical results have much resolving power on this issue.

It may be worth noting that the paper's test for constancy of the model across subperiods seems to show little evidence of shift in form of the autoregressive equations. (This is what Geweke calls coefficient stability in table 1.) Two of five variables show shifts marginally significant at the 5 percent level on this measure, with only one of these test statistics much above 2. The Akaike criterion, which, roughly speaking, attempts to retain rejectable restrictions only when they are far enough wrong to worsen mean square error, would sharply reject stability for only one of the equations. Applied to the joint models Geweke uses, it might well favor parameter stability. Of course the variance decompositions Geweke presents would be strongly affected by changes in the variances of shocks to the system, which are clearly important.

The above argument provides another reason for paying attention to moving average representations, which are little affected by changes in relative variances of shocks. The pattern of much stronger evidence for changes in the sizes of shocks to autoregressive structures than for changes in their coefficients is one which I have observed in work of my own with other sets of variables as well. It is encouraging in that it implies that autoregressive structures may continue to extrapolate fairly well even when there have been substantial shifts in the nature of policy or nonpolicy disturbances to the economy.

This paper deserves close attention for the insight it provides into cyclical interactions of wages and labor market conditions, though readers should recognize that the policy conclusions consistent with the statistical results may include more than the range of conclusions presented explicitly in the paper.

Comments by Robert Hall

First of all, this paper has a very neat econometric idea worked out in it. It provides a method to decompose variance into a set of parts that add together to give the overall effect of one variable on another. This decomposition by frequency is very informative. The only quibble I have is that this is not altogether a new issue. To talk about how variables are related by frequency is exactly to talk about how distributed lag shapes look. A strong, low-frequency association is something that we often talk about. For instance, in Bob Gordon's work it has been particularly evident; it is simply a long, smooth, distributed lag. An association that is very much at high frequencies is more like a first difference of something that involves the very short end of a distributed lag. Frequencies are a different way of expressing a set of ideas that we have already had in terms of distributed lags, but the methodology is much more neatly worked out and much easier to talk about.

So much for the econometrics. I find the economics in the paper rather casual in some respects. There are no references to the literature of the 1970s on monetary surprises and real activity, on the Phillips curve and its relatives, or on long-term employment contracts. How can a paper on the money-employment-inflation issue cite Bailey but not Baily?

What I found most interesting are the results on the feedback from wages to other variables in the economy. In the paper that I gave at the Brookings panel in 1980, I pointed out an implication of the strongest form of contract theory: the wage has no allocational role in the economy. (That point was missed in the Mitchell-Kimbell paper, by the way.) In a contract economy, the wage is not the variable that is equated to the marginal product of labor in determining employment. Thus, the wage determines income distribution, not employment.

In Geweke's terms this should mean, in particular, that there is no feedback from the wage rate to the labor market tightness variables—unemployment or the quit rate—and, according to a very strict version of contract theory, no feedback to prices either. To my great surprise these predictions are confirmed. In Geweke's words: "It is evident that feedback is essentially unidirectional; there is little evidence of feedback of likely economic consequence from the rate of wage inflation to any of the other variables."

I think that result is terrific, but I find a complete absence of any mention of contract theory and its implications in the paper. If I were to send Geweke back to the library, it would be to read the papers on contract theory that come to exactly the conclusion that this is the way the economy should work. Notice what a great contradiction that is to standard IS-LM analysis, in which any wage surprises should have very important real effects. A wage surprise should be turned into a price surprise right away, and then create an important real surprise very soon in the IS-LM model.

The extreme version of contract theory, in contrast, suggests that even if there is a very large, positive wage surprise, it should not discourage employment at all, because that IS-LM apparatus is wrong in claiming that employment is determined by equating the value of the marginal product of labor to the wage. Instead, contracts have employment provisions that embody the principle of equating the marginal product to the value of labor's time. Wage payments are just labor's share of the total revenue of the firm. Wages do not determine marginal costs. Therefore, they do not determine prices or real output.

The other side of this story is the feedback from real variables to wages, a modern reexamination of Phillips curve ideas. There Geweke finds the feedback to be very strong. This supports the idea that if something goes wrong that is signaled by an unemployment rate that is too high or too low, then indeed wages do move in the market-clearing direction, and that is true even at low frequencies. If this is interpreted in terms of time domain and distributed lags, it means that a long distributed lag on real variables helps predict wages.

The next interpretive question is whether we expect from conventional ideas that a large weight should be given to lagged money in a wage regression. Geweke finds that labor market variables dominate money in predicting wages. But if money affects unemployment a lot and unemployment affects wages, then I do not think these findings contradict anyone's theory of the long-run neutrality of money. Long-run neutrality does not automatically mean that the sum of the coefficients on money in the wage equation is equal to one. Whether or not that sum is equal to one is actually a very subtle question. I do not think that the poor performance of money in predicting wages in competition with the unemployment rate really tells us anything about long-run neutrality.

To conclude, I think that the most interesting and relevant finding goes back to the issue of the allocational role of wages. Maybe my interpretation is completely wrong, but it seems that there are some results here that very much bear on the contract labor market idea and they should be pushed.

DANIEL J. B. MITCHELL *and* LARRY J. KIMBELL

Labor Market Contracts
and Inflation

THE GAP between theory and practice in wage determination has been difficult to bridge. Economists have long acknowledged that wage determination does not much resemble an auction process. In particular, the response of wages to labor market tightness or slack is surprisingly limited. But it was not until recently that the economics literature began seriously to explore the discrepancies.[1]

There are many characteristics of the labor market that are difficult to interpret in a simple demand-supply framework with its assumptions about costless wage adjustments and free labor mobility. The most important of these is that the response of employers to changes in business conditions focuses much more heavily on quantity adjustments (hours and employment) than on wage rates. In addition, wage rates seem to be adjusted in response to variables (such as the consumer price index) or in ways that are hard to explain in a simple market context.

A number of implications flow from this irregular behavior. It can be expected that the wage-determination process will have significant linkages to price setting and inflation. In turn, these linkages suggest that the response to orthodox anti-inflation policies—such as monetary restraint—could be affected by particular wage-determination char-

---

1. The discrepancies were the subject of an early debate between institutionalists and theorists in the 1940s. See Richard A. Lester, "Shortcomings of Marginal Analysis for Wage-Employment Problems," *American Economic Review*, vol. 36 (March 1946), pp. 63–82. By the 1960s, macroeconomic textbooks simply included assumptions about wage rigidity in their models without much analysis of why the rigidity existed. For example, see Gardner Ackley, *Macroeconomic Theory* (Macmillan, 1961), p. 403. More recent texts have tended to rely on empirical observation of limited wage sensitivity to labor market tightness or looseness. See Robert J. Gordon, *Macroeconomics* (Little, Brown, 1978), pp. 311–15.

acteristics. One purpose of this paper is to explore the qualitative impact such characteristics may be expected to have on the effectiveness of anti-inflation policy.

Although the labor market is the site of important deviations from simple economic models, there are other areas of the economy where special characteristics may also be present. Thus, a second important question is the relative significance of labor market processes when set in a realistic empirical macroeconomic model. For example, a particular characteristic of wage determination might tend to reduce the effectiveness of monetary policy in reducing inflation. But there may be processes in other sectors that have the same effect. In a simple model in which the labor market was the only source of anomalous behavior, changing the labor market characteristic might have a much more dramatic effect than it would in the real world.

A third issue is the assessment of tightness in the labor market. Policymakers interested in measuring this concept have a choice of alternative indexes that may give divergent impressions. They can look at indicators such as unemployment rates, vacancies, and measures of turnover (quits, layoffs, accessions) that appear directly related to the degree of excess demand and supply. Or they can watch wage developments. Obviously, alternative models of wage determination will lead to different assessments of these different types of indexes.

Wage-Determination Practices

Substantial differences in the processes of wage determination are found in the U.S. labor market. A common distinction is between union and nonunion wage-setting practices. However, even within these two divisions considerable variation exists. Over time the relative size of the two sectors has changed and internal practices have evolved.[2] There is no single theory that can honestly purport to explain completely what is currently practiced and why it has evolved. However, there are some institutional and legal constraints that provide useful insights.

2. Union and association membership in 1978 was estimated to include 22.2 percent of the labor force and 26.6 percent of employees in nonagricultural establishments. These figures have generally declined since the mid-1950s. See U.S. Department of Labor, Bureau of Labor Statistics, "Labor Union and Employee Association Membership—1978," press release USDL:79-605, September 3, 1979, p. 2.

And newer theories of contracting and employer-employee linkages are helpful in understanding what is observed.

Property Rights in Jobs

Some labor markets function on a very casual basis. In such markets, individuals may be hired to perform a specific task for a day or other short periods of time. Haggling over the payment to be made for the service may occur for each separate transaction. However, such arrangements are rare. More commonly, the word *job* implies some type of ongoing relationship between the employer and employee.

Usually, when an individual is hired, there is an initial understanding about terms and conditions of employment. These terms may eventually be changed. But for a significant period of time, the initial arrangement is expected to stand, a practice that imparts a certain rigidity to wage determination. At some point in the future the employer may find that he has a surplus or shortage of labor. In the case of a surplus, the employer typically reduces hours per worker, or numbers of workers, or both. Explicit wage cuts are unusual, although not unknown. When shortages occur, the employer may attempt to use the existing work force more intensively (say, by increasing overtime) or decrease hiring standards. Use of these quantitative adjustments suggests a resistance to viewing the wage-setting mechanism as the appropriate vehicle for cyclical adaptations. It also suggests a preference for tying internal labor market adjustments in the firm to a tangible indicator: the level of output.

These observations could be consistent with a property right in jobs of employees. If employees did have a formal property right, the value of that right would clearly be affected by either a price or quantity adjustment. Such rights could flow from an implicit or explicit contract with the employer. And such contracts might have contingency arrangements linked to the employer's demand for labor. It is in the nature of contingency provisions that they are linked to observable conditions, and that the responses they call forth are linked to those conditions in some reasonable way. An understanding that if output fell by, say, 10 percent, the employer could reduce labor input by up to 10 percent meets these criteria. It would surely be more reasonable than an arrangement that allowed the employer to reduce wages by whatever amount he felt appropriate whenever he felt that business conditions were bad.

All of this depends, however, on there being a property right in jobs. In the case of union agreements, such rights can be negotiated.[3] And in the public sector, civil service statutes generally provide such rights. However, in the nonunion private sector, property rights in jobs are either the creation of the employer or the by-product of some regulatory program.

Nonunion employers do make unilateral offers of property rights.[4] A nonunion firm may well provide its employees with company rule books that contain provisions similar to those in union contracts— grievance procedures, for example, or even arbitration in the event of unresolved grievances. Nonunion firms may establish policies of progressive discipline (a hierarchy of penalties typically starting with a warning) for misbehavior. Seniority may be given some weight in layoff, recall, and other decisions. General wage adjustments may occur only at stated intervals, often once a year. Formal progression plans, based on merit reviews with explicit criteria for evaluation, may be used to determine where an individual worker stands in the wage structure.

In general, good personnel management is thought to be character-ized by formality, central control, and the elimination of situations in which individual workers are subject to arbitrary treatment by super-visors. Thus, employees of a firm with good personnel management policies can expect to hold their jobs for as long as the firm needs to have the job performed, assuming satisfactory performance. They can expect to advance through the wage structure and possibly up a promotion ladder on the basis of unbiased merit reviews and perfor-mance evaluations. An interesting question is why employers should want to offer such terms. As will be discussed later, it was not always the case that they did.

---

3. For discussion of the concept of property rights in jobs, see Frederic Meyers, *Ownership of Jobs: A Comparative Study*, Monograph Series:11 (Los Angeles: University of California, Los Angeles, Institute of Industrial Relations, 1964).

4. Unfortunately, information on nonunion practices is more difficult to obtain than that on union practices because of the absence of written contracts. Examples of available sources are Ronald Berenbeim, *Nonunion Complaint Systems: A Corporate Appraisal*, Conference Board Report No. 770 (New York: Conference Board, 1980); and Bureau of National Affairs, *Layoff and Unemployment Compensation Policies*, Personnel Policies Forum Survey No. 128 (Washington: BNA, 1980).

Legal Reinforcement of Property Rights

In some countries, the legal nature of the employment contract is specified in great detail. Systems of labor courts function in a manner similar to private arbitrators under union agreements in the United States. After a period of time, workers acquire tenure in their positions. No such formal arrangements exist in the American legal system.

There are certain public policies, however, that encourage formalized personnel management practices. First, the right to organize is protected by statute, and procedures are provided for union representation elections. In recent years, unions have been winning less than half of such elections.[5] Nevertheless, the threat of organization exists for many employers and may influence their behavior. The notion of the "threat effect" in wage determination is familiar to labor economists.[6] However, in response to potential organization by a union, management may adopt personnel practices similar to those in the union sector. In recent years, a subspecies of management consultants has developed whose function is to help nonunion firms retain their unorganized status. The heavy-handed tactics of these consultants have received considerable publicity, particularly from unions. However, much of their advice consists of suggesting that management demonstrate to its nonrepresented employees that no gains would accrue from unionization.[7]

A second source of legal reinforcement of formalized personnel management comes from the various equal employment opportunity laws that have been adopted since 1964. Under title 7 of the Civil Rights Act of 1964, employers are forbidden from engaging in discriminatory practices on the basis of race, sex, religion, or national origin.[8] The first two categories have been the most important and have sparked a substantial volume of litigation. Federal government contractors are subject to more detailed scrutiny and are expected to implement

5. Unions won 45 percent of all NLRB representation elections in fiscal year 1979. See National Labor Relations Board, *Forty-Fourth Annual Report of the National Labor Relations Board for the Fiscal Year Ended September 30, 1979* (Government Printing Office, 1979), p. 297.

6. H. G. Lewis, *Unionism and Relative Wages in the United States: An Empirical Inquiry* (University of Chicago Press, 1963), pp. 23–24.

7. Jules J. Justin, *Managing Without a Union: Private and Public Sectors* (New York: Industrial Relations Workshop Seminars, Inc., 1978).

8. 78 Stat. 253.

programs of affirmative action. Equal employment opportunity policy now extends to older workers, the handicapped (including mental and physical impairments), and Vietnam-era veterans. Many states have similar laws or ones more strict than the federal regulations and statutes.[9]

A by-product of this shift in public policy has been substantial scrutiny of existing personnel policy by government and the courts. This scrutiny, in turn, has elevated and enhanced the importance of personnel departments in firms. An employer charged with discrimination in hiring, promotions, layoffs, or wage setting will be hard-pressed to mount a defense without being able to demonstrate that uniform personnel practices are in place. Given that demonstration, the issue turns on whether those practices meet the regulatory agencies' and courts' current criteria for nondiscrimination. There is considerable incentive, therefore, for management to adopt uniform policies, to vest enough authority in the personnel department to ensure that those policies are implemented, and to hire experts to keep up with current regulations.

Direct regulation of the terms and conditions of employment is a third public policy that enhances the modern personnel function. In 1970, the federal Occupational Safety and Health Act created a new system of regulation with its accompanying litigation, experts, and stress on personnel management.[10] In 1974, detailed federal regulation of private pension plans was established.[11] Concern over rising medical costs has also thrust federal policy into employment-related insurance programs.

In addition, older regulatory programs have become more complex. For example, under state workers' compensation programs, the notion of occupational stress as a job-related injury has developed and raised concerns about rising employer costs.[12] Personnel departments are also charged with dealing with the requirements of unemployment insurance, minimum wage, overtime, child labor, and other laws.

There have been periodic bouts of wage-price controls and guidelines

9. For a survey of EEO regulation, see Geraldine Leshin, *Nineteen-Eighty Report on Equal Employment Opportunity and Affirmative Action: The Roots Grow Deeper* (Los Angeles: UCLA Institute of Industrial Relations, 1980).

10. 84 Stat. 1590.

11. Employee Retirement Income Security Act of 1974 (88 Stat. 829).

12. Rosalind M. Schwartz, ed., *Occupational Stress, Proceedings of the Conference on Occupational Stress* (Los Angeles: UCLA Institute of Industrial Relations, 1977).

since the beginning of World War II. Although these programs have varied considerably in scope and detail, they have also fostered centralized and formalized personnel management. Controls and guidelines authorities look for regularities and documentation in considering cases and appeals. Program rules—sometimes inadvertently—will favor particular types of practices over others. Experts are required to keep up with the regulations and the regulators.

Historical Evolution of Modern Personnel Practices

Employers—even large employers—did not always find it advantageous to offer working conditions in accord with current personnel management principles. A recent study by Sanford Jacoby finds that such practices are basically a twentieth-century invention.[13] At the turn of the century, employers commonly relied on foremen to recruit, retain, and supervise their labor forces. These foremen functioned as quasi-independent labor contractors. They were held accountable for meeting cost and production targets. But the details of how their goals were achieved was not considered a proper concern of management. Firms did not have personnel departments or personnel managers. Individuals in the employ of a single firm might well be paid different wages for identical work.

The development of internal labor markets in firms coincided with general corporate evolution toward internalizing, centralizing, and rationalizing other management functions. A literature on personnel management began to evolve. The implementation of personnel policies and the reduction in authority of foremen were linked by some of the early originators of personnel management to other social reform movements of the time.

A major breakthrough in the widespread adoption of personnel management techniques occurred in the World War I period, according to Jacoby, who notes the period coincided with a substantial increase in unionization.[14] During the 1920s, employers retreated somewhat from the new personnel management techniques, while unionization of the work force also generally declined. However, the retreat was

13. Sanford Jacoby, "The 'Human Factor': An Historical Perspective on Internal Labor Markets in American Manufacturing Firms," working paper no. 21 (Los Angeles: UCLA Institute of Industrial Relations, 1980).
14. Ibid.

by no means total. Indeed, doctrines of welfare capitalism that evolved during this period as an employer alternative to unionization encompassed the offering of fringe benefits and other forms of paternalism. Personnel management received a second substantial boost in the 1930s, another period of rapid increase in unionization.

The historical connection between unionization and personnel management, combined with the policies advocated by modern consultants for nonunion employers, suggests that threat effects and union-to-nonunion spillovers occur in a broader sense than economists have considered. Union-type practices, concepts of equity, as well as wage rates, all have an influence on nonunion employers. Thus, it is important to investigate the special nature of union wage and employment policies.

The Modern Union Sector

A primary feature of the union sector is the explicit, fixed-duration contract. Such contracts are typically two or three years in duration and cover wages, fringe benefits, and workplace rules.[15] Virtually all union agreements provide for grievance procedures to settle disputes arising during the term of the contract. Such disputes may involve individual protests of unjust discipline or any issue of contract interpretation.

There is nothing in the legal system that would prevent nonunion employers from offering explicit, long-term agreements to their workers. As already noted, some nonunion employers do offer conditions that resemble those of their union counterparts. But few go as far as the union sector. Some recent court decisions have suggested that nonunion employees may have more implicit rights than has heretofore been the general interpretation.[16] And there have been suggestions that nonunion employers should be compelled by law to provide greater

15. Analysis of typical contract provisions in union agreements can be found in U.S. Bureau of Labor Statistics, *Characteristics of Major Collective Bargaining Agreements, January 1, 1978,* bulletin 2065 (GPO, 1980).

16. In one case, a union employee working for a private federal contractor was deemed to have certain protections by virtue of his employer's intimate involvement with the federal government. For a discussion, see Benjamin Aaron, "The Impact of Public Employment Grievance Settlement on the Labor Arbitration Process" in Joy Correge, Virginia A. Hughes, and Morris Stone, eds., *The Future of Labor Arbitration in America* (New York: American Arbitration Association, 1976), pp. 21–23. Some recent cases in California have granted employees rights previously confined to union contract situations.

employee protection and rights.[17] However, these are the concerns of the future; at this time it is safe to say that some other consideration explains the discrepancy in practices between the union and nonunion sectors.

That other consideration is the economic damage that unions are capable of inflicting on employers in case of an impasse. The effectiveness of strikes and their costs to employers vary from situation to situation. But it is difficult to find other plausible explanations of why employers should make concessions to union negotiators that they would not otherwise unilaterally give their employees.

Employer concessions tend to tighten the linkage between firm and worker. Wage premiums make alternative opportunities less attractive to employees, thus reducing quits. So do the fringe benefits and industrial jurisprudence processes that are associated with unionization.[18] The union political process is likely to reflect the special interests of more senior workers, and the seniority systems that are formalized in union agreements work to shield such workers from layoffs and resultant income losses. Since seniority is valuable, workers who have acquired it are likely to remain with the firm.

By themselves, wage premiums and the shielding effect of seniority systems should reduce the sensitivity of union wages to external labor market tightness or looseness. If there is generally a queue of workers waiting to be hired at the premium wage, it is not clear why fluctuations in the length of the queue should matter to either party in negotiations. Furthermore, if a firm reduces its employment by laying off or terminating only workers with low seniority, senior workers will have little interest in whether or not there are layoffs.[19]

It has also been argued that models that postulate substantial union perception of the wage-employment trade-off implicit in the demand for labor are unrealistic.[20] Most of the anecdotal evidence on union

17. See Clyde W. Summers, "Protecting *All* Employees Against Unjust Dismissal," *Harvard Business Review,* vol. 58 (January–February 1980), pp. 132–39. See also the symposium on "Due Process for Nonunionized Employees" in Barbara D. Dennis, ed., *Proceedings of the Thirty-Second Annual Meeting,* Industrial Relations Research Association Series (Madison, Wis.: IRRA, 1980), pp. 155–86.

18. R. B. Freeman, "Individual Mobility and Union Voice in the Labor Market," *American Economic Review,* vol. 66 (May 1976, *Papers and Proceedings, 1975*), pp. 361–68.

19. Daniel J. B. Mitchell, "Union Wage Determination: Policy Implications and Outlook," *Brookings Papers on Economic Activity, 3:1978,* p. 538. (Hereafter *BPEA.*)

20. Daniel J. B. Mitchell, "Union Wage Policies: The Ross-Dunlop Debate Reopened," *Industrial Relations,* vol. 11 (February 1972), pp. 46–61.

wage concessions in the face of shrinking employment opportunities comes from extreme cases in which the demand curve itself is threatened with extinction. It is the ultimate threat to survival rather than the slope of the curve that provokes a reaction.

Collective Bargaining and Wage Determination

Union wage determination is a bargaining process. While capable of threatening economic damage to the firm—and obtaining concessions from this threat—strikes involve the loss of wage income to workers. Union strike benefits are generally modest.[21] Unemployment insurance is not usually available to replace lost income during strikes.[22]

Since each negotiation raises the potential for strike costs to both sides, both parties have an incentive to reduce bargaining costs. They do so by extending contract duration and thus reducing the frequency of bargaining. Longer horizons for wage setting tend to attenuate the significance of short-term labor market tightness or looseness at negotiation time. They require that the parties make projections concerning developments during the life of the contract and/or include contingency clauses with formulas to deal with future events. The most common contingency clause is the cost-of-living escalator that gears wage adjustments to the consumer price index (CPI).[23] But there

21. Sheldon M. Kline, "Strike Benefits of National Unions," *Monthly Labor Review,* vol. 98 (March 1975), pp. 17–23.

22. Two states, New York and Rhode Island, provide unemployment benefits to strikers under certain conditions. See Gordon Falk Bloom and H. R. Northrup, *Economics of Labor Relations,* 9th ed. (Irwin, 1981). In some cases, workers idled by a dispute who are not directly on strike can receive unemployment insurance payments. Some states provide benefits for workers who are locked out by employers. Thus, there is an incentive for employers to provoke a strike rather than to lock out employees overtly.

23. Some contracts include reopener clauses conditioned on inflation or other occurrences. Others contain "most favored nation clauses" (terminology borrowed from international trade negotiations) in which one party or the other agrees to revise the contract if more favorable terms are granted to a third party. See U.S. Bureau of Labor Statistics, *Characteristics of Major Collective Bargaining Agreements,* pp. 21, 51. Contracts where wage adjustments are triggered by external wage developments rather than price developments are rare, but not unknown. For example, a 1980 contract covering nurses at Kaiser-Permanente facilities in southern California makes wage partially contingent on a community wage survey. See Bureau of National Affairs, *Daily Labor Report,* July 11, 1980, p. B-2. Escalator clauses geared to prices covered 58.8 percent of workers under major collective bargaining agreements (those covering 1,000 or more workers) in November 1979. See Edward Wasilewski, "Scheduled Wage Increases and Escalator Provisions in 1980," *Monthly Labor Review,* vol. 103 (January 1980), p. 10.

are limited examples of other contingency clauses. In short, bargaining costs reinforce long-term horizons and give rise to the need to project future inflation—probably by some type of extrapolative process—or to link wage movements to price inflation mechanically.

The bargaining process reduces the need for unions to recognize the wage-employment trade-off explicitly.[24] Unions do not unilaterally determine wages; collective bargaining is bilateral. Generally, management resistance can be relied on to prevent a move too far up the demand curve, since the resulting wage cost increases cut into profits. In cases where management does not resist, for example because substitutes for union labor are available, unions can push for contract language limiting such substitutions.

Bargaining may also contribute to a certain rigidity of wage goals on both sides. The theory of strikes has suggested that strikes should be viewed as costly mistakes, and—in a variation of rational expectations analysis—that strikes should not be predictable.[25] This stems from the idea that both parties would benefit if they could agree to settle, without a strike, upon the terms that a strike would eventually bring about. The saving in strike costs would be an added gain that could be split between the two parties.

However, it has long been known that strike data exhibit cyclical regularities and can be partially explained by various economic indicators.[26] Thus both parties may have incentives to "stick to their guns," even when they both can see that a strike is likely to result from such behavior. This contradicts the idea developed above; the best explanation may be that in a long-term relationship, such as often exists between union and management, the objective is to minimize strike costs over the duration of the relationship, and not necessarily to minimize these costs in any particular negotiation.

Long-term strategy for minimization of strike costs suggests that

24. Daniel J. B. Mitchell, *Unions, Wages, and Inflation* (Brookings Institution, 1980), pp. 68–72.

25. This view is often associated with the early analysis of J. R. Hicks. Hicks did suggest, however, that unions might strike periodically simply to remind employers of their potential to carry out a work stoppage. See his *The Theory of Wages* (New York: St. Martin's Press, 1963), pp. 140–47.

26. Albert Rees, "Industrial Conflict and Business Fluctuations," *Journal of Political Economy*, vol. 60 (October 1952), pp. 371–82; Orley Ashenfelter and George E. Johnson, "Bargaining Theory, Trade Unions, and Industrial Strike Activity," *American Economic Review*, vol. 59 (March 1969), pp. 35–49; Daniel J. B. Mitchell, "A Note on Strike Propensities and Wage Developments," *Industrial Relations*, vol. 20 (Winter 1981), pp. 123–27.

the parties should strive to understand each other's goals. Both sides have an incentive to establish their most important objectives. For example, the union might seek to establish over a period of time that keeping up with the CPI or with some comparison groups was a key objective and that the rank and file stood ready to bear substantial costs to obtain this goal. Management might seek to establish objectives such as profitability, competitive costs compared with rival firms, or the preservation of certain management prerogatives. Obviously, both sides have incentives to bluff about their objectives, and neither can be sure about the other side's true feelings.

If one side feels uncertain about the other's key objectives, it may feel impelled to probe the relationship. For example, if management began to suspect that keeping up with the CPI was not a key union objective, it might suggest capping or eliminating the escalator clause to probe the union's reaction. If management's suspicions were not put to rest by the union's response at the bargaining table, the employer might be tempted to push the issue to an impasse. Thus, anything that creates uncertainty about bargaining positions increases the probability of a strike.[27] This logic makes concessions and conciliatory behavior difficult. Today's goodwill gesture could be misinterpreted and probed in future negotiations. Perhaps an artful mediator or special circumstances (for example, imminent bankruptcy) may make it possible to label a concession temporary, unusual, and without precedent—but not always.[28]

Historical Evolution of the Union Contract

The union contract is not a recent invention. Analysis of the development of contractual language suggests a process of evolution, helped along at times by public policy. Prior to World War II, union

27. Strike probabilities at the time of a renegotiation are not negligible. One study of major contract expirations in manufacturing found that about 14 percent led to a strike during 1954–75. These strikes involved 17 percent of the workers covered by these negotiations. See Bruce E. Kaufman, "The Propensity to Strike in American Manufacturing," in Barbara D. Dennis, ed., *Proceedings of the Thirtieth Annual Winter Meeting*, Industrial Relations Research Association Series (Madison, Wis.: IRRA, 1978), p. 423.

28. The contract view of strikes presented above suggests that the incidence of strikes should tend to decline as the parties gain more experience with each other. For some empirical support of this hypothesis in a paper developing a similar theme, see Melvin W. Reder and George R. Neumann, "Conflict and Contract: The Case of Strikes," *Journal of Political Economy*, vol. 88 (October 1980), pp. 867–86.

agreements were mainly of one year's duration.[29] However, longer contracts with deferred wage adjustments, sometimes qualified by reopener clauses, were known at the time. Use of arbitration to settle disputes arising from contracts was well established, although many contracts provided for grievance mechanisms without final arbitration. Fringe benefits such as pensions and health insurance were quite rare. Escalator clauses were known but not common. Even private unemployment benefits—a forerunner of today's supplemental unemployment benefit (SUB) plans—had prewar precedents.[30] Generally, contracts of that period were shorter and less complex than their present-day descendants.

As the parties became more experienced in bargaining, longer contracts became more common. It became evident that strike costs during contracts could be minimized if management accepted arbitration of contract disputes in exchange for no-strike clauses. As escalators, which helped permit longer contracts, became more common, it was discovered that clever formulas and qualifications could help reduce some of the uncertainty that they created for management.[31]

29. Examples of early contract language can be found in Bureau of National Affairs, *Collective Bargaining Contracts* (Washington: BNA, 1941); and U.S. Bureau of Labor Statistics, *Union Agreement Provisions,* Bulletin 686 (GPO, 1942). Mitchell has been collecting pre–World War II union contracts from various sources for analysis. Some of the statements in the text result from analysis of those contracts.

30. William E. Simkin provided a 1931 contract between the American Federation of Full Fashioned Hosiery Workers and the Full Fashioned Hosiery Manufacturers Association, Inc., for the contract collection cited in the previous footnote. The agreement provides for a fund whose proceeds are to be used for "alleviation of distress caused by unemployment."

31. Some employers have a need to know in nominal terms what their future labor costs will be for purposes of bidding. Thus escalator clauses are rare in construction. Presumably this need to know the future nominal wage is attributable to lack of escalators in agreements signed by successful bidders. More generally, employers cannot be sure that their ability to pay will move with the CPI. While there have been examples in the past of contracts with wages geared to the price of the employer's product, such contracts do not necessarily protect worker purchasing power. (For examples of such contracts, see Bureau of National Affairs, *Collective Bargaining Contracts,* p. 603.) Profit-sharing arrangements effectively reflect the employer's price. A more common compromise is to use the CPI but include constraints on the operation of the escalator. For example, contracts may contain caps that stop the escalator above a certain limit. Or they may contain corridors that specify that a certain minimum amount of inflation must occur before the escalator comes into effect. Also, the escalator formulas often provide less than 100 percent protection against inflation, so that a 10 percent price increase may trigger less than a 10 percent wage increase. The art of qualifying escalators seems to have developed gradually. During 1968–77, the annual degree of protection

By smoothing out annual incomes in the face of layoffs, SUB plans helped cope with the standard practice of negotiating the wage level and allowing management to determine employment.

Fringe benefits might have been expected to be favored by unions, in keeping with their orientation toward senior workers. The wage control authorities stimulated interest in such benefits during World War II (and in subsequent programs), and the tax code provided favorable treatment for them. Controls and guidelines programs have also provided incentives for the use of long-term contracts and escalators.[32]

In short, the modern union contract is the product of various forces. It reflects the logic of bargaining and bargaining costs. It evolved in part from practices that were probably in use by management before unionization.[33] And it reflects the influence—deliberate or inadvertent— of various government policies. As the contract developed, it contributed to general social norms regarding what a good employer should

---

from escalators contained in major contracts averaged 57 percent. Escalators in the 1950s apparently were much more likely to provide full protection. See Victor J. Sheifer, "Cost-of-Living Adjustment: Keeping Up with Inflation?" *Monthly Labor Review,* vol. 102 (June 1979), p. 15.

32. Controls and guidelines authorities are reluctant to override agreements signed prior to the beginning of their programs. As a result, wage increases pursuant to preexisting long-term contracts are more likely to go unchallenged. Thus, in periods when programs of wage controls are likely to be established, unions may feel it advisable to lock future wage goals into long-term contracts. On the other hand, during controls programs, the parties may shorten their contract durations so as not to be locked into contracts influenced by controls in the event the program is ended. This was the experience during the Nixon controls program. Escalators were granted favorable treatment under both the Nixon and Carter administration programs. Under the Nixon program, a time-weighting procedure was applied to the costing of escalator increases, which tended to lower the percentage increase attributable to them. The Carter guidelines program permitted escalators to be costed using assumed inflation rates substantially below actual rates of inflation. On the Nixon program, see Arnold R. Weber and Daniel J. B. Mitchell, *The Pay Board's Progress: Wage Controls in Phase II* (Brookings Institution, 1978), pp. 56–63, 363–67. There has been little analytical work published on the Carter program as yet. A critical discussion can be found in the U.S. General Accounting Office, *The Voluntary Pay and Price Standards Have Had No Discernible Effect on Inflation* (GPO, 1980). This report was especially critical of the treatment of escalators (pp. 90–92). However, the analysis presented below in the text provides some rationale for encouraging their use.

33. As David E. Feller notes, "Rules . . . contained in a collective agreement have their genesis as much in the nature of modern industrial enterprise as in collective bargaining, and there are substantial reasons apart from coercion why some employers accept the incorporation of those rules." See his "A General Theory of the Collective Bargaining Agreement," *California Law Review,* vol. 61 (May 1973), p. 721.

provide to workers, whether union or nonunion. Personnel managers, and their consultants and textbooks, today reflect the influence of union wage practices.

Modern Economic Analysis of Contracting

Recent economic literature has attempted to find micro-level explanations of the limited responsiveness of wage determination to labor market tightness or looseness. Since much of the work force is nonunion, the theory has sought explanations other than collective bargaining costs for the phenomenon. One possibility is that turnover costs are high enough to make both employers and employees desire to enter into contractlike relationships.[34] Such relationships would give nonunion wage determination a unionlike character. Wage changes would be made relatively infrequently, thus reducing responsiveness to immediate conditions.

Generally, turnover costs are considered to include recruitment, screening, and specific training costs for the employer, and loss of income by the employee while searching for a job. In the face of such costs, both parties have an incentive to reduce turnover. Employers with particularly high turnover costs would follow high-wage strategies to reduce the attractiveness of other labor market opportunities for their workers. Employers might hoard labor during temporary downturns in demand, producing the well-known procyclical fluctuation of productivity. If employers had made layoffs and demand then picked

---

34. The discussion below owes much to Arthur M. Okun, *Prices and Quantities: A Macroeconomic Analysis* (Brookings Institution, 1981). See also Michael L. Wachter and Oliver E. Williamson, "Obligational Markets and the Mechanics of Inflation," *Bell Journal of Economics,* vol. 9 (Autumn 1978), pp. 549–71. One of the important strands in the literature that led to the turnover-cost approach to wage setting dealt with the impact of specific capital on employment and hours fluctuations over the business cycle. See Walter Y. Oi, "Labor as a Quasi-Fixed Factor," *Journal of Political Economy,* vol. 70 (December 1962), pp. 538–55; Sherwin Rosen, "Short-Run Employment Variation on Class-1 Railroads in the U.S., 1947–1963," *Econometrica,* vol. 36 (July–October 1968), pp. 511–29; John H. Pencavel, "Wages, Specific Training, and Labor Turnover in U.S. Manufacturing Industries," *International Economic Review,* vol. 13 (February 1972), pp. 53–64; Donald O. Parsons, "Specific Human Capital: An Application to Quit Rates and Layoff Rates," *Journal of Political Economy,* vol. 80 (December 1972), pp. 1120–43; Dale T. Mortensen, "Specific Capital and Labor Turnover," *Bell Journal of Economics,* vol. 9 (Autumn 1978), pp. 572–86.

up, they might attempt to recall previously laid-off workers before engaging in new hiring. In short, the turnover-cost theory can be called upon to explain a number of real-world phenomena.[35]

Turnover costs by themselves do not fully explain why labor market arrangements favor inflexible wage decisions and give the employer the right to determine employment and hours. For example, individual haggling costs have to be considered.[36] Just as retail stores find it advantageous to post prices rather than bargain with each customer, so employers would find continuous negotiations with each employee to be costly. Such costs would favor uniform wage policies applied to broad classes of employees.

Another consideration is the bilateral relationship and the inherent possibility of "exploitation" on both sides. The payment of a wage premium, the existence of specific job skills, and the search costs of finding a new job mean that there is a potential surplus to be divided between worker and employer. Once a relationship has begun, management can limit its vulnerability to exploitation by refusing to haggle, that is, by establishing uniform wage policies. But workers also would prefer some protection.

While it would be difficult for workers and management to agree on precise formulas that will determine wage payments indefinitely into the future, there may be understandings that future wage deter-

35. For example, the internal labor market literature and the analysis of the "dual" labor market can be analyzed in terms of the turnover-cost approach. See Peter B. Doeringer and Michael J. Piore, *Internal Labor Markets and Manpower Analysis* (Lexington Books, 1971); Michael L. Wachter, "Primary and Secondary Labor Markets: A Critique of the Dual Approach," *BPEA, 3:1974*, pp. 637–80. Doeringer and Piore originally pointed to the neoclassical interpretation of their findings (pp. 14, 76). Later, however, Piore became critical of this interpretation (see his comments on the Wachter paper, pp. 684–88).

36. The importance of minimizing haggling costs in employment contracts is emphasized in Oliver E. Williamson, Michael L. Wachter, and Jeffrey E. Harris, "Understanding the Employment Relation: The Analysis of Idiosyncratic Exchange," *Bell Journal of Economics*, vol. 6 (Spring 1975), pp. 250–78, especially pp. 270–71. In an earlier paper, Simon noted that employment contracts typically contain an unspecified element. The worker agrees to permit the employer—within some reasonable range—to assign tasks, which may be pleasant or unpleasant to varying degrees. Under the implicit contract, however, the detailed tasks on a day-to-day basis may not be delineated. If the worker can be confident that the employer will take his preferences into account, he would presumably be willing to work for less than if his preferences are ignored. Hence an area of surplus is created, which can be divided as part of a long-term understanding. See Herbert A. Simon, "A Formal Theory of the Employment Relationship," *Econometrica*, vol. 19 (July 1951), pp. 293–305. Such a long-term understanding is an alternative to haggling on a daily basis about wages for each day's tasks.

minations will be "fair."[37] Such understandings can be viewed as worker protection provisions. What is fair may be a subject of disagreement, but there is no reason why the definition should be centered on labor market tightness or looseness. Possible sources of guidance to what is fair might be wage decisions made by other employers or movements in the CPI.[38]

The fairness criterion might also explain the preference for flexibility in employment and hours rather than for wage adjustments to cyclical movements in demand. As already noted, an employer might have a difficult time convincing workers that a wage cut was justified by financial conditions. However, workers can readily see that output is declining, and cuts in the quantity of labor used to produce that output may be acceptable because of the obvious relationship between inputs and outputs.

Since fairness is an ambiguous concept, popular definitions of what is fair might change over time, or might vary from society to society. In particular, in the United States the publicity surrounding major union achievements and practices may influence the concept of fairness of nonunion workers. Thus, the coincidence of rapid unionization growth and the development of personnel management techniques noted earlier can be linked.

Obviously, the encompassing nature of the turnover theory is both a strength and weakness. It says that employers have an incentive to offer fair treatment, so virtually any practice that seems fair can be explained by the theory. In addition, it has a self-reinforcing tendency that might be used to explain whatever is observed. If employers in seeking to reduce turnover costs adopt centralized, formalized, and uniform wage policies, workers seeking jobs will be confronted with take-it-or-leave-it offers from some employers and "no vacancies" at

37. General understandings of fairness are common in business dealings, even if they are not set down in legal language. See Stewart Macaulay, "Non-contractual Relations in Business: A Preliminary Study," *American Sociological Review*, vol. 28 (February 1963), pp. 55–67.

38. On wage imitation, see Robert J. Flanagan, "Wage Interdependence in Unionized Labor Markets," *BPEA, 3:1976*, pp. 635–73; George E. Johnson, "The Determination of Wages in the Union and Non-Union Sectors," *British Journal of Industrial Relations*, vol. 15 (July 1977), pp. 211–25; Susan Vroman, "Union/Non-Union Wage Spillovers," *British Journal of Industrial Relations*, vol. 18 (November 1980), pp. 369–76; and Daniel J. B. Mitchell, "Union-Nonunion Wage Spillovers: A Note," *British Journal of Industrial Relations*, vol. 18 (November 1980), pp. 372–76. The use of outside wage comparisons is an important element of public-sector wage setting. See Geraldine Leshin, *The Prevailing Wage Concept in Public Sector Bargaining* (Los Angeles: UCLA Institute of Industrial Relations, 1977), chap. 1.

others. Job applicants will not be given the opportunity to underbid existing job holders. This will increase search costs, thus making employees all the more anxious to avoid such costs and establish contractlike relationships with their employers.

Empirical testing of a theory in which anything is possible is obviously difficult. The problem is complicated by lack of a clearcut guide as to what should be measured.[39] For example, specific training is often cited as a source of turnover costs. But if employers attach premiums to the obtaining of specific training, workers will have incentives to invest in it. In addition, if the labor market arranges itself in a way that leads employers to believe that workers are likely to remain, employers might be willing to invest in general training. Thus, the distinction that human capital theory makes between specific training and general training does not exist in many real-life situations.[40]

It is also unclear how to differentiate the turnover-cost model of implicit employer-employee understandings from alternative models of implicit contracting. Some authors have used differential risk preferences between workers and employers to explain such contracting.[41] There is some connection between the two models; if turnover costs lead to special treatment of senior workers—including a reduced probability of layoff—then the risk aversion of these workers will be automatically catered to by employers.

39. The Los Angeles-based M & M Association, an employers' group, did produce estimates of turnover costs from a member survey for 1979. The average cost of replacing an employee was $3,378.50 for production and maintenance workers, $1,975.83 for office and technical workers, and $9,115.83 for salary-exempt workers. Of these totals, 38 percent for the first two categories and 75 percent for the last went for advertising; travel expenses for recruiters and applicants; expenses for interviewing, reference checks, paperwork, and testing; and medical examinations. The rest went for induction procedures, substandard production by new employees, and time spent by supervisors and fellow workers performing on-the-job training. However, no distinction is made between specific and general training. Exit costs for the three categories were estimated as $233.25, $315.67, and $1,240.33. Hence, the costs of turnover in a steady-state situation were $3,611.75, $2,291.50, and $10,356.16. It should be noted that the M & M Association included data only from firms that could provide detailed information. Firms that could provide only rough estimates of totals estimated steady-state turnover costs for the three categories of $1,029.09, $1,332.84, and $4,260.39. Not surprisingly, those firms that thought it worthwhile to collect detailed data were the ones with the higher costs of turnover. Source: M & M Association, *Turnover and Absenteeism Manual* (Los Angeles: M & M, 1980), sec. III, tables I and II.

40. Mark Blaug, "The Empirical Status of Human Capital Theory: A Slightly Jaundiced Survey," *Journal of Economic Literature*, vol. 14 (September 1976), p. 837.

41. An early incorporation of risk-sharing behavior in contracting was made by

Generally, the risk aversion models of contracting need some supplementation to produce the kinds of contracts and practices actually observed. For example, the lack of contracts fully specified in real terms—even when escalators are used—presents a theoretical problem.[42] In the union sector, the bargaining considerations involved in protecting a union-induced wage premium may be part of the explanation. Sometimes contracting models suggest complete guarantees of wage income, including guarantees against fluctuations in employment.[43] Since employment and hours fluctuations are permitted in the real world, institutional arrangements that reduce the income effects of employment fluctuations, such as unemployment insurance, may need to be invoked. If unemployment insurance systems are not fully experience-rated (and they are not), an incentive is provided to use layoffs as an adjustment mechanism, rather than offering complete income guarantees or maintaining employment and adjusting wages.[44]

Steven N. S. Cheung in connection with landlord-tenant relationships in agriculture. See his "Transaction Costs, Risk Aversion, and the Choice of Contractual Arrangements," *Journal of Law and Economics,* vol. 12 (April 1969), pp. 23–42. Examples of the labor market literature include Costas Azariadis, "Implicit Contracts and Underemployment Equilibria," *Journal of Political Economy,* vol. 83 (December 1975), pp. 1183–1202; Martin Neil Baily, "Wages and Employment under Uncertain Demand," *Review of Economic Studies,* vol. 41 (January 1974), pp. 37–50; and Robert E. Hall and David M. Lilien, "Efficient Wage Bargains under Uncertain Supply and Demand," *American Economic Review,* vol. 69 (December 1979), pp. 868–79.

42. In reviewing the evidence on contracting, one author finds lack of support for the notion that wage contracting is conducted in real terms. He views this finding as weakening the case for the risk aversion theory of implicit contracting. See James E. Pearce, "Trade Unionism, Implicit Contracting, and the Response to Demand Variation in U.S. Manufacturing," research paper number 8003 (Federal Reserve Bank of Dallas, April 1980).

43. Indeed, as Robert E. Hall noted in comments on an earlier version of this paper, an extreme form of contract theory suggests that firms would not use labor costs as a guide to pricing decisions. Labor costs would become totally fixed and would not affect marginal decisionmaking. It is sometimes argued that Japanese firms, for example, with their "lifetime" employment contracts, undercut foreign prices during recessions because their labor costs are fixed. However, Japanese firms can lend their permanent workers to other firms and make use of nonpermanent workers and suppliers who do not offer lifetime commitments. Hence, it would be difficult to come up with real-world examples of such extreme contracting behavior. In addition, the transactions cost view suggests that in the product market, firms might use cost markups to guide pricing decisions in ways that seem fair to customers. Thus, labor costs might enter pricing through the markup channel. See Arthur M. Okun, "Inflation: Its Mechanics and Welfare Costs," *BPEA,* 2:1975, pp. 362–63.

44. Martin Feldstein, "The Effect of Unemployment Insurance on Temporary Layoff Unemployment," *American Economic Review,* vol. 68 (December 1978), pp. 834–46.

In short, recent economic analysis of wage determination provides many insights into real-world behavior without abandoning assumptions of economic rationality. The most rigorous versions of contracting theory, however, often do not predict precisely the form of employer-employee wage arrangements that characterize actual practice. In contrast, the turnover-cost models are general enough to encompass almost any form of behavior. These models, with their emphasis on the use of fair standards for wage setting, do provide a link with the historical development of personnel management techniques and unions.

Contracting in a Macroeconomic Model

Contracting or contractlike behavior can be expected to be associated with three important characteristics of wage setting. First, the influence of labor market tightness or looseness will be attenuated. Fluctuations in indexes such as the unemployment rate need not be associated with dramatic shifts in wages or even the rate of change of wages. Second, at any moment in time some observed wage behavior is occurring pursuant to previously determined arrangements. Thus, it is possible that past circumstances—such as previous rates of wage or price inflation—are carried into the present. Third, in the most extreme form of contracting, written union-management agreements, use of explicit escalation is common. Thus, inflation of the present (or very recent past) is mechanically reflected in some wage adjustments. The degree to which these three characteristics are present or absent in the labor market should have some influence on the responsiveness of the inflation rate to anti-inflation policy. However, in order to predict what the effect will be, a model that includes behavior in other markets must be specified.

Initially, we examine a simple four-equation model. This model is relatively general in form and probably reflects the relationships many macroeconomists carry about in their heads. It is first solved algebraically for the next-period values of critical variables. Because the dynamic implications are also of interest, a simulation over a multi-period horizon is also presented. The goal is to explore the influence of the three contract-related characteristics on the effectiveness of monetary and fiscal policy in influencing the inflation rate.

While a simple four-equation model can be expected to give some insight into the probable qualitative impact of these contract-related characteristics, it cannot offer much guidance on the quantitative impact. A larger model with an empirical basis is needed for such estimates. Thus, after the four-equation model is explored, we try similar experiments on the large-scale quarterly UCLA business forecasting model. This model is similar in broad outlines to other large-scale models such as those maintained by Data Resources, Inc., and Wharton. As it turns out, although the big model produces the same qualitative effects as the four-equation model, it suggests that inertia in other areas of the economy reduces the importance of variations in contract-related behavior in the labor market.

Contracting in a Simple Model

Contracting in the labor market suggests that the process of wage-change determination will be altered to reflect a multiperiod horizon. Continuous decisions about wages are not made. Instead, a wage policy is established for some duration. Generally, the longer the horizon for the contract, the less attention will be paid by wage setters to short-term transitory phenomena. In particular, it might be expected that longer contracting horizons will attenuate the influence of the real state of the labor market on wage decisions. This should be the case for both explicit and implicit understandings with employees in the nonunion sector.

In a simple classical model, the labor market clears and determines a real wage. It is the real wage that is equated with marginal productivity on the demand side and with the marginal utility of leisure on the supply side. While it is true that the classical model operates on a real basis with money as a veil and nominal values of little or no consequence in equilibrium, in disequilibrium situations *nominal* values must adjust. In the case of an excess supply of labor and a given money supply, the nominal wage will fall until such time as the market clears. Past rates of wage or price inflation, or even current rates of price inflation, should not alter this prediction. In a simple classical model, nominal wages must fall absolutely so long as there is excess supply.[45]

45. This does not mean that the price level is irrelevant to how far the nominal wage must fall. All other things equal, a higher price level would lead to a higher *equilibrium* nominal wage. However, the text is explicitly focused on situations of disequilibrium.

In the spectrum from the simple classical auction-type labor market to the contracting market, past and current values of price inflation and/or past values of wage inflation become more and more relevant in determining current wage changes, and demand and supply conditions in the labor market become less relevant. Where negotiating costs in union settings induce a combination of long-term agreements and escalator clauses, the importance of current price inflation is accentuated. Hence, the major contrasts between classical auction processes and contracting processes in the labor market can be highlighted by adjusting the wage-change determination equation in a macro model to reflect differences in the response to particular explanatory variables. Specifically, in a classical market an excess supply or demand variable should be the primary determinant of wage change. Nonescalated contracting markets should show little wage-change sensitivity to excess supply or demand, but will probably be particularly sensitive to lagged wage and/or price inflation. Escalated contracting markets should put major emphasis on current price-change determination and little emphasis on anything else.

Consider the following model featuring a money market, a labor market, and a product market.[46] Traditional monetary policy is represented by exogenous manipulation of the money supply, M^s, while traditional fiscal policy is represented by deliberate changes in net government expenditures (expenditures minus taxation), E. Manipulations of monetary and fiscal policy will have some impact on the rate of price inflation and hence the absolute level of prices, $\dot{P}$ and P, respectively, and on wage inflation and the absolute level of wages, $\dot{W}$ and W. Also affected will be the overall level of real output, Y, employment of labor, L, and the rate of interest, r.

In the money market, it is assumed that the demand for money, M^d, is equated with supply, and that money demand is a positive function, A, of the price level and the level of real output, but a negative function of the interest rate. That is:

(1) $M^s = M^d = A\,(P, Y, r); \partial A/\partial P > 0, \partial A/\partial Y > 0, \partial A/\partial r < 0.$

The labor market is initially assumed to be characterized by the classical economic condition, wage = marginal revenue product of

---

46. Since an interest rate appears in this model, there is implicitly a securities market in the background. However, by Walras's law, explicit treatment of this market is unnecessary.

labor. This can be expressed more generally as a function, B, linking employment, L, and the real wage, W/P. Thus,

(2) $$L = B(W/P); \partial B/\partial(W/P) < 0.$$

Following the classical assumption, increases in the real wage have a negative effect on labor demand. Therefore, increases in W have a negative effect, while increases in P have a positive and offsetting effect. Equation 2 can be solved for P and viewed as a price markup equation.

Also in the labor market, a dynamic process occurs that determines wage change, $\dot{W}$, at any point in time. Under purely classical conditions, wage change might be assumed to be only a function of demand and supply conditions. If the labor supply is greater than the level of employment, wage increase should be retarded. Indeed, as noted earlier, nominal wages should fall absolutely. Much of the empirical work on wage determination, however, suggests that current and lagged price inflation, $\dot{P}$ and $\dot{P}_{-1}$, and lagged wage inflation, $\dot{W}_{-1}$, might play some role in the determination of wage change. Thus, a general specification of the dynamic wage-change process[47] can be represented, using the function C, as:

(3) $$\dot{W} = C(\dot{P}, \dot{P}_{-1}, \dot{W}_{-1}, L); \partial C/\partial \dot{P} > 0, \partial C/\partial \dot{P}_{-1} > 0,$$
$$\partial C/\partial \dot{W}_{-1} > 0, \partial C/\partial L > 0.$$

It is generally assumed that lagged and current price inflation has a positive effect on current-period wage inflation, as does lagged wage

---

47. The simplified model and the UCLA macroeconometric model (discussed below) determine wage rates without explicit reference to the union and nonunion sectors. The assumption implied is that the presence of these and other differentiations within the labor market can be embodied in the parameters of a single wage equation, without keeping track of the many different labor markets that exist. In response to Robert Flanagan's discussion of an earlier version of this paper, the authors simulated a version of the model that explicitly assumed two labor markets, with different wage levels and parameters specified for the union and nonunion sectors. The simulation results were identical to five decimal places for all variables, *assuming* that the unionized sector held a fixed share of the labor market. A slow drift in the union share would not change the results significantly. Considerable variation in the unionized share might, however, imply that no single wage equation, with fixed parameters, could adequately appropriate the results that would be observed using a more disaggregated approach. A full two-sector (or multisector) model would have to include equations that determined the size of the sectors in response to changes in relative wage levels. Such a model is beyond the scope of this paper.

inflation.[48] Higher levels of employment are also generally assumed to have a positive effect on wage inflation.

Finally, there is the product or goods market. It may be assumed that the demand for output determines total output unless the economy is bumping against a capacity constraint. Output demand can be assumed to be a function, D, that increases with real money balances (wealth effect), decreases with the interest rate (higher interest rates make investment in plant and equipment and consumer durables less attractive), and increases with net government expenditures, E (stimulative fiscal policy). Thus:

(4) $\quad Y = D(M^s/P, r, E); \partial D/\partial(M^s/P) > 0, \partial D/\partial r < 0, \partial D/\partial E > 0.$

The system of equations 1 through 4 is quite general. Since the model described is meant to be short run, no assumptions need be made about the stability of particular relationships. In particular, the wage-determination system of equation 3 might or might not be assumed to have "accelerationist" tendencies over several periods.

To close the model, a fifth relation between output and labor input (a short-run production function) can be added, that is, $Y = f(L)$. This permits the substitution of L for Y in equations 1 and 4. In addition, the following identities permit the substitution of $\dot{W}$ and $\dot{P}$ for W and P in all equations: $W = (1 + \dot{W})W_{-1}$, $P = (1 + \dot{P})P_{-1}$, and $M^s = (1 + \dot{M^s}) M^s_{-1}$. The functions A, B, and D become A^*, B^*, and D^* as result of the substitutions. A modified system of four equations with four unknown or endogenous variables ($\dot{P}$, L, r, and $\dot{W}$) and four predetermined or exogenous variables ($\dot{M^s}$, $\dot{W}_{-1}$, $\dot{P}_{-1}$ and E) emerges:

(1') $\quad \dot{M^s} = A^*(\dot{P}, L, r) \qquad$ Money market
$\qquad\qquad\quad\; \overset{+}{}\;\; \overset{+}{}\;\; \overset{-}{}$

(2') $\quad L = B^*(\dot{W}, \dot{P}) \qquad\qquad$ Classical labor market
$\qquad\qquad\quad \overset{-}{}\;\; \overset{+}{} \qquad\qquad$ (wage = marginal revenue product)

(3') $\quad \dot{W} = C(\dot{P}, \dot{W}_{-1}, \dot{P}_{-1}, L) \qquad$ Wage-change determination process
$\qquad\qquad\quad\;\; \overset{+}{}\;\; \overset{+}{}\;\;\; \overset{+}{}\;\;\; \overset{+}{}$

(4') $\quad L = D^*(\dot{M^s}, \dot{P}, r, E) \qquad$ Product market
$\qquad\qquad\quad\;\; \overset{+}{}\;\;\; \overset{-}{}\;\; \overset{-}{}\;\; \overset{+}{}$

48. The role of lagged prices and wages can obviously be rationalized by assuming adaptive expectations on the part of wage earners. Even if wage earners are entirely concerned about future prices and are willing to "let bygones be bygones," their observable behavior, in the absence of direct measures of expectations of future prices or wages, may resemble adaptive expectations. A further discussion of expectations can be found below.

The expected signs of influences of the right-hand side variables on the left-hand side variables are shown under the equations.

Suppose that inflation, $\dot{P}$, is running at a higher than acceptable rate and that the monetary and fiscal authorities wish to exercise their policies in order to slow the rate of price increase. The effectiveness of monetary and fiscal policy is measured by the magnitude of the overall impact (worked through the complete system) of changes in the rate of growth of the money supply and of the flow of net government expenditure on the rate of price inflation. In algebraic terms, effectiveness is measured by $d\dot{P}/dM^s$ and by $d\dot{P}/dE$. It may then be asked how contracting in the wage-change determination process affects these two magnitudes.

Contracting

Contracting is most likely to enter the model through the wage-change determination process. First, if contracts attenuate supply-demand influences on wage determination, the impact shows up in the model in the linkage between the wage-change determination and L. In a simultaneous-equation system, such an influence is not confined just to that linkage; rather, it spreads throughout the system in complex ways. Second, a stronger linkage of past wage and price inflation and current wage change can be expected due to contracting. Finally, the use of escalator clauses in explicit union contracts may strengthen the linkage between current price inflation and current wage inflation.

How do the contracting impacts on wage change affect the effectiveness of monetary and fiscal policy? One way to deal with the question is to linearize the equations and solve for the two measures of effectiveness, $d\dot{P}/dM^s$ and $d\dot{P}/dE$. The contracting impact can be summarized in a linear system by increases or decreases in the magnitudes of particular coefficients. Then the impact of changes of those magnitudes on the two measures of efficiency can be calculated. These calculations are described in an unpublished appendix (available from the authors). The results are shown in table 1.

Two aspects of the contracting impact cause difficulty for monetary and fiscal policy in fighting inflation. Although the intent of demand restraint is often obscured in public statements by government officials, its primary mechanism is the creation of economic slack. In the context of the four-equation model, this slackness appears as a reduction in

Table 1. *Summary of One-Period Impact in Four-Equation Model*

Contracting impact	Influence of monetary/ fiscal policy on inflation	Implication for inflation restraint
Attenuation of supply-demand linkage to wage-change determination	Reduction in effectiveness	If inflation has occurred in the past, difficulty in slowing inflation through demand restraint is increased.
Long-term contracts (ignoring escalation)	No change	If inflation has been high in the past, it will tend to be high in the present.
Escalator clauses	Increase in effectiveness	If inflation has occurred in the past, difficulty in slowing inflation through demand restraint is reduced.

employment, L. A lower value of L reduces the rate of wage change. Given the assumed linkage of wage and price change, the rate of inflation is then indirectly reduced. But if the initial linkage between L and $\dot{W}$ is reduced, then so is the indirect effect on price inflation. In the context of the simple simultaneous model presented above, the complex interactions of the variables do not offset this chain of reasoning.

Long-term wage contracts have a different influence from the attenuation effect in strengthening the importance of past wage and price inflation as determinants of current wage inflation. Since the past cannot be changed, monetary and fiscal policy can influence only the present. In the wage-change equation, the only real present influence is L. Whatever the effectiveness of monetary and fiscal policy (operating through L) may be, the inflation rate today will be more closely linked to past inflation rates (operating through $\dot{W}$). In particular, if the inflation rate has been high in the past, it will tend to be high in the present.

Escalators, on the other hand, create a contemporaneous echo effect that enhances the efficiency of monetary and fiscal policy. Wage change is more dependent on a current variable (price inflation) with an escalator clause. To the extent that some price moderation is induced by demand restraint (by inducing economic slack and reducing wage inflation), the price moderation reinforces the wage-moderation effect, which in turn reinforces the price-moderation effect in a continuing cycle.

Dynamic Simulations of the Four-Equation Model

The algebraic solution of the linearized model indicates the first-period qualitative directions of change in the measures of effectiveness of monetary and fiscal policy with respect to changes in parameters that represent the influences of long-term contracts, escalators, and attenuation of slack in the labor markets. Obviously, a critical issue is the speed of response of prices and wages to changes in monetary or fiscal policy. To examine this feature, dynamic simulations of the four-equation model were performed.

Given any arbitrary rate of growth of the money supply, the rate of inflation in both prices and wages will eventually equal this rate, and the rate of unemployment will stabilize at a level that has been set for convenience at 6.0 percent. Results in the base case are roughly equal to those simulated by Tobin.[49]

The model was specified and initialized to yield a steady-state solution with the same chronic (expected) inflation in both wages and prices, which is also equal to the initial rate of growth of the money

49. See James Tobin, "Stabilization Policy Ten Years After," *BPEA, 1:1980*, pp. 19–71, especially pp. 66–68. Since full employment is eventually restored regardless of the rate of money growth, there is no long-run trade-off between unemployment and inflation. The presence of inertia in wage adjustments, however, does imply short-run trade-offs exist. As John B. Taylor noted in comments on an earlier draft of this paper, the interpretation of the source of wage inertia can be critical to the policy implications of the model. Specifically, if rational expectations are assumed, then wage earners should not persistently err in their estimates of real wages. A thoroughly convincing announcement of an anti-inflation policy would then permit prices to be reduced with far less unemployment than would be implied by adaptive expectations. Nevertheless, even under the assumption of rational expectations, if wage and price decisions are staggered over time, and multiperiod contracts overlap, then inertia will emerge. Taylor has estimated empirically a model of the U.S. economy, with constraints imposed that were developed assuming rational expectations. See John B. Taylor, "Estimation and Control of a Macroeconomic Model with Rational Expectations," *Econometrica*, vol. 47 (September 1979), pp. 1267–86. Simulations of his model give short-run trade-offs similar to those presented here. Taylor has also developed an approach for distinguishing wage expectations from wage inertia. See his "Aggregate Dynamics and Staggered Contracts," *Journal of Political Economy*, vol. 88 (February 1980), pp. 1–23, especially pp. 18–20. He concludes that rational expectations matter greatly despite the existence of contracts.

supply. The real output level is constant in steady state, as is the level of employment and the interest rate. (Alternatively, one can regard the results as deviations from trend increases in real output, employment, and real wages.)

Union contracts and similar institutional practices in the nonunion sector may have three types of effects on wage determination. First, in the absence of these practices, higher unemployment rates or other indicators of slack in the labor market might lead to stronger effects on wage rates than has been observed. Second, explicit union contracts and informal implicit long-term understandings in the nonunion sector may act to lengthen the period of adjustment to anti-inflationary policies that create slack in the labor markets. Third, wider use of escalator clauses may speed the transmission of price reductions (or increases) to wage determination. A base-case equation and three alternative wage parameter specifications were designed to indicate the potential effects of these features, as follows:

Base wage equation
(5a) $\dot{W} = 0.30\,\dot{P} + 0.70\,\dot{P}_{-1} + 0.0\dot{W}_{-1} + 0.1(L - 100)$

Wage equation with stronger unemployment effects
(5b) $\dot{W} = 0.30\,\dot{P} + 0.70\,\dot{P}_{-1} + 0.0\,\dot{W}_{-1} + 0.2(L - 100)$

Wage equation with long-term contracts
(5c) $\dot{W} = 0.10\,\dot{P} + 0.20\,\dot{P}_{-1} + 0.70\,\dot{W}_{-1} + 0.1(L - 100)$

Wage equation with escalators
(5d) $\dot{W} = 0.90\,\dot{P} + 0.10\,\dot{P}_{-1} + 0.0\,\dot{W}_{-1} + 0.1(L - 100)$

The equations with stronger unemployment effects (5b) doubles the weight given to the measure of labor-market slack, holding constant prices and wages. The equation with long-term contracts (5c) shifts part of the weight from current and previous prices to previous wage rates. Finally, equation 5d reflects more widespread use of escalators by shifting much of the weight from previous prices to current prices.

Four experiments were run, one for each of the four wage equations. In each experiment the model was initialized at steady-state 10 percent inflation. The money supply, starting in year 0, was held constant throughout the rest of the twenty-year simulation. That is, money growth that had been 10 percent per year was abruptly cut to zero.

Table 2. *Results of Simulations of Four-Equation Model*[a]

Year	Base equation		Stronger unemployment equation		Long-term equation		Escalators equation	
	$\dot{P}$	U	$\dot{P}$	U	$\dot{P}$	U	$\dot{P}$	U
0	10.0	6.0	10.0	6.0	10.0	6.0	10.0	6.0
1	7.4	7.4	7.1	7.4	7.9	7.5	2.9	6.6
2	5.2	8.4	4.6	8.2	7.0	8.8	2.9	6.7
3	3.4	9.0	2.4	8.6	5.9	9.8	0.5	6.6
4	2.0	9.3	0.7	8.8	4.8	10.6	−0.3	6.5
5	0.8	9.5	−0.7	8.6	3.6	11.2	−0.4	6.5
6	−0.2	9.4	−1.6	8.4	2.4	11.6	−0.5	6.4
7	−0.9	9.3	−2.1	8.0	1.2	11.7	−0.4	6.3
8	−1.4	9.0	−2.3	7.5	0.1	11.8	−0.3	6.3
9	−1.7	8.7	−2.3	7.1	−0.9	11.6	−0.3	6.2
10	−1.9	8.4	−2.1	6.7	−1.9	11.3	−0.2	6.2
11	−1.9	8.0	−1.8	6.3	−2.7	10.9	−0.2	6.1
12	−1.9	7.7	−1.4	6.0	−3.3	10.3	−0.2	6.1
13	−1.7	7.3	−1.0	5.8	−3.8	9.6	−0.1	6.1
14	−1.6	7.0	−0.6	5.7	−4.1	8.9	−0.1	6.1
15	−1.4	6.8	−0.3	5.6	−4.3	8.1	−0.1	6.1
16	−1.2	6.5	−0.1	5.6	−4.3	7.3	−0.1	6.1
17	−1.0	6.3	0.1	5.7	−4.1	6.4	−0.1	6.0
18	−0.8	6.2	0.2	5.7	−3.8	5.6	−0.0	6.0
19	−0.6	6.0	0.3	5.8	−3.4	4.9	−0.0	6.0
20	−0.5	5.9	0.3	5.8	−2.9	4.3	−0.0	6.0

a. $\dot{P}$ = inflation rate; U = unemployment rate.

The simulation results for the rate of inflation and the rate of unemployment are summarized in table 2.

The base equation implies that an abrupt termination of money growth could eliminate inflation in five years. The unemployment rate would rise until year 5, with a peak of 9.5 percent, and would remain above 8.0 percent until year 12. It would take about twenty years for inflation to be eliminated and full employment restored.

This model, like that simulated by Tobin, shows damped oscillatory behavior in all four simulations. Zero money growth therefore leads to a period when prices are falling before the steady state is reached. The greatest rate of deflation, using the base equation, is −1.9 percent, and it comes about ten periods after the anti-inflationary policy is introduced.

If the wage-determination process were more responsive to labor market conditions, as simulated with the stronger unemployment equation, demand policies would be significantly more effective. Inflation would be essentially ended by year 4 and the unemployment rate would not exceed 9.0 percent.

Long-term contracts seriously worsen the period of adjustment. Inflation is not brought to zero until nearly ten periods have passed, and the peak rate of unemployment is 11.8 percent, more than 2 percent higher than the peak rate in the base case simulation. The oscillation period is longer and the overshooting problem is intensified. Deflation peaks at −4.3 percent and the unemployment rate is almost 2 percent below full employment by year 20. A considerable period would have to elapse before steady state would be reached.

According to the four-equation model, escalators offer considerable promise in reducing the pain and speed of adjustment to anti-inflationary policies. Inflation ends after two periods, and the peak unemployment rate is 6.7 percent.[50] Escalator clauses would, of course, worsen the situation when exogenous price shocks cause temporary increases in the overall rate of inflation. Crop failures that lead to food price increases, OPEC crude oil price increases, and other such price shocks would raise wages more quickly if escalators were more extensively adopted.

Dynamic Simulations of the UCLA Macroeconomic Model

UCLA's Business Forecast Project uses a large-scale, empirically estimated model for economic forecasting.[51] The key wage equation in the UCLA model determines the annual percentage rate of change of the hourly index of wage compensation in the nonfarm business sector. This index was chosen as the critical wage indicator because it corresponds exactly with the numerator of the index of unit labor costs in the nonfarm sector published by the U.S. Bureau of Labor Statistics. Standardized unit labor costs, in turn, provide the key path from wages to the implicit price deflator for gross domestic product in the nonfarm sector, which is the pivotal price term in the model.

Wage changes are predicted as a function of the current rate of

50. Real-world escalators generally do not provide for wage decreases due to price deflation. In principle, equation 5d should be modified to reflect this fact. The limited oscillation suggests that such modification would have little effect.

51. Thomas Y. Miracle, ed., *The UCLA Business Forecast for the Nation and California in 1981*, Proceedings of the Twenty-ninth Annual Business Forecasting Conference (Los Angeles: UCLA Business Forecasting Project, December 1980).

change in the implicit price deflator for consumption expenditures, lagged price changes, and the inverse of the unemployment rate, adjusted for demographic changes. The demographic adjustment, developed by Data Resources, Inc., is nearly zero in 1956, rises gradually to a value of about 0.5 percent in 1966 and is 1.4 percent in 1979. The lagged price term is:

(6) $GPCLAG(t) = GPCLAG(t-1) + 0.6\,[GPCLAG(t-1)$
$- GPCLAG(t-2)]$
$+ 0.04\,[GPC(t) - GPCLAG(t-2)],$

where *GPC* is the current percentage change in the consumption deflator and *GPCLAG* is the lagged price term.

In equation 6, the lagged price term is a second-order Pascal lag specification. Current adaptive inflationary expectations, *GPCLAG*, equal the expectations in the previous quarter, plus 60 percent of the change in expectations in the previous quarter, plus 4 percent of the difference between the current rate of inflation and expectations two quarters previously. If 10 percent inflation had been the actual inflation rate long enough to make the lagged price term also equal to 10 percent, and then the consumption deflator were to become perfectly stable, with zero change, then the lagged price variable would drop to 5 percent in seven quarters and would be 2 percent in thirteen quarters. This specification means that if inflation has been rising in the past it will be "extrapolated" to rise more rapidly in the future unless offset by a substantially lower rate of inflation in the current quarter. First-order adaptive expectations specifications do not have this extrapolative component, and a brief variation, such as took place in the third quarter of 1980, will produce lower inflationary expectations immediately. The second-order specification, on the other hand, can ride over a temporary deviation because of the trend component.

Quarterly data over the period from the first quarter of 1956 through the second quarter of 1980 were used to estimate the base forecasting equation (*t*-statistics in parentheses):

(7a) $GJRWSSNF = 0.96 + 0.292*GPC + 0.546*GPCLAG$
$\qquad\qquad\quad (3.05) \qquad (3.88)$
$\qquad + 9.352*[1/(RU - RUADJ)],$
$\qquad (2.77)$

$\bar{R}^2 = 0.565$; Durbin-Watson = 2.13

where *GJRWSSNF* is the annual percentage change in the hourly wage and benefit compensation index for the nonfarm business sector, *RU* is the rate of unemployment, and *RUADJ* is the demographic adjustment. An increase in the adjusted unemployment rate from 5 to 10 percent would slow the rate of change in wages by about 1 percent.[52] A sustained 1 percent increase in inflation would eventually increase wage compensation by 0.83 percent.

This equation reflects, to some extent, each of the three effects of unions and informal contracts on wage determination discussed above. First, long-term contracts and implicit long-term understandings between employers and employees are reflected in the significant weight given to past price movements. Second, the coefficient of the inverse of the adjusted unemployment rate is rather small. An increase in adjusted unemployment from 5 percent to 10 percent would reduce the rate of increase in wage compensation by only about 1 percent. Finally, the effects of escalator clauses on wage gains are captured in the coefficient of the current inflation term. This equation implies considerable inertia in wage adjustments, so it is used for simulations entitled "long-term contracts."

To simulate the effects of more widespread use of escalators, the coefficients of this equation were altered to shift much more weight to the current rate of inflation. This alternative equation, called the "escalators" equation, is as follows:

(7b) $$GJRWSSNF = a + 0.7*GPC + 0.13*GPCLAG + 9.35*[1/(RU-RUADJ)].$$

The constant term, *a*, in equation 7b was adjusted to yield the same prediction as the base forecasting equation for the first quarter of the simulation period (the third quarter of 1980).

Stronger impacts of unemployment on wage determination were simulated by raising the coefficient of the inverse of adjusted unemployment to 109.35, a value almost ten times larger than the empirical estimate. This larger coefficient means that an increase in the adjusted unemployment rate from 5 percent to 10 percent would reduce wage

52. The results of the UCLA macroeconometric model also agree roughly with Okun's review of six macroeconomic Phillips curve estimates; all six pointed to a very costly short-run trade-off between unemployment and inflation. See Arthur M. Okun, "Efficient Disinflationary Policies," *American Economic Review*, vol. 68 (May 1978, *Papers and Proceedings, 1977*), pp. 348–52.

compensation gains from an initial value of 10 percent to virtually zero. The following equation is therefore called the "stronger unemployment" version of the wage equation:

(7c) $GJRWSSNF = a + 0.29*GPC + 0.55*GPCLAG$
$+ 109.35*[1/(RU-RUADJ)]$.

The constant term, a, was adjusted to yield the same forecast for the first quarter of the simulation period as the base forecasting equation (7a).

Four simulations were performed to evaluate the effects of changing the wage equations as described above (see table 3). The first simulation is the base UCLA macroeconometric forecast presented in September 1980, called the "base forecast." All other simulations (labeled "spending cuts") examine the effects of a fiscal policy designed to reduce the rate of inflation. In four quarters, starting in the third quarter of 1980, real federal government expenditures for goods and services are reduced until the spending cuts reach $30 billion in 1972 dollars. These reductions are sustained until the last quarter of 1984.

The empirical estimates of the wage equation reflect a considerable lag between a given reduction in the rate of increase in prices and the full transmission of reduced inflation in wages. Therefore, the simulation using the empirically estimated wage equation is labeled "long-term contracts." A third simulation involved a change in the basic model's wage equation with a switch to the specification with stronger escalation features, as described above. This simulation is called "escalators." Finally, the key wage equation was altered to show a much less attenuated response to unemployment. This simulation is called "stronger unemployment."

The annual results of these simulations for four variables are presented in table 3. The variables are: (1) the percentage change in real GNP, (2) the official rate of unemployment, (3) the percentage change in the implicit price deflator for gross domestic product in the nonfarm business sector (hereafter called the inflation rate), and (4) the percentage change in the index of hourly compensation in the nonfarm business sector (hereafter called wage changes).

The results for real GNP, under all simulations reported in table 3, continue to reflect the business cycle features of the base forecast. Spending reductions initiated in 1980 would not, of course, alter very

Table 3. *Impact of Alternative Wage Equations on the Effectiveness of Monetary and Fiscal Policy, 1980–84*

Percent

Wage equation	1980	1981	1982	1983	1984
Change in real GNP					
Base forecast	−1.3	1.2	4.4	2.4	2.8
Spending cuts					
Long-term contracts	−1.5	−0.9	4.5	2.7	2.9
Escalators	−1.5	−0.9	4.5	2.7	3.1
Stronger unemployment	−1.5	−1.0	4.5	2.9	3.2
Rate of unemployment					
Base forecast	7.4	7.8	7.5	7.5	7.2
Spending cuts					
Long-term contracts	7.5	8.6	8.2	8.2	7.7
Escalators	7.5	8.6	8.3	8.1	7.7
Stronger unemployment	7.5	8.6	8.3	8.1	7.6
Inflation rate					
Base forecast	9.6	9.2	9.1	9.1	8.6
Spending cuts					
Long-term contracts	9.6	8.9	8.6	8.8	8.2
Escalators	9.6	8.9	8.5	8.3	7.5
Stronger unemployment	9.6	8.9	8.2	8.1	7.5
Wage changes					
Base forecast	10.0	10.8	10.4	10.3	10.1
Spending cuts					
Long-term contracts	9.9	10.6	10.1	10.0	9.7
Escalators	9.9	10.2	8.9	8.5	8.2
Stronger unemployment	9.9	9.4	8.7	9.0	9.5

substantially the results for 1980. Real GNP declines in 1981 under all alternatives, but it is predicted to show only modest recovery under the base forecast. For 1981, a maximum deviation in real GNP results is shown. After this period, real GNP recovers in 1982 under all alternatives, and then returns to potential GNP growth (approximately 2.7 percent) in 1983 and 1984.

Bear in mind that the assumed $30 billion (1972 dollars) federal spending reduction is substantial measured by feasible spending reductions, but it is not too large relative to total real GNP. (In 1979, real GNP was $1,431.6 billion in 1972 dollars.)[53] Results for the unemployment rate are correspondingly small. In 1981, the predicted

53. U.S. Department of Labor, *Employment and Training Report of the President* (GPO, 1980), p. 380.

unemployment rate is 8.6 percent for all spending cut alternatives. (Recall that all alternative wage equation results include the cut in spending.)

Unemployment rate differences among the alternative wage equations are not discernible in the first year. By 1984 the unemployment rate is reduced by amounts that vary only slightly among the alternatives. The difference between the rate in the base forecast and those in the three alternative wage equations is about one-half as large in 1984 as in 1981. This reflects a process in the model to restore full employment after a deflationary period.

The lowest inflation rates are predicted using the equations with a stronger unemployment effect and more widespread escalators. Both of these equations imply that inflation could be lowered more than 1 percent below the base equation forecast inflation in 1984. Spending cuts alone, as simulated in the model without alteration of equation 7a, imply that inflation would be reduced by only 0.4 percent in 1984.

Comparisons between the Two Models

The four-equation model differs from the UCLA macroeconometric model in numerous respects; those relevant to the effectiveness of monetary and fiscal policy are summarized below.

In the four-equation model, a lag was specified between price changes and wage adjustments, but no lag was specified between wage changes and price adjustments. The UCLA macroeconometric model reflects lagged price adjustment as well as lagged wage adjustment. A temporary increase in productivity does reduce prices as much as it reduces unit labor costs. Unit labor costs are standardized to reflect more permanent changes.

Higher unemployment does not immediately and substantially reduce wages in the four-equation model. However, product market slack acted instantaneously in the price equation. Product market slack is measured in the UCLA macroeconometric model by the gap between actual and potential real GNP. But product market slack does not instantaneously reduce prices, given unit labor costs, just as labor market slack does not immediately and substantially reduce wages, given prices. The labor markets are not alone in showing considerable attenuation of adjustments with respect to temporary periods of slack.

There was only one price in the four-equation model, whereas there are numerous prices in the UCLA macroeconometric model. More strategically, some key prices are not linked to wages or the GNP gap as strongly as others. Energy prices are dominated by the price for imported petroleum and domestic decontrol policies, not domestic wage changes. Similarly, food prices are strongly influenced by changes in producers' prices at the farm level, which are treated as exogenous. External price changes are therefore more important than is recognized in the simplified model.

Automatic stabilizers were not represented in the four-equation model, whereas the UCLA macroeconometric model has several significant mechanisms that prevent reductions in employment and wage income from reducing disposable income immediately in the same proportion. Increases in unemployment compensation and other transfer payments and reduced personal income taxes paid to federal, state, and local governments all cushion income from reductions in employment.

The four-equation model treated the expenditures on the GNP as identical to the income received by consumers. In the UCLA macroeconometric model, corporate profits absorb a larger share of short-run variations in national income than wages do. Furthermore, dividends do not vary proportionately with profits. Although the long-run adjustment leads to a stable dividend payout ratio, the short-run variation in national income is greater than the variation in personal income. These mechanisms lengthen the time from an initial reduction in GNP to the full consumption adjustments.

Changes in the money supply led to immediate adjustment of the (single) interest rate used in the four-equation model, and interest rate adjustments passed immediately into the (implicit) investment equations. In the UCLA macroeconometric model, changes in the money supply affect short-term rates but do not affect long-term interest rates as quickly. Long-term rates reflect longer-term inflationary expectations. Business fixed investment is a function of the cost of capital, which is tied to long-term rates; therefore a change in the money supply does not affect investment as quickly as in the four-equation model. The four-equation model, since it had no lag between changes in the money supply and full investment adjustments, exaggerates the speed of response of investment to monetary developments.

In summary, most of the differences between the four-equation model and the UCLA macroeconometric model imply longer adjustment periods and weaker responses than were represented in the smaller model. Even if widespread use of escalators made wages adjust rapidly to prices, other mechanisms would slow down the speed of adjustment. According to the UCLA macroeconometric model, widespread use of escalators would not permit monetary and fiscal policy to eliminate inflation in two years with less than 1 percent increase in the employment rate, as suggested by the smaller model.

Implications for Labor Market Measurement

The institutional and analytical models developed in this paper suggest a rationale for the attenuated influence of traditional measures of labor market slackness or tightness (such as the unemployment rate) on wage-change determination. Given this attenuation, it must be concluded that measures of excess demand or supply in the labor market should not be judged primarily on their ability to predict wage inflation. Changes in prices are by far better predictors of wage change than is the unemployment rate. If the wage-change prediction test were applied literally, one would be led to the absurd conclusion that labor market slackness or tightness is better measured by movements in the CPI than by the unemployment rate.

Since the contracting model suggests that employers substitute layoffs and unfilled vacancies for wage adjustments as adaptations to changing demand levels, special interest is focused on these measures. However, data on layoffs, quits, and other measures of turnover are currently confined mainly to manufacturing, although manufacturing represents less than one-fourth of nonfarm payroll employment. It would be desirable to have such data on a more comprehensive basis.[54] In addition, the U.S. Bureau of Labor Statistics ceased collecting vacancy data in 1973. Since that time, analysts have had to rely on proxies for vacancies, such as help-wanted advertising indexes. The contracting model suggests that employers will vary in their vacancy

54. Technical details of the turnover survey can be found in U.S. Bureau of Labor Statistics, *BLS Handbook of Methods for Surveys and Studies,* Bulletin 1910 (GPO, 1976), chap. 4, pp. 43–48. Unfortunately, after this paper was prepared, budget cuts at the BLS led to elimination of the turnover series in December 1981.

strategies according to factors such as industry or firm size. But the help-wanted advertising indexes cannot be disaggregated in this fashion. Some of the observed cyclical response in help-wanted advertising could reflect changes in employer mix rather than changes in employer policy.[55]

Tenure on the job is of special interest to researchers in contracting because contracting theory suggests long-duration employer-employee relationships. The Labor Department currently collects biennial data on tenure on the job. Unfortunately, the two-year collection interval makes analysis of cyclical adjustment in job tenure difficult. More frequent collection would be helpful to researchers, particularly since some industry and occupational disaggregation is already possible.[56]

Finally, the contracting approach suggests that nonunion employers will exhibit certain unionlike characteristics in terms of wage determination and other practices, despite the absence of formal, written agreements. Yet detailed information on employment practices (such as the availability of grievance machinery or the use of merit plans) is collected only for union contracts. Obviously, such information is easier to collect from union agreements since analysts need only read the contract. The obtaining of similar data from nonunion employers would require survey and questionnaire techniques. At present, such information is available only from limited surveys conducted by private organizations such as the Conference Board and the Bureau of National Affairs.[57] It is difficult to determine from such surveys how representative the respondent firms are of the universe of nonunion employers. Indeed, union and nonunion firms are sometimes mixed together in the surveys.

55. There are technical problems with vacancy data, but many of these are mirror images of the difficulties in defining and measuring unemployment. For example, employers' searching activities must be defined, and individuals may often be hired for positions for which no vacancy (defined by some criteria) appeared to exist. In measuring unemployment, individuals' searching activities must also be defined; many individuals leave or lose jobs and drop out of the labor force without entering the state of unemployment. However, the latter problems have not been raised as arguments for not collecting unemployment data, while the former have been cited as reasons not to collect vacancy information. See National Commission on Employment and Unemployment Statistics, *Counting the Labor Force* (GPO, 1979), pp. 118–22.

56. The latest available data on job tenure are for January 1978. See Edward S. Sekscenski, "Job Tenure Declines as Work Force Changes," *Monthly Labor Review*, vol. 102 (December 1979), pp. 48–50.

57. As cited in footnote 4.

Conclusions

The story of labor market contracting can be derived either from analytical models based on turnover costs and/or risk sharing, or from the historical and institutional analysis of wage determination in the union and nonunion sectors. The story is one of labor markets far removed from auction processes, in which workers willing to work at the prevailing wage may have trouble finding employment and employers are sometimes unable to find workers to fill vacancies at the wages they are willing to pay. Thus, contracting models inevitably take on a Keynesian flavor. Real fluctuations in employment and output are possible because wage (and price) changes in response to excess demand and supply are limited. The partial detachment of the wage and price mechanism from real market forces makes possible the existence of ongoing inflation momentum.

There are some hidden features in a contracting world, however. In particular, in the collective bargaining sector, where contracting is most formalized and where negotiating and impasse costs contribute to the long-range horizon, there is an incentive to write contingency clauses to avoid contract reopenings. The main example of such contingency clauses in the real world is the escalator, which links wages to prices. To the extent that price inflation is sensitive to real economic fluctuations, the use of escalators can create a backdoor channel for wage inflation sensitivity to those fluctuations. A real slowdown's anti-inflation effect is amplified by the wage-price interaction inherent in escalator behavior. Escalators obviously pose a symmetrical danger during periods of economic expansion. And they may speed the reaction of wage inflation to price inflation (or deflation) that stems from exogenous sources of the OPEC type.

Is contracting a help or hindrance to anti-inflation demand-restraint policies? The answer is obvious, but ambiguous. In a pure auction model, anti-inflation policy would be highly effective. But in such a model, it is not clear why anyone would care much about inflation. If all markets were able to adjust costlessly to depreciation of the *numeraire,* leaving relative prices unaffected, inflation would not be a problem. Thus, in the extreme case, contracting is the villain that creates both unemployment and the *problem of* inflation. However, if the question is simply whether more or less contracting within a world of significant contracting behavior is helpful to traditional anti-inflation policy, the answer is "it depends." The attenuation of the influence of real output on wage and price inflation is harmful. But escalator clauses may have the (presumably unintended) effect of increasing rather than attenuating the real-output effect.

At the macro level, the impacts of contracting can be described by the use of lagged coefficients (to convey lethargy and long-term horizons), alternative degrees of wage sensitivity of price change (to simulate escalators), and weakened coefficients of real output indexes—such as unemployment rates—in wage-change equations (to simulate the attenuation effect). In this paper, whether the model used was a simple four-equation set of relationships or an elaborate many-equation forecasting model, the results were qualitatively similar. Escalators helped reduce inflation under a regime of demand restraint; other aspects of contracting made inflation reduction more difficult. Our opinion is that the limited scope of escalators (they cover very few nonunion workers, and many union workers, especially in short contracts, are uncovered) suggests that quick and painless cures for inflation are not likely to be developed solely through induced labor-market slack.

Although the UCLA macroeconometric model and the four-equation model gave qualitatively similar results, the specifications and calibrations used led to significantly more pessimistic quantitative estimates in the large-scale model. The only source of inertia in the four-equation model came from the wage equation; all other adjustments were instantaneous. In the large-scale model there are other substantial sources of inertia, especially in the price-adjustment sector. Product market slack, like labor market slack, does not immediately lower prices. Significant external price shocks keep unit labor costs from fully determining the prices to which wage earners are reacting. In fact, there are many areas of the economy that are characterized by lethargy. Plans are made in advance and continue in the face of changed circumstances. It may well be that the explanation for such behavior is similar to the turnover-cost theory invoked for the labor market; if decisionmaking is itself costly, then it pays to make long-term plans that cut down on the frequency of decisions. In any case, the stickiness associated with contracting in the labor market is likely to be reinforced in other sectors of many-equation models and the real world.

Comments by Robert J. Flanagan

The paper by Mitchell and Kimbell reports on simulation experiments that were designed to explore a very important issue—just how much influence will alternative contractual arrangements in labor markets have on the speed of adjustment of the rates of inflation and unemployment to changes in macroeconomic policy?

I have two broad reservations concerning the simulations and some of the implications that the authors draw from them. First, the simulation work does not complement the general discussion of contractual arrangements as well as it might. Early in the paper, much is made of the difference between contractual arrangements in the union (explicit-contract) and nonunion (implicit-contract) sectors, and I believe that this is appropriate. No matter how much one may wish to emphasize the importance of implicit contracts, there are important empirical differences in the wage-adjustment functions of the union and nonunion sectors that cannot be overlooked. (Most important, the labor market effects are stronger in the nonunion sector, but the price effects are weaker.) These differences are in effect noted but play no real role in the simulations. The paper effectively contrasts the behavior of a one-sector economy operating under different contracting arrangements with a one-sector economy that is not. What is needed to complement the earlier discussion is a two-sector model in which one sector exhibits contracting characteristics much more strongly than the other.

The importance of a two-sector exploration is that *differences* in contractual arrangements can be an important source of wage inertia. Differences in contractual arrangements will be reflected in sectoral differences in the speed of macroeconomic adjustments. But the variable response of sectors with different contract arrangements will itself open up intersectoral wage differentials that will feed back into the wage-determination process and contribute to the sluggishness of wage adjustments to macroeconomic stimuli.

The problem becomes acute when the feedback is asymmetrical. Where wage changes in one sector (such as unions with long-term explicit contracts) are sensitive to changes in relative wages with respect to another sector (such as nonunion firms that revise their wages annually), but the reverse is not true, the full effect of contracting arrangements will not be captured by one-sector simulation experiments such as those performed by Mitchell and Kimbell. That is because in this situation macroeconomic stimuli may create relatively rapid responses in the nonunion sectors, but the response will alter relative wages. By the time long-term contracts in the unionized sector come up for renegotiation the macroeconomic posture may have changed significantly, but the "disequilibrium" in relative wages may continue to drive union wage demands. Something like this appears to have contributed to wage inertia in the early 1970s. Although the effects of wage inertia were very much tied to the structure of contractual arrangements, they would not be captured in the simulation developed by Mitchell and Kimbell.

The difficulty seems most important in the discussions of policy implications in the paper. The analysis is an effort to consider the macroeconomic returns to policies that might alter certain contractual arrangements. But that question is not really answered for the United States by comparing a one-sector contracting model against a one-sector base case. The approach taken in the paper might be more appropriate for countries where collective bargaining arrangements effectively determine wages for the entire economy. An interesting and largely unexplored question for the United States concerns the macroeconomic implications of a mixed contract and noncontract economy.

A related question concerns the macroeconomic behavior of an economy with staggered contracts. This question would be germane even if there were no sectoral differences in contractual arrangements other than the timing of negotiations. One effect of a system of staggered contracts would be to alter wage differentials between sectors, and these disturbances could be an independent source of inertia. Something like this is believed to occur regularly in the construction industry and, more generally, in the United Kingdom, where the synchronization of contract negotiations—a relatively mild form of incomes policy—has been proposed.

The second broad reservation I have about the suitability of simulations for policy judgments stems from the separate treatment of various contractual influences. Although separating the effects of long-duration contracts and escalator arrangements has a certain pedagogical value, in practice cost-of-living adjustments are a part of—indeed a quid pro quo for—long-term contracts. As the authors point out early in the paper, this is one of the most common sorts of contingency arrangements found in collective bargaining agreements. The simulations of the "wage equation with escalators" in both the four-equation and UCLA models are different from the actual world of escalation. A closer approximation of contractual reality would be to combine the features of an equation with long-term contracts and an equation with escalators. Until such a model is explored, the rather favorable comments that the authors advance on the potential value of widespread escalation for macroeconomic adjustment may be premature. The larger issue that this raises is the endogeneity of contracts and contract issues. This is a relatively unexplored aspect of the recent work on contract theory, but until the endogenous aspects of contracts in labor markets are modeled, it is risky to draw strong policy conclusions from simulation models.

Comments by John B. Taylor

The Mitchell-Kimbell paper is divided into two largely distinct parts. I like the first part very much. The critical review of the invisible handshake literature is extremely useful and informative. However, the second part of the paper is rather uninformative with respect to the central issue raised, that is, the relationship between wage contracts and inflation.

To illustrate some of my reservations and why I do not think the simulation experiments are informative, consider equation 5a, which is the wage-change determination equation. Equation 5a is varied in 5b, 5c, and 5d to represent alternative forms of contracts. For example, according to this methodology, if one wants to investigate the effects of longer-term contracts on the inflationary process, the authors suggest varying the coefficient of the lagged wage. Alternatively, if one wants to represent different forms of indexing, the coefficient on the price feedback would be adjusted.

Consider this technique as it applies to adjusting the coefficient on lagged wages. There is no indication given as to how this coefficient would correspond to contract length, or how one would go about matching up a certain set of contractual institutions with the coefficient. Essentially, the numerical value of this coefficient is arbitrary. Moreover, the lagged variables in equation 5 could represent expectations of inflation as much as they represent previous contract decisions. Hence, simulation of the model with alternative values of this coefficient conveys no direct information about the effect of contracts. The coefficient represents a conglomeration of the expectations and contract effects on inflation inertia.

There are other ways to go about achieving the important objective of finding out the effect of contracts on inflation. In my own recent research I have emphasized two features of the contracting mechanism that I do not think are emphasized here. One is the overlapping of contracts—the simple fact that all contracts in the economy are not signed at the same point in time; the second—an issue alluded to above—is that not only are contracts part of the inertial mechanism of inflation, expectations of inflation also play an important part. In any simulation study, it is necessary at least to discuss how one would go about extracting that expectation component from the contractual component.

In my own research I have assumed as a behavioral idea that the contract wage is set relative to the expected prevailing wage during the contract period. Wage decisions would also be influenced by other variables, such as the unemployment rate emphasized in the Mitchell-Kimbell paper. With this formulation, the coefficients representing expectations emerge rather explicitly, and it is possible to estimate these coefficients using rational expectations or adaptive expectations, whichever one feels is appropriate.

I have worked with simulating models of this kind with fairly realistic parameter values and find, perhaps not surprisingly, that the trade-off between inflation and unemployment is not nearly as pessimistic as is found in the Mitchell and Kimbell simulations. That result largely depends on the expectations being influenced by policy—by a change in the policy regime.

There is one additional way to go about distinguishing between contracts and expectations, or between forward-looking and backward-looking wage-setting behavior. This is to use actual contract data. The Bureau of Labor Statistics has a systematic data file on union contracts, which can be referenced by a computer program. Although the data set is expensive to reference, it could be used to help distinguish between expectations and inertia. The main difficulty with this approach is that many wage contracts are implicit and arise in the nonunion sector. In this respect the BLS data on union contracts is incomplete.

PIERRE FORTIN *and* KEITH NEWTON

Labor Market Tightness and Wage Inflation in Canada

SINCE World War II the Canadian labor force has grown at rates virtually unsurpassed by those of any other industrialized country. Nevertheless, with the exception of the period 1958–62, the unemployment rate did not exceed 5.5 percent until the 1970s, though this overall performance was flawed by regional disparities and seasonal and cyclical fluctuations. In the 1970s, by contrast, the unemployment rate fell *below* 5.5 percent on only one occasion (1974). Furthermore, inflation, which had been gathering some momentum during the previous decade, accelerated sharply in the early 1970s and has maintained historically high levels thereafter—albeit with some amelioration during the period 1975–78, when wage and price controls were in place.

An examination of this apparent deterioration is clearly in order and the present paper is intended to draw attention to a number of related labor market developments in recent years, to examine some of the analytical studies that have addressed these factors and their interrelationships, and to consider their policy implications.

Overview

The Canadian unemployment rate in 1979 reached 7.5 percent, a level unattained since the Depression ended and higher than that of

We thank Jean-Pierre Aubry, David Backus, Martin Neil Baily, Ronald G. Bodkin, Jean-Marie Dufour, David Foot, Bernard Fortin, John Helliwell, Robert Lacroix, David Laidler, James Mackinnon, Michael Parkin, James Pesando, Louis Phaneuf, and participants in the Brookings conference for helpful comments; and Sylvie Dillard and Doris DesJardins for assistance. We are grateful to the Social Research Council of Quebec, the Social Sciences and Humanities Research Council of Canada, and the Economic Council of Canada for financial support.

any major industrialized country.[1] The rate of growth of output per man-hour averaged only 1.8 percent per year in the 1970s, compared to 3.4 percent in the 1960s, and unit labor cost increases followed a path similar to that of the general rate of inflation. Add to this a record of time lost due to strikes that in some years was exceeded only by Italy, and the despondency of labor market observers may be appreciated.

The interpretations of the malaise reveal a variety of emphases—though the majority appear to cite institutional and demographic changes as significant factors—which are in turn reflected both in the official responses of governments and in the foci of researchers. Early speculations ran in terms of an outward shift of the trade-off relation due to worsening structural unemployment, and attempts were made to demonstrate the existence of previous shifts in the relation between inflation and unemployment or vacancies and unemployment.[2]

In the search for factors to explain these changing circumstances, a number of candidates soon began to emerge. The changing composition of the labor force was readily apparent in the form of increasing proportions of women and young people. In 1966, 15- to 24-year-olds accounted for 24.2 percent of the labor force, males 25 to 54 for 44.3 percent, and women for 31.3 percent. A decade later the corresponding figures were 26.9 percent, 39.5 percent, and 37.6 percent.[3] Clearly, the attitudes, characteristics, and labor force behavior of the majority of labor force participants in recent years no longer coincided with those of the prime working-age male breadwinner who formerly dominated the market. In any case, the data show that the unemployment rates of women and young people are higher than the aggregate rate. In 1981, the unemployment rate for women was 8.0 percent and for 15-

1. Canadian unemployment rates during the Depression were close to 20 percent. See Frank T. Denton and Sylvia Ostry, "Historical Estimates of the Canadian Labour Force," 1961 Census Monograph Programme, Dominion Bureau of Statistics (Ottawa, 1967). Recent data about unemployment rates and other labor force statistics used throughout this paper are from Labour Force Survey results, published monthly in Statistics Canada, *The Labour Force,* catalogue 71-001.

2. Michael Skolnik and Farid Siddiqui, "The Paradox of Unemployment and Job Vacancies: Some Theories Confronted by Data," *Industrial Relations/Relations industrielles,* vol. 31 (1976), pp. 32–56; and Economic Council of Canada, *People and Jobs: A Study of the Canadian Labour Market* (Ottawa: Information Canada, 1976).

3. The trend has continued: by 1979, young people accounted for 27 percent of the labor force, women for nearly 40 percent, and prime-age males for only 38 percent. Statistics Canada, *The Labour Force.*

to 24-year-olds it was 12.9 percent, compared to an aggregate rate of 7.3 percent.[4]

One of the most important institutional changes is thought to have been the amendment of the Unemployment Insurance Act.[5] This amendment, which came into force in 1972, considerably liberalized unemployment insurance (UI) provisions by extending coverage, reducing eligibility requirements, increasing the benefit rate, and extending the duration of benefits. As indicated below, the empirical evidence concerning the impact of UI changes is rather mixed. Of the studies indicating a significant effect, the addition to the official unemployment rate ranges from a little less than 1 percentage point— from 6.5 percent to 7.5 percent—in a number of early studies[6] to as high as 1.3, 1.5, and 1.9 percentage points in three recent studies.[7] It should be pointed out, however, that amendments to the UI legislation in 1975, 1977, and 1979 have rendered the overall provisions less generous.

A second institutional arrangement often cited is the minimum wage. The argument proceeds from standard microtheoretic propositions concerning the disemployment effects of a minimum wage[8] and suggests these effects may be expected to be strongest for precisely those groups whose labor force share is increasing, thus exacerbating the interplay of the demographic and UI factors mentioned above. Mini-

4. Statistics Canada, *The Labour Force* (December 1981).
5. 1971 Can. Stat. chap. 48.
6. Herbert G. Grubel, Dennis Maki, and Shelley Sax, "Real and Insurance-Induced Unemployment in Canada," *Canadian Journal of Economics*, vol. 11 (May 1978), pp. 174–91; Christopher Green and Jean-Michel Cousineau, *Unemployment in Canada: The Impact of Unemployment Insurance* (Ottawa: Supply and Services Canada, 1976); Samuel A. Rea, Jr., "Unemployment Insurance and Labour Supply: A Simulation of the 1971 Unemployment Insurance Act," *Canadian Journal of Economics*, vol. 10 (May 1977), pp. 263–78.
7. Ronald G. Bodkin and André Cournoyer, "Legislation and the Labour Market: A Selective Review of Canadian Studies," in Herbert G. Grubel and Michael A. Walker, eds., *Unemployment Insurance: Global Evidence of its Effects on Unemployment* (Vancouver: Fraser Institute, 1978), pp. 62–88; Fred Lazar, "The Impact of the 1971 Unemployment Insurance Revisions on Unemployment Rates: Another Look," *Canadian Journal of Economics*, vol. 11 (August 1978), pp. 559–70; Frank Reid and Noah M. Meltz, "Causes of Shifts in the Unemployment-Vacancy Relationship: An Empirical Analysis for Canada," *Review of Economics and Statistics*, vol. 61 (August 1979), pp. 470–75.
8. Edwin G. West and Michael McKee, *Minimum Wages: The New Issues in Theory, Evidence, Policy, and Politics*, Economic Council of Canada and the Institute for Research on Public Policy (Quebec: Supply and Services Canada, 1980).

mum wages exist not only in the federal jurisdiction but also in each of the provinces of Canada, so that their potential for good or ill is frequently, and hotly, debated. There is as yet no overwhelming body of empirical evidence, although, as reported below, several recent studies claim disemployment effects. There is clear evidence of substantial upward adjustments in minimum wages in all jurisdictions in 1974, 1975, and 1976. As an example, in 1974 the average upward adjustment was 20.3 percent.[9]

Other government programs may also have contributed to a change in the characteristics of the Canadian labor market and of its participants. For example, since the late 1960s the federal Canada Manpower Training Program has served about 300,000 clients per year and Canada has disbursed more training funds per labor force member than any other developed country save Sweden.[10]

For these reasons, some observers have felt that the Canadian labor market today is very different from that of even a decade ago, and that traditional measures of performance—such as the aggregate unemployment rate—do not adequately capture the changed circumstances.[11] One of the official responses to this perception has been to stress that the labor market is actually characterized by a good deal more tightness than meets the eye. Indeed, a significant development on the statistical front was a new published series for the employment-to-population ratio, which highlights Canada's impressive job creation record.[12] This series and other indicators of labor market performance are shown in appendix table 4.

Some of the studies reviewed in the following section indicate increased natural or equilibrium unemployment rates in the 1970s compared to the 1960s: several estimates place recent natural rates at 6 percent or more.[13] They are therefore consistent with the view that

9. Ibid., p. 22.

10. Employment and Immigration Canada, *Annual Report 1979–80* (Ottawa: Minister of Supply and Services, 1980); and R. A. Jenness, "Comparative Manpower Strategies," *Industrial Relations/Relations industrielles*, vol. 32 (1977), pp. 94–107.

11. Economic Council of Canada, *People and Jobs*, pp. 23–25, 191–211.

12. Green suggests that the use of the employment-population ratio rather than the unemployment rate is sufficient to reestablish the trade-off: Christopher Green, "The Employment Ratio as an Indicator of Aggregate Demand Pressure," *Monthly Labor Review* (April 1977), pp. 25–32. See also P. A. Della Valle and E. Primorac, "Potential Labour Surplus," *International Labour Review*, vol. 116 (November–December 1977), pp. 279–88.

13. Concerning the question of the voluntary nature of recent unemployment, the

there is little scope for stimulatory measures before inflation accelerates. However, other evidence suggests more slack than meets the eye, represented by labor hoarding and discouraged workers.[14] Neither concept is captured by the official unemployment count. The presence of such phenomena may mean that initial doses of stimulus will serve only to absorb the less visible labor market slack without any appreciable effect upon the official unemployment count.

The fear of the inflationary consequences of addressing the unemployment problem stems from the fact that Canada has recently experienced double-digit inflation for the first time since the Korean War. The inflation rate had already gathered momentum during the 1960s; then in 1971 the government responded to rising unemployment by liberalizing the unemployment insurance legislation and implementing a highly expansionary monetary policy. It is possible that these policies were partly offsetting in their impact on unemployment. In any event, the unemployment rate declined only moderately, and both inflation and the rate of increase of wages increased, especially in 1974 and 1975.[15] A direct result was the introduction, in October 1975, of a program of controls on compensation, prices, and profits administered by the Anti-Inflation Board (AIB).

Compensation was regulated under the AIB by means of a guideline rate of increase comprising a basic protection factor (geared to anticipated inflation rates of 8, 6, and 4 percent during the three years of the program), a national productivity factor of 2 percent (the approximate average rate of growth of productivity during the twenty preceding years), and an experience adjustment factor not to exceed 2 percent.[16] This last factor was designed to permit "catch-up" for

---

promise of the search-theoretic framework has as yet been little exploited in Canada. A notable exception is the series of discussion papers by Abrar Hasan and Surendra Gera, *Job Search in Canada: Theory and Evidence* (Ottawa: Economic Council of Canada, forthcoming).

14. G. Marion and Byron G. Spencer, "Labour Hoarding and the Wage Share," *Industrial Relations/Relations industrielles*, vol. 34 (1979), pp. 70–83; and Tom Siedule and Keith Newton, "Another Labour Market Indicator: Some Estimates and Implications of Labour Hoarding in Canada," *Canadian Public Policy*, vol. 6 (Winter 1980), pp. 101–05.

15. While the unemployment rate, even in 1973 and 1974, remained relatively high by historical standards, other indicators suggested labor market buoyancy. Job vacancies, for example, increased at unprecedented rates in the period 1971–74.

16. Reginald S. Letourneau, *The Impact of the Anti-Inflation Program: A Framework for Analysis* (Ottawa: The Conference Board in Canada, 1979), pp. 1–3.

groups that had experienced below-average rates of increase prior to inception of the program. Increases in prices were limited to the amounts required to cover cost increases, and profits were controlled mainly through year-end tests based on companies' profit histories.

The controversy precipitated by the imposition of the controls program was subsequently mirrored in the interpretation of its performance. On the face of it, figures show that the rate of increase of hourly earnings declined from 14.74 percent per year in the two years before controls to an average of 10.19 percent per year during the three years of controls ending in October 1978.[17] The annual rate of increase of the consumer price index (CPI) dropped from 11.10 percent before controls to an average of 7.88 percent per year during the control period.

What is more difficult to estimate is the effect of controls versus what would have happened without them. Most studies to date show some modest reduction in the rate of wage inflation and very little impact on the rate of price inflation. Indeed, one recent study suggests that one of the principal effects of the AIB was to redistribute income from persons to business.[18] In addition to the administrative costs of the program, organized labor deplored its interference with free collective bargaining, businessmen railed against its incursion in the free market, and many economists raised questions about the implications for resource allocation of rigidities in relative wages and prices. The labor movement's contention that the program restrained wages but not profits and prices seems, in retrospect, to have been substantially correct. Nevertheless, recent public opinion polls in Canada suggest majority support for controls.

An important feature of the program is that its scope was quite severely constrained. About 40 percent of the price level for final goods and services in the Canadian economy is determined on world markets in the form of trade prices and raw materials prices, and the AIB did not attempt to control these. Indeed, the international sector has frequently been associated with inflationary pressures in Canada. Only in 1975–77 did unit labor costs contribute more to the increase in the price level than unit materials costs and import prices combined.[19]

17. Frank Reid, "Unemployment and Inflation: An Assessment of Canadian Macroeconomic Policy," *Canadian Public Policy*, vol. 6 (Spring 1980), pp. 283–99.

18. Letourneau, *The Impact of the Anti-Inflation Program.*

19. Reginald Letourneau, *Inflation: The Canadian Experience* (The Conference Board in Canada, 1980), p. 76.

Furthermore, while Canada was to some extent insulated from the initial shock administered by the OPEC oil cartel, energy prices and food prices have increased rapidly in the last decade.[20]

The amelioration in the rate of wage inflation has so far carried over into the postcontrols period, largely because of generally recessionary conditions. Since real wages have actually declined in the last two years, however, there is likely to be considerable pressure for catch-up. This may, in our view, be supported by the recent emergence of severe shortages in a number of occupations. The energy-related "megaprojects" in the Canadian West are expected to make particularly large demands for a variety of skilled occupations that are already in short supply across the country.[21] A major policy concern of government is now to facilitate mobility and mount the training programs that will help reduce bottlenecks and alleviate inflationary wage movements.

Alternative Measures of Labor Market Tightness

One suggested way of measuring labor market tightness appropriately is to correct the official unemployment rate for the evolving demographic circumstances and public policy measures that presumably have their main impact on its structural, not its cyclical, component. This approach has been popularized in the United States by Perry and Wachter. However, Perry's weighted unemployment rate (*UP*) and Wachter's *UGAP* have actually remained confined to the demographic correction, although in principle Wachter's measure can also handle policy changes.[22] In Canada, the sweeping revision of the Unemployment Insurance Act (1971), the substantial increase in the relative minimum wage (1968–76), and the progress of unionization in the public sector (1965–78) may also have influenced the meaning of the official unemployment rate as an index of the excess supply of labor.[23]

20. It is now common to see price indexes for Canada calculated with the exclusion of energy and food prices.

21. Gordon Betcherman, *Skills and Shortages*, Economic Council of Canada (Ottawa: Supply and Services Canada, 1980).

22. See George L. Perry, "Changing Labor Markets and Inflation," *Brookings Papers on Economic Activity, 3:1970*, pp. 411–41 (hereafter *BPEA*); and Michael L. Wachter, "The Changing Cyclical Responsiveness of Wage Inflation," *BPEA, 1:1976*, pp. 115–59.

23. Another candidate is simply the unemployment rate of adult males.

A second approach substitutes some measure of the job vacancy rate (*VAC*) for the official unemployment rate in wage equations. Denton, Feaver, and Robb have recently constructed one by linking three independent overlapping data series: the National Employment Service data in the 1950s, the Department of Finance's help-wanted index in the 1960s, and Statistics Canada's Job Vacancy Survey data in the 1970s.[24] The resulting vacancy rate is vulnerable to the same criticism as the official unemployment rate: demographic and policy changes in the 1960s and 1970s may have changed its meaning over time as an index of labor market tightness. Despite this misgiving, we will test its performance below in our wage equation.

A third approach exploits the fact that the cyclical changes in the employment status of the work force are but one aspect of the cyclical changes in the demand for labor, the other being changes in the work effort (output per person-hour and hours per person employed) relative to trend. Robert J. Gordon has explored a few such alternatives in conjunction with or in place of the (corrected) unemployment rate.[25] Most of them are tested in our wage equation.

A Canadian *UGAP*

Our Canadian *UGAP* corrects the official unemployment rate not only for demographic changes, as in Wachter's own work, but also for unemployment insurance revisions, minimum wage developments, and public-sector relative wages.[26]

Unemployment Insurance Policy

The 1971 revision of the Unemployment Insurance Act in Canada increased the aftertax wage-replacement ratio approximately from 66

24. Frank T. Denton, Christine H. Feaver, and A. Leslie Robb, "Patterns of Unemployment Behaviour in Canada," Discussion Paper No. 36 (Economic Council of Canada, 1975).

25. See Gordon, "Inflation in Recession and Recovery," *BPEA, 1:1971*, pp. 105–58; and "Comments by Robert J. Gordon," *BPEA, 1:1980*, pp. 249–57. Among the alternatives are the actual-to-potential output gap and the unemployment of hours, or, equivalently, the measure of labor hoarding constructed by Tom Siedule and Keith Newton, "Tentative Measure of Labour Hoarding, 1961–1977," Discussion Paper No. 128 (Economic Council of Canada, 1979).

26. Details of the construction of our *UGAP* may be found in Pierre Fortin and

to 80 percent for individuals earning the average industrial wage or less. It also legislated a substantial increase in the ratio of the maximum number of benefit weeks to the corresponding minimum number of employment weeks required for eligibility. Under the new act, anybody with only eight weeks of employment in the previous year qualified for twenty-eight weeks of UI benefits on average, and for up to forty-four weeks in high-unemployment regions. Since the weekly benefit replaced about 80 percent of net wage, each of the employment weeks in the qualifying period allowed the eligible unemployed to collect benefits equivalent to 2.8 weeks of full pay on average ($0.8 \times 28 \div 8$), and to 4.4 weeks of full pay in depressed regions ($0.8 \times 44 \div 8$). These implicit wage subsidies of 280 and 440 percent to those who are forced into or prefer to remain in the most unstable segment of the labor market can be compared with a subsidy of only 33 percent under the old act, which required two employment weeks per benefit week ($0.66 \times 0.5 = 0.33$). Subsequent revisions of the act in 1975, 1977, and 1978 have reduced the generosity of the UI program, but in 1981 the wage subsidy for unstable employment still ranges from 72 to 302 percent, with an observed average of 180 percent.[27]

By comparison, in the United States, even when federally extended benefits are taken into account, the approximate range for the subsidy is 42 to 146 percent, with a median of about 63 percent.[28] Put more sharply, the least generous of the Canadian regions is still more generous for high-unemployment workers (72 percent) than the median

---

Louis Phaneuf, "Why is the Unemployment Rate so High in Canada?" working paper 8115 (Laval University, Department of Economics, 1981).

27. The maximum number of benefit weeks and the minimum number of employment weeks are determined by the act. They vary across forty-nine regions according to the regional unemployment rate. Data were obtained from a quarterly publication by Statistics Canada, *Statistical Report on the Operation of the Unemployment Insurance Act,* catalogue 73-001.

28. For the United States we use a liberal assumption of 72 percent for the net wage-replacement ratio. A low-subsidy state is one for which the ratio of the maximum benefit duration (B) to the (corresponding) minimum length of employment qualifying period (E) is 0.5 (for example, Georgia, Texas). The regular subsidy is then 36 percent (0.72×0.5), and the extended subsidy is 50 percent higher, or 54 percent. Hence under the assumption that federally extended benefits are triggered on one-third of the time, the average subsidy is 42 percent ($0.36 \times 0.67 + 0.54 \times 0.33$). A high-subsidy state (for example, Hawaii) is taken to be one with $B = 26$ weeks and $E = 15$ weeks. Then the regular subsidy is 125 percent, the extended subsidy 188 percent, and the average subsidy 146 percent. The assumption for the median state is $B/E = 0.75$, which yields a regular subsidy of 54 percent, an extended subsidy of 84 percent, and an average subsidy of 63 percent.

American state (63 percent), and the median Canadian region subsidizes the wage (180 percent) more than the most generous American state (145 percent) and almost three times as much as the median American state.

This description of the 1971 revision of the Unemployment Insurance Act and the comparison between Canada and the United States serves to underline two points. First, the revision may have exerted an upward pressure on the aggregate unemployment rate, not only through the increased subsidization of unemployment of workers who are a permanent part of the labor force, but also through the heavier subsidization of unstable employment in the secondary labor market, which may have drawn into or retained in the labor force groups of persons bound to experience higher than average unemployment rates. Second, the figures of the parameter changes involved in the Canadian revision are huge by any standards and make it likely that the greater generosity of the Canadian unemployment insurance program had an important upward effect on the aggregate unemployment rate.

This is borne out by the evidence from a wide variety of empirical studies (macroeconomic structural models, reduced-form models, and microeconomic models based on individual files or on Labour Force Survey data). They indicate that the 1971 revision of the Unemployment Insurance Act did raise the official unemployment rate by an amount ranging from 0.7 to 2.0 percentage points.[29] As far as we know, there is no study arguing that changes in U.S. unemployment insurance regulations since the early 1960s have increased the aggregate unemployment rate by more than 0.25 percentage point.

Minimum Wage Policy

The average minimum wage in Canada increased very rapidly in the first half of the 1970s relative to the average Canadian industrial wage and the U.S. federal minimum wage. In 1975 the ratio of the average of provincial minimum wages to average hourly earnings in manufacturing was 12.5 percent higher than in 1968, and in 1977 the average minimum wage in Canada was 25 percent higher than in the United States.[30]

29. D. Peter Dungan and Thomas A. Wilson, "Notes on the Equilibrium Unemployment Rate" (Economic Council of Canada, 1979), have recently presented a summary of the various point estimates.
30. Denis Guidon, "The Non-Accelerating Unemployment Rate in Canada: A

Furthermore, one should expect that minimum wage increases in Canada in the 1970s had a stronger positive impact on the unemployment rate than in the United States for four basic reasons: (1) Canadian minimum wage regulations cover almost 100 percent of nonfarm wage earners, compared to a much lower figure in the United States (75 percent in 1975); (2) there is some evidence that the disemployment effect of the minimum wage is nonlinear and increases with its level, which was higher in Canada than in the United States;[31] (3) in a more open economy like that of Canada, firms are likely to adjust to higher minimum wages more through employment reductions and less through price increases; and (4) the high wage subsidy provided to unstable employment by unemployment compensation should weaken the discouraged-worker effect and exacerbate the effect on the measured unemployment rate of any minimum wage increases.

The available national and regional evidence supports the presumption of a substantial impact of the minimum wage (although more tentative than in the case of UI) on the measured unemployment rate, particularly for youth and in high minimum wage provinces. On the basis of the few existing empirical studies, we would estimate that a 10 percent increase in the relative minimum wage from its average level for the 1970–78 period has an effect on the measured unemployment rate of between 0.2 and 0.5 percentage point.[32] Our argument also makes clear why we believe it very likely that minimum wage developments in the early 1970s have had a greater cumulative effect on the aggregate unemployment rate in Canada than in the United States.

Reexamination," presented to the Société canadienne de Science économique, May 1981.

31. Pierre Fortin, *Une évaluation de l'effet de la politique québéçoise du salaire minimum sur la production, l'emploi, les prix et la répartition des revenus: annexe technique* (An Evaluation of the Impact of Quebec Minimum Wage Policy on Output, Employment, Prices, and Income Distribution), prepared for Quebec Department of Labour and Manpower (Quebec City, 1978).

32. This range is based on the point estimates we have calculated from four studies: Fortin, *Une évaluation;* Jean-Michel Cousineau, "Impact du salaire minimum sur le chômage des jeunes et des femmes au Québec" (The Effect of the Minimum Wage on Unemployment among Youth and Women in Quebec), *Industrial Relations/Relations industrielles,* vol. 34 (1979), pp. 403–16; Robert Swidinsky, "Minimum Wages and Teenage Unemployment," *Canadian Journal of Economics,* vol. 13 (February 1980), pp. 158–71; Dennis R. Maki, "The Effect of Changes in Minimum Wage Rates on Provincial Unemployment Rates, 1970–77," *Industrial Relations/Relations industrielles,* vol. 34 (1979), pp. 418–29.

Public Wage Policy

Robert Hall has argued on the basis of search theory that wage increases in the nonentrepreneurial sector greater than those in the entrepreneurial sector would raise unemployment by encouraging rational job seekers to wait longer for nonentrepreneurial job openings rather than accept entrepreneurial job offers immediately.[33] Although presented as an explanation of wage rigidity and the persistence of unemployment over the business cycle, his analysis is perfectly general and applicable to the case of permanent wage differentials as well.

We are skeptical about the empirical validity of Hall's argument mainly because, from a career point of view, a lower-wage job held temporarily in the entrepreneurial sector while waiting for a higher-wage offer to materialize in the nonentrepreneurial sector would seem to dominate the option of living out the wait on UI benefits or social assistance. Be that as it may, the Canadian experience with rising public-sector unionization and rising relative public-sector wages since the middle 1960s provides an interesting opportunity to test Hall's proposition. This is the more so since the generous UI program in Canada reduces the cost of longer unemployment duration and increases the likelihood that if the wage differential effect exists at all, Canadian data will be apt to reveal it.

In general, the youth and female unemployment rate equations used in the construction of the Canadian *UGAP* reveal strong demographic and UI influences. The effects of minimum wages are imprecisely identified and Hall's conjecture on the unemployment consequences of the relative public-sector wage does not fare well, but the final verdict should not be rendered before more reliable public wage data series become available. The final *UGAP* series appears in the appendix (table 3) for further reference.

An Annual Canadian Wage Equation

In the following sections, our goal is to generate new macroeconomic evidence on the link between labor market tightness and the process

33. Robert E. Hall, "The Rigidity of Wages and the Persistence of Unemployment," *BPEA*, 2:1975, pp. 301–35.

of wage inflation in Canada for the period 1957–78. We will demonstrate that the actual behavior of wages over this twenty-two-year span has been a relatively stable function of only a few arguments, and that the Phillips curve remains a meaningful concept for policy planning even in the small and open Canadian economy. This is in contrast to the apparent lack of success of quite a few Canadian and U.S. researchers in identifying a reliable Canadian Phillips relation at the macro level.[34] We also trust that some of our results may bear some relevance for the understanding of U.S. wage behavior.

Our basic wage equation stems from the application of the standard disequilibrium adjustment hypothesis to the balance between labor demand and supply in the private commercial sector. It has the following general form:

$$W = \beta_0 + \beta_{11}W^* + \beta_{12}PP^* + \beta_{13}PC^*$$
$$+ \beta_{21}(WM - W^*) + \beta_{22}(WG - W^*) + \beta_{23}(WF - W^*)$$
$$+ \beta_3 x + \beta_{41}TD + \beta_{42}TI + \beta_{43}UIR$$
$$+ \beta_5 Q + \beta_6 C7678.$$

The left-hand variable (W) is the annual rate of change in total hourly compensation in the private commercial sector. The first set of

---

34. Examples of this relative lack of success are: S. F. Kaliski, *The Trade-Off Between Inflation and Unemployment: Some Explorations of the Recent Evidence for Canada,* Special Study No. 22 (Ottawa: Information Canada for Economic Council of Canada, 1972); J. C. R. Rowley and D. A. Wilton, "Empirical Foundations for the Canadian Phillips Curve," *Canadian Journal of Economics,* vol. 7 (May 1974), pp. 240–59; George L. Perry, "Determinants of Wage Inflation around the World," *BPEA, 2:1975,* pp. 413–17; Robert J. Gordon, "World Inflation and Monetary Accommodation in Eight Countries," *BPEA, 2:1977,* pp. 437–39 and 454–55; and Jeffrey D. Sachs, "Wages, Profits, and Macroeconomic Adjustment: A Comparative Study," *BPEA, 2:1979,* pp. 269–319. More satisfactory results were achieved by Bank of Canada researchers, namely Charles Freedman, "The Phillips Curve in Canada," Research Memorandum 76-189 (Bank of Canada, 1976); Daryl L. Merrett, "Estimation of a Simple Phillips-Curve Wage Equation," Research Memorandum 78-159 (Bank of Canada, 1978); and Michel Gosselin, "Modifications apportées à l'équation des salaires et estimation du taux de chômage naturel" (Modifications to the Wage Equation and Estimation of the Natural Unemployment Rate), Research Memorandum 80-39 (Bank of Canada, 1980). Recent Canadian research on wage dynamics has relied heavily on micro data. See Jean-Michel Cousineau and Robert Lacroix, *Wage Determination in Major Collective Agreements in the Private and Public Sectors* (Ottawa: Supply and Services Canada for Economic Council of Canada, 1977); William Craig Riddell, "The Empirical Foundations of the Phillips Curve: Evidence from Canadian Wage Contract Data," *Econometrica,* vol. 47 (January 1979), pp. 1–24; and D. A. L. Auld and others, *The Determinants of Negotiated Wage Settlements in Canada (1966–1975): A Micro-econometric Analysis* (Hull, Quebec: Supply and Services Canada, 1979).

right-hand variables reflects inertia in the inflationary process from inflation in past wages (W^*), producer prices (PP^*), and consumer prices (PC^*). This inertia can arise from backward-looking elements like ongoing multiyear labor contracts as well as from forward-looking, or expectational, behavior. Among the foremost modern proponents of the wage-wage feedback are James Tobin, Arthur Okun, and Robert E. Hall, whose views are rooted in the labor economics tradition dating back to John Dunlop, John Hicks, and John Maynard Keynes. The price-wage feedbacks were recently emphasized by researchers in the Phillips curve tradition, in particular Robert J. Gordon, who stressed that the numerical importance of producer price inflation relative to consumer price inflation is an increasing function of the size of the ratio of the real-wage elasticities of labor demand and supply.[35] The relatively inelastic aggregate labor supply curves that arise from most econometric studies of labor supply would be consistent with a relatively small coefficient for consumer price inflation and a relatively large coefficient for producer price inflation. We do not take sides in the wage-wage versus price-wage debate, but instead let the data reveal their comparative importance in wage determination. Furthermore, we point out that the increased *variance* of price inflation in the 1970s relative to the 1960s may have operated to increase the importance of the wage-wage feedback and decrease that of the price-wage feedback, to the extent that economic agents therefore began to discount recent price performance more heavily than previously. However, this movement could have been offset by the substantial shortening of labor contracts observed in Canada in the 1970s.[36] Here again, we have the data determine the actual direction of the change (if any).

The second set of right-hand variables focuses on three possible sources of wage inflation: relative movements in minimum wages ($WM - W^*$), public-sector wages ($WG - W^*$), and foreign (U.S.) wages ($WF - W^*$).[37] These variables can operate through three channels.

35. Robert J. Gordon, "Interrelations between Domestic and International Theories of Inflation," in Robert Z. Aliber, ed., *The Political Economy of Monetary Reform* (Chicago: Graduate School of Business, University of Chicago, 1977), pp. 126–54.

36. The proportion of one-year contracts among major new settlements rose from 18 percent in 1967 to 47 percent in 1975, and to 52 percent in 1978. See W. D. Wood and Pradeep Kumar, eds., *The Current Industrial Relations Scene in Canada, 1980* (Queen's University at Kingston, Industrial Relations Centre, 1980), p. 597.

37. Among others, Martin Neil Baily and James Tobin, "Macroeconomic Effects of

First, minimum wage changes will affect the left-hand variable directly by raising the compensation of minimum wage workers. Second, all three relative-wage fluctuations can influence private-sector wage inflation through emulation effects. Third, however, the demand-side reaction to changes in relative minimum wages, public-sector wages, or foreign wages tends to create a change in the supply of labor in the private commercial sector that may partially offset the emulation effects. This consequence would appear to have its greatest effect on public wage movements because governments adjust their demand to the cost of labor, but less effect on minimum wage adjustments, because of the near-total absence of an uncovered sector in Canada, and on foreign wage changes, because of the relative international immobility of labor.

The third set of right-hand variables is a measure or a vector of measures of labor market tightness (x), which we have discussed in the preceding two sections and have submitted to extensive testing.

The fourth set of variables comprises changes in rates of taxation and transfer: direct payroll and personal income taxation (TD), indirect taxation (TI), and the unemployment insurance wage-replacement ratio (UIR). Our formulation allows for lagged direct taxation changes, so that the long-run effect on gross wages may be different from the short-run effect. In particular, there is room for the long-run effect to be small or even zero in conformity with the relative inelasticity of the aggregate labor supply in the long run. The impact of changes in indirect taxation on the left-hand variable will be smaller to the degree that it is easier for firms to shift the burden onto consumers. Increases in the UI ratio have two opposite effects on aggregate wage developments. They reduce the cost of waiting and correspondingly increase the reservation wages of persons already active in the labor force. However, they also induce higher participation rates and lower the reservation wages of persons who are higher unemployment risks, since the same rate of return from being an active labor market participant can now be obtained at a lower wage rate.

The fifth set of variables reduces to actual productivity changes (Q). Trend productivity growth is picked up by the regression constant and by various dummy variables that were used to test for its recent

Selective Public Employment and Wage Subsidies," *BPEA, 2:1977*, pp. 511–41, have been strong proponents of relative-wage effects.

downward shift. Actual productivity changes may also serve as a proxy for changes in product and labor market tightness.

The last explanatory variable (*C7678*) is a dummy variable meant to reflect the wage control experience of 1976–78. It takes on the value 0.5 in 1976, 1 in 1977 and 1978, and 0 in all other years. This follows our own testing and agrees with the microeconometric evidence, adduced by Christofides and Wilton, that the first-year impact of controls on wage inflation was only half as large as the second- and third-year impacts.[38] We do not test for the presence of a postcontrol rebound effect, as our sample period ends with the last year of controls.

Estimation Results

We estimated the above wage equation with annual Canadian data from 1957 to 1978. The exact definitions and sources of the variables are given in the appendix. On the right-hand side of the equation, wage, producer price inflation, and consumer price inflation lagged more than one period never entered significantly.[39] All other variables appear only contemporaneously, except those for changes in direct taxation and the UI wage-replacement ratio, for which one-period lags could be retained by reasonable statistical standards (*t*-statistics greater than one). Actual productivity growth and a series of dummy variables starting in 1973 that were meant to account for the recent downward shift in the productivity trend had to be rejected, except to the extent that the shift has been highly collinear with the controls dummy. Indirect tax changes and public-sector and U.S. wage inflation were similarly found to play no net role in the private wage-inflation process.[40]

38. L. N. Christofides and D. A. Wilton, *Wage Controls in Canada (1975:3–1978:2): A Study of Their Impact on Negotiated Base Wage Rates* (Hull, Quebec Supply and Services Canada, 1979).

39. In particular, this brings about rejection of a crude version of the "catch-up" hypothesis, which implies that past *changes* in the rates of producer price or consumer price inflation do affect wage inflation.

40. Concerning the effect of public-sector wage policy, Auld and others, *The Determinants of Negotiated Wage Settlements* (chap. 4) found that wage spillovers are important in individual collective agreements, but only within the same geographical region and industrial sector. That would exclude spillovers from public to private wage settlements. Robert Lacroix and François Dussault, "L'effet des ententes salariales du secteur public sur celles du secteur privé, Canada, 1967–1978" (The Impact of Public-Sector Wage Agreements on Those in the Private Sector, 1967–1978) (University of

Thus, equation 4-1 of table 1 starts with the estimation results for the entire 1957–78 period with β_{22}, β_{23}, β_{42}, and β_5 already set equal to zero and an equality constraint imposed (after testing) on the coefficients of the current and one-period lagged values of the variable for changes in the UI wage-replacement ratio (*UIR*).

The statistical properties of equation 4-1 make it interesting to test for three additional constraints on the model. First, it is sensible to impose the theoretically desirable price homogeneity restriction that the coefficients of $W(-1)$, $PP(-1)$, and $PC(-1)$ sum up to 1, since their sample sum is actually 0.96. The ultimate consequence is verticality of the long-run Canadian Phillips curve if purchasing power parity is granted. Second, given its large standard error, it is natural to constrain the small negative coefficient of $PC(-1)$ to zero because of consistency with the near-vertical aggregate labor supply curve generally observed in econometric studies. Third, for the same reason the long-run effect on wage inflation of changes in direct taxation should also be zero. This means that the sample coefficients of *TD* and $TD(-1)$, which are 0.46 and -0.41 respectively, should be set equal and opposite in value. Equation 4-2 imposes the three constraints simultaneously, and the null hypothesis of their joint validity cannot be rejected statistically; sample $F = 0.09 < 3.49 = F(5, 10)$ at the 95 percent confidence level.

Equation 4-3 illustrates the misleading nature of the most popular version of the Canadian Phillips curve, which excludes wage and producer price feedbacks, minimum wage developments, and tax and transfer measures. Because of lack of competition, the consumer price feedback steals the influence that in fact belongs to the other types of feedback, and demand management working through the labor market tightness variable appears twice as effective (albeit with a larger standard error) as it really is.

Equation 4-4 is the final specification we obtain after testing the stability of equation 4-2 over time. When equation 4-2 was reestimated for the 1957–69, 1957–73, and 1957–75 subperiods, the validity of the

---

Montreal, Department of Economics, February 1981), found evidence of such spillovers by breaking down the contract micro data further into occupational categories (blue collar, white collar, and others). However, that takes care only of the emulation effect, not of the overall net effect on the total private sector. Our result is subject to the reservation that the public wage here is measured as compensation per employee (not per hour), excluding fringe benefits.

Table 1. *Estimated Annual Wage Equation with Alternative Specifications for the Private Commercial Sector, Canada, 1957–78*[a]

Independent variable or summary statistic	Equation			
	4-1	*4-2*	*4-3*	*4-4*
Independent variable				
Constant	−0.50	−0.75	−0.75	−0.92
	(1.23)	(0.83)	(1.47)	(0.76)
$W(-1)5769$	0.54	0.58	. . .	0.51
	(0.15)	(0.09)		(0.09)
$W(-1)7078$	0.54	0.58	. . .	0.76
	(0.15)	(0.09)		(0.09)
$PP(-1)5769$	0.47	0.42	. . .	0.49
	(0.17)	(0.10)		(0.10)
$PP(-1)7078$	0.47	0.42	. . .	0.24
	(0.17)	(0.10)		(0.10)
$PC(-1)$	−0.05	. . .	1.05	. . .
	(0.20)		(0.12)	
$WM\text{-}W(-1)$	0.11	0.12	. . .	0.11
	(0.05)	(0.04)		(0.04)
$UGAP$	2.87	2.93	5.72	3.33
	(1.35)	(0.91)	(1.80)	(0.84)
TD	0.46	0.44	. . .	0.44
	(0.28)	(0.15)		(0.14)
$TD(-1)$	−0.41	−0.44	. . .	−0.44
	(0.24)	(0.15)		(0.14)
UIR	0.04	0.04	. . .	. . .
	(0.02)	(0.02)		
$C7678$	−1.79	−2.03	−3.50	−2.99
	(0.76)	(0.55)	(1.21)	(0.57)
Summary statistic				
Standard error of regression	0.70	0.63	1.33	0.59
Autocorrelation statistic[b]	−2.67	−1.97	1.85	−1.27

a. Symbols are defined in the appendix. In all equations the left-hand variable is W. The numbers in parentheses are the standard errors of the estimated coefficients. In equations 1 and 2, the coefficients of $W(-1)5769$ and $W(-1)7078$ are constrained to be equal. Equation 4-2 imposes three additional constraints on equation 4-1: the coefficient of $PC(-1)$ is set equal to zero; the sum of the coefficients of $W(-1)$ and $PP(-1)$ is set equal to one; and the sum of the coefficients of TD and $TD(-1)$ is constrained to zero. Equation 4-4 relaxes the equality constraint on the coefficients of $W(-1)5769$ and $W(-1)7078$ in equation 4-2. The *t*-statistic for the validity of this constraint is $t = 3.34 > 2.13 = t\,(15)$ at the 95 percent confidence level.

b. For equations 4-1, 4-2, and 4-4, which contain the lagged dependent variable, this is Durbin's (asymptotically normal) *h*-statistic. For equation 4-3, this is the usual Durbin-Watson statistic.

three constraints embedded in it was confirmed, and the stability of the estimated coefficients was generally satisfactory, but with one important exception: the weight of $W(-1)$ relative to that of $PP(-1)$ significantly shifted up in the 1970–79 period compared to the 1957–69 period. This lends credence to the expectational argument, which is based on the greater variance of inflation in the 1970s, and to this argument's dominance over the opposite effect from the shorter average duration of wage contracts. Once the shift in the relative weight of $W(-1)$ and $PP(-1)$ in the 1970–78 period is introduced, the predictive performance of the resulting equation (4-4) improves substantially, and no other statistically significant shift in the coefficients of $W(-1)$, $PP(-1)$ or any other variable actually occurs further in the 1970s.[41] One implication that is important for the historical record is that the so-called wage explosion of 1974–75, which led to wage controls in late 1975, was not actually a case of wages getting exogenously out of control. Instead, this episode is given an entirely endogenous explanation by our equation 4-4. The main source of the sharply accelerating trend of wages in those years—from 10 percent in 1973 to 15 percent in 1975—was the equally sharp acceleration in producer price inflation one year earlier—from 5 percent in 1972 to 15 percent in 1974. Either equation 4-2 or equation 4-4 reestimated over the 1957–73 sample period actually slightly overpredicts wage inflation in 1974–75.

We have relied on equation 4-4 of table 1 for an examination of the comparative performance of various measures of labor market tightness as explanatory variables in the wage-formation process. The results are reported in table 2. The broad picture that emerges is that the most effective measures in terms of goodness of fit (t-statistics of the variables and standard errors of the regressions) are measures of the change in the employment status of the labor force: Wachter's $UGAP$, the inverse of the adult male unemployment rate (UMA), the job vacancy rate (VAC), and the inverse of Perry's weighted unemployment rate (UP). When measures of the change in the work effort (labor hoarding) are entered to substitute for or to complement $UGAP$, the statistical properties of the wage equation deteriorate, sometimes substantially. This is the case for the deviation from trend of productivity ($PGAP$), hours worked per employed person ($HPEGAP$), aggregate hours of work ($HGAP$) and output ($YGAP$). It seems that as a predictor of wage inflation, disguised unemployment within firms, however measured, does not carry any useful information that is not already contained in "street" unemployment. Our final verdict is that among all the candidates, $UGAP$, $UMA(-1)$, VAC, and $UP(-1)$ are

---

41. The relevant regression results and F-statistics for sample subperiods are available from the authors on request. One apparent consequence of the specification improvement from equations 4-1 and 4-2 to equation 4-4 is the drop of Durbin's h-statistic to statistical insignificance.

Table 2. *Estimated Annual Wage Equation with Alternative Labor
Market Tightness Variables for the Private Commercial Sector,
Canada, 1957–78*[a]

Equation number and labor market tightness variable	Summary statistic	
	t-statistic	*Standard error for equation*
5-1		
UGAP	3.98	0.586
5-2		
UMA(-1)	3.85	0.596
5-3		
VAC	3.83	0.597
5-4		
UP(-1)	3.74	0.605
5-5		
PGAP	0.24	
		0.606
UGAP	3.40	
5-6		
PGAP	0.53	
HPEGAP	0.77	0.615
UGAP	3.14	
5-7		
PGAP	-1.18	
		0.685
HGAP	2.44	
5-8		
HGAP	2.65	0.694
5-9		
YGAP	1.90	0.755
5-10		
PGAP	-1.40	0.790

a. All symbols are defined in the appendix. Equation 5-1 is the same as equation 4-1. Replacing *UGAP* with other labor market variables in this equation yields equations 5-2 to 5-10.

the most desirable labor market tightness measures in the sample period 1957–78. However, the recent (1978) termination of Statistics Canada's Job Vacancy Survey and the absence of any direct account for policy-induced variables in the construction of Perry's weighted unemployment rate leave *UGAP* and the adult male unemployment rate as our favorite measures of labor market tightness for future research on labor market dynamics.

Implications for Anti-Inflationary Policy

Consequences of Inflationary Feedbacks

It should be noted at the outset that the great openness of the Canadian economy and the substantial variability of its terms of trade in the 1970s have at times pushed wages, producer prices, and consumer prices onto widely divergent paths in the short run. The consequent econometric return is a smaller sample multicollinearity between these variables in Canada than in the United States and better identification of the relative importance of the wage-wage and price-wage feedbacks than in the U.S. Phillips curve studies. Given the similarity between the wage-setting institutions of the two countries, we trust that our results add useful information on the elusive nature of inflationary feedbacks in the United States.

One striking aspect of our equation 4-4 is the practical irrelevance of consumer price inflation for aggregate wage determination. The widespread popular fear that workers would successfully resist the downward adjustment in their real wages after a depreciation of the currency, a decline in the terms of trade, or a boost in food prices does not seem to be warranted as far as Canadian experience is concerned. If these shocks filter through to wages, it is via their lagged impact on business ability to pay, as measured by producer prices, which now carry only 25 percent of inflationary inertia. For example, if the short-run (one year) partial elasticity of producer prices to the exchange rate is of the order of 0.25, a 5 percent depreciation of the Canadian dollar would imply a lagged inflationary impact of only about 0.3 percentage point for wages ($5 \times 0.25 \times 0.25 = 0.31$). Hence the inflationary consequences of short-run variability in the exchange rate are considerably less than is often thought. One crucial lesson for the conduct of Canadian monetary policy is that the inflationary cost for Canada of absorbing more of the short-run volatility of U.S. interest rates in the form of greater exchange rate fluctuations and smaller domestic interest rate fluctuations—if such an interest rate policy is deemed suitable—is not as high as claimed by Bank of Canada officials.[42]

42. This issue has been central to Canadian monetary debates since early 1980. See the *Bank of Canada Review* (Ottawa: Bank of Canada), various issues, for official policy views on the subject.

A further result with high policy relevance is the dominance of the wage-wage feedback (75 percent) over the producer price-wage feedback (25 percent). As Arthur Okun emphasized, the more important the wage-wage channel is relative to the price-wage channel, the less efficient (in terms of bang per buck) direct price-reducing policies are within a disinflationary strategy, and the greater role direct wage-reducing policies—like tax-based incomes policies or thorough wage controls—have to assume if an alternative is sought to pure demand-reducing policies.[43]

Our Canadian wage equation is also just about price-homogeneous, so that if purchasing power parity holds, the implied long-run Phillips curve is vertical. Hence, although hardly measurable with any precision in the context of a wage equation alone, the concept of a nonaccelerating inflation rate of unemployment (NAIRU) receives empirical support. A number of recent Canadian studies have offered estimates for the overall impact on structural unemployment of the demographic changes and policy measures of the last twenty-five years. Moreover, a few of them have ventured into locating the approximate level of the NAIRU in recent years by solving structural wage and/or price equations or reduced-form price equations for the steady-state unemployment rate. A quick survey of a dozen or so of these studies would locate estimates of the increase in Canadian structural unemployment over two decades in the range between 1.7 and 3.3 percentage points, with a median of 2.5, which is about 1 percentage point higher than the comparative figure for the United States over the same time span. As a result, the available Canadian NAIRU estimates for the period 1977–78 fall between 6.5 percent and 7 percent, compared to 5.5 percent to 6 percent in the United States. The main source of this intercountry differential is most probably the much wider coverage and greater generosity of the Canadian unemployment insurance program, with smaller contributions from somewhat more significant demographic changes and the higher relative average minimum wage in Canada. We would argue, however, that in the last three years the Canadian NAIRU has been lowered by the 1977 and 1978 UI revisions and by swift deceleration of the average relative minimum wage, and that it is now closer to the 6 percent level.

43. Arthur Okun, "Efficient Disinflationary Policies," *American Economic Review*, vol. 68 (May 1978, *Papers and Proceedings, 1977*), pp. 348–52.

The Inflationary Impact of Minimum Wage Increases

The sample magnitude of the effect of Canadian minimum wage changes on aggregate wage inflation is far from negligible, since equation 4-4 indicates that a 10 percent increase in the relative minimum wage would push aggregate wages up by as much as 1.1 percent. This point estimate of 0.11 for the minimum-wage elasticity of aggregate wage inflation would seem on the high side to U.S. observers in view of, say, Gramlich's finding of a 0.03 elasticity for the United States.[44] Conceptually, this elasticity (call it ξ) is the product of three terms: $\xi = \alpha\,\delta\,\mu$, where α is a percentage of workers earning the minimum wage, δ is the ratio of the minimum wage to the average industrial wage, and μ is a wage emulation multiplier. Given the shape of the wage distribution, both α and μ are increasing functions of δ, which in turn is influenced by market forces and minimum wage and other policy measures. Thus, increases in δ push ξ upward and the impact is even more than proportional. A low minimum wage policy (with smaller coverage) holding δ at 0.4 could mean $\alpha = 0.04$ and $\mu = 2.0$, so that $\xi = 0.032$, while a high minimum wage policy (with wider coverage) with δ at 0.5 could push α to 0.08 and μ to 3.0 and send ξ to 0.12. Canadian minimum wage policy in the 1968–76 period was of the latter sort.

The Cyclical Responsiveness of Wage Inflation

The empirical evidence generated by our wage equation indicates that the effect of labor market tightness, as measured by *UGAP*, is small and stable over time.

Based on equation 4-2, an increase of 1 percentage point for a full year in the national unemployment rate from 6 percent to 7 percent reduces wage inflation by only 0.3 to 0.5 percentage point.[45] With Okun's law in the background, this is just as pessimistic as are most

44. Edward M. Gramlich, "Impact of Minimum Wages on Other Wages, Employment, and Family Incomes," *BPEA*, 2:1976, pp. 426–30.

45. *UGAP* is the ratio (u_s/u) of a "normalized" unemployment rate (u_s) to the official unemployment rate (u). In 1978, u_s was equal to 5.1 percent (as a check, $5.1 = 8.4 \times 0.606$, where 8.4 percent was the official unemployment rate in 1978 and 0.606 was the value of *UGAP* in that year; see appendix table 3). It then follows from equation 4-4 that $\partial w/\partial u = (3.33)\,(5.1)u^{-2} = 0.40$ for $u = 6.5$ percent. The 0.3 to 0.5 interval is derived from the one-standard-error confidence interval around 3.33.

U.S. estimates for the social cost of disinflationary policies based on demand restriction alone, save for the direct impact of aggregate demand pressure on prices. The other striking feature of our results is the great precision and stability of the cyclical responsiveness of wage inflation to labor market tightness, as measured by the *UGAP* coefficient across the sample subperiods for which our basic wage equation was estimated. If these numbers are to be believed, there is no basis for claiming that the Canadian Phillips curve, that is, the slope of the aggregate partial relationship between wage inflation and a proper measure of labor market tightness, has collapsed in the 1970s, though it has clearly shifted for various identifiable reasons. Canadian wage inflation was neither more nor less sensitive to aggregate demand stimulation or restriction in the 1970s than in the 1960s. Rather, it is the growing size of the task of anti-inflationary policy in the 1970s that has made the powers of traditional demand management look so limited.

The Inflationary Content of Direct Tax and Transfer Increases

Our estimated wage equation 4-4 is able to identify the short-run inflationary consequences of increases in direct taxation. About 45 percent of the change is translated into faster aggregate wage inflation within the same year. However, our results are also consistent with the long-run inelasticity of labor supply, which is that after another year the inflationary effect is just about reversed. This is a warning that penalty or reward-oriented incomes policies based on direct taxation may not have permanent anti-inflationary effects. Further experiments conducted in order to separate out the effects of payroll taxation and personal income taxation seemed to indicate that this result is valid for total direct taxation. Hence, we were unable to generate evidence that a shift from payroll taxes to personal income taxes would carry anti-inflationary benefits even in its first year of enforcement.

Concerning transfer policy, equation 4-2 raises the possibility that on balance the 1971 revision of the Unemployment Insurance Act, which increased the net replacement ratio from about 65 percent to about 80 percent, did push reservation wages up in the segments of the market where labor supply is elastic, but the aggregate inflationary impact of this measure did not apparently exceed 0.05 percentage point equally spread over 1972 and 1973. However, because over the sample period *UIR* is more or less a dummy variable with value 0.3 in 1972 and 1973, and 0 in all other years, it is correlated with any other factor intervening in 1972 and 1973. Hence it is no surprise that its coefficient loses statistical significance when the 1970–78 value of the coefficient of $W(-1)$ is left free to differ from its 1957–69 value. Accordingly, our verdict is that unemployment insurance reform probably had no net direct inflationary consequence on aggregate wages.

The Effectiveness of Wage Controls

Our experiments strongly suggest that the wage controls administered by the Anti-Inflation Board from 1976 to 1978 were generally successful in bringing down wage inflation. First, the coefficient of the dummy variable for controls in equation 4-4 implies that after its three years of operation the AIB was able to "shock" wage inflation (not only wage levels) down cumulatively by 7.5 percentage points.[46] This corroborates the microeconometric findings of Cousineau and Lacroix, Christofides and Wilton, and Reid.[47] However, for the private sector our results are more general, because these studies were limited to the analysis of base wage rates in collective agreements free of cost-of-living-adjustment clauses, while our wage variable is private hourly compensation for the whole economy.

Second, the relatively large weight (76 percent) attributed to the wage-wage feedback by equation 4-4 ensures that a significant proportion of the cumulative shock actually remained in the observed rate of wage inflation at the end of the control period (1978), even if very conservative assumptions are made on the proportion of the decline in the rate of increase in wages that is translated into a decline

46. The cumulative value of the variable over 1976, 1977, and 1978 is $0.5 + 1.0 + 1.0 = 2.5$, and it interacts with an estimated coefficient of about -3.0. The one-standard-error interval for the cumulative shock is 6 percent to 9 percent.

47. Jean-Michel Cousineau and Robert Lacroix, "L'impact de la politique canadienne de contrôle des prix et des revenus sur les ententes salariales" (The Impact of the Canadian Wage and Price Controls Program on Wage Agreements), *Canadian Public Policy*, vol. 4 (Winter 1978), pp. 88–100; Christofides and Wilton, *Wage Controls in Canada;* and Frank Reid, "The Effect of Controls on the Rate of Wage Change in Canada," *Canadian Journal of Economics*, vol. 12 (May 1979), pp. 214–27.

in the rate of increase of producer prices.[48] This adds a very important
time dimension to the efficiency of wage controls during the enforcement period.

However, the swift impact of wage controls on *nominal* wage
inflation resulting from the high coefficients on the wage control dummy
variable and the wage-wage feedback variable is likely to have significantly reduced *real* wage growth in the 1976–78 period. Indeed, the
degree of transmission of lower wage inflation into lower consumer
price inflation must have been low, not only because of less than
perfect absorption of lower wages into lower producer prices, but also
because of the slippage from lower producer prices to lower consumer
prices. These two attenuating factors are, of course, highly relevant
in the very open Canadian economy in the short run, when purchasing
power parity does not hold. In addition, since for any given degree
of openness the short-run negative real-wage effect of wage controls
is an increasing function of their nominal-wage effect, the policymakers
are caught in a dilemma: the more efficient wage controls are as an
inflation-reducing device, the greater the consequent distortion in the
functional distribution of income will be, and the harder it will prove
to reach a political consensus on this type of policy, unless offsetting
measures like tax reductions or effective price controls are included
in the disinflationary package.[49]

There are two respects in which our empirical results are not
definitive. First, there is a serious possibility that our dummy variable
for controls picks up some of the labor market consequences of the
declining productivity trend. Future data points will no doubt help us
resolve this issue, but in our judgment they are unlikely to overturn
the conclusion that wage controls significantly altered the path of wage
and price inflation in 1976–78. In fact, the magnitude of the fall in
average labor productivity growth since 1973, which has been somewhat

48. Even under the assumption that *no* reduction in producer price inflation followed
the decline in wage inflation, over 80 percent of the cumulative shock would have
actually remained in the observed rate of wage increase at the end of 1978.

49. Price controls were actually introduced by the Anti-Inflation Act of 1975, but
the real purpose of the program was to control wages, not prices, as recently demonstrated
in Allan M. Maslove and Gene Swimmer, *Wage Controls in Canada, 1975–78: A Study
of Public Decision Making* (Montreal: Institute for Research on Public Policy, 1980).
This view is consistent with the study by Thomas A. Wilson and Gregory V. Jump,
*The Influence of the Anti-Inflation Program on Aggregate Wages and Prices: A
Simulation Analysis* (Ottawa: Anti-Inflation Board, 1979) which found no evidence of a
direct impact of controls on prices.

below 2 percentage points in the private sector, would have caused the rate of aggregate wage increase to fall by less than the cumulative impact of wage controls (7.5 percent) implied by our regression estimate over the 1976–78 period.

Second, since our sample period ends with the last year of the wage controls experiment (1978), our results do not test the validity of the postcontrol "rebound" hypothesis, whereby the 1976–78 controls would have a positive effect on wage inflation, say, in the 1979–81 period. One story behind this hypothesis is that in a labor market environment where wages are largely set on the basis of long-run contracts between employers and workers, producer prices would be geared to long-run expected wages and not to short-run observed wages. Consequently, the mirror image of the downward shock of controls on nominal and real wages would be a temporary profit buildup providing for a postcontrol nominal and real wage rebound, which would bring compensation back to its long-term path. Be that as it may, a direct test of the rebound hypothesis has to wait for the availability of post-1978 data.

Summary and Conclusions

A number of points emerge from the foregoing analysis. It does appear, for example, that, with the exceptions noted above, Canadian wage inflation has been a stable function of a few main variables since the late 1950s. Moreover, the results with respect to the shifts in the coefficients of the lagged inflation variables are interesting in themselves, for they indicate that as price inflation increases and becomes more variable, wage setters tend to discount recent price inflation more heavily.

Another important result has to do with the apparent inappropriateness of the consumer price variable in the wage equation: this causes the impact of food and energy price shocks on the wage bargain to be felt not by way of the consumer price index, but by way of producer prices.

As far as controls are concerned, the evidence favors the view that they were effective, though caution is advised because of the possibility of collinearity with the declining trend rate of growth of productivity. With respect to their effectiveness, it should also be noted that the more open the economy, the greater the slippage between wages and producer prices and the greater the impact on income distribution as real wages are eroded; and the greater the coefficient on lagged wage inflation, the more effective are controls on nominal wage restraint during the control period. Future research will have to test the postcontrol rebound hypothesis.

A result with important implications for the use of traditional anti-inflationary tax policies is that increases in direct taxation appear to have inflationary consequences only in the first year, after which the burden of the increase is borne by labor. Moreover, there was no evidence that a shift from payroll to direct taxes carries anti-inflationary consequences. On the transfer side, the estimates do not support the hypothesis that the 1971 unemployment insurance revisions affected the rate of wage inflation.

The political economy of minimum wage policy in Canada provides some clues as to the recent upward pressure on wage rates, as we have seen. The finding that a 10 percent increase in the relative minimum wage could cause a rise of 1.1 percent in the rate of wage inflation may appear surprising to American observers, but the relatively higher impact in the Canadian case may be explained by such factors as Canada's wider coverage and higher levels of minimum wages.

While minimum wages, unemployment insurance, and demographic change are explanatory factors common to both U.S. and Canadian studies of recent labor market developments, these factors appear to have played a more important role in the Canadian case. At the height of these factors' influence, empirical studies place the natural rate of unemployment in the range of about 6.5 percent to 7 percent. In the last years of the 1970s, however, their impact has eroded—unemployment insurance provisions, for example, have been made less generous—and recent estimates of the NAIRU are close to 6 percent.

As far as the tests of labor market tightness variables are concerned, the broad conclusion is that measures taking into account work effort are unable to add to what is already explained by the employment status variables.

Finally, the prospects for the role of demand-management policies in Canada appear less than sanguine since the results suggest that an increase in the aggregate unemployment rate from 6 percent to 7 percent serves to ameliorate the wage inflation rate by an amount ranging from 0.3 percent to 0.5 percent. Moreover, the openness of the Canadian economy presents slippage problems in the relationship between producer prices and wages. Nevertheless, there are indications that inflation is regarded as the primary macroeconomic target in Canada at the present time and that the generous unemployment insurance provisions render the recessionary approach to anti-inflation policy more palatable by spreading the social costs of the attendant unemployment.

Appendix

The symbols for the variables used in the wage equation (tables 1 and 2) are defined as indicated below. The suffix (-1) at the end of a variable name indicates that the variable is lagged one year. When four numbers in a row (for example, 7078) appear at the end of a variable name, the result is a new variable equal to the old variable in the sample subperiod indicated by the numbers (1970–78) and to zero in the rest of the sample period. All variables except *C7678* and *UGAP* are measured in percentage points. Methodology and data are available on request for all variables, including those not retained in tables 1 and 2 (U.S. wage, public wage, indirect tax rate).

C7678: A dummy variable for wage controls, equal to 0.5 in 1976, 1 in 1977 and 1978, and 0 in other years.

HGAP: Percentage deviation of hours worked in the commercial nonagricultural sector from their (quadratic) 1957–78 trend. The source series is in Statistics Canada, *Aggregate Productivity Measures, 1946–1978,* catalogue 14-201 (October 1979). The log-linear trend is 4.28 + $0.163t + .00189t^2$. The hours index is 100.0 in 1971.

HPEGAP: Percentage deviation of hours worked per person employed in the commercial nonagricultural sector from their (quadratic) 1957–78 trend. The source is the same as for *HGAP.* The log-linear trend is $4.70 - 0.00353t - 0.0000764t^2$. The index of hours per person is 100.0 in 1971.

PC: The year-over-year logarithmic difference in the consumer price index, obtained from Statistics Canada's CANSIM data bank.

PGAP: Percentage deviation of output per person-hour in the commercial nonagricultural sector from its (quadratic) 1957–78 trend. The source of the productivity data is the same as for *HGAP.* The

log-linear trend obtained by ordinary least squares regression is 3.96
+ 0.0404t − 0.00317t^2, where t is 1 in 1957, 2 in 1958, etc., and the
productivity index is 100.0 in 1971.

PP: The year-over-year logarithmic difference in the implicit price
deflator for gross national expenditure minus current government
expenditure. The source series were obtained from Statistics Canada's
CANSIM data bank.

TD: The change in the effective rate of direct taxation. The rate
was computed as the sum of the effective rates of payroll taxation
and of income taxation. The former is the ratio of total payroll taxes
(UI contributions, workmen's compensation, and Canada and Quebec
Pension Plans contributions) to total compensation (wages and salaries,
military allowances, and supplementary labor income). The latter is
the ratio of total personal income taxes to total personal income. The
source series were obtained from Statistics Canada's CANSIM data
bank. *TD* is actually equal to the logarithmic difference of $1/(1 − T)$,
where T is the effective rate of direct taxation.

UGAP: The ratio of standardized unemployment rate to actual
aggregate unemployment rate. The standardized unemployment rate
is calculated after Michael L. Wachter, "The Changing Cyclical
Responsiveness of Wage Inflation," *BPEA, 1:1976,* pp. 115—59. It is
extended to include policy-induced changes in the labor market, as
described in Pierre Fortin and Louis Phaneuf, "Why is the Unemployment Rate So High in Canada?" working paper 8115 (Laval
University, Department of Economics, 1981). The *UGAP* series is
reported in table 3.

UIR: The change by UI benefits in the aftertax replacement ratio
of the aftertax wage. The aftertax wage benchmark is the net wage
received by a person earning about 75 percent of Statistics Canada's
average weekly wage in manufacturing (CANSIM data bank). Taxes
are deducted according to the standard income tax forms. Some
allowance for the opportunity cost of work (meals, clothing and
transportation) is also made in the construction of the net wage. The
gross UI benefits are set equal to the product of the gross wage and
the gross replacement ratio defined in the Unemployment Insurance
Act. The net benefits are the same as the gross benefits, except after
1971 when benefits become taxable. Hence, starting in 1972, the
(marginal) income tax is subtracted from the gross benefit to yield the
net benefit. The net replacement ratio is the ratio of net benefits to

Table 3. *Annual Canadian* UGAP *Series, 1956–78*

Year	UGAP
1956	1.165
1957	0.813
1958	0.544
1959	0.663
1960	0.552
1961	0.550
1962	0.664
1963	0.726
1964	0.863
1965	1.058
1966	1.153
1967	1.033
1968	0.899
1969	0.922
1970	0.731
1971	0.690
1972	0.757
1973	0.889
1974	0.940
1975	0.733
1976	0.717
1977	0.639
1978	0.606

Source: Pierre Fortin and Louis Phaneuf, "Why is the Unemployment Rate So High in Canada?" working paper 8115 (Laval University, Department of Economics, 1981).

net wage. The *UIR* variable in the wage equation is actually the simple average of this year's and last year's changes in the replacement ratio.

UMA: The unemployment rate for males aged twenty-five and over, obtained from Statistics Canada's CANSIM data bank. From 1956 to 1975, Statistics Canada's data were adjusted to match the definition of the new Labour Force Survey according to a procedure supplied by the Bank of Canada Research Department.

UP: Perry's weighted unemployment rate. The unemployment rates of the four main age-sex groups (males 15 to 24 and 25 and over and females 15 to 24 and 25 and over) are weighted by their relative importance in the aggregate wage bill.

VAC: The job vacancy rate. This series comes from two sources. From 1953 to 1970, it is the series constructed by Frank T. Denton, Christine Feaver, and A. Leslie Robb, "Patterns of Unemployment Behavior in Canada," Discussion Paper No. 36 (Economic Council of

Table 4. *Selected Canadian Labor Market Indicators, 1960–79*
Percent

Year	Unemployment rate	Employment ratio	Vacancy rate	Increase in gross national expenditure per man-hour	Increase in hourly earnings	Increase in real hourly earnings	Unit labor costs	Consumer price index	Gross national expenditure deflator
1960	7.0	50.4	0.39	2.1	4.4	3.1	2.0	1.2	1.3
1961	7.1	50.2	0.39	2.4	3.8	2.9	0.0	0.9	0.4
1962	5.9	50.7	0.52	4.3	4.4	3.2	−2.0	1.2	1.4
1963	5.5	50.9	0.53	3.5	4.9	3.1	0.0	1.7	1.9
1964	4.7	51.6	0.63	3.9	5.9	4.0	2.0	1.8	2.4
1965	3.9	52.3	0.76	3.2	7.3	4.8	2.0	2.4	3.3
1966	3.4	55.4	0.79	4.0	9.9	6.0	5.8	3.7	4.4
1967	3.8	55.7	0.67	1.1	8.5	4.7	5.5	3.6	4.0
1968	4.5	55.0	0.58	6.5	9.4	5.1	1.7	4.0	3.3
1969	4.4	55.3	0.68	2.7	9.0	4.2	3.4	4.6	4.4
1970	5.7	54.5	0.55	2.5	8.3	4.8	4.9	3.3	4.6
1971	6.2	54.5	0.40	5.2	8.4	5.4	3.1	2.9	3.2
1972	6.2	54.9	0.70	3.3	8.7	3.7	4.6	4.8	5.0
1973	5.5	56.4	0.89	2.6	10.6	2.8	7.3	7.5	9.1
1974	5.3	57.3	1.00	. . .	15.7	4.3	13.5	10.9	15.3
1975	6.9	56.9	0.61	−0.4	14.5	3.4	14.3	10.8	10.8
1976	7.1	56.7	0.49	2.1	12.0	4.2	8.4	7.5	9.5
1977	8.1	56.6	0.40	1.8	9.5	1.4	6.8	8.0	7.0
1978	8.4	57.4	0.40	−0.8	4.7	−3.9	4.6	9.0	6.4
1979	7.5	58.6	. . .	. . .	. . .	. . .	7.8	9.1	10.3
1960s average	5.0	. . .	. . .	3.4	6.8	4.3	2.0	2.5	2.7
1970s average	6.7	. . .	. . .	1.8	10.3	2.8	7.5	7.5	8.1

Sources: Statistics Canada CANSIM data bank and Economic Council of Canada CANDIDE data bank; vacancy series up to 1970 from Frank Denton, Christine H. Feaver, and A. Leslie Robb, ''Patterns of Unemployment Behaviour in Canada,'' Discussion Paper No. 36 (Economic Council of Canada, 1975).

Canada, 1975). For 1971 to 1978, it is based on Statistics Canada, *Quarterly Report on Job Vacancies* catalogue 71-002 (December 1978). The job vacancy rate is expressed as a percentage of the labor force.

W: The year-over-year logarithmic difference in total compensation per person-hour. The source is the same as *HGAP*.

WM: The year-over-year logarithmic difference in a weighted average of the provincial minimum wages, unadjusted for coverage. For 1966–78, the provincial data were supplied by Labour Canada. For 1956–65 it was obtained from selected issues of Department of Labour, *Labour Gazette.* The highest rate for experienced adults was selected in all cases. The provincial weights are fixed and equal to the average 1956–75 provincial shares in the Canadian labor force.

YGAP: Percentage deviation of real gross national expenditure in millions of 1971 dollars from its (quadratic) 1957–78 trend. The real GNE series was obtained from Statistics Canada's CANSIM data bank. The log-linear trend is $3.63 + 0.0567t - 0.000129t^2$.

Comments by Ronald G. Bodkin

The first part of the paper is a qualitative summary of what has happened in Canada. Fortin and Newton identify three factors that are very important. The Canadian unemployment insurance system was "reformed" in late 1971. There have been a number of studies of how much the unemployment rate has increased just due to this "reform." Estimates range from 0.5 percentage point to 2 percentage points, with about 1 or 1.25 being median estimates.

Then there is also minimum wage policy. Canada increased its minimum wage relative to the average industrial wage from about 30 percent in the middle of the 1960s to about 45 percent in 1976 or 1977.

Finally, Fortin and Newton mention increasing unionization of the public sector. Since the market operates somewhat differently in this sector, coercive comparisons might emanate outward from it.

The discussion of these three factors is by way of introduction to the wage equation that Fortin and Newton have fitted to see whether the labor market has changed. Is wage inflation generated in a way that is different in the 1970s from the way in which it was generated in the 1950s and 1960s? The conclusion about the nonaccelerating inflation rate of unemployment or NAIRU is already implicit in what is said, namely, that there has been a pronounced increase in this critical rate of unemployment. In particular, if the policymakers target on the same rates of unemployment in the 1970s as in the 1960s, this will have drastic inflationary consequences. Everybody agrees about that. But subject to such a change, has there been a change in labor market behavior?

They have a formulation that is a wage-wage formulation plus the producer price index, rather than the consumer price index. The *UGAP* variable is the ratio of the standardized or normalized unemployment rate to the actual rate. They also include a measure of direct taxes and the unemployment insurance replacement ratio. Looking at their results, one can conclude that the coefficients of multiple determination are certainly respectable, and the regression coefficients have reasonable signs. About the stability, there seems to be relatively little evidence of structural shifts with this formulation, if one takes account of the regime of wage and price controls that Canada had beginning in the fourth quarter of 1975 through 1978. The only shift that shows up is that wage-wage inflation becomes more important and producer price feedback becomes less important; this shift is apparently statistically significant.

Their results imply, as they show later on, an increase in the NAIRU, as calculated on the basis of the wage equations. Of course, that was in a previous study by Fortin, which, in a sense, was a Robert J. Gordon-style semireduced-form price equation. But this result is corroborated directly here in the wage equation itself.

Then the paper looks at some alternative measures of labor market tightness. A number of these hold up well, such as the adult male unemployment rate and the vacancy variable. But the output gap and the hours-worked gap do not do so well. In any case, those more standard ones seem to be retaining their validity as measures of the overall state of the labor market, which is interesting and confirms other well-known research results on the Canadian economy.

Their findings have implications for stabilization policy. If you think the NAIRU is, say, 7 percent or close to it, then you would not fault the Canadian government for failing to stimulate in the present [1980] context, when the measured rate of unemployment is about 7.5 or 7.6 percent. On the other hand, if you think the NAIRU is only about 6.25 percent, then the present budget is a bit conservative because there is a large amount of purchasing power being taken out of the economy with the oil price increases, with increases in unemployment insurance premiums, and with higher taxes on sin (liquor and tobacco taxes), and there is little independent stimulation to aggregate demand.

What I liked about the paper was the discussion of sectoral influences on inflation. The authors made the point that the composition between producer prices and consumer prices might have an appreciable role to play, and I thought that that was quite reasonable. I also liked the discussions on the limitations of demand-management policies. In particular, I agree that unemployment rates do not mean what they used to. I think all of the qualified observers agree on this point, and that is important. I also liked the authors' caution in interpreting the effect of the dummy variable to measure the shift associated with controls. As in the U.S. case, controls were correlated with a decline in the productivity trend, and that is worth emphasizing.

The final point that the authors made about institutional changes was interesting. These changes make a big difference in how restrictive a demand-management policy one might be willing to have. If everyone is on unemployment insurance, then the individual pain associated with a demand-restriction policy is rather small. People are quite willing to take a bit of time off, because they are getting 80 to 85 percent of their income. And, remember, they do not have work-related expenses when they are home making a few desultory telephone calls to see whether there is anything doing in their particular line of endeavor. This point should be recognized. Of course, socially, there is nevertheless a fairly large loss of real output, usually roughly double what the wage earner is earning. Hence, unless the marginal value of leisure is about double what these people would be earning at work, there is a net social loss entailed. This point is implicit in the paper, but perhaps it should be made explicit.

What are some of my quibbles? First, the Canadian wage equation is approximately homogenous, so that the resulting long-run Phillips curve is vertical. This might be true for a largely closed economy like that of the United States, but it is not likely to be true under a fixed exchange rate regime or quasi-fixed exchange rate regime of the sort that we have now in Canada. To make things really simple, say that the rate of change in domestic prices is some proportion of the rate of wage change plus some proportion of the rate of change of import prices. I am ignoring the productivity term, because that would just go into the constant anyway. Now say that the rate of change of domestic wages is the rate of change of expected domestic prices plus some measure of excess demand in the labor force and, of course, a constant term. In the steady state, the rate of change of prices is equal to the rate of change of expected prices. If you solve out such a system, there is still a long-run trade-off curve.

I next ask: How about the introduction of wage-wage and producer price? A group at the University of Guelph has studied this fairly extensively, and they have come up with the influence of consumer prices captured by two split formulations—catch-up and anticipated inflation—which seems to function pretty well, at least in their explanation of micro contract data.

A final quibble: Has the NAIRU really shifted downward in Canada from 1977 to the present date? This is an important political issue at the present. It may well be that the view that it is shifting down from nearly 7 percent to something more like 6.25 or at least 6.5 percent is too optimistic. Seven, or something close to it, is probably close to the right target, if one can judge by the unpublished research of Jean-Pierre Aubry and Charles Freedman at the Bank of Canada.

Before I terminate, let me just say something about the issue of statistics on vacancies. When interest first arose in excess demand as an explanatory variable in labor market adjustments, this interest focused on British data. In the mid-1950s J. C. R. Dow published a paper, "An Index of Excess Demand in the Labor Market," on the basis of which he and L. A. Dicks-Mireaux later analyzed British wage experience, and this approach worked reasonably well. But then along came Phillips and others, and they simply used unemployment rates, and this simpler variable seemed to do just as good a job. So why go to all the trouble to generate an indicator of excess demand for labor based, in part, on vacancy data when unemployment data would do the trick? We may have been led down the primrose path, because although the unemployment data generated explanatory variables that were quite good for the 1950s and 1960s, for the 1970s that appears to be no longer the case, and perhaps we always should have had reason to be skeptical.

On that basis, I think this paper and also the Medoff and Abraham paper corrects an omission of which some of us have been guilty in the past. As such, it is most welcome.

KIM B. CLARK *and* LAWRENCE H. SUMMERS

Unemployment Insurance and Labor Market Transitions

AN UNEMPLOYMENT rate above 4 percent was once regarded as synonymous with slack in the economy. That view is no longer widely held. Indeed, some observers today believe that rates of unemployment below 6 percent place unsustainable inflationary pressure on the economy. This change in viewpoint has been the result of both labor market developments and new perspectives on the causes of unemployment. The apparent upward trend in unemployment has been a source of major concern to policymakers and the focus of research by a number of economists. Central to many explanations of the rising natural rate of unemployment is the role of government transfer programs.

The impact of transfers on measured unemployment includes both real effects on the intensity of search and the willingness to accept offers, and a pure reporting effect. Where program participation depends on registration for possible employment, the measured rate of unemployment could be higher simply because some individuals change the way they report otherwise unchanged behavior. A full evaluation of the impact of transfers on conventional measures of labor market tightness requires an assessment of both real and reporting effects. Although most analyses of transfer programs focus on changes in incentives to find jobs, these programs' effect on the reporting of constant behavior may also be quite significant.

This study reports preliminary estimates of an econometric simulation model capable of a comprehensive evaluation of the effects of unemployment insurance (UI) on measured and actual employment, unemployment, and nonparticipation. The data are longitudinal, comprising information from 75,000 households sampled in the Current

We are indebted to Tom Chesterman and Daniel Smith for valuable research assistance. This research was supported by the Office of the Assistant Secretary for Policy, Evaluation, and Research of the U.S. Department of Labor.

Population Survey (CPS) of March and April 1978. A computer program was developed to impute UI benefits conditional on becoming unemployed for each individual in the sample. The program uses information on each state's benefit formula and eligibility rules, as well as information on federal and state tax codes to calculate a hypothetical replacement rate for each individual in the March sample.

The simulation model is constructed from multinomial logit equations characterizing individuals' labor force transitions. These equations express an individual's probability of transiting between labor force states as a function of his characteristics and of variables reflecting UI benefits (such as the replacement rate and the potential duration of benefits). This technique makes it possible to estimate the impact of UI on both the length of unemployment spells and their frequency. The former depends on UI effects on the probability of exit from employment, while the latter depends on UI effects on the probability of transition into unemployment. The model also can be used to examine the effect of UI reforms on both the level of employment and rate of nonparticipation.

The methodology and data used here have several advantages over previous studies of the effects of UI. Most important, they permit a comprehensive evaluation of the effects of the program. Previous studies have typically focused on the effects of UI on just one labor force transition. Our study provides the first estimate of UI effects on the rate of job loss, labor force exit, and labor force entrance into unemployment. The common data and methods in this study make it possible to combine the estimates of UI effects on individual transition probabilities to yield an estimate of overall impact.

Second, this evaluation of UI makes use of data from the CPS. As has been well documented, measures of unemployment derived from different surveys diverge widely.[1] The use of CPS data means that the results obtained here can be used as a basis for evaluating the effects of UI on unemployment as it is officially measured. The focus here on the reporting effects of UI as well as its behavioral effects also improves the realism of our estimates of the impact of UI on measured unemployment. Recognizing reporting as well as behavioral effects is crucial when using CPS data, as almost half of all unemployment spells culminate in labor force withdrawal.

1. For example, see Richard Freeman and James Medoff, "Why do Youth Unemployment Rates Differ Across Labor Market Surveys?" in Richard Freeman and David Wise, eds., *The Youth Labor-Market Problem: Its Nature, Causes, and Consequences* (University of Chicago Press, 1982).

A third advantage of the approach used here is that it takes account of the effect of UI on the composition of the unemployed and employed populations. Previous studies have been flawed by the failure to take account of the fact that UI will affect the mix of persons becoming unemployed. If, for example, UI induces many short-term layoffs, it may reduce the average duration of unemployment even while increasing spell lengths for each individual. The transition probability approach taken here avoids this difficulty, because explicit account is taken of the effect of UI on the flow into unemployment.

Many previous efforts to evaluate the effects of UI have failed to take account of the taxes that are necessary to finance the system. This study also attempts an examination of the effects of the payroll taxes used to finance UI on levels of employment and unemployment.

It should be clear at the outset that estimating the impact of social insurance programs on the measured unemployment rate is in no way equivalent to examining their desirability. One important goal of social insurance is to make it possible for persons for whom work is likely to be very burdensome (the aged or disabled) to subsist without holding jobs. An important function of UI is facilitating the mobility between jobs that is necessary to accommodate changing product demands. This does mean encouraging persons to become unemployed. Moreover, the reporting effects of social insurance programs have little welfare significance. If UI encourages workers who would otherwise withdraw from the labor force to engage in nominal search activity and report themselves as unemployed, there is no real social cost.

However, an evaluation of the impact of social insurance programs on the level of unemployment is crucial to interpreting labor market conditions. If UI has induced a large increase in the measured unemployment rate, then current high rates of unemployment are not a warrant for public policies to promote employment. If the increases in unemployment cannot be linked to UI or other social programs, the case for policies to combat the increase may be strengthened.

A Theoretical Framework

The relationship between UI and unemployment has been extensively studied.[2] Most previous studies have focused on the relationship

2. An excellent survey of this large literature is Alan Gustman, "Analyzing the Relation of Unemployment Insurance to Unemployment," National Bureau of Economic Research working paper 512 (Cambridge: NBER, July 1980).

between unemployment duration and UI. This is only a small part of the story. There may also be important linkages between UI and the rate of flow into unemployment. Martin Feldstein has argued that UI encourages temporary layoffs and irregular work scheduling.[3] Daniel Hamermesh has suggested that UI may actually increase the labor force participation of some workers.[4] He points out that labor force entrance is more attractive if part of the compensation for employment includes the chance to take advantage of unemployment insurance. UI may also encourage quits in states where job leavers are eligible for benefits.[5]

In order to model these various effects it is necessary to use a framework that takes account of labor market dynamics. The approach taken here builds on the work of Hall, Perry, and Marston, which treats transitions between labor market states as a Markov process.[6] Specifically we assume that each individual's behavior can be characterized by a matrix of transition probabilities given by

$$(1) \qquad \mathbf{p}^i = \begin{bmatrix} p_{ee}^i & p_{eu}^i & p_{en}^i \\ p_{ue}^i & p_{uu}^i & p_{un}^i \\ p_{ne}^i & p_{nu}^i & p_{nn}^i \end{bmatrix}$$

where, for example, p_{en}^i represents the probability that the ith worker would be not in the labor force (NILF) in month $t + 1$, conditional on being employed in month t. Since a worker must always be in one of the three labor force states, the rows of p sum to one.

From the transition probability matrix $\mathbf{p}^i$, it is possible to calculate the proportion of the time individual i spends in each of the three labor force states. Let π_j^i be the fraction of time that individual i spends in state j. We solve for the π_j^i by finding the root of the linear equation system

3. Martin Feldstein, "The Effect of Unemployment Insurance on Temporary Layoff Unemployment," *American Economic Review*, vol. 68 (December 1978), pp. 834–46.

4. Daniel S. Hamermesh, "Entitlement Effects, Unemployment Insurance and Employment Decisions," *Economic Inquiry*, vol. 17 (July 1979), pp. 317–32.

5. The quantitative importance of this effect has been questioned in Stephen Marston, "Unemployment Insurance and Voluntary Employment," report to the National Commission on Unemployment Compensation (Washington, D.C.: NCUC, October 1979).

6. Prominent contributions include Robert Hall, "Why is the Unemployment Rate so High at Full Employment?" *Brookings Papers on Economic Activity, 1970:3*, pp. 369–410 (hereafter *BPEA*); George Perry, "Unemployment Flows in the U.S. Labor Market," *BPEA, 1972:2*, pp. 245–92; and Stephen T. Marston, "Employment Instability and High Unemployment Rates," *BPEA, 1976:1*, pp. 169–210.

(2) $$\mathbf{p}^i \boldsymbol{\pi}^i = \boldsymbol{\pi}^i,$$

for which $\pi_u^i + \pi_e^i + \pi_n^i = 1$.[7] The unemployment rate, the fraction of the labor force which is unemployed, is given by $\pi_u/(\pi_u + \pi_e)$. The steady-state distribution of the population across labor market states can be found by averaging individual probabilities. That is,

(3) $$\Pi_j = \frac{1}{N} \sum_{i=1}^{N} \pi_j^i$$

where N is the size of the population. The aggregate unemployment rate is given by $\Pi_u/(\Pi_u + \Pi_e)$.

In table 1 we provide the 1974 averages of the individual transition probability matrices for various demographic groups. The striking feature of the table is the importance of flows into and out of the labor force. It is instructive to consider the group with the greatest labor force attachment and contact with the UI system, prime-age males. Even though the participation rate in the group averages 92 percent, over one-third of employment entrances came from outside the labor force, and 28 percent of employment spells ended in labor force withdrawal. This suggests the potential importance of UI effects on reported participation as well as on employment.[8]

The approach taken in this paper is to use multinomial logit analysis to estimate the impact of individual characteristics and UI on individual transition probability matrices $\mathbf{p}^i$. These estimates are then combined using equations 2 and 3 to generate estimates of UI impacts on the unemployment and participation rates. This "transition probability" approach has the virtue of being closely linked to theories of labor market choice that emphasize the role of transition decisions. The use of Markov transition matrices involves the assumption that individuals' transition decisions do not depend on how long they have been in a state. This assumption of no state dependence has been examined in earlier work with mixed results. Econometric identification of state

7. Note that any one equation of system 2 is linearly dependent on the others. Hence, a unique root satisfying $\pi_j^i + \pi_e^i + \pi_n^i = 1$ exists. This theorem, which is proved in any textbook in Markov processes, assumes that all the p_{jk}^i are positive. The vector $\mathbf{\Pi}$ can be calculated as the eigenvector corresponding to the unit eigenvalue of the matrix $\mathbf{P}$. The vector $\mathbf{\Pi}$ is the ergodic steady state corresponding to the matrix $\mathbf{P}$.

8. A much more extensive discussion of the significance of observed labor force transitions may be found in Kim B. Clark and Lawrence H. Summers, "Labor Market Dynamics and Unemployment: A Consideration," *BPEA, 1979:1*, pp. 13–72; and Kim Clark and Lawrence Summers, "The Dynamics of Youth Unemployment" in Freeman and Wise, eds., *The Youth Labor-Market Problem*.

Table 1. *Labor Market Transition Probabilities, by Age and Sex, 1974 Annual Average*

	Men			Women			
Probability	16–19	20–24	25–59	16–19	20–24	25–59	Total
Unemployment to employment	0.284	0.287	0.309	0.250	0.255	0.172	0.254
Unemployment to nonparticipation	0.286	0.133	0.105	0.318	0.159	0.272	0.208
Employment to unemployment	0.045	0.032	0.011	0.033	0.026	0.012	0.020
Employment to nonparticipation	0.102	0.033	0.004	0.133	0.047	0.042	0.033
Nonparticipation to employment	0.144	0.180	0.071	0.093	0.071	0.050	0.050
Nonparticipation to unemployment	0.085	0.079	0.032	0.067	0.034	0.013	0.020

Source: Unpublished tabulations by the Bureau of Labor Statistics adjusted by the Urban Institute as described in Jean E. Vanski, "Recession and the Employment of Demographic Groups: Adjustments to Gross Change Data," in Charles C. Holt and others, *Labor Markets, Inflation, and Manpower Policies*, final report to the U.S. Manpower Administration (Washington, D.C.: Urban Institute, 1975), pp. C-1 to C-14.

dependence is difficult because any heterogeneity among individuals in their transition probabilities will lead to apparent state dependence. The assumption here is necessitated by the absence of data on how long individuals have occupied their initial states.

UI and the Unemployed

The duration of unemployment spells has been the focus of most research on UI and the unemployed. In terms of the framework developed here, this is equivalent to studying the relationship between UI and the transition probabilities p_{ue}^i and p_{un}^i. The duration of completed spells of unemployment is related to the transition probabilities p_{ue}^i and p_{un}^i by the identity:

$$(4) \qquad D_u^i = \frac{1}{p_{ue}^i + p_{un}^i}.$$

In thinking about the impact of UI on the duration of unemployment, it is crucial to distinguish between individuals who are searching for work and those on layoff from jobs to which they are permanently attached.

We begin by analyzing the decision problem faced by workers who are eligible for UI but not attached to permanent jobs. Dale Mortensen's excellent theoretical study of the decision problem faced by these workers brings out the crucial effects.[9] He finds that the impact of an increase in the UI benefit level on the probability of reemployment is likely to be positive but is theoretically ambiguous. Increases in UI benefits will tend to increase the length of spells by reducing the opportunity cost of both leisure and job search. The consequent rise in the reservation wage tends to prolong unemployment. However, it is possible that for some workers this effect will be offset by another. Since jobs are not permanent, workers will recognize that the sooner they take a job, the sooner they will again be eligible for UI. This effect is likely to be particularly important for persons near exhaustion of benefits.

Mortensen's analysis does not treat the question of UI's impact on the probability of labor force withdrawal. Increases in UI are likely to reduce labor force withdrawal through both real and reporting effects. By raising the rewards of working, increases in UI reduce the incentive to withdraw from the labor force. In most states, eligibility for UI requires a worker to be available and actively looking for work. When enforced, this will cause some workers to search for work rather than withdraw from the labor force. However, this requirement is usually very poorly enforced. Disqualifications from UI are quite rare, affecting fewer than 0.1 percent of claimants. Nonetheless, knowledge of the requirement is likely to lead at least some persons to profess to be looking for work even if they are not in fact seriously seeking a job. This effect may also occur because workers regard mandatory registration with the state employment service as a form of job search.

It is important to be clear about the relationship between this analysis and statements about the impact of UI on the average duration of unemployment. The question examined here is the impact of an increase in UI on a given worker's probability of reemployment. The average duration of unemployment will be affected by changes in this probability, as well as by changes in the composition of the unemployed. Even if UI reduced the probability of exiting unemployment for any given individual, the average length of unemployment spells might also be reduced if persons with high reemployment probabilities were encouraged to become unemployed. This problem would seem to be

9. Dale T. Mortensen, "Unemployment Insurance and Job Search Decisions," *Industrial and Labor Relations Review*, vol. 30 (July 1977), pp. 505–17.

a serious drawback of previous studies that have relied on comparisons of averages of unemployment durations.

Similar considerations suggest that increases in the potential remaining duration are likely to reduce the probability of unemployment exit by delaying returns to employment. An additional complication is posed by those who are waiting to receive benefits. This group (mostly quitters) will also be sensitive to increases in benefits, even though benefits are not received contemporaneously.

UI and Exit from Layoff Unemployment

The importance of distinguishing between the behavior of workers who are attached to permanent jobs and those not attached has been recognized since the influential work of Feldstein.[10] In an ex-post sense, the duration of layoff spells is determined by the employer rather than the employee. In an ex-ante sense, of course, this is not the case. Explicit, or more likely implicit, contracts will determine the length and frequency of spells of temporary layoff unemployment. These contracts will depend on both workers' tastes and the availability of UI. The nature of these interactions is discussed in more detail below. However, in the presence of imperfect experience rating, increases in UI at the margin will lead to longer and more frequent layoffs.

A second consideration suggests a positive relationship between benefit levels and the length of spells of layoff unemployment. A large fraction, perhaps as great as 50 percent, of those in the temporary layoff category do not in fact return to their original employer. For this group, the considerations discussed above for ordinary job losers should be relevant. It does not appear on theoretical grounds that there should be important effects of UI on labor force withdrawal from layoff unemployment.

UI and the Flow into Unemployment

Previous research on demographic, cyclical, and regional differences in unemployment rates has all found that most variations can be attributed to differences in the rate of flow into unemployment rather

10. Martin S. Feldstein, "The Importance of Temporary Layoffs: An Empirical Analysis," *BPEA, 1975:3*, pp. 725–45.

than the duration of unemployment spells. This suggests the importance of examining the relation between UI and the rate of entrance into unemployment. While most of the research in this area has examined the relationship between UI and temporary layoff unemployment, it is also likely that there are important effects of UI on permanent separations.

UI and Employment Exit

In order to examine the relationship between UI and permanent separations, it is necessary to provide a model for determining the duration of employment. We use the framework developed by Robert Hall to attack this problem.[11] The optimal separation rate is determined by the interaction of workers' tastes and employers' cost functions.

In general it is reasonable to suppose that employers have some optimal turnover rate. If jobs are too short, costs of staffing and training become prohibitive. If they are too long, the ability to adjust to changing product market conditions is likely to be impaired. This suggests that the employers' isoprofit curves between wages and separation rates look like that depicted by *EE* in figure 1. Workers also are likely to prefer intermediate durations. If jobs are too short, they will have to incur excessive search costs. If they are too long, they lose flexibility.

The set of tangencies of indifference and isoprofit curves trace out an expansion path in wage separation space. The condition that the supply and demand for labor be equated determines the level of wages and separations. In general, it is clear from the configuration of these curves that the optimum, or equilibrium, separation rate can involve either a positive or negative rate of substitution between wages and separations.

Consider first the impact of introducing a non-experience-rated UI system. Employers' isoprofit curves are unaffected. However, since UI reduces the costs of changing jobs, it is reasonable to suppose that the shape of workers' indifference curves changes from *I* to *II* as shown in figure 1. At any given level of wages and the separation rate, the introduction of UI reduces the rate of substitution between wages and separations. Graphically, the associated slope of the indifference

11. Robert Hall, "A Theory of the Natural Unemployment Rate and the Duration of Employment," *Journal of Monetary Economics,* vol. 5 (April 1979), pp. 153–69.

Figure 1. *Equilibrium Wages and Separations
without Experience Rating*

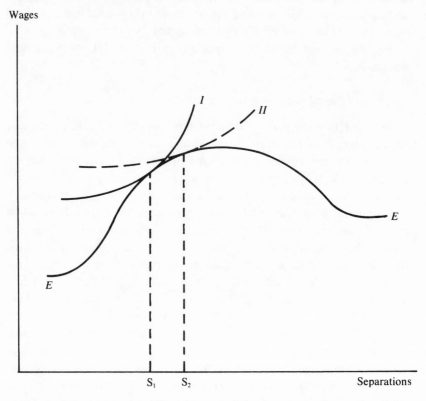

curve at each point declines. This means that the introduction of UI
leads to a new equilibrium with a higher separation rate (S_2). The
magnitude of the impact of UI on the equilibrium level of rates and
separations depends on the shape of the indifference curves. The figure
would seem to suggest that UI represents a Pareto improvement. This
is a consequence of deferring consideration of the taxes necessary to
finance the program.

The basic result, that UI raises the equilibrium separation rate,
should not be surprising. Since it subsidizes job search, it makes
separation less costly for workers. This directly encourages quits.
Employer-initiated separations are also encouraged. Since workers
will demand less compensation for a high risk of layoff, employers
will find it profitable to shift to production methods involving a higher
risk of separation.

Figure 2. *Equilibrium Wages and Separations*
with Experience Rating

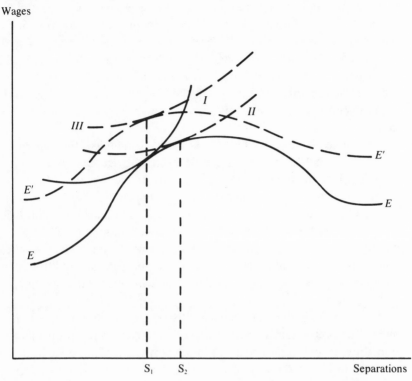

The UI system considered so far was not experience rated. That is, an employer's contribution to the system was assumed to be independent of his own separation experience. Consider now the extreme opposite case of perfectly experience-rated UI. In this case, depicted in figure 2, the employers' isoprofit curve is shifted (from *EE* to *E'E'*) in a fashion parallel to the change in workers' indifference curves. Hence the separation rate at the point of tangency (between indifference curve *III* and isoprofit curve *E'E'*) is unaffected. A fully experience-rated system of UI will have no impact on the separation rate.

This result can be seen intuitively. Efficiency considerations dictate an optimal rate of substitution between wages and separation rates. The announcement by the government that the employer must make transfers to the employee in the case of separation will have income effects, but will not affect the optimal contract.

The extent of experience rating in the UI system is examined below. At this point, it is useful to point out that if wages are taxed, a fully experience-rated system requires that the employer pay the full UI costs of separations, and that the government receive the revenue it would have received if the UI benefits had been paid out as wages. If UI benefits are not taxes, and if the firm is not charged for the government's forgone revenue on those benefits, there will be an inducement toward separations. Thus, even if the UI system is perfectly experience-rated internally, there is still a distortion because of forgone tax revenue on benefits.

This analysis suggests that UI is likely to increase the separation rate. This conclusion is not affected by taking account of additional complexities. In many states, separations labeled as quits leave the worker ineligible for UI. This will tend to reduce the effect considered here and give a strong inducement for quits to be labeled as job loss. If implicit contracts can be enforced, even separations induced by the employee will be labeled as layoffs. If one assumes that implicit contracts are not enforceable, and that employers are indifferent to their reputations, then only quit decisions will be affected by the level of UI benefits.

A final issue is the state occupied by persons exiting from employment. The prediction is an unambiguous increase in the probability of transiting from employment to unemployment. The effects of an increase in UI on the rate of transition from employment to NILF is ambiguous since workers who would otherwise enter this state are likely to become unemployed instead in order to collect benefits.

This analysis suggests that the effect of UI on the permanent separation rate is theoretically unambiguous. However, UI may have an ambiguous effect on the division of separations between quits and job loss.

UI and Permanently Attached Workers

The relationship between UI and temporary layoff unemployment has been extensively studied. Martin Feldstein has presented a theoretical analysis demonstrating that the introduction of an imperfectly experience-rated UI system encourages this form of unemployment.[12]

12. Martin Feldstein, "Temporary Layoffs in the Theory of Unemployment," *Journal of Political Economy*, vol. 84 (October 1976), pp. 937–57.

Table 2. *Effect of Unemployment Insurance on Labor Market Transition Probabilities*

	Final labor market state		
Initial labor market state	*Employment*	*Unemployment*	*Nonparticipation*
Employment	–	+ +	–
Unemployment	–	+ +	– –
Nonparticipation	?	+ +	–

The nature of long-term contract arrangements has been discussed in detail by Robert Hall.[13] He shows that optimal contracts involve employing workers wherever their marginal product exceeds their marginal valuation of time out of work. Since UI raises the marginal valuation by workers of time out of work, it increases the number of states of the world where workers are laid off. This effect will occur unless firms are perfectly experience rated, in which case the UI system will have no impact on layoff unemployment.

UI and Labor Force Entrance

As Daniel Hamermesh has pointed out, the entitlement effect of UI is likely to increase labor force entrance. This effect is similar to the proemployment effects for the unemployed described above. The ability to collect UI after a spell of work raises the effective wage and so is likely to encourage labor force entrance. This entry may be through either the unemployment or NILF states. Some workers outside the labor force may be immediately eligible for benefits if they reenter the unemployment state. For this group, who have been recently employed, the impact of UI is likely to be particularly pronounced.

In table 2, the conclusions of this section are summarized. The theoretical analysis leads to predictions regarding the effects of UI on all the transition probabilities except for the movement between nonparticipation and employment. Note that the effect of UI on total unemployment is almost certain to be positive, because the transition rate into unemployment from each of the alternative states is increased.

13. Robert E. Hall, "Employment Fluctuations and Wage Rigidity," *BPEA, 1980:1*, pp. 91–141.

Financing the UI System

The UI system is financed partially out of a payroll tax levied at a variable rate on the first $6,000 of income on a given job. This tax, which reduces after-tax wages, will tend to discourage transitions into employment and to encourage labor force withdrawal. It will tend to offset the entitlement effect of UI discussed above. In considering UI reform, it may be reasonable to assume that the taxes and benefits are changed simultaneously. Alternatively, it may be appropriate to consider the case where marginal UI funds come from other expenditure programs so that the tax system is unaffected. Both cases are considered in the empirical work below.

Imputing UI Benefits

A complete analysis of UI and labor market flows imposes formidable information requirements. We require an estimate not only of the level and potential duration of benefits received by the unemployed, but also of what the system would provide other individuals if they were to join the jobless ranks. Furthermore, theory suggests that the variables affecting economic decisions are the after-tax replacement ratios; thus we require an estimate of the applicable marginal tax rate. In order to derive these data, we have designed a computer program embodying federal tax rules and each state's UI laws and tax codes. The UISIM program determines UI eligibility, calculates basic and dependent benefits (where available), establishes the maximum allowable duration of benefits, and estimates federal and state marginal tax rates.

The program has been designed to use information from the annual work experience survey conducted in March 1978 as a supplement to the regular Current Population Survey. Federal extended benefits and supplemental assistance were not in force at that time, so that variation in UI parameters depended only on differences in state laws. Since information on income and work experience in the CPS is not as detailed as the law requires, a number of assumptions underlie our calculations.[14]

14. The work experience survey provides no information on the pattern of earnings (high quarter, low quarter, etc.) throughout the year, nor on the timing of spells of unemployment. Furthermore, earnings above $50,000 are not reported, and nonwage and salary income tend to be underreported.

The UI System: Rules and Definitions

An individual's participation in the UI system—the level and duration of benefits—is conditioned by previous work experience. The specific rules for eligibility, benefit amounts, and duration are determined by each state. Though no two states are identical, a number of common elements are present. In order to highlight the basic structure of the system, table 3 presents key rules for a hypothetical "typical" state.

Within limits, the weekly benefit amount in our typical state is defined as 1/26 of the individual's wages in the high quarter of the base period (that is, four quarters prior to the quarter in which the claim is filed); the minimum and maximum benefit limits are $20 and $110 respectively.[15] To be eligible for benefits, a claimant must be available for and actively seeking work, and must not have left the last job voluntarily without "good cause."[16] In addition, base-period earnings must be at least $800 and must exceed 125 percent of high-quarter wages. Once determined, benefits are fixed for a period (fifty-two weeks) called the benefit year.[17] Within that period, all eligible claimants receive benefits for at least ten weeks; the maximum number of weeks for receipt of benefits is twenty-six. Actual potential duration is chosen so that total potential benefits are less than or equal to one-third of base-period earnings.

While variations on this theme are legion, the basic structure—including eligibility for and level of benefits linked to past work experience and minima and maxima for benefits and duration—is found in each state. Most of the interstate variations reflect either different numerical formulas (for example, 1/23 versus 1/26) or different reference values (for example, average weekly instead of high-quarter wages).

15. In this example, the benefit year is specifically individually determined. In a few states the benefit year is fixed for all individuals by statute, but administrative rulings have the effect of making it specific to the individual.

16. The definition of "good cause" varies greatly by state; while usually restricted to action by the employer, a number of states make exceptions for "compelling personal reasons."

17. Three states and the District of Columbia employ a "bracket step down" in determining eligibility. If a claimant does not meet the basic test, a second, less restrictive, test is applied; passing the second test brings a lower benefit. The number of such brackets ranges from three to five. U.S. Department of Labor, Employment and Training Administration, Unemployment Insurance Service, *Comparison of State Unemployment Insurance Laws* (Government Printing Office, 1978), pp. 3–28.

Table 3. *Parameters of the Unemployment Insurance System in a Typical State, and Common Variations*

Parameter	Typical state rule	Common variations
Weekly benefit amount	1/26 of high-quarter wages (minimum $20, maximum $110)	50 percent of average weekly wage
Eligibility	Able/available for work Base-period earnings more than 125 percent of high-quarter wages and at least $800 Quit disqualification	Earnings test supplemented by a weeks-of-employment requirement Quitters qualified after waiting period
Maximum potential duration of benefits	Given weekly benefit amount, choose longest duration possible that is at least 10 weeks and no more than 26 weeks; weekly benefit amount times duration is less than or equal to one-third of base earnings	Maximum of 39 weeks Secondary limit based on weeks of employment

Source: U.S. Department of Labor, Employment and Training Administration, Unemployment Insurance Service, *Comparison of State Unemployment Insurance Laws* (Government Printing Office, 1978).

Actual formulas can be quite complex. In twelve states, for example, the fraction of high-quarter wages received in weekly benefits depends on previous work experience and earnings. There are two variations, however, of a more fundamental nature. Twelve states provide additional benefits to claimants with dependents (usually ranging from $3 to $5 per dependent per week), and sixteen states allow quitters to receive benefits after a waiting period, varying from five to fourteen weeks, has elapsed. Although these provisions are found in a minority of states, they are potentially applicable to a significant fraction of the unemployed. In March 1978, for example, states with dependents' benefits accounted for 32 percent of all the unemployed; for quitters' benefits, the figure was 24 percent.

The UISIM Program

Our model of the UI system incorporates the rules for eligibility and the determination of benefits and taxes for each state. The program is designed to use information available in the CPS work experience survey conducted in March 1978. Information on family income, marital status, and dependents is used to calculate federal and state marginal tax rates, including social security taxes.[18] Data on weeks worked and wage and salary income from the previous year provide the basis for determining eligibility and the level of benefits. For those out of the labor force in March 1978 who had no work experience in 1977, we imputed an average weekly wage (described below). The output of the program consists of a weekly benefit, maximum potential duration, the quit disqualification period (where applicable), the marginal tax rate, and weeks of employment needed to qualify for benefits (NILF only).

The federal tax module in the program is based on previous work conducted at the National Bureau of Economic Research. We modified the NBER's TAXSIM program to work with CPS data and to interact with a new state tax module especially developed for UISIM. State income taxes have not received as detailed attention in the public finance literature or the empirical work on UI as have federal taxes. While state marginal tax rates are much lower than the federal taxes, they are not insignificant. In several states, marginal rates as high as 10 percent are not uncommon. Moreover, variation across states and across income classes within states may be important. In light of these considerations, it seems inappropriate both to ignore state taxes and to apply an average for each state. UISIM thus includes a module with an income tax algorithm for each state. Both the federal and state tax modules incorporate provisions in force as of March 1978.

Given an individual's basic earnings and employment information, the bulk of the program is a relatively straightforward and mechanical application of tax laws and state UI rules. There are three parts of UISIM, however, which required a good measure of approximation. First, in order to derive marginal tax rates we had to determine whether an individual would itemize deductions and how large the deductions would be. Information from the CPS by itself provides no guidance. Our approach to the problem involved two steps. We first used tax return information from the NBER TAXSIM file to calculate the frequency of itemization and average deductions for itemizers by income class and filing status.[19] The second step was to calculate two

18. The program for calculating tax rates uses a modified version of the federal and state tax simulation models developed at the National Bureau of Economic Research.

19. For a description of TAXSIM see Martin Feldstein and Daniel Frisch, "Corporate Tax Integration: The Estimated Effects on Capital Accumulation and Tax Distribution of Two Integration Proposals," *National Tax Journal*, vol. 30 (March 1977), pp. 37–52. The data are based on 1976 returns and were updated to reflect 1978 income levels.

marginal tax rates, one assuming the standard deduction and the other assuming average itemized deductions as estimated from the sample of returns in TAXSIM. We then computed a weighted average with weights based on the frequency of itemization.

The second major area of uncertainty in the design of the simulator was the calculation of potential duration and the problem of the benefit year. At the time an initial claim is filed, weekly benefits and maximum duration are determined and fixed for the benefit year. If the individual files another claim (that is, begins a second spell of unemployment) within the benefit year, benefits available for the second spell are equal to the initial entitlement minus benefits already paid in the benefit year. For individuals with no unemployment in 1977 (the previous year) this presents no problem, since the current spell of unemployment (captured in March) can be taken as the first spell of the benefit year. For those with previous unemployment, however, the calculation is more complex. The easiest way to illustrate our approach is to consider the case of an individual who had just become unemployed at the time of the survey (March) and who had one ten-week spell of unemployment in the previous year.

In calculating maximum continuous duration of benefits in the current spell, there are three possibilities.[20] If last year's spell of unemployment began before March, the current spell marks the beginning of a new benefit year and the individual receives the maximum duration consistent with previous work experience; let this amount be *MAX*. If last year's spell began after March (actually after the week of the March survey), one of two conditions holds. Assume that the survey occurs in week number 10, and define the critical week *(CW)* to be $CW = MAX - U_{t-1} + 10$, where U_{t-1} is weeks of unemployment last year (ten in our example).[21] If last year's spell began after the

20. The "continuous" aspect of this calculation deserves emphasis. Note that we ignore the possibility that an individual could exhaust benefits, wait for a short period until the beginning of a new benefit year, and resume receipt of benefits if qualified. Our calculation stops at the point of exhaustion unless a new benefit year is reached.

21. Since the individual is assumed to have just become unemployed at the time of the survey, there is no need to adjust for weeks of benefits already received in the current spell. The adjustment incorporated in the program is as follows: if U_t is weeks in the current spell, $CW = MAX - U_{t-1} + 10$. Our calculation assumes that all weeks of unemployment in the previous year were accumulated in one spell. This formula assumes no overlap between benefit years. The true formula is weeks to exhaust + *MAX2*. We have no information on the point at which the spell of unemployment began and therefore have ignored the overlap problem. The effect is to overstate somewhat potential duration.

critical week, say in week number 38, the individual is still in the first benefit year, and will exhaust benefits before the beginning of the second benefit year is reached; maximum potential duration is thus $MAX - U_{t-1}$ (note that we assume in this example that the current spell has just begun). If U_{t-1} began after March but before CW, the individual will reach the end of the first benefit year without exhausting benefits, and will be allowed to begin a new benefit year with a new MAX (call it $MAX2$) and weekly benefit. $MAX2$ will be conditional on whatever work experience has been accumulated during the base period (which now includes some part of the old benefit year). If the individual meets eligibility requirements for the second benefit year, maximum potential duration (continuous) for the current spell would be $MAX - U_{t-1} + MAX2$.[22]

Unfortunately, the annual work experience survey does not tell us when spells of unemployment occur. Thus, in order to derive an expected maximum potential duration, we compute a weighted average of the three possibilities. The weights are determined under an assumption that the probability of becoming unemployed is distributed uniformly across weeks. For the individual in our example, the calculation is as follows:

$$DUR = w_1(MAX) + w_2(MAX - U_{t-1}) + w_3(MAX - U_{t-1} + MAX2)$$

where

$$w_1 = \frac{10}{52},$$
$$w_2 = \frac{CW - 10}{52},$$
$$w_3 = 1 - w_1 - w_2.$$

The third major issue in the design of the simulator was the whole problem of people out of the labor force at the time of the survey. The CPS provides sufficient information to determine current eligibility

22. The possibility of overlapping benefit years may reward some individuals who have experienced some unemployment in the previous year. Consider the case of two individuals, each laid off at the same time. Assume that one has no previous unemployment experience, while the other was unemployed for four weeks nine months ago. Given sufficient earnings and weeks of unemployment, the first individual will begin a benefit year and have a maximum potential duration of twenty-six weeks. The second individual, however, will reach the end of the first benefit year in twelve weeks, and, subject to eligibility tests, will receive an additional twenty-six weeks in the second benefit year. Thus the individual with unemployment experience has a potential duration of thirty-eight weeks, while the first individual has twenty-six.

status and, where applicable, to calculate marginal tax rates, weekly benefits, and potential duration. Thus some in the NILF group have enough work experience and previous earnings to qualify for benefits immediately. Others would be eligible for benefits only after some minimum period of work experience. For individuals currently ineligible, we calculated taxes and UI benefits assuming that weeks employed just satisfied minimum requirements. The applicable weekly wages were either taken from the previous year where available or imputed using an earnings function. The earnings function was estimated using data on the employed population from the May 1978 CPS; estimated earnings were corrected for selectivity bias using Mills's ratio.[23]

Simulation Results

The use of CPS information necessarily entails significant assumptions in the design of the simulator. It is clear that some error is possible because work experience data is not as detailed as the law requires and some tax information has to be estimated. Furthermore, the raw CPS data, particularly reported annual income, may not be accurate. With respect to the parameters of the UI system, however, substantial effort has been made to ensure their accuracy. We have made extensive use of internal Department of Labor documents made available to us by the Employment and Training Administration. We have also directly verified provisions for a large number of the states and in a few instances have engaged in extensive discussions with state officials to determine the appropriate specifications.

The results of the simulation suggest that the program provides a plausible description of the UI system. Table 4 presents estimates of the distribution of marginal tax rates, after-tax replacement ratios, and potential durations for the employed and the unemployed. If we look

23. The sample used to estimate the earnings function was composed of employed individuals who participated in both the March and May 1978 CPS. The specification included controls for years of schooling, race, age, region, weeks worked in the previous year, location (SMSA, central city), sex, marital status, and Mills's ratio. The dependent variable was the log of usual weekly earnings. Mills's ratio was estimated using a probit model of employment status. For Mills's ratio, see James J. Heckman, "The Common Structure of Statistical Models of Truncation, Sample Selection and Limited Dependent Variables and a Simple Estimator for Such Models," *Annals of Economic and Social Measurement*, vol. 5 (Fall 1976), pp. 475–92. The results are available on request.

Table 4. *Estimated Marginal Tax Rates, Replacement Ratios, and Potential Durations of Employed and Unemployed*
Percent unless otherwise indicated

Parameter	Employed	Unemployed
Marginal tax rate		
0	1.0	1.6
0–20	17.0	53.3
20–30	31.7	26.7
30–40	33.6	14.3
40–50	12.3	3.3
Over 50	4.3	0.7
Replacement ratio		
0	19.2	60.7
0–25	1.1	1.5
25–40	7.2	2.8
40–60	25.2	10.8
60–80	39.9	18.4
Over 80	7.4	5.8
Potential duration (weeks)		
0	19.2	61.1
0–5	0.1	2.9
5–10	0.4	5.9
10–15	1.6	8.5
15–20	2.0	8.0
Over 20	76.7	13.4

first at tax rates for the employed, the results appear to be consistent, both internally and with estimates generated by existing tax simulation models. The exclusion of wage income above $50,000 and the underreporting of other incomes appear to have only moderate effects on the overall distribution of rates. The fact that the bulk of the unemployed are found in the bottom tax bracket reflects the marginal income position of many of these individuals, as well as the use of the previous year's income, which may understate potential earnings.

The evidence on net replacement ratios accords with previous estimates. We find that 61 percent of the unemployed receive no benefits, while those who do have an average replacement ratio of 66.6 percent. This compares with 55 percent reported in Feldstein.[24] It should be noted that the calculations for the unemployed assume that all leavers are ineligible for benefits. The calculations for the employed predict what they would receive if they were to lose their

24. Feldstein, "The Effect of Unemployment Insurance."

jobs. We find that 19 percent are ineligible for benefits, while about 40 percent of the unemployed would receive benefits replacing 60 percent to 80 percent of the after-tax wage.

It is instructive to compare the employed and unemployed groups after adjusting for eligibility. If we look only at those receiving or potentially receiving benefits, we find that close to 15 percent of the unemployed recipients have replacement ratios above 0.8; the comparable figure for the employed is 0.9. The other categories are quite close together, with a greater fraction of the employed in the lower ranges. These calculations are suggestive of the disincentive effects of UI.

The distribution of durations for the unemployed and employed appear quite reasonable. After correcting for eligibility, we find that more than 34 percent of the unemployed have a potential duration that exceeds twenty weeks, while 7.5 percent are within five weeks of exhausting remaining benefits. The remainder of the eligible unemployed are quite evenly distributed between five and twenty weeks. Among the employed the distribution is skewed toward eligibility for long durations. Clearly work of the employed group has accumulated sufficient wage credits and work experience to qualify for weeks close to the maximum (usually twenty weeks).

As a further check on the consistency of the program, we compared predicted benefits with those actually paid out in March 1978.[25] Estimates of weekly benefits are quite close to the actual values, while the program overestimates total weeks compensated by about 9 percent.

	Actual	Predicted
Average weekly benefits	$85.45	$83.51
Total weeks compensated (millions)	11.124	12.08

One explanation of the difference is the tendency for only some job leavers to receive benefits, a fact that we have not reflected in the predicted values. Both the internal checks on consistency and the actual-predicted comparisons suggest that UISIM provides plausible, relatively accurate values of the principal variables of interest.

25. U.S. Department of Labor, *Unemployment Insurance Statistics*, March 1978, table 3c.

Empirical Analysis

Our analysis of UI and labor market transitions is based on the flows between labor market states captured in the March and April 1978 Current Population Surveys. The CPS focuses principally on labor market activity, but also provides a good deal of information about other personal and family characteristics, generally obtained from one (presumably knowledgeable) member of the household. In addition to the regular or basic questionnaire, the Census Bureau administers short supplementary questionnaires on a variety of topics. Data on usual weekly earnings, for example, are obtained in May, while school attendance is dealt with in October. The supplement to the March CPS referred to earlier covers employment and earnings experience in the previous year and is the most extensive of the supplementary interviews.

The structure of the CPS allows us to follow individuals through four months of labor market activity. A given household in the survey is interviewed in four consecutive months, then is dropped from the survey for eight months before returning for a final four months of interviews. By watching individuals and households in successive months, flows between labor market states can be estimated.

The probability framework relating UI to transitions assumes that alternative states of the labor market are clearly defined, and that changes in status reflect meaningful changes in behavior. It is well known, however, that the definitions of unemployment and nonparticipation in the CPS are somewhat ambiguous. Observed movements into and out of these states may occur because otherwise unchanged behavior is reported in a different way. While the results should thus be interpreted with caution, it is our view that the estimated transition probabilities convey useful information. Clearly, reporting problems are likely to be less important in flows involving employment. Moreover, the available information on reasons for unemployment can be used to enhance the reliability of results. The layoff category, for example, is likely to be somewhat less affected by arbitrary distinctions.

Variable Definition and Empirical Specification

The theoretical analysis has treated UI as an exogenous aspect of the choice set facing individuals and firms. Yet the earlier discussion makes clear that both the level and duration of benefits depend on previous work experience and earnings. These factors are likely to have an independent effect on transitions. In order to isolate the effects of UI, it is necessary to control for the level of wages and weeks worked. Transition decisions are also influenced by differences in opportunities and constraints related to demographic characteristics, marital status, education, and local labor market conditions. Table 5 presents definitions and mean values of the variables in the CPS that we use to control for these factors.

Two specifications are used to estimate the impact of UI on transitions between labor market states. The first and simplest is the linear probability model given by

$$(5) \qquad p_{hk}^i = a_0 + b_1 UIBEN_i + \sum_{j=2}^{n} b_j x_j^i,$$

where p_{hk}^i is the probability of transition from h to k, and x_j^i represents the jth characteristic for the ith individual. In estimation, p_{hk}^i takes on the value one if a transition occurred from month t (March) to month $t + 1$ (April), and zero otherwise. The assumption of linearity in equation 5 has significant limitations. First, the data come in the form of observations on individuals' labor force states in succeeding months. Since the dependent variable is essentially trichotomous (movement into one of three states), there is no natural scale, and standard regression techniques are inappropriate. A linear specification also fails to enforce the constraint that the probabilities lie between zero and one.

Because of these limitations, the linear probability model is used only to illustrate the effect of alternative specifications. Inferences about the effects of UI on specific transitions and analysis of the overall impact of UI on unemployment and labor force participation will make use of estimates based on the cumulative logistic probability function. In this framework, the logarithm of the odds of a transition occurring (rather than the probability) is a linear function of the characteristics of the individual. Although in the present case there are three possible states, and three transition probabilities for a given base period, the logistic form and the adding-up constraint imply that coefficients for only two of the transitions need be estimated; the third equation can be derived from the other two.

Table 5. *Basic Current Population Survey Variables, by Labor Market State*

	Labor market state[a]		
Variable (mean)	Employ- ment	Unem- ploy- ment	Nonpar- tici- pation
UIBEN (replacement ratio: ratio of benefits to after-tax wage)	0.494	0.249	0.484
AWW (average weekly wage)	198.56	111.96	68.05
WKSWKD (weeks worked in 1977)	44.75	21.35	5.08
Age	38.05	29.76	48.3
Marital status by sex			
MARRYM (1 = male, married; 0 = other)	0.43	0.23	0.17
MARRYW (1 = female, married; 0 = other)	0.24	0.18	0.47
SINGLEM (1 = male, single; 0 = other)	0.16	0.33	0.12
SINGLEF (1 = female, single; 0 = other)	0.17	0.26	0.24
SCHOOL (years of schooling)	12.5	11.5	11.0
SMSA (1 = living in SMSA; 0 = otherwise)	0.58	0.57	0.56
CCITY (1 = living in central city; 0 = otherwise)	0.23	0.27	0.24
UMARCH (state unemployment rate in March 1978)	6.43	6.79	6.49
HSGRAD (1 = high school grad; 0 = otherwise)	0.78	0.61	0.55
WKSND (weeks needed to qualify for benefits)	. . .	. . .	9.1
RACE (1 = nonwhite; 0 = otherwise)	0.10	0.23	0.11

a. Numbers in survey sample: employed, 42,593; unemployed, 3,057; nonparticipant, 24,173.

In order to illustrate the approach more formally, consider the case of the transitions out of unemployment. The model is given by:[26]

$$(6) \qquad \ln(p^i_{ue}/p^i_{uu}) = \alpha_{ue} + \beta_{ue}UIBEN_i + \sum_{j=2}^{n} \gamma_j x^i_j;$$

$$(7) \qquad \ln(p^i_{un}/p^i_{uu}) = \alpha_{un} + \beta_{un}UIBEN_i + \sum_{j=2}^{n} \delta_j x^i_j,$$

where the x^i_j are defined as before, and the βs measure the effect of UI on the odds of a transition relative to remaining unemployed.

26. In the general case, a given probability for the ith individual can be written as

$$p^i_j = \frac{\exp(x_i\beta_j)}{1 + \sum_{j=1}^{} \exp(x_i\beta_j)},$$

where j indexes choices, and the Xs are characteristics. The likelihood function can be formed as a product of the appropriate probabilities, and maximized with conventional nonlinear techniques.

Similar models can be written for transitions out of employment and into the labor force. Estimates of the coefficients in these models are obtained by maximizing the likelihood function.[27] The coefficients can be used to derive an estimate of the derivative of a given probability with respect to *UIBEN*. The formula for p_{ue}, for example, is:

$$(8) \qquad \frac{\partial p_{ue}}{\partial UIBEN} = \hat{\beta}_{ue}(1 - p_{ue})p_{ue}$$

where $\hat{\beta}_{ue}$ is the estimated coefficient on *UIBEN*.

Throughout the analysis, the effect of UI on the transition probabilities is captured by the replacement ratio. Theory provides little guidance about the form this variable ought to take. Our use of a linear specification reflects the fact that more complicated nonlinear expression failed to dominate the simple approach. We examined several alternative UI variables, including category dummies, a quadratic term, and linear splines. The results were uniform and consistent; none of the variants produced significant value added when compared to the linear form.

In addition to its linearity, *UIBEN* also stands alone in capturing the effects of UI. We found that maximum potential duration provided little additional insight or explanatory power. Moreover, since duration is likely to interact with *UIBEN*, its presence in the equation significantly complicates attempts to use parameter estimates to assess the impact of changes in replacement rates. We did find, however, that other aspects of the UI system, notably adjustments for weeks of employment needed for eligibility, were important. These will be noted and reported below.

The expected impact of UI on the transitions has been extensively discussed. Other variables are expected to have a significant influence on movements in the labor market. Wide variations across demographic groups in the propensity to leave and enter the labor force or employment are well known. For a given demographic mix, conditions in the local labor market as measured by the state unemployment rate influence available opportunities. We expect individuals in states with higher rates of unemployment to have greater difficulty in finding work

27. Such models have been developed and used in several places. See Daniel McFadden, "Conditional Logit Analysis of Qualitative Choice Behavior," in Paul Zarembka, ed., *Frontiers in Econometrics* (Academic Press, 1974), pp. 105–42, for a discussion and review of the statistical literature.

and to be at a greater risk of job loss. It is possible that job finding and labor force entrance will be affected by residential location. *SMSA* and *CCITY* are included to capture the possibility of mismatches between the location of jobs and workers.

The demographic variables and other personal characteristics are included to control for differences in preferences and individual opportunity. As noted above, the generosity of UI is likely to be related to personal factors, which are correlated with transition decisions. Two of the most important of these variables are weeks worked last year (*WKSWKD*) and average weekly wage (*AWW*). The *WKSWKD* variable is designed to capture two effects. First, it is likely to be highly correlated with job tenure and thus will capture some of the effects of seniority on the possibility of layoff and recall. Second, it should reflect both attachment to the labor force and personal stability. If these are important aspects of individual heterogeneity, *WKSWKD* may help to isolate the effects of UI that do not depend on individual quality. The wage variable plays a similar role.

Transitions from Unemployment

Table 6 presents the coefficients estimated from a multinomial logit model of transitions from unemployment. Estimates are presented by destination state (such as employed, NILF) for the total unemployed population, and for each of three unemployment groups: those on layoff, quitters, and other job losers (including reentrants). In the layoff and loser regressions, *UIBEN* is entered as calculated by UISIM. In the quit regression, however, an adjustment was made to reflect the possibility of outright disqualification and the effect of the waiting period where applicable. Where quitters are disqualified, we set *UIBEN* to zero. For potentially eligible quitters, an adjusted *UIBEN* is given by:

$$(9) \qquad UIBEN_i^* = UIBEN_i \left(\frac{k - q_i}{k} \right),$$

where q is the number of weeks a quitter must wait until benefits will be received, and k is the expected remaining duration of the unemployment spell. The parameter k is given by:

$$(10) \qquad k = \frac{1}{p_{ue} + p_{un}}.$$

Table 6. Multinomial Logit Estimates of Transitions from Unemployment, by Reason for Unemployment[a]

Transition	Constant	UIBEN	SMSA	CCITY	RACE	AWW	WKSWKD	UMARCH	SCHOOL
					Independent variable				
Unemployment to employment									
Layoff	-0.541	-0.700	-0.120	-0.054	-0.585	-0.002	0.027	0.195	-0.014
	(0.756)	(0.436)	(0.190)	(0.273)	(0.328)	(0.001)	(0.008)	(0.072)	(0.059)
Quit	-2.150	0.185	-0.204	0.471	-0.452	0.001	0.013	-0.102	0.115
	(0.938)	(0.719)	(0.190)	(0.264)	(0.356)	(0.001)	(0.004)	(0.067)	(0.067)
Loser	0.898	0.269	0.112	-0.581	-0.469	-0.0004	0.007	-0.111	-0.064
	(0.369)	(0.135)	(0.096)	(0.129)	(0.121)	(0.0003)	(0.003)	(0.030)	(0.028)
Total	0.469	0.162	-0.036	-0.254	-0.560	-0.0001	0.012	-0.076	-0.055
	(0.325)	(0.180)	(0.102)	(0.124)	(0.123)	(0.0003)	(0.003)	(0.028)	(0.025)
	0.092	0.032	-0.007	-0.050	-0.110	-0.00001	0.002	-0.015	-0.011
Unemployment to not in labor force									
Layoff	-2.331	-1.878	-0.129	0.663	-1.187	-0.003	0.012	0.200	0.072
	(1.345)	(0.778)	(0.247)	(0.406)	(0.624)	(0.001)	(0.015)	(0.085)	(0.091)
Quit	-2.518	1.557	0.658	-0.173	0.440	0.002	-0.010	-0.022	0.107
	(0.987)	(0.766)	(0.317)	(0.348)	(0.345)	(0.001)	(0.005)	(0.041)	(0.081)
Loser	-0.417	0.132	-0.153	0.127	0.055	-0.002	-0.012	0.006	0.023
	(0.100)	(0.217)	(0.101)	(0.126)	(0.117)	(0.0004)	(0.004)	(0.016)	(0.008)
Total	-1.273	0.116	-0.067	0.213	0.067	-0.002	-0.020	0.028	0.057
	(0.386)	(0.230)	(0.118)	(0.131)	(0.117)	(0.0006)	(0.004)	(0.031)	(0.029)
	-0.207	0.019	-0.011	0.035	0.011	-0.0003	-0.003	0.004	0.009

a. The numbers in parentheses are standard errors; the value given below the standard error for the total results is the derivative of the probability with respect to the variable. All equations include age-sex dummies and controls for marital status and high school graduation.

Average values of p_{ue} and p_{un} for the entire quit sample were used to calculate average k. Variation in *UIBEN** thus reflects variation in *UIBEN* and q.

Looking just at the results for the three categories of unemployment, the effect of UI is generally inconsistent with expectations, although the large standard errors preclude clear conclusions. We do find negative effects among those on layoff, where the impact of UI on withdrawal from the labor force is quite strong. Among the other groups, however, the coefficients are positive, though relatively imprecise. When the evidence is pooled by estimating the model for the total sample, we find very weak and insignificant effects. In addition to the logit coefficients, we report the derivatives of the probability for the total sample. It can be seen that the estimated effects are not only statistically weak, but substantively small. In the case of entering employment, for example, the derivative (0.032) implies that changing the replacement rate by 0.10 would change the probability of finding a job by 0.003. This compares with an average job-finding probability of 0.31.

In light of the strong theoretical arguments and previous empirical evidence on duration and transitions, the relatively weak effects of UI are surprising. Furthermore, the positive effects for losers and quitters remain a puzzle. A possible explanation of the findings for job losers and of the general imprecision of UI estimates in table 6 is individual heterogeneity. If unmeasured quality differences are positively correlated with eligibility for UI (and the level of benefits), as well as the likelihood of finding work, then the coefficient of UI would be biased upward.

A possible correction for this heterogeneity problem is to introduce the duration of the current spell of unemployment as a control variable. The argument is simply that current duration indicates the degree of success in finding work and is thus an indicator of individual quality. While this procedure apparently does reduce the upward bias, the general character of the results is unaffected. The signs remain unchanged, while the size of the coefficients declines slightly.

The heterogeneity argument does not explain the positive effect of UI on labor force withdrawal by quitters. It would seem that more able individuals would find work more easily whether the previous separation were initiated voluntarily or not. A somewhat more plausible explanation is the absence of any controls for other income, especially

Table 7. Linear and Multinomial Logit Estimates of the Probability of Leaving Employment[a]

Transition	Constant	UIBEN	SMSA	CCITY	RACE	AWW/ 1,000	WKSWKD/ 100	UMARCH/ 100	School/ 100	R²	Standard error
Linear probability models											
Employment to unemployment											
Layoff	0.013 (0.002)	0.005 (0.001)	-0.001 (0.001)	0.001 (0.001)	0.0001 (0.0010)	-0.001 (0.002)	-0.023 (0.002)	0.069 (0.018)	-0.050 (0.013)	0.004	0.003
Loser	0.029 (0.003)	0.0001 (0.0016)	-0.001 (0.001)	0.0001 (0.001)	0.004 (0.001)	-0.005 (0.003)	-0.046 (0.003)	0.031 (0.026)	-0.025 (0.020)	0.013	0.006
Quit	0.007 (0.002)	0.002 (0.001)	0.0000 (0.0003)	0.0010 (0.0006)	-0.002 (0.0007)	-0.002 (0.002)	-0.009 (0.002)	-0.009 (0.010)	-0.015 (0.011)	0.003	0.002
Total	0.049 (0.004)	0.008 (0.002)	-0.002 (0.001)	0.002 (0.001)	0.002 (0.002)	-0.008 (0.004)	-0.077 (0.005)	0.090 (0.035)	-0.091 (0.026)	0.016	0.011
Employment to not in labor force											
Total	0.148 (0.006)	-0.042 (0.003)	0.0003 (0.002)	0.0000 (0.002)	-0.0001 (0.003)	-0.038 (0.006)	-0.200 (0.007)	0.046 (0.053)	-0.002 (0.040)	0.062	0.027
Multinomial logit models											
Employment to unemployment											
Total	-1.804 (0.354) -0.020	0.791 (0.238) 0.009	-0.142 (0.116) -0.002	0.119 (0.135) 0.001	0.088 (0.149) 0.001	-2.552 (0.561) -0.028	-5.133 (0.403) -0.057	9.048 (3.108) 0.100	-9.442 (2.517) -0.104	...	...
Employment to not in labor force											
Total	-2.171 (0.276) -0.045	0.694 (0.158) -0.014	-0.002 (0.085) -0.0000	0.114 (0.098) 0.002	0.025 (0.112) 0.001	-3.491 (0.446) -0.072	-3.570 (0.271) -0.074	4.878 (2.358) 0.101	2.221 (1.896) 0.046	...	...

a. The numbers in parentheses are standard errors; the value given below the standard error for the multinomial logit totals is the derivative of the probability with respect to the variable. Each regression includes age–sex dummies and controls for marital status and high school graduation.

the income of the spouse. Since marginal tax rates are based on family income, secondary earners may have both high replacement rates and high family income. Without controls for other income, strong income effects could lead to individuals with high replacement rates leaving the labor force. Once again, however, it is not clear why this effect should apply only to quitters. And indeed adding other income variables has only negligible effects. The impact of UI on labor force exit by quitters remains paradoxical.

Transitions from Employment

In contrast to rather weak results on the unemployed, the evidence on the impact of UI on employment decisions is quite strong. Two sets of estimates are presented. We first use the linear probability model to study the impact of UI on unemployment transitions, with particular emphasis on subsamples defined by the reason for becoming unemployed. For comparison, linear probability estimates for the total sample are provided. Linear probability models are used because the computational cost of multinomial logit with many destination states is prohibitive. In the second set, we estimate the transitions from employment using the multinomial logit framework and present coefficient estimates and the associated derivatives. The linear probability estimates in table 7 reveal a significant positive effect on the flow into unemployment. The bulk of this effect occurs in the layoff group, where the *UIBEN* coefficient is well over half the size of the average transition probability from employment to layoff unemployment. These results are consistent with the evidence presented by Feldstein. While the layoff group dominates in the UI effect, we also find a statistically significant positive impact on quit behavior. The flow of other job losers, however, appears to be unaffected by rates of replacement.

The theory suggests that the flow out of employment will depend on the extent of experience rating of firms. The UI tax system allows only partial experience rating over a limited range of tax rates and previous unemployment behavior. Maximum and minimum tax rates are built into all the state tax laws. These have the effect of setting the marginal cost of a layoff to the firm (net of separation costs) to zero. The experience-rating hypothesis was tested using data on fraction of covered weeks at the minimum and maximum in each state. Using various combinations of minima and maxima, we found experience rating to have no effect on the flow out of employment. The conclusion

Table 8. *Transitions into the Labor Force*[a]

					Independent variable							Summary statistic	
Transition	Constant	UIBEN	WKSND/100	AWW/1,000	WKSWKD/100	UMARCH	SCHOOL/100	HSGRAD	RACE	MARRYW	SINGLEM	R²	Standard error
Linear probability models													
Not in labor force to unemployment													
1. Without eligibility													
variable	0.009	0.007	...	0.057	0.076	0.003	-0.060	-0.002	0.022	-0.017	0.009	0.029	0.024
	(0.008)	(0.004)		(0.020)	(0.009)	(0.001)	(0.060)	(0.004)	(0.004)	(0.004)	(0.005)		
2. With eligibility													
variable	0.010	0.015	-0.040	0.051	0.065	0.003	-0.060	-0.002	0.022	-0.017	0.009	0.029	0.024
	(0.008)	(0.006)	(0.021)	(0.020)	(0.011)	(0.001)	(0.060)	(0.004)	(0.004)	(0.004)	(0.005)		
Not in labor force to employment													
3. Without eligibility													
variable	0.088	-0.017	...	-0.199	0.406	-0.003	0.002	0.004	-0.0005	-0.005	0.001	0.070	0.050
	(0.012)	(0.006)		(0.029)	(0.013)	(0.001)	(0.001)	(0.005)	(0.0050)	(0.005)	(0.007)		
4. With eligibility													
variable	0.085	-0.030	0.064	-0.188	0.424	-0.003	0.002	0.004	-0.001	-0.006	0.002	0.070	0.050
	(0.012)	(0.008)	(0.031)	(0.029)	(0.015)	(0.001)	(0.001)	(0.005)	(0.005)	(0.005)	(0.007)		
Multinomial logit models													
Not in labor force to unemployment													
5. Estimated coefficient	-4.055	0.148	...	0.959	3.124	0.100	-3.649	-0.148	0.616	-0.930	0.368	...	...
	(0.335)	(0.174)		(0.449)	(0.284)	(0.028)	(-2.377)	(0.147)	(0.121)	(0.144)	(0.195)		
6. Effect on probability	-0.095	0.004	...	0.022	0.073	0.002	-0.086	-0.003	0.014	-0.022	0.009	...	...
Not in labor force to employment													
7. Estimated coefficient	-2.582	-0.336	...	-0.143	4.560	-0.048	4.400	0.027	0.068	-0.185	0.069	...	...
	(0.237)	(0.114)		(0.049)	(0.169)	(0.021)	(1.787)	(0.105)	(0.110)	(0.107)	(0.133)		
8. Effect on probability	-0.127	-0.017	...	-0.071	0.225	-0.002	0.217	0.001	0.003	-0.009	0.003	...	...

a. The numbers in parentheses are standard errors. Each regression includes age-sex dummies and controls for location (SMSA, central city). Rows 6 and 8 contain the derivatives associated with the logit coefficients.

applied to transitions into all of the different states of unemployment and NILF.

We argued earlier that UI may raise the gain to labor force attachment and thus reduce the probability of leaving the labor force from employment. The evidence in table 7 indicates overwhelming support for this hypothesis. It appears that higher UI benefits discourage labor force withdrawal. While the direction of the effect is consistent with the theory, the magnitude of the impact in the linear probability model is implausible. The logic of the connection between UI and labor force withdrawal requires an offsetting flow into unemployment. This is because the decision to remain employed is based on the attractiveness of becoming unemployed at some point in the future. If the negative effect of UI on p_{en} were due to the attractiveness of unemployment, we would expect to see a flow into unemployment of comparable magnitude.

Much of the disparity in the estimates disappears in the logit framework. There we find that the derivative of UI in the p_{eu} equation is 0.009, while the estimated effect in the p_{en} equation is -0.014. Although the p_{en} effect is still somewhat larger (in absolute value), the difference between them is not statistically significant.[28] It appears that imposition of linearity distorts the evidence on labor force withdrawal. When a more appropriate functional form is applied, estimates are obtained that are reasonably consistent with the notion of offsetting flows. Overall, the evidence points to UI as a major factor in decisions to leave employment.

Transitions into the Labor Force

Estimates of the effect of UI on movements into the labor force are examined in table 8. Both linear probability results and results from

28. Inspection of the data set for left-out variables that may lie at the foot of the unrealistic p_{en} coefficient suggests one possibility. Because of technological differences and differences in required skill and ability, an individual's occupation and industry may be an important determinant of labor force exit. In order to test this possibility, we estimated a new set of regressions with broad industry and occupation dummies. In doing this we run the risk of "overcontrolling" possible effects of *UIBEN* that may work through occupational choice or the decision of where to work. The results are instructive. We find that the industry and occupation dummies reduce the coefficient of *UIBEN* on p_{en} from 0.042 to 0.027. All of the impact occurs through the occupational variables, suggesting that the omitted variables of interest have to do with skills and training, rather than conditions of demand or risk shifting through contracts. This view is supported in the layoff regression. There we find that the industry and occupation dummies have virtually no effect on any of the previous coefficients.

the logit specification are presented. The results are based on an estimate of what benefits would be available if one were eligible and became unemployed.[29] We have also calculated the number of weeks of employment needed to qualify for benefits and estimated its impact.

It is evident in both sets of results that UI encourages the flow into unemployment through the benefit structure. In row 2, however, we find that eligibility rules and attachment tests appear to cut the other way. The results indicate a negative effect of *WKSND*, while *UIBEN* is positive and statistically significant. The sign of *WKSND* seems reasonable. We would expect that individuals with a requirement of a week or two would appear in the unemployment category sooner and more readily than those where weeks needed were sizable. This is particularly true in light of the fact that an important part of the NILF group (10 percent) has accumulated sufficient weeks and earnings to qualify for benefits. While a large number of those individuals are likely to have quit their most recent job, it is quite likely that some significant number are essentially eligible for benefits immediately.

The contrast with the flow into employment is symmetric; higher benefits are associated with reduced movements into employment, while weeks needed has a positive association. It is likely that the signs of these effects are more than coincidence. One explanation for the negative effect of benefits on p_{ne} is that those with very attractive replacement ratios choose to enter unemployment. Likewise, the *WKSND* variable reveals the eligibility effect—people choosing to enter employment over remaining out of the labor force or becoming unemployed tend to require more weeks worked in order to qualify for benefits.

In order to simplify later analysis of UI and rates of employment and unemployment, we have dropped *WKSND* from the logit specification. The evidence in rows 5–8 is consistent with our previous remarks: UI has a positive effect on the flow into unemployment, and tends to reduce the flow into employment. As in the case of movements out of employment, we find that decisions regarding labor force entry are apparently interrelated, although the orders of magnitude of the derivatives suggest that unmeasured differences in individuals may be affecting the results.

In summary, the evidence in tables 6–8 points to a significant and

29. Where wage data were not available, we imputed a wage based on an earnings function (see footnote 23).

consistent impact of UI on the flow into unemployment out of employment, a strong effect on the transition from employment to nonparticipation, generally mixed results for the unemployed, and some indication of influence on flows into the labor force.

Estimating the Impact of UI on the Unemployment Rate

This section uses estimates of the multinominal logit model to assess the impact of UI on the measured rate of unemployment, the employment ratio, and the nonparticipation rate. At the outset it is important to realize that the estimates here can be regarded only as an approximation to a fully dynamic stochastic simulation.

The approach we have adopted makes use of the steady-state relationship between transition probabilities and the fraction of the population in the three labor market categories. If we let P indicate the 3×3 matrix of probabilities, and use Π to represent the 3×1 vector of proportions, then we know that in steady state $P\Pi = \Pi$. The P matrix is not of full rank, but we can use the fact that the elements of Π sum to one, together with the steady-state identity, to solve for Π as a function of P.

The first step in estimating the impact of UI is to obtain an estimate of Π using actual values of the independent variables including *UIBEN*. A P matrix is estimated for each individual using the logit coefficients in tables 6–8 (total sample estimates) and the individual's characteristics. We then solve for the Π vector associated with each individual (that is, the fraction of time the individual could expect to spend in each state) and cumulate across individuals to get the aggregate proportions.

In order to gauge the impact of UI, two situations are examined. In the first, we reduce potential UI benefits by 10 percent, while potential UI benefits are eliminated completely in the second. In both cases, a new P matrix and a new Π are calculated for each individual, and new aggregate steady-state proportions are derived. These can be compared to the original steady-state estimates to see the change induced by UI.

Table 9 presents estimates of the impact of changes in UI on the employment ratio, the unemployment rate, and the rate of nonparticipation. The first line presents average values of these indicators as

Table 9. *Impact of Changes in Unemployment Insurance on Employment and Unemployment with No Change in Wages*
Percent

Simulated UI situation	Labor force state		
	Employ-ment ratio	Unemploy-ment rate	Nonpartici-pation ratio
Actual rates, 1978	59.4	6.0	36.8
UI down 10 percent	−0.02	−0.08	0.08
No UI	−0.62	−0.65	1.11

measured by the CPS during 1978. The unemployment rate averaged 6.0 percent in that year, while a little over 59 percent of the population was employed. The estimated effect of UI is examined in the next two lines. First, the change in UI is applied to the whole sample, and the difference between the steady-state proportions with and without the change is reported. The first entry in the employment column, for example, indicates that reducing UI by 10 percent would lower the steady-state fraction of the population employed by 0.02 percentage point. Unemployment would be reduced by 0.08 point, and nonpartic-ipation would increase by a similar amount.

When UI benefits are eliminated, however, these magnitudes are much larger. In the case of unemployment, for example, we estimate that elimination of UI would lower the unemployment rate by more than half of a percentage point. With the overall rate on the order of 6 percentage points, the effect is sizable. Coupled with a decline in the employment ratio of 0.62 point, the unemployment effect leads to a significant increase in the rate of nonparticipation. Indeed, the dominant effect of UI in these data appears to be its impact on movements into and out of the labor force. As the coefficient estimates suggested, it is likely that transitions into and out of employment play a significant role in the overall effect.

The estimates in table 9 are derived under assumptions about changes in UI, but no changes in other variables are introduced. Many of the independent variables would be unaffected, but it is likely that wages, in particular, would be affected by changes in UI. Table 10 presents estimates of the UI impact on labor market states allowing for the effect of taxes on wages. We assume that the burden of the UI tax falls entirely on labor, so that reductions in the tax are fully

Table 10. *Impact of Changes in Unemployment Insurance on Employment and Unemployment, with Wages Adjusted for Tax Changes*
Percent

Simulated UI situation	Labor force state		
	Employ-ment ratio	Unemploy-ment rate	Nonpartici-pation ratio
Actual rates, 1978	59.4	6.0	36.8
UI down 10 percent	0.00	−0.08	−0.06
No UI	−0.59	−0.65	1.09

reflected in an increase in the wage. The tax rate used was 0.86 percent. It was calculated by dividing total UI receipts by total wage and salary income for 1978. The rate is small both because the UI tax applies to only a portion of total earnings and because the rate is not large to begin with.

The basic algorithm used to identify the effect of UI is the same, with the only change being an adjustment in the wage in addition to changes in UI. It is clear from the table that the tax adjustment has little impact on the estimated UI effect. In the results for elimination of UI, for example, comparison with table 9 shows that employment would fall somewhat less and nonparticipation would rise somewhat less if wages were adjusted for tax changes. But the differences are trivial. At least with the estimated coefficients and tax rates used here, failure to address the tax issue has a negligible effect on inferences about the UI effect.

Overall, the results suggest that UI has a sizable impact on the rates of unemployment and labor force participation. Taken literally, the estimates indicate that the growth of UI over the last decade may have played an important role in the upward trend in participation. However, the estimates also imply that UI raises employment, a result which probably reflects the relative size of the UI effect in the p_{en} and p_{eu} equations. Since these estimates may reflect errors of measurement, or nonlinearities in the UI variable, further analysis seems in order.

In spite of the preliminary nature of the evidence, the analysis does underscore the importance of studying the effect of UI on other labor market groups besides the unemployed. Much empirical work in this area has concentrated on the behavior of the unemployed, but the impact of UI is clearly much broader. It appears that transitions into and out of the labor market, particularly in and out of employment, play a central role in the overall effect of UI.

Conclusions

The results in this paper are all based on microeconometric evidence. The information used is basically a comparison of the behavior of persons receiving high UI benefits with those receiving lower benefits. This approach assumes that the effect of a general change in UI would simply be the sum of the individual effects. Previous experience suggests that extrapolating micro relationships to the macro sphere is perilous. Here we list some of the biases in our procedure.

First, the estimates reported here may underestimate the impact of UI on some of the transition probabilities. Consider, for example, the relation between UI and temporary layoffs. Employers can tailor their layoff policy to the UI situation of their typical worker but not to each individual worker. Hence increases in the general level of UI will tend to cause greater increases in layoffs than would be implied by comparisons of individuals receiving more or less generous benefits. A similar point applies with respect to permanent separations.

Second, the calculation described here depends on the assumption that the transition probabilities are determined independently. While this is reasonable in considering cross-sectional variation among workers, it may not be tenable in assessing policies with large impacts. Consider, for example, a measure that sharply reduced the flow from unemployment to employment. This would raise employers' hiring costs, and so would be likely to reduce the optimal separation rate. A similar point applies to the relation between the flows from nonpartic-ipation to unemployment and from unemployment to employment.

Third, changes in UI may have important macro effects. The role of UI as an automatic stabilizer has been discussed frequently. The program's impact on the extent of wage rigidity may be as important. By making unemployment more palatable, UI is likely to reduce the downward pressure it places on wages. This will tend to reinforce the stickiness of wages, which according to many theories is the cause of unemployment. The cross-sectional analysis presented here has no way of taking account of these effects.

Fourth, there are strong reasons to believe that the effects of UI depend on the overall unemployment rate. The rate of unemployment was 6.0 percent in 1978. The results might be very different at business cycle troughs and peaks. One would expect that the effect of UI is most pronounced when labor is in excess demand, and least pronounced when jobs are being rationed. These propositions could in principle be tested by replicating this study with data sets drawn at different parts of the business cycle.

Beyond the difficulties inherent in the microeconometric approach taken here, there are a variety of ways in which the results can be refined. The preliminary results regarded here consider only small variations in theoretical form. Only crude account is taken of the potential duration of UI benefits. A crucial problem is errors in variables. The UI variables used here necessarily involve some imputation error. Perhaps more important, there is evidence that the dependent variables suffer from significant measurement error. It appears that the rate of flow between labor force states may be exaggerated by as much as a factor of two or three. In future work we hope to address these issues. It is also hoped that it will be possible to explore a broader menu of alternative reforms.

Several conclusions emerge from our research at this stage. UI has large effects on the decisions to seek and leave employment. The possibility of becoming eligible for benefits attracts many workers into the labor force. The program also encourages persons leaving employment to enter unemployment rather than leave the labor force. To some extent this may be a reporting rather than a behavioral effect. Taken together, these results imply that UI has a substantial positive effect on labor force participation. Our econometric estimates suggest that eliminating the program would reduce the labor force participation rate by about 1 percent. This drop-off would come from a decline of about half a percent in the employment ratio, and about two-thirds of a percent in the employment rate.

Our results suggest that a focusing on unemployment effects of UI, as has been done in most previous research, may be very misleading. Our estimates imply that the program simultaneously increases both employment and unemployment. Future research should concentrate on the direct employment impact of the UI program.

These results must be used cautiously in interpreting labor market developments. The effects of the UI program probably increased somewhat during the 1970s as benefits and coverage levels were raised. Of equal importance, rising marginal tax rates, due primarily to increasing social security payroll taxes, raised replacement rates. The results suggest that these developments may have contributed to the increase in the national unemployment rate and participation rate that were observed during the decade. Since the increase in the level of the average replacement rate was probably less than 20 percent, it is doubtful that the effects studied here can account for a large part of the movements that have taken place. It may be that other social insurance programs have contributed to the remaining increase. This question is left for future research.

Comments by Martin Feldstein

This is an impressive paper. As someone who has previously tried to develop a microsimulation model for imputing unemployment insurance benefits, I know just how much work is involved. They worked very carefully to take account of not only federal but also state income taxes and to get the marginal tax rates right. They then went on to estimate all nine of the labor market transition probabilities and used their estimates to calculate the net effect of changes in unemployment insurance on the equilibrium unemployment rates, nonparticipation rates, and employment rates.

However, I think the theory of what they set out to do is more interesting and successful than the final empirical results. It is important to distinguish between their results on the flows from employment into unemployment and their results for the other types of transition. The theory is much clearer on the former and the statistical results are much more reliable.

The basic finding for transitions from employment into unemployment is that there is a very powerful effect of unemployment insurance. The coefficient on the UI benefit for the linear model in table 7 is 0.008 with a standard error of 0.002. Since benefits average about 50 percent, this implies that the monthly flow out of employment into unemployment is increased by 0.004. Since the average monthly flow is about 0.02, this means that unemployment insurance accounts for about one-fifth of the total. The multinomial logit estimate gives a slightly larger coefficient of 0.009, suggesting that UI accounts for between one-fifth and a quarter of the total flow into unemployment.

Despite the fact that Clark and Summers estimate this large effect of UI on transitions into unemployment from employment, when these results are combined with their estimates for the other transition probabilities the overall effect of the UI system on unemployment is pretty small. This is because they find that UI induces employment— it reduces the flow from employment to nonparticipation very substantially—and because UI benefits increase the flow out of unemployment.

I think there are good reasons to believe that the estimated effects on the transitions from employment to unemployment are plausible, but that many of the other estimates are spurious. The first reason is that there is bias caused by the unobserved characteristics of individuals. The second reason is because of differences among unemployment spells. Consider first the individual characteristics. Employees without benefits are those who presumably did not have enough work experience to qualify. These may be the ones who have had a hard time getting jobs, so they have a low probability of going from unemployment to employment, even though their UI benefits are low or zero. The benefit variable is correlated with the disturbance term because of unobserved individual characteristics.

For this reason, the results reported in table 6 are misleading and potentially biased. Despite the fact that Clark and Summers find no statistically significant effect of UI benefits on the flow from unemployment to employment, their point estimate of the coefficient on the benefit variable (0.032), which is perverse in sign, does have a substantial impact on their estimate of the overall effect of the UI program. The same bias is even more apparent in table 7. There they find that UI benefits depress the flow from employment to NILF. That is as it should be. People leave employment for unemployment, rather than dropping out of the labor force. However, their estimates are just not consistent with that explanation. The estimated coefficient from the linear probability model is absurdly high (-0.042), but even the multinomial logit specification gives -0.014. This is higher (in absolute magnitude) than the effect of UI on the flow from employment to unemployment, and therefore makes no sense.

The employees who leave the labor force when they quit or are laid off are likely to be very different from those who stay and look for employment. The dropout group is more likely to be ineligible because they did not work much or because they have exhausted their benefits. Spurious correlation with unobserved characteristics is causing the estimated coefficient on the UI benefit variable to be too large in absolute size.

To explain the second source of bias in their results, I ask you to think back to the old-fashioned regressions that estimated whether or not UI benefits increase the duration of unemployment spells. These regressions found small or even perverse effects, and the reason is that UI induces more short spells of unemployment. An employer is more likely to lay off a worker for two or three weeks if that worker can collect sizable UI benefits. It is quite possible and even likely that UI reduces the average duration of unemployment spells, even though it increases unemployment.

Clark and Summers are correct to focus on transition probabilities rather than average duration, but their estimates still suffer from some of the same bias. When UI benefits are high, firms may provide less job security and employment may be less stable. The high-turnover labor market this creates may actually raise the flow from unemployment to employment, even though the overall effect of UI has been to increase job instability and unemployment. Clark and Summers observe labor market states in successive monthly surveys. But UI encourages the short-term layoffs of a week or a few weeks that are often missed completely by the CPS surveys. Their results are biased, in other words, because the greater the generosity of UI benefits, the greater is the fraction of unemployment spells that they are missing.

These estimation problems, while they exist for the transition out of employment, are likely to be much smaller. Being in the state of employment can be treated as exogenous without causing estimation problems, whereas being in the state of unemployment cannot be. It seems to me that the interesting and plausible results are those for the transition from employment to unemployment. The other results are hard to take seriously. The point estimates are likely to be biased and putting those biased coefficients together with more sensible ones to find the effect of the system on equilibrium unemployment and employment does not produce useful numbers.

I have a few quick points to conclude. First, not everyone in the sample fits the model; federal workers and students, for example, should probably be excluded. Second, I worry about the not-in-the-labor-force definition. Does the fact that people are drawing benefits automatically make them say they are unemployed and searching? Third, the authors say correctly that raising unemployment is not necessarily a bad thing. However, they go too far in arguing that UI is necessary to facilitate job mobility. I understand the theoretical argument, but I doubt in practice whether there is enough of an externality to make the private market work inefficiently. And finally, I disagree with their statement that there are no social costs if the UI program simply changes reported behavior, not actual behavior. Raising taxes to pay the benefits does have distorting effects.

Comments by David S. Coppock

The goal of this paper is to assess the impact of the unemployment insurance system on the natural rate of unemployment. The relevance of this is that it can provide evidence about whether or not recent benefit increases can explain the recent increases in the natural rate. Such evidence is independent of and in addition to the evidence from the Phillips-type equations that others have presented. There is no question but that a comprehensive examination of how the UI system affects flows between all labor force states is a good way to approach this problem. Taken at face value, the results would seem to exonerate the UI system from any major role in increasing unemployment. Although Clark and Summers do not document the amount by which UI benefits have increased in recent years, it is clear that an estimate of the effect of these increases on the natural rate of unemployment would be only a small fraction of a percentage point. However, several methodological issues and puzzling results (especially the positive effect of UI benefits on transitions out of unemployment) prevent me from placing too much weight on the results of the paper.

I would first like to comment on a point that can go part of the way toward explaining the differences between the theoretical predictions and the empirical results. This concerns the pitfalls of interpreting a continuous time process as a discrete time process. Transitions between labor force states can occur at any time between CPS interviews, and individuals are always subject to some instantaneous probability of transiting (often called a hazard rate). The theory linking UI benefits to transition probabilities is really concerned with hazard rates, while the data used by Clark and Summers measure the probability of moving from one state to another over the course of one month. In a two-state model this distinction is not so crucial, but it *is* crucial in a three-state model.

To see this, suppose that an individual is in state a, that he can transit to states b or c, and that the hazard rates governing these transitions are r_{ab} and r_{ac}, respectively. The Markov assumption introduced by Clark and Summers is retained. Let t_{ab} and t_{ac} be the durations until a transition occurs into states b or c. Then the bivariate distribution of t_{ab} and t_{ac} is $f(t_{ab}, t_{ac}) = r_{ab} r_{ac} \exp(-r_{ab} t_{ab} - r_{ac} t_{ac})$. The probability of transiting to state b within one period, $p(ab)$, equals the probability that $t_{ab} < 1$ *and* that $t_{ab} < t_{ac}$ (the possibility of multiple transitions is ignored). It is easily seen that $p(ab) = r_{ab}(r_{ab} + r_{ac})^{-1}[1 - \exp(-r_{ab} - r_{ac})]$. Thus, a theoretical prediction about the effect of UI benefits on r_{ab} would not necessarily be reflected in the effect of UI benefits on $p(ab)$, since the latter would also be affected by the effect of UI benefits on r_{ac}. As it turns out, this cannot explain the positive effect of UI benefits on *both* $p(ue)$ and $p(un)$ for some categories of unemployment. Nevertheless, it should be clear that when assessing the theoretical consistency of the results the nature of the data used should be taken into account.

There are several possible explanations for the results that remain anomalous. The authors mention the possibility of a correlation between UI benefits and heterogeneity in the probability of transiting, and attempt to correct for this by including the duration of the current spell as a control variable. Now it is true that in the presence of heterogeneity current duration should be included to allow for the sorting effect. But it is simply not true that this procedure will eliminate any bias caused by a correlation between heterogeneity and UI benefits. If heterogeneity is present at all, it will also be present among individuals who have been unemployed for equal periods of time, and any correlation between this heterogeneity and UI benefits will still exist.

A second possibility concerns the kind of independent variables used to estimate the UI effects. The UI benefits that an individual is qualified for depend on two factors: the schedule relating his personal characteristics to the benefits for which he qualifies (that is, the UI laws of his state of residence), and his actual personal characteristics. The first of these factors is presumably exogenous and uncorrelated with labor force behavior, while the second factor is not. Thus, UI variables based on the interaction of these two factors will be contaminated by the influence of personal characteristics.

For example, many of the eligibility characteristics are affected by recent periods of unemployment. Since past and present unemployment experience are correlated, this will induce a correlation between present unemployment experience and UI benefits. Also, since the benefit levels are proportional to earnings only up to a certain point, replacement ratios are inversely correlated with earnings.

Clark and Summers realize that this problem exists, and they attempt to correct it by including lagged values of wages and weeks worked. But this procedure depends on the strong assumption that if the UI system did not have any effect on labor market behavior, then the effect of these personal characteristics would be completely captured by the included variables. If this is not true, then any measured effect of UI variables can always be interpreted as a nonlinear effect of personal characteristics.

In view of this problem, my suggestion is that the UI variables used simply be characteristics of the UI laws of the state or residence. This procedure avoids any influence of personal characteristics in the UI variables. After all, the UI laws are the direct policy variables of interest.

My final two comments concern apparent inconsistencies in the paper. First, Clark and Summers promise in the introduction to analyze both the real and the "reporting" effects of the UI system, but I am at a loss to find where they have done so. Indeed, they later explicitly assume that "alternative states of the labor market are clearly defined, and that changes in status reflect meaningful changes in behavior." Second, Clark and Summers interpret the wage as partly serving as a proxy for labor force attachment and personal stability. Under this interpretation, the wage coefficient should not be interpreted as the effect of an exogenous increase in the individual's wage, since the variables being proxied for would not undergo a similar increase. Yet this is exactly the interpretation used when the effect of a change in the UI tax is simulated by changing the wage.

NICHOLAS M. KIEFER *and* GEORGE R. NEUMANN

Wages and the Structure
of Unemployment Rates

THE LABOR MARKET consequences of macroeconomic policy during the past decade present an uncomfortable prospect for the future. Unemployment during the seventies averaged 6 percent of the labor force, reaching a quarterly high of 8.8 percent in 1975. Among some groups, the results were even worse: teenage unemployment averaged over 16 percent for the decade. Inflation, measured by movement in the consumer price index (CPI), averaged over 7 percent and was 11.5 percent in 1979. Consumers and workers face the unpleasant prospect of having to continue to cope with rates of unemployment and inflation well in excess of those considered normal a decade ago.

One "reason" for this bleak state of affairs is that the rate of unemployment consistent with any particular level of inflation has shifted. As Perry has noted, the labor force is increasingly female and young; these groups have historically had high unemployment rates.[1] The growing numbers of these groups, even coupled with their high unemployment rates, appears to have little effect on the rate of wage inflation.[2] This combination of high unemployment rates and little or no reduction in inflation presents a dilemma that appears to be unsolvable by conventional fiscal and monetary policies. However, as

This revised version of the paper presented at the conference reflects the comments of the official discussants, Isabel Sawhill and Christopher Flinn. We also have benefited from comments made by Martin Neil Baily, Kim Clark, Shelly Lundberg, Olivia Mitchell, Melvin Reder, and Lawrence Summers. Support from National Science Foundation Grant SOC 79-12406 is gratefully acknowledged. The views expressed here are those of the authors and not necessarily those of the NSF. Research assistance of David Miller, Ralph Shnelvar, and Caroline Jumper is also acknowledged.

1. George L. Perry, "Changing Labor Markets and Inflation," *Brookings Papers on Economic Activity*, 3:1970, pp. 411–41. (Hereafter *BPEA*.)

2. Robert J. Gordon, "Wage-Price Controls and the Shifting Phillips Curve," *BPEA*, 2:1972, pp. 385–421, provides evidence that the unemployment rates of women and youths have little effect on the rate of inflation.

Baily and Tobin have noted, selective programs of job creation or wage subsidies can reduce the measured level of unemployment attendant to any rate of inflation by reducing the slope of the inflation-unemployment trade-off in the short run and the natural rate of unemployment in the long run.[3]

While the welfare implications of the Baily-Tobin model are subject to debate, the practical matter of the extent of the empirical possibilities of such a program may decide the issue. Would direct job creation for, say, teenagers lower their unemployment rate or would it result, through fiscal substitution and increased labor force participation, in possibly even higher levels of unemployment? Would a wage subsidy program result in greater employment opportunities or simply afford relatively more frequent, albeit more munificent, transitions out of the labor force?

Answers to these questions are not forthcoming from existing literature on unemployment experience, in part because of a lack of data on labor market transitions on an individual basis, but mostly because of a preoccupation with unemployment accounting. Questions about the effect of a wage subsidy or a job creation program require, in the absence of a randomized experiment, a disentangling of demand and supply responses. Without such identification it is impossible to provide evidence on the potential role of a wage subsidy or similar interventionist policy.

The purpose of this paper is to provide evidence on one aspect of the Baily-Tobin model, namely, the effect of a wage subsidy program on steady-state rates of unemployment. Our focus is on the role of wage rates in allocating workers among being employed, unemployed, and not in the labor force. We outline a model of labor market behavior that motivates the subsequent empirical analysis and discuss its relationship to the Baily-Tobin model.

For reasons explained in the text, the customary data set for this type of analysis—gross flow data from the Current Population Survey (CPS)—is inappropriate; we therefore use a less representative sample, namely the control observations from the Denver Income Maintenance Experiment (DIME). These data have some disadvantages, which we discuss at length, but when all caveats are put forth, the net result is

3. Martin Neil Baily and James Tobin, "Macroeconomic Effects of Selective Public Employment and Wage Subsidies," *BPEA*, 2:1977, pp. 511–41.

that these are the only data that allow a careful investigation of the Baily-Tobin or related models.

Since one of the constructs used in this paper and others[4] is that of a steady-state Markov structure for transition rates, diagnostic checks are made on the issue. We use these estimated transition rate functions to calculate steady-state unemployment and labor-force participation rates for various race, sex, and age groups. In turn, these estimates are used to calculate effects of a wage subsidy program. We find significant responsiveness of unemployment rates to wages among adults, but little among teenagers. This is because an increase in the teenage wage increases labor force participation of this group. Thus we are led to conclude that the Baily-Tobin model's theoretical possibility for reducing the natural rate of unemployment does not seem to hold much empirical promise.

Transition Rates and Labor Market Behavior

A central theme of labor market research has been an emphasis on the dynamics of the employment process. In both theoretical and, to a lesser extent, empirical work, the role of turnover has become the critical element for an understanding of unemployment. A stylized view from this perspective is that unemployment is the result of churning among labor market states: jobs are continually being lost and created, and, in the process, individuals spend time searching for employment. One particularly important finding that emerges from this view of the labor market is that the high unemployment rates observed among some groups are not due to an inability to find employment, but rather to an inability to remain employed.[5]

This simple search-cum-turnover story of labor market dynamics,

4. Kim B. Clark and Lawrence H. Summers, "Labor Market Dynamics and Unemployment: A Reconsideration," *BPEA, 1:1979*, pp. 13–60.

5. During the period 1967–73, the highest rate of leaving employment was 21.6 percent for nonwhite male teenagers, while the lowest rate was 1.2 percent for prime-age white males. Thus the ratio of the highest to the lowest rate was 17.5. In contrast, the highest probability of becoming employed from the unemployed state was 39.03 percent for 20–24-year-old white females, while the lowest rate was 17.23 percent for nonwhite female teenagers, implying a ratio of 2.27. Stephen T. Marston, "Employment Instability and High Unemployment Rates," *BPEA, 1:1976*, pp. 169–203, especially table 1, p. 175.

while illuminating, does not provide a complete picture of labor market dynamics. The reason is that a large number of spells of unemployment are ended by withdrawal from the labor force rather than by employment, a point that has been emphasized recently by Clark and Summers.[6] Similarly, part of the instability in employment is manifested by transitions directly from employment to withdrawal from the labor force. These movements into and out of the labor force are not typically explained in standard models of labor market behavior. To account for transitions in and out of the labor market there must be a source of randomness apart from uncertainty over wages or job availability. In a related paper, a model of labor market dynamics is presented in which individuals face random wage offers and random shocks to state-dependent utility functions.[7] In this model, it can be shown that transition rates between states depend upon realized wages, if employed, and on the parameters of the wage-offer distribution.

In particular, using W to denote a realized wage, $\overline{W}$ the mean of wage-offer distribution, and λ_{ij} the transition rate from state i to state j, $i, j \in \{E, U, N\}$ (here E, U, and N denote the states of employment, unemployment, and nonparticipation respectively), the following results can be obtained:

$$(1) \qquad \frac{\partial \lambda_{NE}}{\partial \overline{W}}, \frac{\partial \lambda_{UE}}{\partial \overline{W}} \geq 0;$$

$$(2) \qquad \frac{\partial(\lambda_{EU} + \lambda_{EN})}{\partial W} \leq 0;$$

$$(3) \qquad \frac{\partial \lambda_{UN}}{\partial \overline{W}}, \frac{\partial \lambda_{EN}}{\partial W} \leq 0;$$

$$(4) \qquad \frac{\partial(\lambda_{NU} + \lambda_{NE})}{\partial \overline{W}} \geq 0.$$

6. Clark and Summers, "Labor Market Dynamics and Unemployment," pp. 25–27.

7. Kenneth Burdett and others, "A Markov Model of Employment, Unemployment and Labor Force Participation: Estimates from the DIME Data" (Northwestern University, February 1981). The assumptions needed to generate the results used in this paper are essentially a Markov structure on the arrival rate of job offers and the arrival of random utility shocks. The results for transitions between unemployment and withdrawal from the labor force depend critically upon the arrival rate of job offers being no less in the unemployed state than in nonparticipation. This is equivalent to assuming that there is a real difference between being unemployed and being out of the labor force.

The intuition underlying these results is straightforward. Equation 1 indicates that higher earnings induce workers to leave unemployment faster[8] and decrease the set of random shocks that will make nonparticipation optimal. In other words, the opportunity cost of not working has risen. The second relationship states that the hazard rate of nonparticipation falls with an increase in actual earnings, and the results in equation 4 indicate the opposite side of the coin: higher wages increase the hazard rate out of nonparticipation. The only ambiguity that arises concerns transitions into and out of unemployment. Higher wages make employment more desirable and nonparticipation less so, and thus the net effect on transitions out of unemployment is unclear.

The relationship between wages and labor market transition rates described in equations 1–4 bears directly on the Baily-Tobin model because the transition rates characterize unemployment and labor force participation rates. For example, if the transition rates are constant, a steady state is defined by inflows matching outflows or:

(5a) $$\lambda_{NE}N + \lambda_{UE}U = (\lambda_{EU} + \lambda_{EN})E;$$

(5b) $$\lambda_{EU}E + \lambda_{NU}N = (\lambda_{UE} + \lambda_{UN})U;$$

(5c) $$\lambda_{EN}E + \lambda_{UN}U = (\lambda_{NE} + \lambda_{NU})N.$$

Steady-state unemployment, u^*, and labor force participation rates, lf^*, can be found by solving equation 5, yielding:

(6) $$u^* = U/(E + U) = A/(A + B)$$

(7) $$lf^* = (E + U)/(E + U + N) = (1 + A/B)/(1 + A/B + D/C)$$

where:

$$A = \lambda_{EU} + (\lambda_{EN} \cdot \lambda_{NU})/(\lambda_{NE} + \lambda_{NU});$$

$$B = \lambda_{UE} + (\lambda_{UN} \cdot \lambda_{NE})/(\lambda_{NE} + \lambda_{NU});$$

$$C = \lambda_{NE} + (\lambda_{UE} \cdot \lambda_{NU})/(\lambda_{UE} + \lambda_{UN});$$

$$D = \lambda_{EN} + (\lambda_{UN} \cdot \lambda_{EU})/(\lambda_{UE} + \lambda_{UN}).$$

8. This is a generalization of a result presented for the wealth-maximizing search model in Nicholas M. Kiefer and George R. Neumann, "Estimation of Wage Offer Distributions and Reservation Wages" in S. A. Lippman and J. J. McCall, eds., *Studies in the Economics of Search*, Contributions to Economic Analysis, 123 (Amsterdam: North-Holland, 1979), p. 171.

For steady-state equilibrium, equations 5a through 5c must hold for each labor market group, and thus the aggregate unemployment rate is the weighted average (by labor force share) of each group's unemployment rate, that is:

$$u^* = \sum_j \frac{L_j}{L} u_j^*.$$

Since the transition rates of each group are affected by wage rates, it is possible to change the value of u^* implied by this equation by a judicious choice of wage rates.

Data

A most natural source of data for an inquiry of this sort would be the gross flow data provided by the Bureau of Labor Statistics. These data have the advantage of being representative of the U.S. population and available monthly, and they are particularly useful for studying unemployment. Moreover, because these data have been used by a number of authors, their deficiencies are generally well known.[9] Despite these attractive features, the gross flow data, and even their source, the monthly CPS survey, are not suitable for the analysis described below. The main reason is that the nature of the CPS sampling technique (a unit is in for four months, out for eight, and then in for four months) makes inferences about long spells particularly chancy. If instability in employment or transitions out of the labor force are viewed as important factors in understanding unemployment, then the use of data composed primarily of incomplete spells may lead to serious biases. Indeed, estimates based on incomplete spells alone are entirely dependent upon functional form.[10] In our opinion, this is the

9. Ronald G. Ehrenberg, "The Demographic Structure of Unemployment Rates and Labor Market Transition Probabilities," Cornell University, 1979; Clark and Summers, "Labor Market Dynamics and Unemployment"; Marston, "Employment Instability and High Unemployment Rates."

10. The essential problem is that individuals are observed for only four months, a length of time that is far too short to infer anything about employment duration for most, and probably all, groups in the labor market. This is somewhat less severe in studying unemployment and nonparticipation, depending upon the length of such spells. It should be noted that these problems could be solved at virtually no increase in cost by using a stochastic stopping rule to determine how long a unit should be included in the sample.

most serious drawback to using CPS data for analyzing labor market dynamics, and it effectively precludes the use of matched monthly CPS samples.

As an alternative, one could use the monthly gross flow data to analyze time spent in unemployment (but not the other states). This requires the assumption that the replacement group entering in each month has identical behavior with the departing group, a dubious assumption in light of the well-documented phenomena of rotation group bias.[11] Moreover, the monthly gross flow data contain very little demographic information, eliminating the possibility of controlling for all but the grossest age-race breakdowns. Consequently, the effects of heterogeneity are confounded with duration dependence.[12]

In light of these difficulties we have used data from the Denver Income Maintenance Experiment (DIME). The major feature of this data set is that it provides continuous histories of individual labor market activities over forty-eight months. Moreover, the information available in the DIME data allows one to allocate individuals to labor market states, using the same definitions as the CPS. Because this data source is not as well known as the CPS, we comment briefly on its major features and note the problems that may arise in using it.

The Denver Income Maintenance Experiment was one of the largest programs designed to measure the effects of a negative income tax on labor supply. More than 5,000 individuals participated in DIME, and most of these individuals remained in the experiment for the full forty-eight months. This sample does not constitute a random sample of the Denver area population for two reasons. Eligibility for the program was restricted to individuals who were likely to participate in a full-scale program; excluded were families with heads over fifty-eight or under eighteen years of age at the start of the program, or those with

11. See Hall for a discussion of this phenomenon in terms of unemployment rates. Robert E. Hall, "Why is the Unemployment Rate So High at Full Employment?" *BPEA, 3:1970*, pp. 369–421.

12. See J. J. Heckman and G. J. Borjas, "Does Unemployment Cause Future Unemployment? Definitions, Questions and Answers From a Continuous Time Model of Heterogeneity and State Dependence," *Economica*, vol. 47 (August 1980), pp. 247–83, for an exposition of these difficulties. In the empirical literature on labor market behavior, the problem is best illustrated in the work of Clark and Summers, "Labor Market Dynamics and Unemployment." Clark and Summers were forced to use five observations from gross flow data to estimate the distribution of exit times from unemployment by sex and age. Other considerations such as race or marital status were, perforce, eliminated.

permanently disabled heads; families of four with preexperiment earnings of $9,000 for one-earner families or $11,000 for two-earner families; and individuals who did not belong to a family.[13] An additional source of nonrandomness was that DIME experimentals also had pronounced changes in labor market status.[14]

Of these two major sources of nonrandomness, the experimental effects are the easiest to remove, since 40 percent of the participants in DIME were controls. That is, they did not receive financial guarantees nor were their wages affected. The work reported in this paper therefore uses data on controls exclusively.

The other sources of nonrandomness are more difficult to deal with, in part, because of the dynamics of the experiment. The restriction by age to families with heads less than fifty-eight years old excludes older workers, but since the experiment ran for four years, we actually include individuals up to sixty-two years of age. Restrictions on age for younger individuals are of minor importance because the data includes all persons sixteen and over who are in families, and the fraction of married individuals between sixteen and eighteen is small.

A possibly more serious hindrance to representativeness of the sample arises because of the truncation by preexperiment income levels. As noted above, the cutoff level for eligibility was $11,000 in 1971 income for a two-earner family—a level that was 102 percent of the Denver median family income in 1970.[15] This preexperiment truncation overstates the potential bias, however, because transitory fluctuations in income made some higher-income families eligible for the program. Ashenfelter finds that in the first year of the experiment 22.6 percent of the control families had incomes in excess of $11,204.[16]

13. The original sampling framework eligibility for participation was conditional on being in a "family," where "family" is defined as a one- or two-earner family containing at least one dependent. Subsequently, unrelated individuals (one eligible person comprising an entire family) and two-earner households with no dependents were made eligible.

14. For evidence on the reduction of labor force attachment for DIME experimentals, see Nancy Brandon Tuma and Philip K. Robins, "A Dynamic Model of Employment Behavior: An Application to the Seattle and Denver Income Maintenance Experiments," *Econometrica,* vol. 48 (May 1980), pp. 1031–52; and Michael C. Keeley and others, "The Estimation of Labor Supply Models Using Experimental Data," *American Economic Review,* vol. 68 (December 1978), pp. 873–87.

15. U.S. Bureau of the Census, *Census of Population, 1970,* vol. 1, *Characteristics of the Population,* pt. 7, *Colorado* (Government Printing Office, 1973), table 89.

16. Orley Ashenfelter, "Discrete Choice in Labor Supply: The Determinants of Participation in the Seattle and Denver Income Maintenance Experiments" Princeton

Ashenfelter also finds that in the absence of truncation by income one would have expected to find 34 percent of the control families with incomes in excess of $11,000. This result suggests that the DIME controls are not completely representative of Denver families at the higher income levels. In consequence, since high incomes are well known to be correlated with stable employment patterns, these data are likely to overstate labor market transitions. Table 1 presents some indication of the dimensions of this problem. Unemployment rates for the DIME controls were three times the standard metropolitan statistical area (SMSA) rates over the period, although movements in the two series are closely related. Some part of this difference is accounted for by the rising participation rate of teenagers during this period, but most of the difference is due to the sample composition. For example, blacks and Hispanics account for 65 percent of the sample but only 15 percent of the Denver SMSA population in 1970.[17] If the sample is reweighted to reflect the population weights given in the 1970 census, the results are much closer to the SMSA experience. This is shown in line 3 of table 1. Adjusted unemployment rates average 7.9 percent, somewhat higher than the SMSA average of 3.7 percent, but closer than the unadjusted average of 11.3 percent.

Data Elements

The DIME public-use files are organized in a monthly format with data covering forty-eight months. In addition to the standard demographic variables—race, sex, age, family status—the data contain information of sufficient detail to construct histories of labor market status—employment, unemployment and nonparticipation—using Current Population Survey definitions.[18] There are, however, two points where CPS labor market data differ from DIME labor market data. The CPS sample, being a point-in-time observation, is subject to length bias; that is, short spells of unemployment are less likely to be detected

---

University Industrial Relations Section, working paper 136 (Princeton: May 1980), calculated from data in table 1.

17. U.S. Bureau of the Census (1970), tables 23 and 96.

18. Details about the construction of these labor market histories are given in Shelly J. Lundberg, "Unemployment and Household Labor Supply" (Ph.D. dissertation, Northwestern University, August 1980). It should be noted that the public-use files require significant editing in order to make the definition of, say, unemployment conform to the BLS definition.

Table 1. *Comparison of Unemployment Rates in the Denver*
Standard Metropolitan Statistical Area and the Denver Income
Maintenance Experiment Sample, 1971–74
Percent

Unemployment rates	1971	1972	1973	1974
Denver SMSA unemployment rate	4.0	3.6	3.4	3.7
DIME controls unemployment rate	11.4	11.4	11.0	11.4
Adjusted control unemployment rate[a]	8.3	7.6	7.6	8.1

Source: SMSA unemployment rates are from *Employment and Training Report of the President*, selected years. DIME unemployment rates were calculated using BLS methods.
a. See text for explanation of how this rate was calculated.

than long spells.[19] The DIME sample, being a longitudinal data set, does not have this problem and consequently will contain more short spells of unemployment. If unemployment spells are distributed uniformly across a month, the unemployment rate calculated from a point-in-time sample should not differ from that calculated from a longitudinal basis, so no bias should arise.[20] With regard to length of spells, however, it is obvious that a point-in-time sample will overstate the length of an average spell of unemployment.

A second point where the data may differ is in the transition from unemployment to nonparticipation states. The interview structure used in gathering the DIME data consisted of ten periodic interviews at intervals of three to four months. At each interview the subject was asked if there were any periods since the last interview that were not spent in employment. An affirmative answer resulted in a series of questions about whether the individual was looking for work during

19. For a discussion of this problem, see Hyman B. Kaitz, "Analyzing the Length of Spells of Unemployment," *Monthly Labor Review*, vol. 93 (November 1970), pp. 11–20; and Stephen W. Salant, "Search Theory and Duration Data: A Theory of Sorts," *Quarterly Journal of Economics*, vol. 91 (February 1977), pp. 39–57.

20. This statement presumes that the longitudinal data is being used in the same manner as the point-in-time sample; that is, unemployment rates are calculated as the number of persons unemployed on a given date divided by the number employed plus unemployed on that date.

this period. An affirmative answer to this type of question resulted in the individual's being recorded as unemployed for the entire period between jobs or up to the periodic interview, whichever was less.[21] No further probing was done to inquire whether there were periods of nonparticipation mixed with unemployment. Thus most changes in labor market state from unemployment to nonparticipation, and the reverse, occurred only in months in which there was a periodic interview, and transition rates between these states are understated in these data.

Table 2 presents a comparison of transition rates for white males and females for the DIME and CPS data. The most notable differences are in the $U \rightarrow N$ transitions of young males and females: the CPS data indicate monthly transition rates from unemployment to nonparticipation that are about five times the rate experienced in the DIME data. The lower transition rates in the latter source are no doubt due in part to the form by which labor market status was checked, but are also due to the relatively lower turnover as a whole among DIME participants.[22] The net import of this feature of the DIME data is that durations of unemployment and nonparticipation are likely to be longer than would be measured in the CPS data (if completed spells were available).

To the extent that short spells of nonparticipation are equivalent to "coding errors," as Clark and Summers argue, there is little effect of the DIME coding procedure.[23] However, since the transitions between unemployment and nonparticipation influence the calculation of steady-state values, the caveats noted above should be kept in mind when interpreting such calculations.

The DIME public-use files were used to construct data by labor market spells. Attached to each spell was the length of time of the completed spell and demographic variables relating to each individual

21. There are obvious exceptions to this such as workers on vacation or strikers, which were allocated correctly by use of other information on labor market status.

22. If the only difference between the two sources was the timing of transitions into unemployment or nonparticipation, then collapsing the data into a two-state model—employed versus nonemployed, or participation versus nonparticipation—should yield identical two-state transition rates. As can be seen by aggregating the appropriate rows of table 2, the CPS data indicate higher rates of employment instability than the DIME data.

23. Clark and Summers, "Labor Market Dynamics and Unemployment," pp. 28–30.

Table 2. *Average Monthly Transition Rates, DIME and Current Population Survey Data, by Age and Sex*
Percent

Age and sex	Employment to unemployment		Employment to nonparticipation		Unemployment to employment		Unemployment to nonparticipation		Nonparticipation to employment		Nonparticipation to unemployment	
	DIME	CPS	DIME	CPS	DIME	CPS	DIME	CPS	DIME	CPS	DIME	CPS
White males, 16–19	4.6	4.1	5.1	11.4	20.3	30.1	5.7	30.8	4.8	15.0	1.6	7.2
White males, 25–59	1.6	1.0	1.0	0.3	29.5	32.1	5.0	10.0	11.0	7.2	3.2	3.2
White females, 16–19	4.0	2.9	6.6	13.8	24.1	28.0	6.8	32.7	3.8	10.1	1.2	5.8
White females, 25–29	1.1	1.0	3.4	4.5	16.9	21.3	10.5	26.5	3.9	4.5	0.9	1.2

Source: CPS data are from Ronald G. Ehrenberg, "The Demographic Structure of Unemployment Rates and Labor Market Transition Probabilities" (Cornell University, 1979), table 6, which uses nationwide CPS gross change data for the 1967–77 period. DIME statistics are authors' calculations.

as of the start of the spell.[24] The means of these variables, by age group, are given in table 3. Most of these variables are self-explanatory, the exceptions being the assets and wage variables. Assets were constructed from information on the value of stocks, cash in checking accounts, or equity value in house or cars which was available at each periodic interview. Linear interpolation was used to produce asset values for the intervening months between interviews.

The wage variable used is derived from the reported hourly wage on the longest job worked in a given month. Since the period of the experiment encompasses a wide range of annual inflation rates, all nominal wage rates were deflated by the Denver area CPI for each of the years 1971–74.

Wage rates, however, are defined only for employed individuals. For individuals who are not employed, it is expected wages (more precisely, all the parameters of the wage distribution) that are important. To obtain expected wages, one could either obtain information from other data sources or, equivalently, impute values based on individual characteristics. We have chosen the latter option. The natural log of wages was regressed against age, age squared, education, and race/ethnic status for each of the age/sex groups.[25] This procedure was done by quarters, resulting in sixteen predicted wage rates for each individual. Each labor market spell was matched to the predicted wage appropriate to the quarter in which the spell began.

This imputation of expected wages raises identification questions, both econometrically and conceptually. It is arguable that all personal characteristics that affect labor market transitions—such as age, race, sex—also affect wages and hence one should not use exclusion restrictions on certain variables to secure identification. Technical corrections to imputed wages such as the Mills ratio approach may be sufficient to identify the effects of wages, provided enough nonlinearity

24. In some cases a completed spell length could not be ascertained because the individual left the sample, the spell was in progress when the experiment ended, or the spell was in progress at the beginning of the sample. Spells falling under the first two causes are examples of sample censoring, or truncation from the right, and were explicitly treated in the empirical work. Spells falling under the last cause are problems of initial conditions, or truncation from the left, are much more difficult to handle correctly, and were ignored.

25. In principle, a Mills ratio type of correction could be used in imputing predicted wages. In the DIME data, the correction for truncation appears to make little difference, and, as a practical matter, we ignored it. See James J. Heckman, "Sample Selection Bias as a Specification Error," *Econometrica,* vol. 47 (January 1979), pp. 153–61.

Table 3. Variable Means for DIME Participants, by Age and Sex

Variable	Males 16–21	Males 22–59	Females 16–21	Females 22–59
Education (years)	10.6	11.1	11.0	11.7
Black (percent)	34.5	29.5	31.6	37.0
Hispanic (percent)	31.7	36.2	28.3	28.5
Age (years)	18.2	31.7	18.5	31.8
Age²/100	3.4	10.9	3.4	10.9
Assets/1,000	0.4	0.2	0.3	0.2
ln (wage/p)	4.6	5.5	4.3	4.8
Number of dependent children	0.3	1.0	0.5	0.9
Black *ln (wage/p)	1.5	1.6	1.3	1.8
Hispanic *ln (wage/p)	1.4	2.0	1.2	1.3
Number of separate transitions	1,119	1,571	1,138	2,524
Number of persons in each group in 1973	260	660	326	946

Source: Authors' calculations from DIME data.

is induced by the correction. While this means of identification is possible, and we have exploited it in previous work,[26] a more appealing method of identification is afforded by the longitudinal nature of the data. By obtaining sixteen quarterly expected wages for each individual, it is essentially intertemporal variation in wages that identifies the separate effect of wages. This approach is in the spirit of the model described earlier where tastes, measured, say, by demographic variables, are treated as constant. In the empirical work presented below, when transitions out of the employment state are being considered, ln wage refers to logarithm of the actual real wage; for all other transitions, ln wage refers to the logarithm of the predicted real wage.

Estimation of Transition Rates

The Estimation Procedure

Availability of individual data on labor market behavior affords the advantage of determining the effect of wage rates and individual characteristics on turnover. Since transitions are discrete events and

26. See Kiefer and Neumann, "Estimation of Wage Offer Distributions and Reservation Wages."

there is more than one state to move to, a simple regression strategy for analyzing data is inappropriate. We present an empirical model that handles the discreteness and multiple-state problems.[27] A procedure similar to residual analysis in regression studies can be applied as a check on the specification.

It is useful to introduce the arguments of the transition functions explicitly: $\lambda_{kj} = \lambda_{kj}(t,x)$, with t the random variable "future duration" and x a vector of characteristics. The hazard function associated with state E, that is, the rate of exit from state E at time t is given by

$$(8) \qquad \lambda_E(t,x) = \lambda_{EU}(t,x) + \lambda_{EN}(t,x).$$

Hazard functions for states U and N are defined analogously.[28] Associated with the hazard function $\lambda_k(t,x)$ is the distribution function for duration in state k:

$$(9) \qquad F_k(t,x) = 1 - \exp\left\{ -\int_0^t \lambda_k(u,x)du \right\},$$

and subdensity associated with the time to each transition:[29]

$$(10) \qquad f_{kj}(t,x) = \lambda_{kj}(t,x)[1 - F_k(t,x)].$$

27. The model and simple variations have been used previously in the economics literature by Tony Lancaster, "Econometric Methods for the Duration of Unemployment," *Econometrica*, vol. 47 (July 1979), pp. 939–56; Lundberg, "Unemployment and Household Labor Supply"; and Tuma and Robins, "A Dynamic Model of Employment Behavior."

28. Statistical models for the analysis of duration (or "failure time") data have been widely studied. A recent treatment is John D. Kalbfleisch and Ross L. Prentice, *The Statistical Analysis of Failure Time Data* (Wiley, 1980). The decomposition of the hazard function into the sum of cause-specific hazard functions is the key to the study of "competing risks."

29. The term *subdensity* is used since:

$$\int_0^\infty f_{kj}(u,x)du \neq 1,$$

although

$$\int_0^\infty \left[\sum_j f_{kj}(u,x) \right] du = 1.$$

This usage follows Kalbfleisch and Prentice, *The Statistical Analysis of Failure Time Data*.

Given data (t_i, j_i, d_i, x_i) for a sample of $i = 1, \ldots, N$ independent spells, where t_i is the duration of spell i, j_i indexes the destination state, d_i is an indicator equal to one if t_i is the duration of a completed spell and equal to zero if the individual does not change states over the time of the study, and x_i is a vector of characteristics of the individual experiencing the ith spell, the likelihood function is given by

$$L_k = \prod_{i=1}^{n} \lambda_{kj_i}(t_i, x_i)^{d_i}[1 - F_k(t_i, S_i)].$$

The joint likelihood is given by $L_E L_U L_N$. If there are no restrictions across states on the parameters of hazard functions, then each state-specific likelihood function can be maximized separately without losing efficiency. For expositional purposes, we now concentrate on L_F.

In order to make the model applicable, a functional form for $\lambda_E(t, x)$ must be chosen. A natural and popular specification (the i subscript has been dropped) is:[30]

(11) $\lambda_{Ej}(t, x) = \exp x\beta_j \qquad j = U, N.$

With this specification, the hazard rates are person-specific but not duration-dependent, a specification that has been widely used. Assuming that the hazard functions do not depend on duration is equivalent to assuming that transitions from state to state follow a (continuous-time) Markov process. Structural models generating such a process from optimal behavior by workers are discussed by Burdett and others.[31] With this specification, we have the log likelihood function

(12) $\ln L_e = \sum_{i=1}^{N} [d_i x_i \beta_{j_i} - t_i (\exp x_i \beta_U + \exp x_i \beta_N)]$

and corresponding log likelihood functions for estimating the parameters of transitions from the other states.

30. P. Feigl and M. Zelen, "Estimation of Exponential Survival Probabilities with Concomitant Information," *Biometrics*, vol. 21 (December 1965), pp. 826–38, and Marvin Glasser, "Exponential Survival with Covariance," *Journal of the American Statistical Association*, vol. 62 (June 1967), pp. 561–68, are early references for this specification. D. R. Cox, "Regression Models and Life Tables," *Journal of the Royal Statistical Society*, Series B, vol. 34 (1972), pp. 187–220, provides an interesting generalization.

31. Burdett and others, "A Markov Model of Employment, Unemployment and Labor Force Participation."

The simplicity of the likelihood function (equation 12) is in part a consequence of the Markov assumption that rules out duration dependence. Recent work suggests that this assumption may be overly strong, and hence it should be tested.[32] One way to see the potential effects of duration dependence is to examine the analogs of regression residuals. We have a series of durations t_i whose distributions depend on x_i, and we would like to transform these t_i by a function $Z_i = g(t_i)$ in such a way that the distribution of the Z_i, like the distribution of ordinary regression residuals, does not depend on the x_i. One way to do this is to choose Z_i equal to the cumulative distribution function of t_i evaluated at the observed t_i. The resulting random variables Z_i are identically distributed as uniform on the unit interval, provided the model is correct.[33] The sorted values of the Z_i can then be plotted against a 45° line (the cumulative function of the uniform distribution), and either by specific tests such as Kolmogorov-Smirnov or by eyeballing one can judge the adequacy of the model.

Empirical Results

Table 4 contains estimates of the wage coefficients in the transition functions for the four age-sex groups being considered: males and females aged 16–21, and males and females aged 22–62. (The age is as of the date the spell began.) The variables, including the construction of an instrumental variable for wages, are discussed in detail above. The most significant aspect of these estimates is the powerful role of wage rates on transitions. For all four age-sex groups, higher wages uniformly lead to smaller probabilities of leaving employment and to higher probabilities of moving from unemployment to employment. Moreover, labor force participation significantly increases with the wage rate for all groups except young males, for whom the wage effects on nonparticipation, while negative, are small compared to their standard errors (given in appendix tables 8 through 11). The empirical importance of these wage effects is highlighted by the rather

32. Clark and Summers, "Labor Market Dynamics and Unemployment"; and Nicholas M. Kiefer and George R. Neumann, "An Empirical Job Search Model, with a Test of the Constant Reservation-Wage Hypothesis," *Journal of Political Economy,* vol. 87 (February 1979), pp. 89–108.
33. Maurice G. Kendall and Alan Stuart, *The Advanced Theory of Statistics,* vol. 1, 4th ed. (London: Charles Griffin and Co., 1977), p. 18.

Table 4. *Wage Coefficients in Transition Functions*[a]

Demographic group	Employ- ment to unem- ploy- ment	Employ- ment to non- partic- ipation	Un- employ- ment to employ- ment	Un- employ- ment to non- partic- ipation	Non- partici- pation to employ- ment	Non- partic- ipation to unem- ploy- ment
Males 16–21						
ln *wage*	−0.41	−0.54	0.76	−1.5	0.038	0.62
B ln *wage*	−0.21	−0.64	−0.40	−0.33	−0.25	−0.37
H ln *wage*	−0.37	−0.55	−0.71	0.17	−0.60	0.69
Males 22–59						
ln *wage*	−0.55	−0.83	1.6	1.1	3.8	2.7
B ln *wage*	−0.43	−0.043	0.81	−0.75	1.3	1.5
H ln *wage*	−0.09	−0.49	1.8	0.23	0.40	−0.26
Females 16–21						
ln *wage*	−0.55	−0.80	0.29	−0.85	1.0	1.5
B ln *wage*	0.14	0.33	1.4	0.13	0.30	0.32
H ln *wage*	0.47	0.24	0.22	0.58	0.18	0.83
Females 22–59						
ln *wage*	−0.45	−0.63	1.9	2.3	3.4	5.0
B ln *wage*	−0.33	−0.07	0.72	0.39	−0.14	−1.6
H ln *wage*	−0.22	−0.015	0.63	−0.37	1.1	−1.1

Source: Authors' calculations. Extracted from appendix tables 8–11.
a. B-ln *wage* and H-ln *wage* are interactions between the ln *wage* variable and 0-1 variables for blacks and Hispanics, respectively.

substantial differences across race and sex groups. These empirical results imply that variations in personal characteristics account for substantial variations in labor market behavior. We will use these estimates to construct steady-state distributions of time spent in each labor market state.

Our interpretation of these wage effects is that they reflect real changes in dynamic labor supply. A contrary view would emphasize that the wage rate reflects a number of factors, measurable and nonmeasurable. To the extent that such factors—pluck, determination, effort—are idiosyncratic, the interpretation we give to these results would be misleading. In this view, transitions out of employment are low, not because wages are high, but because an individual is unusually reliable, say, which is reflected in the wage. Higher wages act then as a proxy for these individual fixed effects. Raising wages for a group would not lead to a change in turnover behavior because it would not alter the distribution of these individual effects.

This argument underscores the need for care in interpreting any such estimates. But in the case of transition data there is further information to rely upon. The wage variable used in the nonemployment states is not an actual wage but a predicted wage. As the projection from measurable characteristics, the predicted wage does not contain any idiosyncratic elements. Hence, if idiosyncratic factors were the motivating force in transitions, one would not expect to find a significant effect of predicted wage rates on transitions *into* employment. As table 4 reveals, there are significant effects of wages in the four other transitions. Finally, if the transitions out of employment are reestimated with predicted wages replacing actual wages, the results are virtually unchanged. For these reasons we believe that the estimates do indeed reflect the effect of wage rates on supply behavior.[34]

In order for steady-state calculations to be valid, their underlying transition process must be Markov, an assumption we have exploited in the estimation. As a check on the empirical usefulness of this assumption, we performed a "residual analysis" as described above. An appendix available from the authors presents plots of the cumulative distribution of the duration of unemployment.[35] A formal test of the null hypothesis that the actual and predicted distributions are identical can be made by use of the Kolmogorov-Smirnov statistic. For these three groups we calculate K-S statistics of: 1.44—older females; 0.72—younger females; and 1.30—younger males. The 1 percent critical value obtained from the asymptotic distribution of the K-S statistic is 1.63, and thus we cannot reject the hypothesis that the predicted and observed distributions are identical. Thus, conditional on the individual characteristics that we have included, transitions out of unemployment appear to be Markov for these groups.[36] For adult males, however, the formal test (K-S = 2.68) reveals that the predicted and actual distributions are not in very close agreement. The source of the discrepancy is that we underpredict short spells of unemployment for

---

34. This argument was suggested to us by Isabel Sawhill, to whom we are grateful.

35. In principle, one could analyze the distributions of time spent in all spells. However, since the length of time spent in employment and nonparticipation is long relative to the sample period, usefulness of this technique is lessened.

36. When no allowance is made for individual characteristics—transition rates are assumed constant across age-sex groups—the predicted and actual distributions differ substantially. Thus it appears that the results of Clark and Summers ("Labor Market Dynamics and Unemployment") arise because of their inability to control for interindividual variation in characteristics such as wage rates.

adult males. This suggests that our estimates of equilibrium unemployment rates for adult males may be somewhat too high.

Steady-State Labor Market Distributions

The transition function parameters above, combined with the sample means, yield estimates of the steady-state transition rates across states, which are displayed in table 5 for each of the sex and age groups and within each group by race. We have calculated an overall transition rate for each age-sex group using the overall means for the entire group. Since the transition functions are nonlinear, these overall rates are not equal to the weighted average of the corresponding race groups. Also, the overall transition rates reflect the sample proportions; they have not been reweighted to reflect the Denver SMSA.

From these transition rates, steady-state unemployment and labor force participation rates are calculated as described in equations 6 and 7 and are displayed in table 6. A familiar story is evident from tables 5 and 6. Unemployment rates vary substantially across the population from a low of 4.1 percent for adult white males to a high of 34 percent for young black males. This is in accord with the findings of previous investigators, and it suggests that the DIME participants mirror, to a large extent, forces that exist in the national labor market.[37]

That the steady-state unemployment rates differ substantially by groups is reassuring since it is a precondition for the Baily-Tobin model to be effective. Given these differences, there is the possibility of "cheating the Phillips curve," or of altering the natural rate of unemployment, by making employment opportunities more attractive to certain groups. Whether this can be achieved depends, at least in the case of subsidized wages, on how elastic the responses of the different groups are to wages. In the previous section, we demonstrated that most of the state-specific transition functions were responsive, but as was noted above, the steady-state unemployment and participation rates depend on all six transition rates. Thus the net effect of altering wages for any one group is not immediately obvious, since it depends both on the sign of the individual responses and the relative numbers in each state. To find the sensitivity of the steady-state rates,

37. See Marston, "Employment Instability and High Unemployment Rates" for a discussion of steady-state differences in unemployment rates among race, sex, and age groups.

Table 5. *Steady-State Monthly Transition Rates, by Age, Sex, and Race*
Percent

Demographic group	Employ- ment to unem- ploy- ment	Employ- ment to non- partic- ipation	Un- employ- ment to employ- ment	Un- employ- ment to non- partic- ipation	Non- partici- pation to employ- ment	Non- partic- ipation to un- employ- ment
Males 16–21	6.5	7.6	22.1	7.6	8.0	4.0
Black	6.9	10.1	16.6	9.5	6.3	4.8
Hispanic	7.4	7.7	22.1	6.6	6.4	3.7
White	5.4	5.9	28.6	5.6	11.5	2.9
Males 22–59	1.7	1.4	28.2	4.7	13.7	4.3
Black	1.9	1.1	24.4	3.8	13.7	3.9
Hispanic	1.9	2.0	25.6	5.1	13.1	5.1
White	1.5	1.2	35.5	5.4	14.3	3.6
Females 16–21	4.5	8.2	20.4	9.1	4.9	3.0
Black	5.2	7.1	14.9	10.3	5.1	4.9
Hispanic	4.7	7.9	17.6	8.8	4.1	2.5
White	3.9	9.1	28.4	7.2	5.4	1.9
Females 22–59	1.8	4.7	16.6	10.6	1.0	1.4
Black	1.9	3.2	13.6	11.0	5.1	2.5
Hispanic	1.8	5.8	14.3	7.7	0.3	0.6
White	1.6	5.1	24.8	14.0	4.6	1.3

Source: Authors' calculations from the estimates in appendix tables 8–11 and the mean values of the exogenous variables.

we differentiated the unemployment and labor force participation rates and expressed the changes in elasticity form, as shown in table 7.

There are two messages in these numbers. Unemployment rates are sensitive to wage rates in all groups: the effect of a 10 percent increase in wages ranges from a reduction of adult Hispanic males' unemployment rates by 2.9 percentage points (7.8 percent to 4.9 percent) to a low of 0.3 percentage point (25.0 percent to 24.7 percent) for young Hispanic females. In general, however, the greatest sensitivity of unemployment rates is found among the groups with the highest labor force participation rate. This means that significant changes in the aggregate unemployment rate would require large subsidies to groups that would otherwise have high unemployment rates. The dilemma presented by these findings can be seen in the labor force responses of teenagers. Using the elasticities of the two columns in table 7 and labor force weights reflecting the composition of the U.S. labor force results in a teenage aggregate unemployment elasticity of −0.35, and

Table 6. *Steady-State Unemployment and Labor Force Participation Rates, by Age, Sex, and Race*
Percent

Demographic group	Unemployment rate	Labor force participation rate
Males 16–21	25.0	61.2
Black	34.0	52.9
Hispanic	28.0	57.7
White	16.9	71.1
Males 22–59	6.1	91.8
Black	7.2	93.2
Hispanic	7.8	89.0
White	4.1	92.9
Females 16–21	22.6	48.6
Black	30.2	55.2
Hispanic	25.0	44.7
White	15.4	45.3
Females 22–59	17.9	30.2
Black	12.4	64.6
Hispanic	33.4	9.4
White	7.1	50.9

Source: Authors' calculations from table 5.

Table 7. *Steady-State Unemployment and Labor Force Participation Rate Elasticities, by Age, Sex, and Race*

Demographic group	Elasticity of unemployment	Elasticity of labor force participation
Males 16–21	−0.37	0.35
Black	−0.36	0.69
Hispanic	−0.17	0.44
White	−0.51	0.24
Males 22–59	−2.07	0.30
Black	−2.95	0.33
Hispanic	−3.68	0.51
White	−2.11	0.27
Females 16–21	−0.33	0.90
Black	−0.70	0.71
Hispanic	−0.13	0.95
White	−0.38	0.97
Females 22–59	−1.51	1.77
Black	−2.71	1.03
Hispanic	−1.97	0.73
White	−1.63	1.68

Source: Authors' calculations from tables 5, 6, 8, 9, 10, and 11.

a labor force participation elasticity of 0.61. A relatively modest policy goal of reducing the teenage unemployment rate by 1.5 percentage points—a 10 percent decline—would require a 28.6 percent change in wage rates. The large increases in labor force participation—in this case 17.5 percent, primarily by females and minorities—is what makes even such a modest goal so difficult to attain. As long as the labor market participation decision is sensitive to wages, efforts to reduce unemployment are not likely to appear successful, even though they may have real employment effects.

Conclusions

This paper has examined the effect of wage rate variation on labor market transitions. The evidence presented indicates that labor market transition rates are dependent upon earnings and that, because of this relationship, so too are unemployment rates. Finding such an effect is essential for designing policies that attempt to "cheat the Phillips curve" or to reduce the natural rate of unemployment. The major finding of this paper is that, despite the existence of conditions that make a tax-based employment policy possible, the evidence suggests that the effects on the aggregate unemployment rate are likely to be minor. Essentially, the problem is that an increase in actual or expected earnings for one group induces a large flow into the labor market, which reduces the change in unemployment for that group, while the opposite happens for the group that bears the tax. Although there are several ways to interpret this result, the conclusion that emerges is that this variant of the Baily-Tobin model does not offer great opportunities for reducing unemployment. The offer of more remunerative terms of employment to broadly targeted groups will result in sufficiently greater labor force participation to minimize the unemployment-reducing aspect of the program. If, however, the goal of policy is to improve the employment status of young people and the hard-to-employ, then this paper shows that such a policy could succeed.

Appendix

Tables 8–11 report the estimates underlying tables 4–7 in the text. Newton's method was used to maximize the likelihood functions. The absolute values of the *t*-statistics are given in parentheses.

Table 8. *Transition Function Estimates for Males Aged 16–21*

Variable	Employment to unemployment	Employment to nonparticipation	Unemployment to employment	Unemployment to nonparticipation	Nonparticipation to employment	Nonparticipation to unemployment
Constant	-15.4691 (1.49)	-10.9978 (1.17)	-15.9207 (1.66)	-8.9033 (0.56)	-16.6377 (2.47)	-17.7792 (1.81)
Education (years)	-0.3583 (5.09)	0.0444 (0.51)	-0.0010 (0.01)	0.1058 (0.69)	0.1074 (1.62)	-0.0987 (0.95)
Age (years)	1.9148 (1.71)	-1.1447 (1.10)	1.1493 (1.11)	1.0758 (0.64)	1.1582 (1.56)	1.3800 (1.26)
Age^2/100	-4.9368 (1.63)	2.7047 (0.96)	-2.9876 (1.09)	-2.4367 (0.53)	-2.3284 (1.13)	-3.7750 (1.20)
Assets/1,000	-0.0066 (0.10)	0.0821 (1.95)	-0.0562 (1.52)	0.0102 (0.19)	-0.0143 (0.51)	0.0064 (0.16)
Number of dependent children	0.0572 (0.44)	-0.1529 (0.97)	0.0999 (0.87)	0.2191 (1.11)	0.0851 (0.78)	0.0868 (0.52)
Black	1.1915 (1.23)	2.9494 (3.62)	1.4850 (0.78)	1.9201 (0.61)	0.5389 (0.30)	2.2017 (0.82)
Hispanic	2.0258 (2.02)	2.6893 (2.77)	3.2149 (1.75)	-0.4751 (0.13)	2.1706 (1.25)	-3.0469 (1.03)
ln *wage*	-0.4096 (2.82)	-0.5442 (4.07)	0.7625 (2.07)	-1.4597 (1.72)	0.0377 (0.09)	0.6200 (0.87)
B ln *wage*	-0.2124 (1.07)	-0.6396 (3.53)	-0.4048 (1.01)	-0.3297 (0.47)	-0.2508 (0.64)	-0.3714 (0.61)
H ln *wage*	-0.3695 (1.78)	-0.5463 (2.61)	-0.7143 (1.86)	0.1743 (0.23)	-0.5970 (1.61)	0.6910 (1.07)
Log maximum likelihood function	-851.43	-739.03	-606.77	-289.80	-819.31	-515.19

Table 9. Transition Function Estimates for Males Aged 22–59

Variable	Employment to unemployment	Employment to nonparticipation	Unemployment to employment	Unemployment to nonparticipation	Nonparticipation to employment	Nonparticipation to unemployment
Constant	1.6264 (1.60)	4.2304 (3.53)	-6.9535 (2.20)	-7.7707 (0.88)	-18.0220 (4.21)	-15.1749 (1.84)
Education (years)	0.0186 (0.79)	-0.0001 (0.00)	0.0066 (0.26)	0.0596 (1.00)	-0.0952 (2.72)	-0.0819 (1.32)
Age (years)	-0.1346 (3.11)	-0.2331 (4.46)	-0.1866 (3.33)	-0.1543 (1.50)	-0.2312 (3.64)	-0.1149 (1.10)
Age²/100	0.1442 (2.40)	0.2933 (4.19)	0.2126 (2.81)	0.2466 (1.93)	0.2472 (3.04)	0.1083 (0.82)
Assets/1,000	-0.9922 (5.02)	-0.3346 (2.07)	0.3923 (4.32)	-0.3209 (0.56)	0.1963 (1.87)	-0.3998 (1.05)
Number of dependent children	0.0693 (1.27)	-0.0342 (0.44)	0.1188 (2.14)	0.1002 (0.69)	0.0006 (0.01)	-0.1879 (1.35)
Black	2.4180 (2.75)	0.1911 (0.17)	-5.0105 (1.14)	4.0144 (0.36)	-7.3915 (1.17)	-8.4390 (0.73)
Hispanic	0.7259 (0.73)	2.8305 (2.89)	-10.5040 (2.26)	-1.1940 (0.11)	-2.1147 (0.37)	1.9822 (0.20)
ln *wage*	-0.5539 (4.58)	-0.8277 (6.47)	1.6299 (2.70)	1.081 (0.66)	3.8086 (4.67)	2.7149 (1.75)
B ln *wage*	-0.4322 (2.67)	-0.0431 (0.20)	0.8110 (1.04)	-0.7539 (0.39)	1.3109 (1.18)	1.5087 (0.75)
H ln *wage*	-0.0902 (0.50)	-0.4941 (2.69)	1.8027 (2.21)	0.2288 (0.12)	0.3953 (0.40)	-0.2642 (0.15)
Log maximum likelihood function	-2,087.77	-1,255.98	-1,038.09	-323.23	-783.38	-357.22

Table 10. *Transition Function Estimates for Females Aged 16–21*

Variable	Employment to unemployment	Employment to nonparticipation	Unemployment to employment	Unemployment to nonparticipation	Nonparticipation to employment	Nonparticipation to unemployment
Constant	−20.2854 (2.22)	−25.2351 (3.99)	−1.0345 (0.09)	−11.9666 (0.69)	−5.8334 (0.68)	17.6153 (1.50)
Education (years)	−0.3731 (4.15)	−0.1972 (3.18)	−0.0078 (0.09)	−0.2321 (1.75)	0.0269 (0.43)	−0.1674 (1.87)
Age (years)	2.5252 (2.54)	2.9890 (4.40)	−0.1918 (0.14)	1.6489 (0.82)	−0.0323 (0.03)	−2.5754 (1.82)
Age^2/100	−0.0665 (2.50)	−0.0777 (4.32)	0.6363 (0.18)	−4.3313 (0.83)	−0.3274 (0.12)	6.2507 (1.70)
Assets/1,000	−0.0454 (0.89)	−0.0640 (1.36)	0.1064 (2.36)	0.0778 (0.68)	0.0301 (0.93)	−0.1020 (0.85)
Number of dependent children	−0.6992 (3.82)	0.0009 (0.01)	−0.3123 (2.12)	−0.1781 (1.08)	−0.2151 (1.99)	−0.2272 (1.46)
Black	−0.3313 (0.36)	−1.6977 (2.82)	−6.8361 (2.97)	−0.2206 (0.06)	−1.2658 (0.97)	−0.3549 (0.24)
Hispanic	−1.8682 (1.65)	−1.3201 (2.09)	−1.4145 (0.59)	−2.2939 (0.61)	−0.8858 (0.67)	−3.2725 (1.68)
ln *wage*	−0.5485 (3.35)	−0.8049 (7.89)	0.2861 (0.69)	−0.8527 (1.01)	1.0261 (2.42)	1.4518 (2.34)
B ln *wage*	0.1381 (0.68)	0.3284 (2.47)	1.3809 (2.71)	0.1282 (0.15)	0.3024 (1.00)	0.3191 (0.91)
H ln *wage*	0.4703 (1.90)	0.2443 (1.67)	0.2165 (0.41)	0.5832 (0.67)	0.1781 (0.57)	0.8300 (1.79)
Log maximum likelihood function	−582.11	−918.98	−456.16	−303.58	−1,275.23	−704.51

Table 11. *Transition Function Estimates for Females Aged 22–59*

Variable	Employment to unemployment	Employment to nonparticipation	Unemployment to employment	Unemployment to nonparticipation	Nonparticipation to employment	Nonparticipation to unemployment
Constant	3.0943	2.3540	-2.3364	-7.8167	-10.3372	-17.1868
	(3.09)	(3.71)	(1.08)	(2.56)	(6.46)	(5.79)
Education (years)	-0.0458	-0.0687	-0.1353	-0.2117	-0.1667	-0.2658
	(1.41)	(3.38)	(2.48)	(3.12)	(4.24)	(4.35)
Age (years)	-0.2049	-0.0846	-0.3555	-0.1651	-0.3338	-0.4084
	(4.87)	(2.97)	(4.60)	(1.68)	(6.47)	(5.18)
Age^2/100	0.2090	0.0789	0.4191	0.1789	0.3227	0.3913
	(3.86)	(2.14)	(4.53)	(1.51)	(5.57)	(4.35)
Assets/1,000	-1.0329	-0.0757	0.1038	0.0289	-0.0214	-0.0572
	(4.12)	(1.27)	(1.14)	(0.22)	(0.37)	(0.53)
Number of dependent children	-0.3371	0.1280	-0.1805	0.1407	-0.2348	-0.2489
	(3.74)	(2.49)	(2.67)	(1.78)	(4.91)	(3.10)
Black	1.7380	-0.1358	-4.3931	-2.4317	0.2265	8.1160
	(2.57)	(0.39)	(1.76)	(0.73)	(0.12)	(2.61)
Hispanic	0.9845	0.1574	-3.2420	1.6755	-5.3018	5.2322
	(1.31)	(0.43)	(1.09)	(0.46)	(2.88)	(1.52)
ln *wage*	-0.4547	-0.6316	1.8694	2.2820	3.3638	5.0282
	(4.16)	(12.06)	(2.64)	(2.49)	(6.14)	(5.69)
B ln *wage*	-0.3286	-0.0679	0.7237	0.3936	-0.1364	-1.5789
	(2.35)	(0.92)	(1.44)	(0.59)	(0.37)	(2.51)
H ln *wage*	-0.2161	-0.0150	0.6309	-0.3685	1.0724	-1.0638
	(1.35)	(0.19)	(1.03)	(0.49)	(2.83)	(1.49)
Log maximum likelihood function	-1,371.15	-2,740.44	-946.48	-722.92	-3,139.44	-1,345.19

Comments by Isabel Sawhill

The revised estimates of the "full employment" or "natural" rate of unemployment that have been produced by economists over the past decade are usually adjusted for changes in the demographic composition of the labor force. It should be noted that both George Perry's original article on this topic[38] and the more recent work by Michael Wachter[39] and Paul Flaim[40] indicate that the revision is necessitated not so much because of the greater labor force representation of groups with traditionally high unemployment rates but because of the increased *dispersion* in group rates. It is this dispersion and its increase over time that suggests the desirability of using targeted employment measures (wage subsidies, employment tax credits, or public service employment) to reduce the nonaccelerating inflation rate of unemployment (NAIRU).

As argued by Martin Baily and James Tobin, by targeting any increase in demand on groups experiencing high rates of unemployment, it should be possible to minimize the inflationary costs of the stimulus.[41] However, some upward adjustment of wages for the target groups is likely to occur, making them less attractive to employers and possibly offsetting, or even eliminating, the positive impact of the program in the process. While recognizing this possibility, Baily and Tobin argue that higher wages will lower the equilibrium ("natural") unemployment rates of the target groups by discouraging the kind of excessive turnover commonly observed among low-wage workers.

Kiefer and Neumann attempt to provide some empirical evidence on this hypothesis. I find their test of this particular hypothesis somewhat unconvincing, although I believe the paper has value for other reasons.

I like the general approach of decomposing unemployment into its component flows and then modeling the determinants of those flows, and agree with a point the authors make early in the paper—there has

---

38. "Changing Labor Markets and Inflation."

39. "The Changing Cyclical Responsiveness of Wage Inflation," *BPEA*, *1:1976*, pp. 115–19.

40. "The Effect of Demographic Changes on the Nation's Unemployment Rate," *Monthly Labor Review*, vol. 102 (March 1979), pp. 13–23.

41. "Macroeconomic Effects of Selective Public Employment and Wage Subsidies."

been too much "unemployment accounting" and not enough behavioral modeling. I also think that calculating the sensitivity of equilibrium unemployment and labor force participation rates with respect to changes in some of the key variables in the model is a potentially fruitful research strategy, particularly if there are variables in the underlying models that represent some policies that might be changed.

Returning to the Baily-Tobin hypothesis, Kiefer and Neumann interpret the positive response of equilibrium unemployment rates to real wages among most demographic groups as supporting the general validity of the thesis, although they note that the estimated elasticities are quite small. I am less willing to interpret the regression results this way, because there is nothing about this particular model of the labor market that enables one to separately identify demand and supply. People may leave or enter employment either because they are responding to a change in the wages offered or because higher-wage (more skilled and experienced) workers are in greater demand by employers.

The authors stress the supply-side (search) explanations but I find the demand-side explanations equally, if not more, appealing. If employers lay off low-wage or low-productivity workers before they lay off higher-wage workers with more seniority, one would observe the same negative correlation between employment exit transitions and wage levels that these authors find. Similarly, if employers pick higher-wage, higher-productivity people from the front of the hiring queue, one would observe the same positive correlation between employment entry transitions and wage levels that they find. The inclusion of some productivity-related variables (age, education) in the estimating equations reduces but does not eliminate the likelihood that it is these demand-side phenomena that are being measured.

The above-noted problem is especially serious when one remembers the way the wage rate is measured. It is an instrumental variable based on age, education, and race for each of the demographic groups. As people get older their estimated wage rates rise and their equilibrium unemployment rates fall. But the latter may have as much to do with maturity or other unobservable factors as it does with higher wages.

In short, I would be willing to conclude that a drop in equilibrium unemployment rates may follow a permanent change in the skill and experience levels of target group workers but not that it would necessarily accompany a demand-induced increase in their relative wages.

Comments by Christopher J. Flinn

The paper by Kiefer and Neumann is noteworthy for its attempt to utilize econometric techniques and theoretical frameworks currently popular in labor research at the micro level in order to address issues of interest in policy formulation. Labor economists have for the most part meticulously avoided drawing any connection between the results of their research and issues of interest to policymakers. This is indeed unfortunate since many policy issues are most amenable to analysis at the micro level.

While I commend Kiefer and Neumann for their effort to obtain estimates of parameters necessary to assess the effects of various fiscal and monetary policies on employment, I don't believe the estimates presented in this paper should be considered as anything more than suggestive. The authors seem keenly aware of the well-known Lucas policy critique, and throughout the paper attempt to interpret some parameter estimates as reflecting differences in preferences and others as reflecting differences in wage-offer distributions. I would argue that there is not much basis for this distinction, since what Kiefer and Neumann have estimated is clearly not a structural model of labor market dynamics. It should be considered an interesting reduced form that can provide estimates of the elasticities of transition rates between labor market states with respect to changes in wage rates (for employed individuals) and changes in the mean of the wage-offer distribution (for nonemployed individuals) under certain sets of restrictive assumptions. I also have reservations as to whether the data set and econometric techniques employed are sufficiently rich to estimate even a reduced-form model of labor market dynamics.

I do not believe the authors intend to claim that the model estimated here is a structural one, but readers unfamiliar with theoretical work in this area may get this impression. For example, in the paper by Burdett and others, individuals move between the labor market states of employment, unemployment, and nonparticipation due to shocks to state-dependent utility functions and drawings from known wage-offer distributions.[42] Estimation of a structural version of this model

42. "A Markov Model of Employment, Unemployment, and Labor Force Participation."

necessitates the estimation of parameters of the distribution of shocks to the utility function, parameters of the wage-offer distribution, parameters of the utility function, the discount factor individuals use in the valuation of future rewards, and the rates of arrival of job offers and shocks to preferences. In a recent paper, Heckman and I present estimates of a structural two-state model (employment and nonemployment) of labor market dynamics and discuss identification issues that arise in the estimation of this class of models.[43] Data and computational requirements are stringent, and even in the best of all possible worlds some structural parameters are not estimable. The fact that Kiefer and Neumann have not estimated a structural model is not a criticism. I only wish that they had made a clearer connection between the theoretical model motivating their analysis and the parameters actually estimated.

One final point concerning the theoretical motivation and the model estimated: when examining effects of changes in the wage-offer distribution on rates of transition between labor market states, the authors focus on changes in the expected value of the wage-offer distribution. Even in models in which individuals have linear utility functions (that is, they are risk neutral), the variance of the wage-offer distribution will effect transition rates between labor market states. Programs such as wage subsidies would presumably alter the entire wage-offer distribution, not only the mean. To examine the potential effect of such policies on steady-state transition rates, the dependence of these rates on all the parameters of the wage-offer distribution should be explicitly incorporated.

That aspect of the paper most subject to criticism is the data set employed. There is of course the obvious point that the individuals comprising the sample (members of low-income households in the Denver SMSA) are not representative of the U.S. population. I do not view this as a serious objection for the purposes of conducting basic research in labor economics. As the authors point out, however, policy analysts should use estimates reported here with extreme caution.

A more fundamental criticism concerns the fact that the DIME data are not sufficient to estimate a continuous time, *three*-state model of labor market dynamics. In order to use the econometric techniques

---

43. C. Flinn and J. Heckman, "New Methods for Analyzing Structural Models of Labor Force Dynamics," *Journal of Econometrics* (forthcoming).

described in this paper, the analyst must have access to the beginning and ending date of each spell of employment, unemployment, and nonparticipation that occurred during the sample period (with the exception of the beginning date of the first spell and the ending date of the last spell). This information is available only for employment and nonemployment spells. Generally speaking, there is no information available regarding the starting and ending dates of unemployment and nonparticipation spells within spells of nonemployment. This lack of information not only biases estimates of transition rate functions between the nonparticipation and unemployment states, it results in biased estimates of all six transition rate functions. For example, when an individual leaves employment, it is evident tautologically that he enters nonemployment. However, it is not clear whether the individual entered unemployment (using the standard BLS definition) or nonparticipation. The information collected does not allow one to estimate a three-state model. Only by using arbitrary coding procedures was it possible to break many spells of nonemployment into spells of unemployment and spells of nonparticipation.

The authors are certainly correct in pointing out the problems with using CPS data to estimate the parameters of transition rate functions, the primary limitation being the duration of the sampling period. However, to my knowledge, there currently exist no micro data sets that include all the information necessary to estimate models of the type presented here. Each data set possesses its own sources of bias, and unfortunately there is no data set that uniformly dominates the others. The differences in sampling schemes and populations sampled are even likely to produce disturbingly different descriptive statistics on transition rates, as table 2 convincingly demonstrates.

The econometric models estimated are special cases of more general models available for the estimation of continuous-time models.[44] There is an assumption that the rate of transition from an origin state to a destination state is not a function of the duration of time spent in the origin state (no duration dependence). There is also an assumption that no unmeasured characteristics affect transition rates (no unobserved heterogeneity). Finally, measured characteristics such as age, assets, and number of children are not allowed to vary *within* spells (spell-constant regressors). In the context of estimating a continuous-

44. C. Flinn and J. Heckman, "Models for the Analysis of Labor Force Dynamics," in R. Basmann and G. Rhodes, eds., *Advances in Econometrics* (Greenwich, Conn.: Jai Press, 1982).

time, three-state model of labor market dynamics, Heckman and I found that parameter estimates changed dramatically when we allowed for duration dependence, unobserved heterogeneity, and time-varying regressors. In fairness to Kiefer and Neumann, we did not condition on the wage rate (for employed individuals) or the expected wage (for nonemployed individuals), so that their estimates may be less sensitive to the omission of these generalizations. However, I found their arguments in support of their econometric specification unconvincing.

The argument that Kiefer and Neumann give in support of their omission of unobserved heterogeneity from the model is not compelling. The fact that predicted wages have ''significant'' effects on transitions from the nonemployment states to employment tells us nothing about the relative importance of unobserved heterogeneity in explaining transition rates. To test this assertion it is necessary to estimate a model that allows for unobserved heterogeneity (which may arise through differences in preferences, wage-offer distributions, etc.). It is also the case that significance tests on parameters of transitions out of the two nonemployment states are not correct, since the mean of the wage-offer distribution is not known and must be estimated.

The Kolmogorov-Smirnov tests for the presence of duration dependence in the data are not convincing. The test statistics reported are not appropriate because the duration time distributions depend on parameters that must be estimated.[45] A more convincing test would involve dropping the Markovian assumptions and estimating more general functional forms that include the specification estimated here as a special case. This is not an inherently expensive procedure, and it would have made the empirical analysis more compelling.

While I have raised a number of objections to the Kiefer and Neumann analysis, many of the points are technical in nature and may have little bearing on the estimates obtained or the comparative statics exercises discussed in the conclusion. The most disturbing issue is the appropriateness of the data set for the estimation of a continuous-time, three-state model of the labor market. Unfortunately, the growing sophistication of both theoretical and econometric models such as those presented in this paper has not been met with an increase in the number of data sets of the type required for the estimation of these models. The estimates obtained by Kiefer and Neumann must be viewed as highly speculative, primarily as a consequence of this fact.

45. J. Durbin, *Distribution Theory for Tests Based on the Sample Distribution Function* (Philadelphia: Society for Industrial and Applied Mathematics, 1973).

Conference Participants

with their affiliations at the time of the conference

Katharine G. Abraham *Massachusetts Institute of Technology*
Orley Ashenfelter *Princeton University*
Costas Azariadis *University of Pennsylvania*
Martin Neil Baily *Brookings Institution*
Nancy S. Barrett *U.S. Department of Labor*
Ronald G. Bodkin *University of Ottawa*
Barry Bosworth *Brookings Institution*
Kim B. Clark *Harvard University*
David S. Coppock *University of Chicago*
Roland Droitsch *U.S. Department of Labor*
Martin Feldstein *National Bureau of Economic Research*
Robert J. Flanagan *Stanford University*
Christopher Flinn *University of Chicago*
Pierre Fortin *University of Laval*
John Geweke *University of Wisconsin*
Robert J. Gordon *Northwestern University*
Herchel I. Grossman *Brown University*
Robert Hall *Stanford University*
Timothy J. Hazledine *Queen's University at Kingston*
Nicholas M. Kiefer *University of Chicago*
Larry J. Kimbell *University of California, Los Angeles*
Frank Levy *Urban Institute*
James L. Medoff *Harvard University*
Daniel J. B. Mitchell *University of California, Los Angeles*
George R. Neumann *University of Chicago*
Keith Newton *Economic Council of Canada*
Donald A. Nichols *University of Wisconsin*

Arnold Packer *U.S. Department of Labor*
Joseph A. Pechman *Brookings Institution*
George L. Perry *Brookings Institution*
Daniel H. Saks *National Commission for Employment Policy*
Isabel Sawhill *Urban Institute*
Christopher A. Sims *University of Minnesota*
M. Martin Smith *Brookings Institution*
Lawrence H. Summers *Massachusetts Institute of Technology*
John B. Taylor *Princeton University*
James Tobin *Yale University*
Wayne Vroman *Urban Institute*

Index